PREGNANCY CHILDBIRTH AND THE NEWBORN
THE COMPLETE GUIDE

by Penny Simkin, P.T.;
Janet Whalley, R.N., B.S.N.; and Ann Keppler, R.N., M.N.,
for the Childbirth Education Association of Seattle

Illustrations by Childbirth Graphics, Ltd.
Photographs by Lise Alexander of Beginnings and
Harriette Hartigan of Artemis

Meadowbrook Press
Distributed by Simon & Schuster
New York

Distributed in the UK by
Chris Lloyd Sales and Marketing

Library of Congress Cataloging-in-Publication Data

Simkin, Penny, 1938-
        Pregnancy, childbirth, and the newborn: the complete guide / by
    Penny Simkin, Janet Whalley, and Ann Keppler; illustrations by
    Childbirth Graphics, Ltd; photographs by Lise Alexander and
    Harriette Hartigan.
              p.   cm.
        Includes bibliographical references and index.
        ISBN 0-88166-177-5
              1. Pregnancy--Popular works.   2. Childbirth--Popular works.
    3. Infants (Newborn)--Care.   I. Whalley, Janet. 1945-
    II. Keppler, Ann. 1946-   III. Title.
    RG525.S584 1991
    618.2--dc20   91-29224
                                                       CIP

S & S Ordering #: 0-671-74182-9

Published by Meadowbrook Press, 5451 Smetana Drive, Minnetonka, MN 55343.

BOOK TRADE DISTRIBUTION by Simon & Schuster, a division of Simon and Schuster, Inc.,
1230 Avenue of the Americas, New York, NY 10020.

First Published in the U.K. 1991.
DISTRIBUTION IN THE U.K. AND IRELAND by Chris Lloyd Sales and Marketing, P.O. Box 327, Poole,
Dorset BH15 2RG.

Text © 1979, 1984, 1991 by the Childbirth Education Association of Seattle.

The illustrations in this book were developed by Childbirth Graphics, Ltd., P.O. Box 20540, Rochester, NY 14602-0540.
Illustrations by Karen Martin Tomaselli and Bill Farley © 1991 by Childbirth Graphics, Ltd.

The photographs on pp. 2, 38, 89, 195 © 1988 by Lise Alexander. The photographs on pp. 12, 36, 236, 240 © 1989 by
Lise Alexander. The photograph on p. 241 © 1990 by Lise Alexander. The photograph on p. 288 © 1991 by Lise Alexander.

The photograph on p. 201 © 1979 by Harriette Hartigan. The photographs on pp. 141, 146, 148, 156, 161 © 1985 by
Harriette Hartigan. The photograph on p. 293 © 1988 by Harriette Hartigan.

The cover illustration ©1993 by Vicki Wehrman.

Editor: Kerstin Gorham
Copy Editors: Julie Bach, Bonnie C. Gruen
Cover illustration: Vicki Wehrman
Text design: Diane Hall
Production Manager: Jay Johnson
Production Assistant: Matthew Thurber
Typography: Jocelyn Stecker and K. M. Thill

The contents of this book have been reviewed and checked for accuracy and appropriateness by medical
doctors, midwives, nurses, and physical therapists. However, the authors, editors, reviewers, and publisher
disclaim all responsibility arising from any adverse effects or results that occur or might occur as a result of
the inappropriate application of any of the information contained in this book. If you have a question or
concern about the appropriateness or application of the treatments described in this book, consult your
health care professional.

99   18

Printed in the United States of America

Contents

Dedication and Acknowledgments iv
Preface v
Introduction vii

1. Becoming Parents 1

2. Pregnancy 21

3. Prenatal Care 45

4. Nutrition in Pregnancy 67

5. Drugs, Medications, and Environmental Hazards in Pregnancy 81

6. Exercise, Posture, and Comfort in Pregnancy 91

7. Preparation for Childbirth: Relaxation, Comfort, and Breathing Techniques 103

8. Labor and Birth 131

9. Labor Variations, Complications, and Interventions 165

10. Cesarean Birth and Vaginal Birth after a Previous Cesarean 189

11. Medications during Labor, Birth, and Post Partum 203

12. Postpartum Period 221

13. Caring for Your Baby 239

14. Feeding Your Baby 263

15. Preparing Other Children for Birth and the Baby 289

References 297
Recommended Resources 301
Index 305

Dedication

To our families: Peter, Linny, and Lizzy Simkin; Mary Simkin-Maass and Greg Maass; Andy and Bess Simkin and Freddy, Charlie, and Eva Rose; Doug, Scott, and Mike Whalley; Jerry, Eric, and Heidi Keppler.

To the thousands of expectant and new parents whom we have taught and who have taught us so much.

And to the Childbirth Education Association of Seattle, which since 1950 has educated, supported, and encouraged families in their transition to parenthood.

Acknowledgments

This book was originally conceived as an extension of the childbirth preparation class manual, *Becoming Parents*, published by the Childbirth Education Association of Seattle. Gillian Mitchell edited the first two editions of this earlier book; we revised and edited the last edition. The first edition of *Pregnancy, Childbirth, and the Newborn* was published in 1984 by Meadowbrook Press with the help of editor Tom Grady. Much broader in scope than the original manual, it became a completely new book. Several years and thousands of copies later, we began the necessary task of updating the information in our book.

In revising this book, we have benefited from the help of many people who checked the text for clarity, content, and medical accuracy. We are grateful to the following readers:

Caring parents Nicole Bauer, Cindy Briggs, Neil Chasan, Margaret Farris, Laura Kornfeld, Lisa and Michael Kraft, Lindy Odland, Sharon Reuter, Sandy Roscoe, Sheryl Togashi, Alison and John Unterreiner, Debbie Vonnahme, Connie Wettack, and Lark Young.

Fellow childbirth educators Diane Adam, R.N., C.R.N.; Lynn Bingisser, R.N.; Susan Cassel, R.N.; Melissa Chasan, R.N.; Lauren Collins, R.N., Pam Gaddis, P.T.; Judy Herrigel, R.N.; Judy Higgins, R.N.; Connie Kenyan-Fink, R.N.; Lauren Lawson, R.N., M.N.; Barbara Orcutt, R.N., M.N.; Molly Pessl, R.N., I.B.C.L.C.; Carla Reinke, R.N., M.N.; Denise Reinke, R.N.; Nancy Smith, R.N.; and Sandra Szalay, R.N., F.P.N.P.

Professional consultants Sally Avenson, C.N.M.; Kathy Carr, C.N.M.; Ronald Coe, M.D.; Steven Dassel, M.D.; Douglas Der Yuen, M.D.; Bruce Gardner, M.D.; Charles Heffron, M.D.; James Joki, M.D.; Laurie Karll, C.N.M.; Larry Larson, M.D.; Ken Main, R. Pharm.; Linda Mihalov, M.D.; Kathryn Mikesell, M.D.; Michael Mulroy, M.D.; Nancy O'Neil, M.D.; Kate Sutherland, C.N.M.; Bonnie Worthington-Roberts, Ph.D.; and Kristine Zelenkov, M.D.

We wish to thank our editor for this edition, Kerstin Gorham, for her diligence and thoughtfulness. We thank Jamie Bolane of Childbirth Graphics for her skill and knowledge in coordinating revision of the illustrations, Karen Martin Tomaselli for the new shaded pencil drawings, and Lise Alexander and Harriette Hartigan for the photographs of expectant parents and new families. We thank Lynn Moen of the Birth and Life Bookstore for her assistance in preparing the Recommended Resources. A special thanks goes to our typists Erin Casey, Mary Hueske, and Karen Lundegaard. And we also thank the CEAS office staff—Judy Hulse, Gloria Madche, Cheri McMeins, Barbara Orcutt, Pam Russo, Zene Tefera, and Bronwen Vetromile—for their support and cooperation in many ways.

Lastly we wish to acknowledge our mentor, the late Virginia Larson, M.D., the founder of the Childbirth Education Association of Seattle, whose work with new families was an inspiration.

Preface

Birth never changes. Society and culture change. Maternity care changes. Women, men, and families change. But birth never changes.

This second edition of *Pregnancy, Childbirth, and the Newborn* reflects changes in society and in maternity care that have taken place since publication of the 1984 edition. It also reflects our increased knowledge and understanding of normal pregnancy and birth and early parenting.

We have updated and expanded almost every section of the book, adding numerous illustrations, photographs, and charts to present the information as clearly and accurately as possible. The second edition has two more chapters than the first: one on drugs, medications, and environmental hazards during pregnancy; the other on cesarean birth and vaginal birth after a previous cesarean. Although we discussed these topics in the 1984 edition, so much new information exists on the former and such a change in attitude has occurred among both the public and the medical profession regarding the latter that they require chapters of their own.

Recognizing that today's busy woman has limited time for exercise, we have condensed the sections on exercise and body mechanics. Only those exercises most relevant to pregnancy, birth, and post partum are covered. We heartily recommend high-quality pregnancy exercise classes and comprehensive books on pregnancy exercise for those who want to do more than these essential exercises.

This edition reflects another social change: the growing variety of family configurations. The traditional family, consisting of mother, father, and children, is joined by numerous others, including blended families formed by second marriages, single parent families, and families where a child may have more than two parents, as is the case with lesbian and gay parents, open adoptions, and surrogate mothers. We have tried to acknowledge and respect these different family styles by avoiding, as much as possible, assumptions as to the gender of the woman's partner. At the same time we did not want to neglect the unique contribution and the needs of the biological father; these are addressed as well.

Likewise in keeping with the times, we have tried to avoid gender assumptions regarding the baby and the caregivers. The baby's gender alternates by section. The caregiver is "he or she."

You will never forget the day you give birth and hold your baby in your arms for the first time. We want childbirth to be a marvelous memory. We hope this book, along with the essentials—a competent, caring, and respectful professional caregiving team and a comfortable and secure birth place—will contribute to a safe birth, a healthy baby, and an experience that will always evoke feelings of fulfillment, satisfaction, and accomplishment.

Introduction

The birth of a baby is the birth of a family—a joyous event with long-lasting significance. As childbirth educators, we have found that knowledge, preparation, and teamwork greatly enrich this experience. This book is the result of our desire to provide a complete and practical guide to childbirth and early parenthood. But we wanted to do more than that. We wanted to provide a personal approach. We recognize and respect the differences among women, men, couples, and babies—in personalities, health status, priorities, needs, and wishes. We hope our approach will help each woman and her partner learn what they need to make good decisions, to adapt the labor techniques to suit themselves, and, generally, to begin parenthood with the self-confidence that comes with understanding and active participation.

Although there are many ways to have a baby and many choices to make throughout the childbearing period, we all have some wishes in common. All parents, doctors, midwives, and other health care providers want, first and foremost, a healthy mother and a healthy baby. Everyone also wants emotional fulfillment for the family. In fact, emotional satisfaction is not a separate goal unrelated to health and safety, because psychological well-being enhances the physical health of both mother and baby.

Parents and their professional caregivers can best achieve these goals by working together to discuss and clarify their questions, concerns, and plans for care. This book can enhance their relationship by helping parents gain the information, skills, and confidence necessary to be responsible, active participants in their own care. A look at the table of contents indicates the wide range of topics discussed and the emphasis on responsible self-care.

We have made a special effort to fully describe labor as the normal physiologic process that it is. We hope to take the surprises out of the experience by showing the wide range of variations possible in the normal process. In addition, we have not neglected to discuss difficulties and complications. Throughout the book, we have emphasized what the mother or couple can do using their own resources to keep comfortable and enhance the labor pattern. We have also discussed the medical methods that can help when there are problems.

The psychomotor skills, such as exercise, relaxation, breathing patterns, labor positions, and comfort measures are a vital part of preparation for childbirth. In our combined fifty-eight years' experience in childbirth education, we have found that by presenting these skills within a broad, flexible framework, parents can adapt and individualize them to suit themselves. Thus, this book will be useful to women with differing personalities, individual styles of learning and coping, and unique labor patterns. The role of the partner or labor companion is fully explored to enable each childbearing couple to find the best ways to work together.

Recognizing that the need for preparation is not limited to the birth experience, we have included an extensive discussion of the early parenting period. We present a problem-solving approach to the challenges of early parenthood—breastfeeding, infant behavior, sibling preparation, and changing family relationships.

We have enjoyed our work in bringing this book into existence. We hope you also find it enjoyable as you use it to prepare for a safe and joyful birth and a confident family beginning. If you have any comments about this book, you may direct them to us at the Childbirth Education Association of Seattle, P.O. Box 31234, Seattle, Washington 98103.

Chapter 1

Becoming Parents

Pregnancy is a state of becoming: an un-born baby is becoming capable of living outside the safe, protective, and totally suffi-cient environment of the mother's body, and you and your partner are becoming parents. This state lasts about nine months, and it allows you the opportunity to learn, adjust, plan, and prepare for parenthood. For most people, becoming parents is a greater life change than any other they will experience. Parenthood is permanent, and the physical, emotional, and spiritual nur-turing of a child is both a delightful oppor-tunity and a heavy responsibility.

Like most parents-to-be, you and your partner are probably looking forward to the rewards and joys of parenthood. You want to produce the healthiest baby possible and bring up a happy, secure person who reflects your hopes and dreams. In fact, you might find yourselves spending much time individually and together thinking and dreaming about your child. What kind of person will your child become? What kind of guidance, role models, examples, and dis-cipline are best? As you both begin examin-ing yourselves, evaluating your strengths and weaknesses as parents, you might won-der whether you have the qualities of the ideal parent. You might use the time during pregnancy to develop the characteristics you believe are essential in fulfilling your new roles.

Pregnancy is a positive growth experi-ence for most expectant parents. This is a time to draw on or develop a support sys-tem—to talk to other pregnant women, expectant fathers, or new parents, to find prenatal care and get referrals for assis-tance, to strengthen bonds or "mend fences" with your own parents, to take child-birth preparation and parenting classes, and to read books. This is a time to assess your lifestyle and make changes if necessary to improve the chances of optimal health for mother and baby—changes regarding diet, exercise, and the use of harmful substances.

Birth as Transition

The birth process—labor and delivery—provides the transition from pregnancy to parenthood. In a day or less, the nine-month-long state of pregnancy is over, and the permanent state of parenthood begins. Despite its relative brevity, however, all cul-tures see birth as an event equal in signifi-cance to death. Birth is celebrated everywhere as a joyous event and is surrounded by rituals associated with hope, promise, and new life.

For you as an individual, the birth experience has great and lasting significance. The anticipation of birth and motherhood brings to the surface deep feelings about such things as your sexuality, your childhood, your own mother, your parents' relationship, and your expectations of yourself both in labor and as a mother. Fathers and partners also look at these factors in themselves and in their own backgrounds as they anticipate parenthood.

Your need to complete this major life transition with as much safety and emotional satisfaction as possible leads you and your partner to seek advice, guidance, and help. You turn to experienced parents, your own parents, doctors, midwives, psychologists, nurses, childbirth educators, and authors of books. You will consider their suggestions and advice in light of your own experience, knowledge, common sense, and priorities. From all of these influences, you will choose your own pattern to follow in preparing for childbirth.

You may have been surprised by the vast amount of information available, the number of "experts" ready and willing to advise you, and the number of decisions you have to make. Perhaps this reflects the fact that pregnancy is not only a normal, healthy physical process, but also a highly personal and emotionally significant event. Your participation in your care helps ensure maximum safety for you and your baby and a sense of satisfaction and fulfillment after the birth.

Pregnancy is not a disease, although its extra demands on your body make you more vulnerable to medical complications

photograph by Lise Alexander/Beginnings

Looking forward to the joys and rewards of parenthood.

than you are at other times in your life. For this reason, you and your baby benefit from prenatal care and regular checkups throughout pregnancy. Neither is the birth process an acute illness that ends when the baby is born, although it is a time of stress for both you and your baby that sometimes exceeds normal boundaries and requires medical intervention.

There is no universal agreement among medical professionals or the general public on the single best, safest, and most satisfying way to give birth, especially for the healthy woman experiencing a normal pregnancy. Many types of care are offered; you and your partner should investigate the choices available and decide what kind of care seems appropriate to you, depending on your needs, desires, and priorities. Your choice of a caregiver and a place of birth determine to a great extent the kind of birth experience you will have.

Choosing a Caregiver

Your options for a caregiver are many. Obstetricians, family physicians, midwives, and others provide care to the childbearing woman.

Obstetricians/gynecologists have graduated from medical school or a school of osteopathic medicine and have had three or more years of additional training in obstetrics and gynecology. Much of the focus of their education is on detection and treatment of obstetrical and gynecological problems. To qualify for board certification, they must pass an exam administered by their professional society.

Perinatologists are obstetricians/gynecologists who have received further training in managing high-risk pregnancy and birth. They often consult or accept referrals from other physicians. These specialists practice only in major medical centers.

Family physicians have graduated from medical school or a school of osteopathic medicine and have completed two or more years of additional training in family medicine. The focus of their education is on the health care needs of the entire family. They refer to specialists if their patients develop serious complications. To qualify for board certification, they must pass an exam administered by their professional society.

Certified nurse-midwives (C.N.M.) have graduated from a school of nursing, passed an exam to become registered nurses, and have completed one or more years of additional training in midwifery. Their education focuses on normal health care during the childbearing year, parent education, prevention of and screening for possible problems, and newborn care. They specialize in the care of uncomplicated, normal pregnancies and births. Referrals are made to a physician when needed. To become certified, they must pass an exam administered by the American College of Nurse-Midwives.

Licensed midwives have completed training according to their state's requirements, which vary from state to state. The focus of their education is similar to that of certified nurse-midwives, although a nursing background is not required of licensed midwives. Referrals to physicians are made when needed. To become licensed, they must complete the educational requirements and pass an exam administered by their state licensing department. Only a small number of states recognize licensed midwives.

Others who provide care for pregnant and childbearing women include naturopaths and lay midwives. Their qualifications and standards of care vary—some are well trained and highly skilled, while others are not. Some are legally registered in their state, and others practice without legal sanction.

You will want to know the educational background, training, and experience of any caregiver you consider, especially if you are considering one whose practice is unregulated. Learn about the caregiver's back-up and referral arrangements should you need to transfer to a specialist. An important consideration in choosing your caregiver is how specialized your care should be. This depends on your health care needs. If you are healthy and are experiencing a normal pregnancy, you can choose from any of the specialities offering maternity care. If your pregnancy is complicated or if problems are anticipated during labor and birth, your options are more limited, and an obstetrician or perinatologist should be involved in your care either as your sole caregiver or as a consultant co-managing your care along with your family physician or midwife. Co-management is most likely if you live far away from a specialist, or if you are being cared for in a group practice that provides both midwifery or family practice and obstetrics.

In the United States, obstetricians provide most of the care to childbearing women. Although many family physicians limit their practices and do not provide maternity care, those who do appeal to some parents because they provide medical care for the entire family. Midwives are the usual caregivers in most countries and are becoming increasingly popular in the United States. Midwifery is legal in some parts of Canada as well. Parents choose midwives because midwives offer maternity care, counseling, and emotional support to pregnant women who would like minimal intervention in pregnancy and birth and maximal involvement in their own care. Midwives deliver babies in a variety of settings—homes, hospitals, and birthing centers.

Another important consideration when evaluating caregivers is their general philosophical approach to pregnancy and childbirth, which is influenced by their education, training, and personal experiences. Some caregivers think of pregnancy and birth as a family-centered event and leave much of the decision making to the parents. Some prefer to assume most of the decision making and leave few choices to the parents. Some rely heavily on technology and interventions, such as continuous electronic fetal monitoring, intravenous fluids, medications, episiotomy, and forceps in caring for the healthy, normal childbearing woman. Others believe pregnancy and birth usually do not require intervention. They focus on helping the woman achieve a healthy pregnancy and have confidence in her body's ability to give birth. Look for a caregiver whose philosophical approach appeals to you and who is qualified to provide care appropriate to your health needs.

Initial Interview

As you consider your options, feel free to shop around. Interview more than one caregiver, if necessary, before choosing. Because you will probably be charged for an office visit, you may want to do some initial screening over the telephone. Ask the office nurse about the qualifications and experience of the doctor or midwife. Ask about fees, who takes calls when the caregiver is off duty, and where he or she delivers. Many physicians and midwives have privileges at more than one hospital. Some attend births in homes or birthing centers. Ask your local childbirth education group for suggestions and referrals.

Think of your first office visit as a chance to interview the caregiver; do not assume that it commits you to remaining in his or her care. Try to have a general idea of what you are seeking in a caregiver. Once you decide to make an appointment with a doctor or midwife, be ready to ask questions that will give you an idea of the philosophy and type of care offered.

Since an initial interview will probably last only ten to thirty minutes, you will need to select only a few key questions. Choose from the following list or develop your own.

Questions to Ask

Become as knowledgeable as possible about your questions before your initial appointment. This book will provide background for your questions. Your interview will help you decide if the caregiver is suitable for you.

♦ What do you see as my role and responsibilities during pregnancy and childbirth?

♦ May my partner attend prenatal appointments with me? Are there any restrictions on my partner being with me throughout labor and birth? During a cesarean birth? During my hospital stay?

♦ How do you feel about other family members (children, grandparents, and so on) or friends attending prenatal appointments or being present at birth?

♦ What recommendations do you make on nutrition during pregnancy (for example, foods to eat and to avoid, weight gain)? Do you provide nutritional counseling? Do you have specific recommendations on exercise, sex, and use of medicines and drugs (including over-the-counter drugs; caffeine; tobacco; alcohol; marijuana, cocaine, and other street drugs)?

♦ What are your feelings about childbirth preparation classes or natural, unmedicated childbirth? Approximately what percentage of your clients or patients are interested in natural childbirth? How many of those actually have it?

♦ Do you have routine standing orders for your patients in labor? What are they? Can they be altered to conform to my needs and desires? Would you encourage and help me prepare a birth plan—a written list of my preferences for care during birth and post partum? (See pages 9–12.) Will you check my birth plan for safety and compatibility with your practices and hospital policies?

♦ Does your hospital have birthing rooms, Labor/Delivery/Recovery (LDR) rooms, or Labor/Delivery/Recovery/Postpartum (LDRP) rooms? Do you feel comfortable using these rooms or do you prefer using separate rooms for labor, delivery, recovery, and post partum?

♦ What are the chances you will be present when I deliver? If you are not there, who covers for you? Will I have a chance to meet that person? Will that person respect the arrangements I have made with you? Will the hospital staff?

♦ How often and under what circumstances do you find it necessary to use these procedures: intravenous fluids, artificial rupture of the membranes, continuous electronic fetal monitoring, Pitocin, episiotomy, forceps, vacuum extractor?

♦ How often do you find it necessary to do a cesarean birth? What are the most common reasons for cesareans among the women in your practice? Do you think there are things I can do before and during labor to help reduce the likelihood of a cesarean?

♦ If I should develop complications during pregnancy or labor, would you manage my care? If not, to whom would you refer me?

♦ What are your policies regarding contact between parents and their baby immediately after the birth? Does the baby go to the nursery or may she stay with us? Who will examine the baby after birth? When is this usually done?

♦ What is the usual hospital stay after a vaginal birth? a cesarean birth? How would you feel about my leaving the hospital earlier than that if I wish? Do you or the hospital have instructions for me if I leave the hospital shortly after the birth (early discharge)?

♦ Is follow-up care available for me (home visits by nurse, midwife, or doctor, or phone follow-up)? How soon after discharge may I expect a visit or phone call?

♦ How would you feel about my staying in the hospital longer than the usual stay to get more rest or to stay with my baby if she has to stay longer?

As you discuss these questions, listen as much to how the caregiver answers as to what he or she actually says. Is the caregiver impatient with you, defensive, or open and comfortable with your questions? Do the answers satisfy you? Do you feel confident and trusting of this person? The responses will help you discover how the caregiver feels about prospective parents who take their responsibilities seriously.

What if you have been seeing a caregiver for some time and then, after getting a better idea of his or her practice, you feel uncomfortable with your choice? You should heed those feelings and try to discuss your discomfort or change caregivers. It is a good idea to meet with the new caregiver before making your decision. Although it is an uncomfortable situation, it is better to act than to stay with someone you know makes you feel uneasy.

Choosing Your Childbirth Classes

Many institutions, nonprofit organizations, groups of doctors or midwives, and independent childbirth educators offer childbirth preparation classes. Their programs vary in size, philosophy, cost, number of classes in the series, and topics covered. The background and training of the teachers also vary, as does the quality. Some classes are consumer oriented, with the goal of preparing parents to take responsibility in decision making and self-care. Others are more provider oriented; they inform parents about the type of care their caregivers or hospitals offer, but avoid discussion of alternatives or controversial aspects of maternity care. If you have a choice in your

area, compare the classes available before choosing.

Questions to Ask

♦ Who sponsors the classes? Your hospital, your physician or midwife, an independent childbirth education association, the Red Cross, your public health department, or a nonaffiliated individual? Are they consumer or provider oriented?

♦ What is the background of the teacher: registered nurse, physical therapist, teacher, psychologist, social worker, college graduate, other? What is the teacher's training: national training and certification through such well-known childbirth education organizations as the International Childbirth Education Association (ICEA), the American Society for Psychoprophylaxis in Obstetrics (ASPO), or the American Academy of Husband-Coached Childbirth (AAHCC)? Has the teacher been trained by a reputable local childbirth education association? Trained through apprenticeship or observation of another teacher? Self-taught?

♦ What is the teacher's experience with birth and childbirth education? If the teacher is a woman, has she given birth? If a man, has he participated in a birth? Has the individual cared for or supported women in labor? How long has she or he been teaching? Does the teacher participate in continuing education in the field?

♦ What is the philosophy and approach of the teacher? Does she or he cover normal childbirth and variations from normal? Does she or he describe choices available and their pros and cons? Are techniques for natural or prepared childbirth offered? Does the teacher describe advantages and disadvantages, risks and benefits of various practices, procedures, and medications? Does she or he emphasize the parents' right and responsibility to be informed and to make decisions?

♦ Does the teacher cover topics other than childbirth: nutrition, fetal development, emotional aspects of pregnancy and parenthood, baby care and feeding? Are other classes available, such as early pregnancy, refresher courses for those who already have children, pregnancy fitness, breastfeeding, parenting, baby care, sibling preparation, cesarean preparation, or preparation for vaginal birth after a cesarean?

♦ How long is the class series? How much time is spent in lecture and discussion, how much in practicing exercises, relaxation, and comfort measures?

♦ What is the cost of the series?

♦ Does the educator teach a particular method (such as Lamaze, Bradley, Dick-Read, Kitzinger, or others), or has she or he developed a method from many sources?

♦ What is the ratio of students to teachers? If classes are large, are there assistants or other teachers available to ensure individual attention?

♦ Is there a reunion class after all class members' babies are born?

♦ Is the instructor available to students by phone or in person for questions during and after the course?

After you investigate the classes available, you will find the one most suitable for you. If there is little or no choice in your community, it is still preferable to take whatever class is available and supplement any weak areas with reading. The suggested reading list at the end of this book will be helpful.

Choosing the Place of Birth

In the Hospital

While most people in North America give birth in hospitals, the institutions vary widely in the services they offer, their staffs' attitudes toward patients, and their philosophies of care. You may have no choice in a rural area, but if there is a choice, you should try to learn about several hospitals, take their tours, and choose carefully the one that best meets your needs.

Hospitals committed to family-centered maternity care strive to be flexible and responsive to the mother's needs and family's wishes. Many family-centered hospitals, in an effort to provide a more homelike atmosphere, have introduced birthing rooms or birth centers that are available primarily to low-risk women (healthy women with normal pregnancies). These areas are more attractively decorated than the average labor room and have comfortable furniture, televisions, and other amenities. Fewer medical interventions are used here. If needed, emergency care is readily available. Some hospitals without birthing rooms provide individualized care to their patients. Other hospitals, even those claiming to provide family-centered maternity care, are rigid. Their staffs tend to operate by routine and protocol, treating all patients alike and allowing parents little or no say in their own and their baby's care.

If you have had a difficult pregnancy, or if complications are anticipated for labor or birth, you will need a hospital that is capable of providing intensive care and that has complete obstetrical, anesthesia, blood bank, and laboratory services available twenty-four hours a day.

It helps to know the philosophy, policies, and services of the hospitals in your area so you can choose wisely, work to make some changes, or at least know what to expect in advance. See the chart on pages 14–20 for ideas about specific features to check when comparing hospitals. You might ask about routines while on a hospital tour, or ask your caregiver, since the doctor's or midwife's orders determine your care while you are in the hospital.

Out of the Hospital

A small percentage of low-risk American women give birth outside the hospital—in clinics, birth centers, or at home with midwives or doctors in attendance. In these settings, there are few routines and few medical interventions. In addition, the cost of such care is usually lower than the cost of hospital care.

With an out-of-hospital birth, you are unlikely to have routine interventions such as intravenous fluids, restriction to bed, electronic fetal monitoring, medications, and other procedures of questionable value in uncomplicated labors. By the same token, it is more difficult to get these same interventions if they become desirable or necessary. You should be screened carefully during pregnancy. If there are warning signs (such as premature labor contractions, a rise in blood pressure, bleeding, high blood sugar, protein in the urine, or anemia), you will be transferred to in-hospital care. Even with careful pregnancy screening, between 15 and 27 percent of women who intend to give birth outside the hospital are transferred to the hospital during labor or post partum for problems judged to require obstetrical intervention.[1] Most transfers during labor are for nonemergencies, such as prolonged labor, meconium in the amniotic fluid, or prolonged ruptured membranes—cases where intervention or medication will be helpful or needed but is not an immediate necessity for the welfare of the baby or mother. Outcomes for planned out-of-hospital births, even if a transfer is necessary, are comparable to outcomes for planned hospital births for those women who have had prenatal care and have a competent midwife or doctor.[2]

Emergency transfers are extremely rare for women who have been screened and who have uncomplicated, normal pregnancies. The principal unpredictable life-threatening conditions that can arise during labor and that require immediate medical action are cord prolapse (when the cord slips out of the uterus before the birth); hemorrhage; and the deprivation of the fetus's supply of oxygen during labor (due to bleeding, cord compression, and other factors). After delivery, the main reasons for emergency transfer are hemorrhage, retained placenta, and serious newborn problems.

Any transfer is a disappointment and an added expense for those planning an out-of-hospital birth. When deciding where to have the baby, you should take into account the possibility of transfer, along with the more obvious considerations of autonomy for the parents (which is usually greater outside the hospital) and safety in emergencies (which is greater in well-equipped and well-managed hospitals).

The best place for you is the place where you will feel safe and comfortable and where you can get the help and expertise you want and need as you make the transition to parenthood.

When Your Options Are Limited

Unfortunately for many expectant parents, neither their place of birth nor their caregiver is completely satisfying; either they live in an area where the choices are limited or they have very specific or strong wishes. Communication may be poor or their caregiver may want to manage the pregnancy in an undesirable way. If you discover that your needs and wishes are unlikely to be met by your caregiver or place of birth, investigate your options:

1. Find a more compatible caregiver or change the place of birth, or both.

2. Try to negotiate, with the goal of coming closer to meeting your needs.

3. Accept what your caregiver and place of birth offer.

The first option has already been discussed, and the third needs no discussion. The second option, however, may be the most satisfying one for you, especially if you are reasonably happy or pleased with your care but wish to be sure of particular points. Negotiation is a matter of communicating your wishes to your caregiver, getting feedback, and then both of you compromising to reach agreement on your care. Using a birth plan can help ensure that your care suits your individual needs and preferences.

The Birth Plan

A birth plan is essentially a list of the options you and your partner prefer for your birth experience. There are several advantages to having such a list:

Advantages to you. Preparing a birth plan requires that you find out, think about, and discuss the available options. It helps you clarify your preferences. The birth plan is a concrete vehicle for discussion with your caregiver. By enhancing communication and clarifying your expectations of each other, a birth plan can build trust and understanding among all members of the childbirth team. Throughout labor and birth, the birth plan frees you from having to explain and re-explain your wishes and expectations, especially when there is a change of nursing staff.

Advantages to your doctor or midwife. A birth plan helps your doctor or midwife understand your goals and expectations. Your caregiver can assist you in preparing a realistic plan that all of you find satisfactory. Prior discussion allows your caregiver to note and discuss any areas of misunderstanding or disagreement, allowing you to talk them over and work out a suitable compromise. Of course, the birth plan is not a binding legal agreement, and even if signed or initialed by your caregiver, it is neither a

promise nor a guarantee that circumstances will not require a change in the plan.

Advantages to the nursing staff. The birth plan acts as a guide for the nurses in individualizing your care. When you enter the hospital in labor, you will probably be a stranger to the nurses. A birth plan helps the nurses to quickly become better acquainted with you. It tells them what you really want, as decided by you when you were calm and able to think clearly. Studies show that women have a greater sense of satisfaction with their birth experiences if the desires and expectations they had before birth are met. If not met, they may feel disappointment, anger, or depression. If the nurses know what is important to you, they are more able to fulfill your wishes and expectations.

Getting Started with a Birth Plan

If you decide to prepare a birth plan, tell your caregiver beforehand. This may be a new idea for your doctor or midwife, who may be uncomfortable about it at first, especially if he or she is accustomed to making most of the decisions. You will want to explain why you are preparing a birth plan, emphasizing that you want it to enhance cooperation and trust between you and your caregiver and the nurses. Explain that it will help you to know what to expect under both normal and abnormal circumstances.

Reactions of doctors and midwives vary. Some caregivers believe birth plans are unnecessary, because neither they nor the nurses will make decisions during labor without your consent. Some feel birth plans are a waste of time. They do not realize how helpful it is for you to know in advance whether your desires for care are realistic and acceptable. They may also not realize that without a birth plan you might have to verbally explain your wishes to each doctor, midwife, or nurse involved in your care. This might be more stressful than letting them read what is important to you and discussing your care in the context of your expectations. If your caregiver is opposed to a birth plan, then you have gained valuable insight and can act on it. You can either give in and give up your birth plan, negotiate, or find another caregiver. At the very least, you have clarified your relationship and will not be confused or surprised in labor. When your doctor or midwife is supportive of the idea of a birth plan, it is an excellent opportunity to discuss and plan together how your labor and birth will be managed. Cooperation and trust are built between you. These carry through the birth experience and add much to the satisfaction felt by all concerned. If problems arise during labor, the underlying understanding and trust are most reassuring if you have to adjust to changes in the plan.

Language of a Birth Plan

The wording you choose can have a substantial impact on how your caregivers receive your birth plan. Language that clearly expresses your preferences and reflects a spirit of flexibility and cooperation on your part will be greeted by your caregivers in the same spirit. If your list of preferences reads more like a list of demands, it will be received defensively. Be polite and respectful. Phrases such as "would prefer," "if possible," and "unless medically necessary" indicate that you understand that it may be necessary to modify your plan.

Components of the Birth Plan

Your birth plan should contain an *introduction* and sections on *normal labor and birth, care of the newborn,* and *unexpected events* (a prolonged labor, cesarean birth, a premature or sick baby, the death of the baby).

This book discusses most of the routine practices you may encounter. Use it as background for your birth plan and for discussion with your caregivers. In addition, because routine practices vary from area to area, your childbirth educator can be a helpful resource as you prepare your birth plan, especially if she or he is familiar with the options available in your community. Use your childbirth educator as a consultant on local practices, choices available, wording to use, or any aspect of the birth plan with which you need help.

The Introduction

The introduction is a paragraph that tells the staff a little about you and explains why your birth plan is important to you. For example, you might want to tell the staff if your pregnancy has been pleasant and healthy; if you have had difficulties with infertility, previous miscarriage, or other problems during pregnancy; if you have a fear of childbirth or of hospitals; if you have religious preferences or special needs; or if a natural or home birth is extremely important to you. Also, you might give any helpful information about your partner or others who will be present. Do they have physical or emotional conditions that may influence their participation in your care? Will there be a unique combination of family members present (for example, adoptive parents, lesbian coparents), children present, or stressful family dynamics? Will you be accompanied by an experienced or professional labor support person, in addition to your partner? The nurses can help you more effectively if they have this kind of information. You might also state that you will appreciate the expertise, help, and support of the staff in carrying out your birth plan.

Normal Labor and Birth

When labor and birth are proceeding normally, few interventions are necessary for medical safety. They may be used routinely, however, for reasons other than demonstrated safety. Some, such as intravenous fluids or continuous electronic monitoring, are used in the belief that it is better to use them before rather than after a problem arises. Others, such as the back-lying position for birth, the use of stirrups, and changes of shifts of nurses and other staff, exist for the convenience of the staff or caregiver. Still others, such as the use of silver nitrate or antibiotics for the baby's eyes, are required by law. Some practices, such as enemas, shaving the perineum, the requirement that surgical masks be worn by everyone except the mother, holding the baby upside down by the heels, and so on, became routine at a time when they were believed to be beneficial, but now are known to be of little or no benefit or even harmful. They are rarely done today in most areas of North America. Some routines, such as anesthesia and circumcision, may present an element of risk to mother or baby that may not be worth taking, depending on the circumstances and the benefits to be gained. Others, such as feeding sugar water to the baby, are simply habits, and no one seems to know exactly why they began. Some require your informed consent—that is, your caregiver explains the procedure, its benefits and risks, and the alternatives (including not doing it) and their benefits and risks; your consent is recorded on your chart.

Part of your preparation will be to find out which routines you are likely to encounter, along with the reasoning behind them. Childbirth classes, the hospital tour, and your caregiver can help you find out which routines are used. As you prepare this part of your birth plan, list only the preferences that matter to you. You do not have to hold an opinion on everything.

Care of the Newborn

This section describes how you want your baby cared for during the first few days. There are as many differences in the way healthy newborns are cared for as there are differences in every other aspect of maternity care. Generally, the healthy newborn needs little more than a warm environment, diapers, clothing, and access to her parents' arms and her mother's breast. Certain observations, tests, and procedures are done routinely to discover serious congenital disorders or prevent potentially serious illnesses. In considering the options listed in the chart on pages 242–44, balance concerns for your baby's comfort and well-being with the potential benefits and risks of each procedure.

Unexpected Events

The section on the unexpected may not be needed, but will be most helpful if something unforeseen does arise. A birth plan for a cesarean birth can help you retain some of the priorities of your original birth plan. Though an unexpected cesarean can be a disappointment, you will feel better about the experience if you have thought about this possibility and your choices are considered. Information in chapter 10 will help you with a cesarean birth plan.

Although almost all babies are born healthy and beautiful, there is a slim chance that something could go wrong or that the baby might have a problem. This possibility concerns most expectant parents. You know that prematurity, illness, birth defects, or even death sometimes happen. It is helpful to consider in advance how you would want such misfortunes handled, because if they occur, many decisions have to be made when you are upset and unable to think clearly. Your birth plan can include such possibilities, so that the staff can care for you and your baby according to your preferences. See the chart on page 18 and page 181 for further discussion about the choices to consider in preparing your birth plan.

Once you have made your birth plan

about the unexpected, put it aside. You will probably not need it, but if you do, you will have your own plans to follow at this extremely difficult time.

As you can see, preparing a birth plan requires time, thought, and information gathering. By the time you have finished, you should have a fairly complete picture of what you can expect in your birth experience and immediately afterward. Not only will you and your caregivers have decided how your uncomplicated, normal labor and birth will be managed, but you will also know how unexpected variations and complications will be handled. The decisions you make in advance when you are calm, not stressed, and able to concentrate will help carry you through and guide you and your caregivers at a time when you and your partner need to devote all your mental and physical energies to coping with childbirth.

Decisions to Make for the Postpartum Period

There are many other decisions to make during pregnancy that will affect you and the baby after birth. These also require information gathering, discussion, and introspection.

Choosing a Caregiver for Your Baby

There are several types of health care providers for children; each type has its own advantages.

Pediatricians specialize in children's health care, and their offices are geared for children. Pediatricians have completed medical school and a pediatric residency; they have more training in child development and childhood illness than the following practitioners.

Parenthood is a delightful opportunity and an important responsibility.

—photograph by Lise Alexander/Beginnings

Family physicians provide care for the entire family. They refer seriously ill children to doctors with specialty training. As part of their medical school training, they have had several months in pediatrics.

Pediatric and family nurse practitioners are registered nurses who have additional training in pediatrics or family health. They usually work with a group of physicians or in a clinic providing well-child care and treating common illnesses. Serious problems are referred to a pediatrician. Nurse practitioners are very knowledgeable about children's emotional, social, and physical development.

Naturopaths and other alternative practitioners provide well-child care and emphasize nonmedical treatment of illness. They refer seriously ill children to medical doctors.

Choosing a Health Care Setting

The cost of health care varies depending on the setting you choose.

Private care is more expensive than clinic care, but such care is more personalized and convenient.

Children's health clinics usually cost less, but there is more waiting time and you are less likely to keep the same doctor or nurse practitioner, as the staff may change frequently. Most of the caregivers are doctors or nurse practitioners in training. They are supervised by fully trained caregivers.

Well-child clinics offer free or low-cost checkups and immunizations but usually do not provide care for sick children.

Prenatal Interview

After deciding which type of health care provider and setting suits you best, you may wish to get recommendations from your friends, doctor or midwife, childbirth educator, local hospital, or family. You can make a prenatal appointment for a brief visit with one or more of the practitioners to ask

questions and get to know them. There may or may not be a charge for this visit. If you are not sure exactly what to discuss, check the Baby Care section on pages 17–18, or ask for information or advice on any of the following:

♦ Breast or formula feeding.

♦ Introduction of solid foods.

♦ Employment outside the home and day-care options.

♦ Distance of health care office or clinic from your home or day care.

♦ Who covers when the practitioner is off duty?

♦ Who can answer questions when you call on the telephone?

♦ What hospital would your child go to if necessary?

♦ To whom (if anyone) does the practitioner refer if your child is very ill?

During the interview pay as much attention to how your questions are answered as to what is said. You should be able to sense if this person is competent, caring, and considerate. The right person to provide health care for your baby is someone whose style and philosophy are compatible with yours.

Other Considerations

♦ Will your baby be breastfed or bottle-fed? Chapter 14 discusses the advantages of each method.

♦ Who will help at home after the birth? You will need help with meals and household tasks. Your partner might take time off, your parents or a relative might visit, friends might offer to help out, or you might hire a mother's helper for a few hours each day (ask your childbirth educator or caregiver for referrals).

◆ What preparations and equipment are needed for the baby (car seat, crib, room, clothes, and so on)? See chapter 13.

◆ Will you work outside the home after the baby is born? If so, when? Who will provide child care? Can you and your partner share some or all of the child care? What are your options regarding working—part-time, full-time, length of maternity leave? Will you continue to breastfeed while working? If

finances and your employer permit it, the smoothest transition for mother and baby is to take several months' leave and return to employment part-time at first, then gradually increase your working time.

While this list is by no means complete, it gives you an idea of the kind of planning to begin now. Use the time during pregnancy to plan for post partum; this will ease the transition to parenthood.

Options to Consider for Your Birth

The following is a list of common practices in labor, birth, and post partum, along with options for handling each. Use this book and others, discuss the options with your childbirth educator and caregiver, and take tours of local hospitals to discover what you want. Then make up a rough draft of your birth plan. Go over it with your caregiver and make a final draft. Make several copies—one to keep, one for your chart, an extra to give the staff, if

necessary, and one for your baby's chart. Remember that the following procedures are not all routine everywhere and that some of the options may not be available to you. Find out which are by asking questions on the hospital tour, in childbirth class, or during prenatal care appointments. Most of the following options are discussed in other parts of this book. Check the index for specific pages.

During labor: Procedure or practice	Options
Enema	◆ No enema ◆ Self-administered or given by nurse ◆ If constipated at onset of labor ◆ To start or stimulate labor
Shaving of pubic hair	◆ No removal of pubic hair ◆ Clip hair around vagina ◆ Shave hair around vagina ◆ Shave for cesarean
Presence of partner/others	◆ At mother's discretion ◆ One or more partners present throughout labor and birth ◆ Limit on number of support people ◆ Other children at birth ◆ At doctor's, nurse's, or anesthesiologist's discretion

During labor: Procedure or practice	Options
Position for labor	◆ Freedom to change position and walk around ◆ Confined to bed in various positions ◆ Confined to one position in bed
Onset of labor	◆ Spontaneous (begins on its own) ◆ Self-induced: nipple stimulation, enema, castor oil, sex, acupressure ◆ Medical or surgical induction: artificial rupture of membranes, prostaglandin gel, intravenous Pitocin ◆ Induced with or without tests for fetal maturity and well-being ◆ Induced for medical reasons or for convenience
Food/fluids	◆ Eat and drink as desired ◆ Water, juice ◆ Popsicles ◆ Ice chips only ◆ IV fluids ◆ Heparin lock in case IV fluids needed ◆ No liquids
Rupture of membranes	◆ Spontaneous ◆ Artificial, before or during early or late labor ◆ Replace lost fluid via amnioinfusion, if needed
Vaginal exams	◆ At mother's request ◆ Only when labor changes ◆ Occasionally ◆ Frequently
Monitoring fetal heart rate	◆ Auscultation with stethoscope ◆ Auscultation with Doppler (ultrasound stethoscope) ◆ Intermittent external electronic fetal monitoring ◆ Internal electronic fetal monitoring for medical reasons ◆ Routine continuous electronic monitoring—internal or external ◆ Fetal scalp stimulation (or acoustic stimulation) to confirm fetal distress
Pain relief	◆ Help from partner(s) and nurses or midwife ◆ Relaxation, breathing, comfort measures ◆ Tub bath or shower ◆ Medications, anesthesia only at mother's request ◆ Medications and/or anesthesia encouraged by medical staff

continued

During labor: Procedure or practice	Options
Enhance or speed labor	◆ Walk, change position ◆ Nipple stimulation ◆ Enema ◆ Rupture of membranes ◆ Pitocin
To empty bladder	◆ Walk to toilet ◆ Bedside commode ◆ Bed pan in bed ◆ Catheterization

For birth: Procedure or practice	Options
Position	◆ Mother's choice of position ◆ Caregiver's choice of position ◆ Lithotomy and stirrups
Expulsion techniques	◆ Spontaneous bearing-down ◆ Directed pushing ◆ Prolonged breath-holding and straining
Speed up birth	◆ Gravity-enhancing positions ◆ Prolonged pushing on command ◆ Episiotomy ◆ Forceps or vacuum extractor
Bed for birth	◆ Mother's choice of birth chair, bean bag, tub (water birth), floor, or bed ◆ Birthing bed ◆ Labor bed ◆ Delivery table with or without stirrups
Covering of perineal area	◆ Undraped, mother may touch baby during birth ◆ Sterile drapes around vagina
Care of perineum	◆ Try for intact perineum with massage, support, hot compresses, controlled pushing, and positions to promote perineal stretching ◆ Anesthesia, before or after episiotomy, and stitches ◆ Ice packs immediately after birth

After birth: Procedure or practice	Options
Cord cutting	◆ Clamp and cut after it stops pulsating ◆ Partner cuts cord ◆ Clamp and cut immediately
Delivery of placenta	◆ Spontaneous ◆ Encouraged with breast stimulation, baby suckling ◆ Hastened with massage of the fundus and/or medication (Pitocin) ◆ Manual extraction
Maintaining uterine muscle tone	◆ Frequent checking for uterine tone ◆ Fundal massage by mother, as necessary ◆ Fundal massage by nurse ◆ Medication—IV or by injection
Contact between mother and partner or loved ones	◆ Regulated by mother ◆ Restricted to visiting hours only
Discharge of mother and baby	◆ When desired ◆ Early discharge (within 24 hours after birth) ◆ Standard discharge (1 to 3 days after birth)

Baby care: Procedure or practice	Options
Airway	◆ Baby coughs and expels own mucus; suctioned if necessary ◆ Suction with bulb syringe almost immediately ◆ Deep suctioning with tube down windpipe
Warmth	◆ Baby skin-to-skin with mother with blanket covering both ◆ Wrapped in heated blanket ◆ Placed in bassinet with radiant heater or in electrically warmed bed ◆ Placed in thermostatically controlled, heated isolette
Immediate care	◆ Baby held by parents and suckled by mother; in parents' arms for observation ◆ Kept near parents in bassinet or isolette ◆ Taken to nursery for observation, weighing, and feeding
Eye care	◆ None ◆ Use of nonirritating agent, such as erythromycin or tetracycline ◆ Use of silver nitrate

continued

Baby care: Procedure or practice	Options
Vitamin K	♦ None ♦ Oral doses (after birth and a few days later) ♦ By injection soon after birth
First feedings	♦ Breastfeeding on demand ♦ Scheduled breastfeeding ♦ Supplemental feedings (water, glucose water, formula) to breastfed baby given by parents or nurse ♦ Supplemental feedings (water, glucose water, formula, breast milk) given by medicine dropper, "finger feeding," or bottle ♦ Demand feedings with infant formula ♦ Scheduled formula feedings
Contact between baby and mother/parents	♦ 24-hour rooming-in ♦ Daytime rooming-in ♦ For feedings only, in nursery at other times
Circumcision	♦ None ♦ With one or both parents present to comfort baby ♦ With no anesthesia ♦ With local anesthesia ♦ Out-of-hospital circumcision

Unexpected Events

If problems develop either during labor or afterward, you may have to let go of some of your preferred options, because more interventions may be necessary for safety. The following are some options that are usually available even under such circumstances.

Cesarean birth: Policy	Options
Timing (if cesarean is planned)	♦ After labor begins ♦ Scheduled before labor begins
Presence of partner/others	♦ More than one supportive person present ♦ Father or partner only ♦ Partner seated at mother's head ♦ Partner stands and watches or photographs surgery and birth ♦ No partner present

Cesarean birth: Policy	Options
Anesthesia	♦ Regional anesthesia with little or no premedication ♦ Regional anesthesia with premedication ♦ Sleep-inducing medication for sedation for the first few hours after birth ♦ General anesthesia
Participation	♦ Screen lowered at time baby is delivered ♦ Anesthesiologist or obstetrician explains events ♦ No explanation to parents
Contact between baby and mother/parents	♦ Held by partner soon after birth, where mother can touch and see ♦ Breastfeeding as soon as possible ♦ Sent immediately to nursery or intensive care
Discharge of mother and baby	♦ When desired ♦ Within four to five days
Premature or sick infant: Policy	**Options**
Contact between baby and mother/parents	♦ Parents visit and care for baby as much as possible ♦ If baby is in another hospital from mother, partner goes with baby ♦ Baby separated from parents with little or no visiting
Feeding when baby is able to digest food (before this point baby fed intravenously)	♦ Mother nurses baby ♦ Mother's expresses milk to be given to baby by bottle, dropper, or tube ♦ Formula feeding by bottle, dropper, or tube ♦ Fed by parents or nurse
Contact with support group	♦ Initiated by parents, nurses, or support group ♦ No contact
Stillbirth: Policy	**Options**
Onset of labor	♦ Spontaneous (begins on its own) ♦ Induction of labor
Sedation	♦ No sedatives ♦ Medication that leaves the mother awake and alert ♦ Sleep-inducing medications
Conduct of labor and birth	♦ Participation in decision making and use of labor coping techniques ♦ Management left to hospital staff

continued

Death of a newborn: Policy	Options
Contact with baby after death	♦ See and hold baby as often and for as long as desired
	♦ See and hold baby initially after death
	♦ No contact with baby
	♦ Obtain mementos (photograph, lock of hair, foot prints, naming the baby)
Care of baby after death	♦ Autopsy
	♦ Spiritual services (baptism, memorial service, funeral)
Mother's recovery	♦ On postpartum unit
	♦ In room separate from postpartum unit
	♦ Early discharge
	♦ Spiritual and grief counseling
	♦ Contact with parent support group

Chapter 2

Pregnancy

The normal and healthy process of pregnancy brings profound physical and emotional growth for the expectant mother and psychological changes for the expectant father or partner. This chapter explores the many changes you are likely to experience during pregnancy, and the dramatic fetal growth and development that will take place from conception to birth. But first it will provide information on reproductive anatomy, sexual function, and the process of conception.

Reproductive Anatomy and Sexual Function

The Male

The *external genitalia* of the male include the *scrotum* and the *penis*. The scrotum contains two *testicles,* or male sex glands, which produce *sperm* or *spermatozoa.* Each testicle contains over eight hundred small, tightly coiled tubes, known as *seminiferous tubules,* which produce hundreds of millions of sperm in response to a hormone produced by the *pituitary gland,* which is located in the brain. Another hormone from the pituitary gland stimulates the testicles to produce the male sex hormone *testosterone,*

which is responsible for the male's sexual characteristics (deep voice, facial and body hair, and others) and also ensures adequate development of sperm.

The seminiferous tubules join together to form the *epididymis,* a wider coiled tube that stores the sperm for a few weeks until they are mature and ready to make their way out of the scrotum. As it leaves the scrotum and enters the pelvic cavity, the epididymis becomes the *vas deferens,* a duct that carries and stores the sperm. Into this duct the *seminal vesicles,* the *prostate gland,* and *Cowper's glands* secrete fluids that enhance fertility by nourishing the sperm, aiding their motility. Together with the sperm, these secretions make up the *semen* that is ejaculated into the vagina during sexual intercourse.

The vas deferens empties into the male *urethra,* which leads from the bladder to the end of the penis. The urethra transports both urine and semen from within to outside the man's body. During urination and most other times, the penis is soft or flaccid. With sexual excitement, blood rapidly fills the tissues of the penis, causing it to expand and become firm and erect, facilitating insertion into the vagina during intercourse.

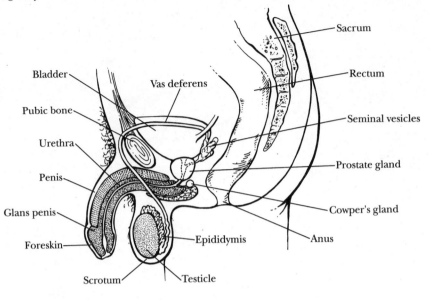

Male Anatomy

With sexual excitement, muscles contract to close the duct to the bladder, keeping urine out of the semen. During orgasm, ejaculation triggers involuntary muscle contractions, which propel two to three milliliters (less than a teaspoon) of semen through the urethra. The ejaculate contains approximately 240 million to 360 million sperm.

The Female

The following description and the accompanying illustrations of the female's reproductive anatomy and physiology provide the background for later discussion of conception, pregnancy, and birth.

A woman's *perineum* includes the pelvic floor muscles, external genitals, urethra, anus, and perineal body (the area between the vagina and anus). The external *genitals* include the vaginal opening, *clitoris, labia majora, labia minora,* and *mons pubis* (the fatty tissue over the pubic bone). The internal reproductive organs are the uterus (or womb), vagina, fallopian tubes, and ovaries. The *uterus* is a hollow, muscular, pear-shaped organ situated in the pelvis—behind the bladder and in front of the rectum. Divided into two parts, the uterus has an upper part called the *body* and a lower part called the *cervix,* which protrudes into the *vagina,* the stretchy canal connecting the internal and external genitals. Two *fallopian tubes* extend from the upper sides of the uterus toward the ovaries.

The two *ovaries,* located on each side of the uterus, are a woman's sex glands. One

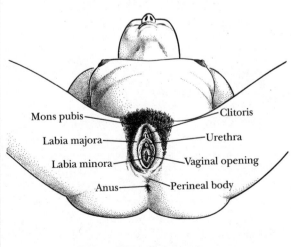

External Female Anatomy

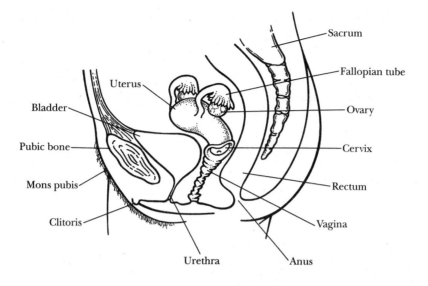

Internal Female Anatomy

of their functions is to produce the female sex hormones *estrogen* and *progesterone*. During adolescence, estrogen, along with other hormones from the pituitary and adrenal glands, stimulates the development of secondary sexual characteristics in the female, such as enlarged breasts and body hair. The ovaries also ripen and expel *ova* (eggs). Of the hundreds of thousands of ova present in the ovaries, only about 400 to 450 actually are expelled (ovulated) in a woman's lifetime.

During a woman's reproductive years, except during pregnancy, the ovaries undergo cyclic changes, which usually occur monthly. The *menstrual cycle* is influenced by pituitary hormones, which cause an ovum to mature and its *follicle* (the sac surrounding the ovum) to enlarge and secrete estrogen. This process then stimulates the growth of the *endometrium* (the lining of the uterus).

Usually only one ovum is released from its follicle each month in a process called *ovulation*, which occurs approximately halfway through the menstrual cycle. After leaving the ovary, the ovum enters the fallopian tube and is propelled slowly to the uterus. Under the influence of another pituitary

hormone, the follicle begins producing progesterone, which stimulates further development of the uterine lining, enabling it to receive and nourish the fertilized ovum. If fertilization does not occur, the levels of estrogen and progesterone decrease, and the uterus sheds its unneeded lining along with the unfertilized ovum. This monthly shedding process is called *menstruation.*

Becoming Pregnant— Conception

Conception occurs as a result of sexual intercourse, or, if that is not possible, alternative procedures such as artificial insemination or *in vitro* fertilization.

Artificial insemination (AI) is a procedure by which previously collected semen is placed at the cervix or in the uterus with a special syringe. This procedure is used when sperm are needed from another source, as in cases of infertility or impotence of the male partner, or if a woman who does not have a male partner desires a pregnancy.

With *in vitro fertilization,* a doctor removes several ova from the mother's (or a donor mother's) ovary, unites them with the father's (or a donor father's) sperm outside the woman's body under laboratory conditions, and then places the fertilized ova into the woman's uterus. This procedure is used when the woman's fallopian tubes are blocked or if she or her partner is infertile for other reasons. Achieving a successful pregnancy often requires several attempts at fertilization. It is not unusual for *in vitro* fertilization to result in a multiple pregnancy.

After sexual intercourse or artificial insemination, sperm travel from the vagina through the cervix, into the cavity of the uterus, and along the fallopian tubes. Conception occurs within twenty-four hours after intercourse or AI when a single sperm penetrates or fertilizes an ovum, forming a single cell; at that moment you become pregnant. The millions of sperm that die before reaching the ovum make your vaginal and intrauterine mucus more receptive to sperm and dissolve the substances that surround the egg, thus making penetration by one sperm possible. Once an ovum is fertilized, a chemical reaction occurs that changes the surface of the ovum and prevents other sperm from penetrating it. Fertilization usually takes place in the outer one-third of the fallopian tube. Then the ovum continues down the fallopian tube to the uterus where, several days later, it embeds into the uterine lining.

At conception, all the inherited characteristics of your child are established. Each ovum and sperm contain twenty-three *chromosomes* (which contain the genetic material), half the number contained in all other human cells. The union of egg and sperm gives the fertilized ovum the full complement of forty-six chromosomes—twenty-three from the mother and twenty-three from the father. These twenty-three pairs of chromosomes combine to form a unique blueprint for your child's development. Your child's body build, physical appearance, sex, blood type, some personality traits, some mental characteristics, and much more are decided immediately. The remainder of growth and development during gestation, infancy, childhood—in fact, your child's entire lifetime—is guided to a great extent by this original genetic blueprint.

Only one pair of chromosomes determines your new baby's sex. Women have a

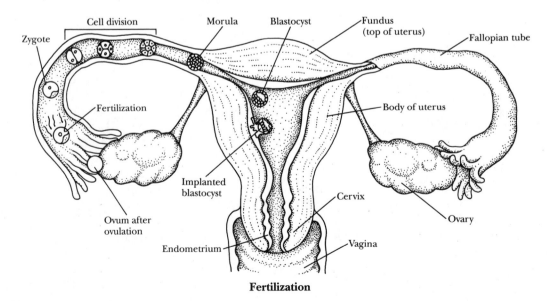

Fertilization

matching pair of X chromosomes (XX); all your ova carry X chromosomes, meaning that your baby will always get one X from you. Men have one X and one Y chromosome in their set of sex chromosomes, so some sperm carry X chromosomes and others carry Y chromosomes. Consequently, the sex of your unborn child is determined by the chromosome that the father contributes. For example, if a sperm carrying an X chromosome fertilizes the egg, the baby is a girl (XX); if the sperm carrying a Y chromosome fertilizes the egg, the baby is a boy (XY).

Occasionally a woman releases more than one egg at ovulation, and each is fertilized by a separate sperm, resulting in *fraternal* or nonidentical twins (or triplets, quadruplets, and so on). Sometimes a single fertilized egg divides into two or more, resulting in *identical* multiples.

Confirming Your Pregnancy

Although pregnancy can be detected soon after you conceive, you might not suspect you are pregnant or test for pregnancy until you have missed a menstrual period. A pregnancy test checks your urine or blood for human chorionic gonadotropin (hCG), a hormone produced only during pregnancy.

Do-it-yourself pregnancy test kits are now available in drug stores. You can test your own urine, reportedly as early as a few days after missing a menstrual period. Although the manufacturers claim accuracy of up to 99 percent, objective testing has found the accuracy of these tests to range from 46 to 89 percent.[1] Accuracy improves to over 80 percent when the test is performed ten or more days after a missed menstrual period. The test could indicate that you are not pregnant when you are, or that you are pregnant when you are not.

Many kits provide supplies for two tests; you can test a week or so after missing a

menstrual period and again a few days to a week later. When used in this way, the tests have a higher rate of accuracy. Professional blood or urine laboratory tests can be performed as early as two to four weeks after ovulation (or at about the time you miss a menstrual period) and are more accurate than the do-it-yourself kits.

If you suspect you are pregnant, whether or not you have used a home pregnancy test, have your pregnancy confirmed by a medical professional, begin prenatal care, avoid environmental hazards, and pay special attention to your nutritional needs.

Early Signs and Symptoms of Pregnancy

Most of the following are caused by changes in hormone production that begin almost immediately after conception and help ensure optimal development of your baby.

- Missed menstrual period
- Breast changes (a heavy and full feeling, tenderness, tingling in the nipple area, and a darkened areola)
- Fullness, bloating, or ache in the lower abdomen
- Fatigue and drowsiness; faintness
- Nausea, vomiting, or both
- Frequent urination
- Increased vaginal secretions
- Positive pregnancy test

Calculating Your Due Date

Your doctor or midwife must know your due date in order to judge whether the growth rate of the fetus is appropriate. Knowledge of your due date is also essential in deciding whether the baby is preterm (before thirty-seven weeks of pregnancy) or postterm (after forty-two or forty-three weeks of pregnancy) and can provide an early clue that you may be carrying twins.

At your first prenatal appointment, your caregiver will determine your due date by asking the date of your last menstrual period (conception takes place about two weeks after your last period). To calculate the date, he or she will subtract three months from the first day of your last menstrual period and add seven days. (Even though it is more accurate to count ahead 266 days from the exact date of conception, this date is rarely known.) Pregnancy lasts an average of 280 days or 40 weeks. When the doctor or midwife says you are twelve weeks pregnant, it means that the fetus is ten weeks old.

If you cannot remember the date of your last menstrual period, or if your last period was scant or unusual, your doctor or midwife will use other methods to determine your due date. An ultrasound scan before the end of the sixth month is the most accurate and common of these methods (see the discussion of ultrasound on page 65).

Remember, normal pregnancies vary in length. Think of your due date as approximate, and expect the baby from two weeks before to two weeks after that date. Two-thirds of all babies are born within ten days of their due dates, but only about 4 percent are actually born on their due date.

Hormonal Changes During Pregnancy

Pregnancy brings profound changes in your body, emotional adjustments for you and your partner, and dynamic growth and development of the fetus. Many of the physical changes that occur are caused by changes in hormone production.

Human chorionic gonadotropin (hCG), produced by the developing placenta, assures that your ovaries produce estrogen and progesterone until your placenta matures and

takes over production of these hormones (approximately three to four months).

Estrogen promotes the growth of reproductive tissues by increasing the size of the uterine musculature, promoting growth of your uterine lining and its blood supply, increasing the production of vaginal mucus, and stimulating the development of the duct system and blood supply in your breasts. The high levels of estrogen in pregnancy probably influence water retention, subcutaneous fat buildup, and skin pigmentation.

Progesterone inhibits smooth muscle contractions. Thus progesterone relaxes the uterus, keeping it from contracting excessively; relaxes the walls of blood vessels, helping maintain a healthy low blood pressure; and relaxes the stomach and bowels, allowing for greater absorption of nutrients. Progesterone stimulates secretion of the ovarian hormone *relaxin*, which relaxes and softens ligaments, cartilage, and the cervix, allowing these tissues to spread during the birth.

Besides estrogen and progesterone, *other hormones* that influence growth, mineral balance, metabolism, and corticosteroid levels are produced in greater quantities and cause many physical changes during pregnancy.

First Trimester Changes for Mother and Baby

Pregnancy is divided into three trimesters, each one lasting approximately three months. The first trimester (the first three calendar months of pregnancy) is called the "developmental period" for the fetus, since by the end of this period all the fetal organ systems are formed and functioning. For you, the first trimester is a time of physical and emotional adjustment to being pregnant.

The First Four Weeks of Pregnancy (conception to two weeks of fetal life)

Fetus

After it has been fertilized, the ovum quickly changes from one cell to many. Within thirty minutes it begins dividing into two cells, then four, eight, sixteen, and so on. By the end of two days the cluster of cells is known as the *morula*. Within five days the morula has made its way along the fallopian tube to the uterus, and, by the end of the first week, it implants, usually in the upper part of the uterus. Now called a *blastocyst*, it develops tiny, rootlike projections (*chorionic villi*) that penetrate the uterine lining and draw nourishment from it.

During the early weeks of pregnancy, the uterine lining (*endometrium*) becomes thicker and more vascular, providing a rich source of nourishment for the developing blastocyst. At the end of the first month of development, the chorionic villi extend well into the uterine lining and become a primitive placenta. Fetal blood circulates through this rootlike formation while your blood circulates into the spaces (intervillous spaces) surrounding the villi. A thin membrane separates the two blood streams, and normally they do not mix.

Through a complex process of cell division and differentiation, the fetus, placenta, and amniotic sac and fluid are formed. The amniotic sac surrounds the blastocyst; later the fluid within the sac (*amniotic fluid*) benefits the fetus by absorbing bumps from the outside, maintaining an even temperature inside, and providing the fetus with a medium for easy movement.

Expectant Mother

While all this is taking place for your baby, you may have noticed only some breast swelling or tenderness, or a slight ache in your lower abdomen. And you are about to miss your menstrual period! The remarkable changes that you will experience have just begun.

The Fifth to Fourteenth Weeks of Pregnancy (third to twelfth weeks of fetal life)

Fetus

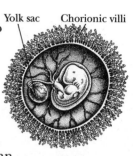

Yolk sac   Chorionic villi

Five Weeks

During the fifth to fourteenth weeks of pregnancy, the baby, now called an *embryo*, develops rapidly. A primitive nervous system, with a brain and a spinal column, begins to form. The circulatory system also develops, with the heart beating by the twenty-fifth day after conception. Although the embryo is only half the size of a pea, the body has a head, with eyes, ears, and a mouth beginning to form. There are simple kidneys, liver, and digestive tract and a primitive umbilical cord. On the twenty-sixth day, arm buds appear, and, two days later, leg buds.

Although your baby's sex is determined at conception, the anatomy of the male and female baby appears the same until the fetus is about seven weeks old. Between the developing leg buds is a slit with a knob of tissue, the *genital tubercle*. Within the abdomen of the embryo are two embryonic sex glands. During the seventh week, if the embryo is male, the Y chromosome stimulates these sex glands to begin producing androgens, male hormones that cause the two sides of the slit to join, forming the scrotum. They also cause the genital tubercle to develop into a penis. Before birth, the testicles descend from the abdomen into the scrotum. In the female, the sex glands begin producing female hormones that cause the slit to become the *vulva* (or external genitals) and the genital tubercle to develop into a clitoris. The sex glands remain within the baby as ovaries.

Developing placenta

Eight Weeks

By the eighth week of fetal life, the embryo is complete. The face has eyes, nose, ears, and a mouth with lips, a tongue, and tooth buds in the gums. The arms have hands with fingers and fingerprints. The legs have knees, ankles, and toes. The new body also functions: The brain sends out impulses that coordinate the functions of other organs, the heart beats strongly, the stomach produces digestive juices, the liver manufactures red blood cells, and the arms move. The embryo grows about one millimeter a day, with different parts developing on different days. Between forty-six and forty-eight days the first true bone cells replace the cartilage in the skeleton. Embryologists have determined that when these first bone cells appear, in the upper arms, the embryonic period is complete. The developing baby is now called a *fetus.*

During the first three months of fetal life, the fetus has become quite active, although you probably do not yet detect any movements. Legs kick and arms move. The fetus can frown or smile, suck his thumb, swallow amniotic fluid, and urinate drops of sterile urine into the amniotic fluid. The fluid is completely exchanged about every three hours. Vocal cords are complete and the fetus makes breathing movements (the chest rises and falls), but of course no air exchange takes place because the fetus is in amniotic fluid. In fact, breathing amniotic fluid into the lungs may actually aid lung development. The heartbeat is strong enough by eight to ten weeks to be detected with a fetal ultrasound stethoscope (often called a Doppler). Eyelids cover the fetus's eyes and remain closed until the sixth month. By fourteen weeks of pregnancy, the fetus is about three inches long and weighs about one ounce.

Placenta

By the third month of pregnancy, the *placenta* is completely formed and serves as an organ for producing hormones and exchanging nutrients and waste products. It is through the placenta that oxygen and nutrients such as simple sugars, protein, fat, water, vitamins, and minerals are passed from your blood supply to the fetus's. The placenta also provides protection against most bacteria in your bloodstream, although most viruses and drugs will cross to the fetus. Waste products from the fetus are exchanged through the placenta and are carried by your blood to your kidneys and lungs for excretion.

With multiple pregnancies, there may be one or more placentas. Most identical twins share the same placenta, although occasionally they have separate ones. Fraternal twins have separate placentas although the placentas sometimes fuse into one large organ.

Expectant Mother

During this period, you may feel unusually tired and require more sleep because of the new demands on your supply of energy and because of the accompanying shift in your rate of metabolism. You may also experience nausea and vomiting during the early months of your pregnancy. Although this is usually called "morning sickness," it may occur at any time of the day and is thought to be caused by human chorionic gonadotropin (hCG), produced by the developing placenta. Ways to cope with the

First Trimester

nausea and vomiting are discussed in chapter 4.

Although your breasts develop in puberty, the glandular tissue that produces milk does not fully develop until you become pregnant. As the levels of estrogen, progesterone, and other hormones increase during pregnancy, your breasts change in preparation for providing milk for your baby. They will enlarge, and you may notice tenderness, more prominent veins, and a tingling sensation in your nipples. The area around each nipple (the *areola*) also enlarges and becomes darker. Little bumps on the areola, called *Montgomery glands*, become more prominent in this area and enlarge to produce more lubricant.

You may need to urinate frequently because of pressure of the enlarging uterus on your bladder. In addition, your vagina and cervix become bluish in color, the cervix becomes softer, and vaginal secretions increase. Because the changes, although dramatic in nature, have been minuscule in size—the top of the uterus reaches barely above your pubic bone—you feel more different than you look.

Along with the physical changes, the early months of pregnancy are often filled with emotional ups and downs. The thought of motherhood may at times be pleasing to you, at other times not. You may cry easily. Mood swings seem more pronounced and may be difficult for you and your partner to understand.

Finding out that you are actually pregnant may bring about a mixture of emotions in you and your partner: pride in your ability to produce a child; fear of losing your independence; apprehension about changes in your relationship; hesitancy to focus on the baby if awaiting results of genetic testing; doubts about your ability to parent; and happiness about becoming parents. Sharing your thoughts and feelings with each other can help you work through this time of transition.

Second Trimester Changes for Mother and Baby

The Fifteenth to Twenty-seventh Weeks of Pregnancy (thirteenth to twenty-fifth weeks of fetal life)

Fetus

The thirteenth week of fetal life marks the beginning of the "growth period," when the already formed organs and structures of the fetus enlarge and mature. Head hair, eyelashes, and eyebrows appear. Fine, downy hair (called *lanugo*) develops on the arms, legs, and back of the fetus. Fingernails and toenails appear. The heartbeat is strong enough by the seventeenth or the eighteenth week that it can be heard with an ordinary stethoscope.

By the end of the twenty-fourth week, the fetus is about twelve inches long and weighs about one and a half pounds. The skin is wrinkled and covered with a creamy protective coating called *vernix caseosa*. At some point during this period, you will probably feel the fetus move (called *quickening*). At first, you may feel a light tapping or fluttering sensation that reminds you of gas bubbles, or the gentle movements of the small fetus may go unnoticed until activity becomes more vigorous.

Expectant Mother

During these middle months of pregnancy, you probably feel physically well, and your nausea and fatigue probably disappear or decline. The growth of your baby continues, and your uterus expands into your abdominal cavity in response to the enlarging fetus, placenta, and increased amniotic fluid. By the end of the fifth month of pregnancy, the top of your uterus (the *fundus*) reaches your navel. During monthly prenatal appointments, your caregiver measures the height of your fundus to check that the fetus is growing adequately and to confirm the length of your pregnancy. Although fetal size and the amount of amniotic fluid can differ, the length of your pregnancy can be approximated by measuring the distance in centimeters between your pubic bone and fundus.

Second Trimester

Your breasts may not increase much in size during the second trimester, but *colostrum* (a yellowish fluid produced before breast milk) is usually present in the milk glands by the middle of pregnancy. Now is the time to examine your breasts in preparation for breastfeeding. See the discussion in chapter 14, on page 265.

Just as your nipples and areola get darker during pregnancy due to hormonal changes, other skin areas also become more pigmented. A dark line (*linea nigra*) between the pubic bone and the navel appears in some women. *Chloasma*, the mask of pregnancy, may appear as darkening of the skin around your eyes and nose. It disappears after the birth of your baby.

The physical changes of advancing pregnancy bring varying psychological responses. Some women enjoy how they look and feel, while others consider themselves unattractive, inconvenienced, and restricted. A heightened sense of growth and creativity may make you more sensitive; a kind word, a beautiful sunset, a touching photograph, or a needy child may elicit unusually strong emotions. You may recall more of your dreams than you did before pregnancy. In the middle months, you may want to start preparing for parenthood by reading books about child care or preparing the nursery and layette (see page 222).

During the second trimester, your pregnancy usually becomes more real for your family and friends. Your partner can feel the baby move when he or she places a hand on your abdomen or when you are in close physical contact. This contact with the developing baby enhances your partner's feelings of involvement and interest in the pregnancy and the baby. Like you, your partner may have a variety of thoughts and feelings about your changing appearance. (See pages 37–40 on sex during pregnancy and the expectant father and partner.)

Third Trimester Changes for Mother and Baby

The Twenty-eighth to Thirty-eighth Weeks of Pregnancy (twenty-sixth to thirty-sixth weeks of fetal life)

Fetus

The third trimester is the "finishing period" for the fetus. Babies born during this period are usually able to survive, although their chances for both survival and an easier transition to independent life improve as they get closer to their due date. In late pregnancy, antibodies pass through the placenta to the fetus, providing short-term resistance to the diseases to which you are immune. The baby born prematurely has received less of this protection than the full-term baby, and is thus more prone to contagious illness.

During the last three months of pregnancy, the fetal features are refined: The fingernails reach the fingertips and may even need cutting at birth, the hair on the head grows, the lanugo almost disappears, fat is deposited under the skin, and buds for the permanent teeth are laid down behind the milk teeth buds.

You can learn much about your baby at this time. The fetus has periods of sleep and wakefulness and responds to bright light. Loud external noises may elicit a reaction and stir her into action. The baby hears and becomes familiar with your voice and after birth will prefer your voice to a stranger's voice. Of course, the baby hears other sounds as well: your digestion and heartbeat, the circulation of blood within your uterus, and other external sounds, such as music and your partner's voice. The baby shows a clear preference for such familiar voices and sounds after birth. These familiar sounds or similar ones (like the rhythmic sloshing sounds of a dishwasher or washing machine) often soothe a fussy newborn.

At some point during the last trimester your baby assumes a favorite position, usually head down. During prenatal visits your doctor or midwife manually palpates your abdomen to determine which position the fetus has adopted. The procedure used is known as *Leopold's maneuvers.*

As your baby continues to grow and gain weight, her activity diminishes since there is less room for her to move. You may feel arm and leg movements rather than whole body shifts. If you feel a series of rhythmic jolts, your baby probably has the hiccups. Your baby may start sucking her thumb while still in the womb. The fetus gains about three and a half pounds and grows about five and a half inches during this part of your pregnancy.

Placenta

The placenta and membranes are part of the complex and intricate fetal-maternal-placental system. In late pregnancy, changes within this system help prepare you physically and psychologically to give birth and to nourish and nurture your infant. They also prepare your baby for labor, birth, and survival outside the uterus.

The elaborate process leading to and including birth is only partly understood.

Here we can barely touch on some of the known steps that bring all the vital elements to readiness for birth.

Changes in placental hormone production cause an increase in the ratio of estrogen to progesterone. Estrogen makes the uterus more sensitive to *oxytocin* (a hormone that causes contractions of the uterus), which means that you will begin to notice more contractions in late pregnancy. The estrogen-oxytocin interaction also seems to trigger release of *prostaglandins,* which ripen the cervix.

The amount of amniotic fluid decreases in the last weeks of pregnancy, from about one and a half quarts at about seven months to about one quart at term.

Expectant Mother

During the third trimester, your uterus expands to a level just below your breastbone. Crowding by the uterus, and the high levels of progesterone, may cause indigestion and heartburn. You may also experience shortness of breath or soreness in your lower ribs as your uterus presses on your diaphragm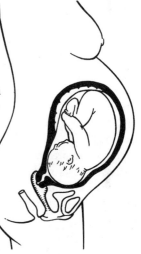

Third Trimester

and ribs. Varicose veins in the legs, hemorrhoids, and swollen ankles sometimes develop due to the increased pressure within your abdomen, the decreased blood return from your lower limbs, and the effect of progesterone, which relaxes the walls of the blood vessels.

During the final months of pregnancy, you may develop small red elevations on the skin, called *vascular spiders.* They may ap-

31

pear on your upper body. Also during this time, you may develop stretch marks on your abdomen, thighs, or breasts. These marks, called *striae gravidarum,* are reddish during pregnancy and become glistening white lines after the birth. Many women attempt to prevent these stretch marks by applying various lotions or oils to their skin, but there is no evidence that they are effective. About half of women develop striae whether they use such lotions or not.

By the ninth month, you will probably start looking forward to the end of the pregnancy, relief from the physical discomforts, and the long-awaited joy of having the baby. You may become more introspective and find yourself thinking more and perhaps worrying about labor, birth, and the baby. Through childbirth education classes, you and your partner can learn more and worry less about labor, birth, and how to cope with the stresses of late pregnancy.

You may feel protective of the developing baby and try to avoid exposing yourself to things that might threaten her well-being. You may also feel more vulnerable and more dependent on your partner and others. As you anticipate the responsibilities of parenthood, you may think more of your own parents and how they parented you. Adjustments in your sexual relationship continue as your abdomen enlarges and you become less agile. Keep the lines of communication open between you and your partner as your sexual feelings, needs, and desires change. (See page 37 for more about your sexual relationship during pregnancy.)

You and your partner may worry from time to time about your health or your baby's well-being. Thoughts of death or injury may come up. This is not surprising, because pregnancy and birth do carry certain potential risks, which can be greatly diminished with good self-care and early and consistent prenatal care. Now in the United States and Canada fewer than ten women per 100,000 die from causes related to child-

bearing; approximately one baby in a hundred dies around the time of birth. If you find yourself worrying or dreaming about death or harm to you or your baby, share these fears with someone who will be supportive—your partner, a relative, your caregiver, a childbirth educator, or an empathetic friend. You might be tempted to avoid telling anyone about such fears, as if talking about them might somehow make them more real or likely to happen. In fact, you will probably be relieved to acknowledge and share such fears. Furthermore, thinking through how you would want such misfortunes handled may ease your mind (see page 181).

The Thirty-ninth and Fortieth Weeks of Pregnancy (thirty-seventh and thirty-eighth weeks of fetal life)

Fetus
During these last weeks, the fetal organs continue to mature to prepare your baby for life outside your uterus. The fetus also adds fat and gains about a pound. At birth, the average baby weighs seven to seven and a half pounds, although normal weight for a full-term baby can vary from five and a half to ten pounds. Newborns average twenty inches in length, but a range of eighteen to twenty-two inches is normal. During the pregnancy, the weight of the fertilized egg has increased six billion times! In the next twenty years, your child's weight will increase only twenty times.

Placenta
The mature placenta is flat and round, six to eight inches in diameter, and one inch thick; it weighs about one-seventh of the fetus's weight. The size and weight vary in proportion to the size of the baby.

The side of the placenta that implants in the uterine wall (the maternal side) is

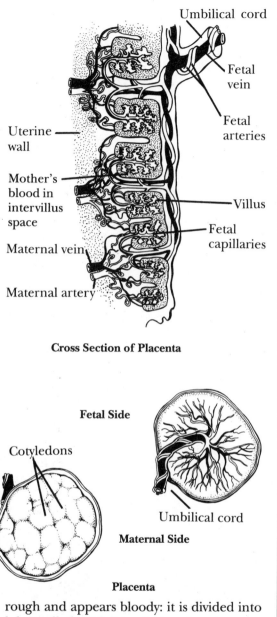

Umbilical cord

Fetal vein

Fetal arteries

Uterine wall

Mother's blood in intervillus space

Villus

Fetal capillaries

Maternal vein

Maternal artery

Cross Section of Placenta

Fetal Side

Cotyledons

Umbilical cord

Maternal Side

Placenta

teries can be seen on the fetal side of the placenta spreading out from the umbilical cord and entering the placenta at various places.

Umbilical Cord

The umbilical cord links the placenta to your unborn baby. It extends from the fetus's navel to the approximate center of the placenta. The average cord length is twenty inches, but twelve to thirty-nine inches is considered normal. The moist, white cord has a twisted or spiral appearance; two arteries and one vein are contained within it. Fetal blood flows at about four miles an hour, keeping the cord stiff, almost like a garden hose full of water. At birth, as your baby breathes, his circulation pattern begins to change, sealing off the blood flow to his navel and rerouting more blood to his lungs.

Expectant Mother

About two weeks before the birth, your profile may change as the fetus descends into the pelvic cavity. This noticeable descent is called *engagement* or lightening. You may feel less pressure on your diaphragm and find it easier to breathe and eat as the fetus becomes engaged in the pelvis. However, as the fetal head descends it presses on your bladder, causing you to urinate even more frequently.

Toward the end of your pregnancy the uterine contractions, *Braxton-Hicks contractions*, become more obvious and more frequent. Though not labor contractions, they serve the useful purposes of enhancing circulation in your uterus, pressing the baby lower in your pelvis and against your cervix, and they are also thought to work with prostaglandins in *ripening* (softening) and *effacing* (thinning) your cervix.

You may find yourself looking forward to the end of pregnancy. Anxiety, light sleep, fatigue, and the usual discomforts of late pregnancy add to this desire. At times you

rough and appears bloody: it is divided into lobes called *cotyledons*. As the placenta ages, hard gritty areas (calcium deposits) begin to appear. The fetal side of the placenta is smooth, pale, and shiny and is covered by the amniotic membrane. The amniotic and chorionic membranes extend from the edge of the placenta to form the sac (bag of waters) that contains the amniotic fluid and fetus. Branches of the umbilical vein and armay feel as though you have been and will be pregnant forever. But at the same time all the customary late pregnancy activities—more frequent visits to your physician or midwife, your childbirth preparation classes, baby showers, preparation of the baby's clothing, equipment, and sleeping area—help you realize that pregnancy will soon be over, and a new stage in your life cycle—parenthood—will begin.

Post-Dates—The Forty-first Week of Pregnancy and Beyond

Fetus

The average length of pregnancy is forty weeks, but many pregnancies last longer. Some post-date pregnancies are cases of mistaken due dates; others involve fetuses who are not quite ready to be born at forty weeks and need more time to grow and mature. Occasionally, the fetus is ready to be born, but for unexplained reasons, labor does not begin on time. In this case, the fetus may become postmature and not receive sufficient nourishment and oxygen from the aging placenta. To determine if the post-date baby is postmature, tests of fetal well-being and placental function are performed. See chapters 3 and 13 for information on the tests and on postmaturity.

Placenta

In many post-date pregnancies, the placenta continues to support the growth and well-being of the fetus, and labor almost always begins by forty-three weeks. In true postmaturity, placental function declines, the amniotic fluid volume drops, and the fetus may be stressed. Under these circumstances, the fetus really needs to be delivered.

Expectant Mother

Physically, you may continue feeling much as you have been during late pregnancy. Emotionally, however, you may find the waiting frustrating, worrisome, or depressing.

The longer the wait, the more difficult it becomes. You may want to try ways to start labor. Clear communication with your caregiver will help you understand your options.

Special Considerations in Pregnancy

Age of the Mother

Statistics indicate that the most favorable age for a woman to bear children is between twenty and the mid-thirties. Fewer problems arise during this period than during the teens, the late thirties, or the forties. Despite this, however, the birth rate among teens and women in their thirties and forties is higher than ever and rising.

Teen Pregnancy

If you are a teenager and pregnant, you have a special set of strengths and needs.

Your young body is probably strong. Your chances for a healthy pregnancy are good, especially if you take good care of yourself by eating well, going to the doctor or midwife early in pregnancy, and staying away from drugs, alcohol, and tobacco.

Teenagers usually give birth well since their bodies are in good condition. Because you are young, your uterus is probably strong and your ligaments and tissues are stretchy. This may not mean a quick or painless labor, but you may not need medical interventions to help the labor along.

Teenagers can love their babies as much as anyone. Let your love for your baby guide you in making decisions about taking care of yourself, going to school, dealing with your parents and your baby's father, and deciding whether to keep or relinquish your baby.

You can get help from your city or county health department, pregnancy counseling organizations, the YWCA, or childbirth education organizations. Look them up in your phone book. Also see Recommended Resources for books on teen pregnancy and parenting.

First Pregnancy after Age Thirty-five

Women today have many reasons for delaying their first pregnancy until they are beyond age thirty-five: career or education priorities, financial considerations, infertility, lack of a partner, and postponement of parenthood until the "biological clock" gives its now-or-never message. Waiting until mid-career before having children is the norm today among well-educated or professional women for whom parenthood is only one of many appealing choices. You have probably heard that the pregnant woman over age thirty-five is at greater risk of medical complications than the younger woman. To an extent that is true, although the reasons are not clear. Age in itself is not a disease, like diabetes or heart disease, although older women seem to be more likely than younger women to develop the problems that caregivers watch for in everyone: high blood pressure, varicose veins, gestational diabetes, growth problems or inherited disorders in the fetus, problems with the placenta, labor complications, and others.

Why are older women at greater risk? Perhaps because the longer a woman lives, the more likely she is to have been exposed to poor health practices, accidents, illnesses, or environmental influences. If, however, you have enjoyed good health over the years and have taken care of yourself, your age is less of a risk factor.

A stressful lifestyle or job, commonplace for women in this age group, may also increase the likelihood of pregnancy complications such as high blood pressure or preterm labor. A demanding job, added to the full-time job of growing a baby, may be too much. You may find it necessary or desirable to reduce the stress of your job and take more time to rest and relax.

Older women are more likely than younger women to carry a baby with a genetic disorder, such as Down's syndrome, which causes mental retardation and physical abnormalities. This condition can be detected with amniocentesis or chorionic villus sampling (see pages 60–61). Women over age thirty-five are offered one of these tests in early pregnancy. If Down's syndrome or another genetic disorder is discovered, you may choose to have an abortion or prepare yourself for life with a child with such a condition.

As an older pregnant woman, your attitudes toward childbearing may be affected by your age and experiences. If you have a history of infertility or miscarriage, you are more likely to be vulnerable to the suggestion that you are "high-risk" or "unhealthy." You may seek assurances that the baby will be normal and healthy through extensive testing and procedures designed to detect and treat problems. Some women find the testing stressful in itself, especially because the tests are not always accurate and cannot detect every possible problem. (For discussion of pregnancy complications and the relevant tests and treatments, see chapter 3.) As for labor complications, it is true that the cesarean rate for women over thirty-five is higher than average (approximately 40 percent), but the reasons are not clear. It may be that problems arising in the older woman's labor are more likely to be treated by a cesarean than the same problems in a younger woman's labor.[2]

If you are thirty-five or over and pregnant, what should you do to help improve the possibilities of a good outcome and emotional satisfaction? Really, you should do no more and no less than any pregnant woman having a baby. Take good care of yourself, reduce stress, get good prenatal care with a competent and caring physician or midwife, consider your options regarding the tests and procedures available, and deal with problems if and when they arise. Take childbirth classes to learn what to expect, how to work with your partner to participate

—photograph by Lise Alexander/Beginnings

Because of the older child's need for care, you may focus less on this pregnancy than your first.

in decisions, and how to help yourselves deal with the stresses of labor.

Although problems will arise in some women and you might be one, the problems are almost always treatable or manageable. And even though you may be older than other pregnant women, you are correct to expect a healthy outcome.

When You're Pregnant Again

We usually refer to a woman expecting her second (or more) baby as a multipara or multip. As a multip, you may find this pregnancy is not as emotionally exhilarating as the first. Pregnancy is not new and may have lost some of its luster. For this reason, and because of the older child's needs for care, you may focus less on this pregnancy than the first.

Although each pregnancy is different, second pregnancies share some predictable differences from the first. You can expect to feel the baby's movements about one month earlier, because you will recognize the sensation sooner. Because your abdominal muscles tend to relax more easily in a subsequent pregnancy, your abdomen may enlarge sooner so that the pregnancy becomes noticeable earlier. Your pelvic ligaments may soften sooner this time. You may also feel you are carrying the baby lower. Braxton-Hicks contractions may be more noticeable and numerous, especially toward the end of pregnancy. While you may not be delighted at these earlier discomforts and physical changes, it might be reassuring to realize that pregnancy changes take place more readily in a body that has done it before.

You may feel less emotionally involved in this pregnancy than you were the last. Your attention shifts from thoughts about the fetus to thoughts about integrating a new baby into the family. This is partly because you have a clearer picture of yourself this time as a mother of a newborn. Your partner may also be less involved, less attentive to you during this pregnancy, which could be due to his or her own added experience and diminished fears about you and your baby's health.

Should you participate in childbirth preparation classes at this time? Even if you attended excellent classes with your first pregnancy, there are some good reasons to attend classes again, particularly refresher classes designed for your needs. Refresher classes prepare you for how this labor may differ from the first; they offer ideas on preparing siblings and managing the household with more than one child.

Anxiety about the upcoming labor is not uncommon among multiparas. If you had a straightforward and positive birth experience before, you may wonder if you can "do it again." If your previous birth was difficult or disappointing, you may be burdened with worries that these problems will arise again. These normal doubts are worth talking about with your partner, caregiver, or childbirth educator. Much can be done to overcome these self-doubts, to increase your self-confidence, and to improve your birth experience.

Many second-time mothers worry whether they can possibly have enough love for another child. You may feel that all your love goes to the first child and the second will be short-changed. Or you may wonder if your love for your first will lessen when the new baby arrives. It helps to remember that you do not have a limited amount of love to share. You do not run out of love. Just as the flame of a candle can light other candles without ever using up the flame, you will find you can spread love without using it up.

Sex during Pregnancy

What happens to your sexual relationship during pregnancy? Your feelings? Your partner's feelings? Is intercourse safe? Is orgasm safe?

For most women and their partners, pregnancy brings changes in the sexual relationship, but these changes are not the same for everyone. While one woman may feel ripe, beautiful, and sexual, another may feel clumsy and fat. While one woman may feel secure and loved by a caring and considerate partner, another may be alone or in a difficult relationship. One woman may be concerned about her health or the baby's, while another feels robust and wonderful. One partner may feel anxious about the woman's health or turned off by her changing appearance, while another relishes the entire process.

Many expectant fathers have never felt so deeply in love.

Your partner's and your feelings about pregnancy and its associated changes will undoubtedly influence your sexual relationship. So will the bodily changes, such as nausea, fatigue, weight gain, breast tenderness, changes in circulation, and hormonal changes. As these physical factors fluctuate, so may your sexual feelings. The kinds of things that excite and please you may also fluctuate. At times you may feel more desire than usual; at other times, less or none. Your partner may or may not understand and accept your changing sexuality. Pregnancy can create tensions between the two of you, so open communication is important at this time.

What about safety? Reports or rumors of associations between intercourse or orgasm and vaginal bleeding, infection, miscarriage, or preterm labor are scary. In addition, you may have questions about whether deep entry of the penis into your vagina and your partner's weight on top of your abdomen can endanger the baby.

On close examination of the information now available, it appears that intercourse or orgasm may cause problems if you are at risk for a miscarriage or preterm labor, if you have had vaginal bleeding during pregnancy, if you have continuing or painful cramps after intercourse, or if you have a new sexual partner who has a sexually transmitted disease. If you are at risk, you should avoid intercourse. The only other warning usually given is that your partner should not blow air into the vagina, since this can cause an *air embolus*—an air bubble in the bloodstream—which is a very serious complication.

Otherwise, most medical caregivers recommend sexual activity as desired by both partners. The contractions resulting from orgasm seem to be handled well by a healthy fetus. Gentle, more shallow penetration and the use of positions that avoid placing your partner's weight on your abdomen help prevent discomfort and alleviate the worry you may feel about the baby. Remember that the baby is protected by the cushioning effect of the amniotic fluid and the seal provided by the amniotic sac and cervical mucus.

Pregnancy can be a time to explore new ways to please each other sexually and a time to more openly express your needs and desires to each other.

The Expectant Father

Waiting for fatherhood is a unique emotional experience—less understood, but no less significant than waiting for motherhood, yet fathers' needs and concerns are often not addressed. Many have never felt so important yet so ignored, so married yet so abandoned, so deeply in love and sexual yet so afraid of sex, and so creative yet so drained of energy. Paying attention to these new feelings and sharing them with their partner or close friends will help men through this rich but challenging time. Counseling or discussions with others in similar circumstances are also helpful. When expectant fathers get together and share their feelings and concerns, several themes come up:[3]

Responsibility. Many men feel that they are leaving freedom behind. The happy-go-lucky days are almost over, and it is time to be a responsible and mature provider and parent. The role of wage-earner becomes more pressing. The pregnant mother's more vulnerable state and increased emotional needs may make a father feel overwhelmed with duties and responsibilities he is not quite ready to accept. He may at times yearn for the good old days when he was relatively independent. Sometimes getting away for an afternoon or a day helps relieve the pressure.

Life and death. Pregnancy and the impending birth of a child often prompt thoughts about the biological life cycle and immortality. Continuing the family for another generation is a source of pride and fulfillment. Many expectant fathers also fear the death or injury of their spouse and/or unborn child. Some even worry about their own death. These concerns may lead a man to buy life insurance, change jobs from one that involves physical danger to a safer one, or become more protective of his partner (urging seat belt use, urging her to avoid potentially risky activities or exposure to illness, encouraging the use of any obstetric test or popular remedy that claims to improve the chances of a healthy outcome, and so on). As long as the protectiveness is reasonable and not overdone, it is probably constructive and appreciated by the mother.

Displacement. A man sometimes feels left out as the mother focuses inward and becomes more preoccupied with the baby, especially if she also turns more to others for some emotional support. He may feel she is less available to him emotionally, physically, and sexually, while he, at the same time, is expected to give more than ever in their relationship. To complicate it all, he may also feel guilty for any resentment or lack of enthusiasm about the pregnancy. It may help to discuss these feelings with a friend who has experienced this, but it is also very important to explain these feelings to his partner, who may be unaware of what he is feeling.

Anxiety about his role during labor and birth. "How will I perform during labor? What about blood? Will I faint or get sick? Can I handle it?" Every expectant father questions himself in this way—some more than others. Childbirth preparation classes, films, books, and discussions with other fathers are all very helpful in building confidence and helping to prepare him for his role in childbirth. It is also a good idea to consider having another support person at the birth to help both the father and the laboring woman. A friend, relative, or a trained labor support person can help the couple with comfort measures and also offer perspective and advice.

Physical discomforts. Many men experience physical symptoms, sometimes called the Couvade (Fathering) Syndrome, during their partner's pregnancy. Weight gain, food cravings, abdominal bloating, nausea, vomiting, backaches, toothaches, loss of appetite, or abdominal cramps may be among the symptoms, which reflect empathy and identification with the pregnant woman or perhaps some anxiety. If an expectant father becomes preoccupied with pregnancy-like symptoms, counseling may be in order.

If You Have No Partner

If you are pregnant and without a partner, you face a different set of challenges. Although there are millions of single parents in North America, little support is provided by society. You may notice that people seem uncomfortable, hostile, or pitying when they learn you are single.

In a sense you are taking on a role usually shared by two people—the parenting role. It is hard work and there may be times when you doubt whether you can or want to do it. You may feel lonely or vulnerable at times and wish for a reliable partner. At other times, however, you may be relieved that

you are not burdened with an incompatible partner. This is a time to reach out to others for help and emotional support.

If Your Partner Is Not the Baby's Biological Father

If your partner is not the father of your baby, you both may encounter new and different challenges as you go through the pregnancy and become parents. If your partner is a new lover or a lesbian lover, his or her role is less defined by society than the role of husband/father. If your baby was conceived by artificial insemination due to your male partner's infertility, your partner may have had to make some difficult emotional adjustments.

The lack of a biological tie may cause your partner to feel less involved in the pregnancy—that it is "your" pregnancy rather than "our" pregnancy—or to question his or her role in decision making and support. If the biological father is also involved, your partner's role is even less clear. You and your partner need to anticipate that your relationship with each other and with the baby may be challenged by misplaced or unrealistic expectations and assumptions made by friends, acquaintances, society, and yourselves. Honest and open discussion, coupled with extra patience and a willingness to try different, nontraditional solutions will help.

Calendar of Pregnancy: First Trimester

	Four weeks	*Eight weeks*	*Twelve weeks*
Fetal growth	♦ Is less than ⅒ inch long ♦ Beginning development of spinal cord, nervous system, gastrointestinal system, heart, and lungs ♦ Amniotic sac envelops the preliminary tissues of entire body ♦ Is called an "ovum"	♦ Is less than 1 inch long ♦ Face is forming with rudimentary eyes, ears, mouth, and tooth buds ♦ Arms and legs are moving ♦ Brain is forming ♦ Fetal heartbeat is detectable with ultrasound ♦ Is called an "embryo"	♦ Is about 3 inches long and weighs about 1 ounce ♦ Can move arms, legs, fingers, and toes ♦ Fingerprints are present ♦ Can smile, frown, suck, and swallow ♦ Sex is distinguishable ♦ Can urinate ♦ Is called a "fetus"
Placental and uterine changes	♦ Uterine lining is thick with increased blood supply; uterus is enlarging ♦ Cervix becomes softer, more blue in color ♦ Implantation of ovum is usually in upper back portion of uterus ♦ Placenta and umbilical cord are forming ♦ Chorionic gonadotropin, produced by chorionic villi (which become placenta), is present in mother's blood and urine and is used for pregnancy test	♦ Uterus is size of a tennis ball ♦ Umbilical cord has definite shape ♦ Amniotic fluid cushions fetus, maintains even temperature, and allows easy movement	♦ Uterus is size of a grapefruit ♦ Fundus is just above pubic bone ♦ Amniotic fluid fills uterine cavity and is continually replaced ♦ Placenta is small but complete; there is full exchange of nutrients and waste products ♦ Placenta is now major source of estrogen and progesterone

First Trimester

Common physical changes in mother	♦ Is not menstruating ♦ Has fullness, bloating, or ache in pelvic cavity ♦ May be constipated ♦ Has vasocongestion in genital area ♦ May be nauseated, may vomit ♦ Is tired ♦ Has increased vaginal secretions	♦ May feel faint ♦ Has to urinate more frequently ♦ Breasts are fuller, nipples may tingle or feel tender, areola is darker ♦ May lose or gain up to 5 pounds
Common emotional changes in mother	♦ Feels anxiety, hope, while awaiting confirmation of pregnancy and results of tests for genetic disorders ♦ Focus is on body changes	♦ Moods vary widely ♦ "Motherhood" feelings are being sorted out ♦ May fear miscarriage ♦ Time seems long
Common emotions of father/ partner	♦ Reality of pregnancy may be a shock ♦ Is concerned with partner's mood swings and fatigue	♦ May experience weight gain, occasionally nausea ♦ Pregnancy seems unreal
Common changes for both	♦ Parenting roles and priorities are questioned ♦ Sexual relationship may change ♦ May fear sexual intercourse will harm fetus ♦ May feel ambivalent toward pregnancy: joy and excitement vs. resentment and anxiety	♦ Feelings toward own parents are examined ♦ Finances may affect attitudes about approaching parenthood ♦ Well-being of baby may be a concern

continued

Calendar of Pregnancy: Second Trimester

	Sixteen weeks	*Twenty weeks*	*Twenty-four weeks*
Fetal growth	♦ Is about 5½ inches long and weighs about 4 ounces ♦ Heartbeat is strong ♦ Skin is thin, transparent ♦ Downy hair (lanugo) covers body ♦ Fingernails and toenails are forming ♦ Has coordinated movements; is able to roll over in amniotic fluid	♦ Is 10 to 12 inches long and weighs ½ to 1 pound ♦ Heartbeat is audible with ordinary stethoscope ♦ Sucks thumb ♦ Hiccups ♦ Hair, eyelashes, eyebrows are present	♦ Is 11 to 14 inches long and weighs 1 to 1½ pounds ♦ Skin is wrinkled and covered with protective coating (vernix caseosa) ♦ Eyes are open ♦ Meconium is collecting in bowel ♦ Has strong grip
Placental and uterine changes	♦ Uterus is 3 inches above pubic bone ♦ Placenta performs nutritional, respiratory, excretory, and most endocrine functions ♦ Amount of amniotic fluid increases	♦ Uterus is at level of navel ♦ There are 2 to 3 pints of amniotic fluid ♦ Placenta is fully developed and covers about half the inner surface of uterus	♦ Uterus is above level of navel ♦ Placenta covers less of inner surface of uterus as uterus grows

Second Trimester

Common physical changes in mother	♦ Fetal movement is noticeable ♦ Nausea is usually gone ♦ Breasts are usually less tender ♦ Linea nigra may appear ♦ Mask of pregnancy (chloasma) may appear ♦ May be constipated ♦ May have food cravings or nonfood cravings (called pica) ♦ May have nasal congestion	♦ Pelvic joints are relaxing (due to relaxin, a hormone) ♦ May have leg cramps ♦ Gums or nose may bleed ♦ Side or groin may be painful from round ligament contractions ♦ Voice may change due to effects of hormones ♦ Weight gain is from 13½ to 15½ pounds (0.8 to 1 pound per week)
Common emotional changes in mother	♦ May be more dependent ♦ Pregnancy is accepted and there is more interest in baby and parenting ♦ May be introspective ♦ Daydreaming and dreaming at night increase	♦ Sense of growth and creativity may develop ♦ Changing appearance brings varying feelings about body image ♦ Time seems short
Common emotions of father/ partner	♦ Has varying feelings about partner's changing appearance ♦ May feel left out of mother-fetal relationship	♦ Is evaluating readiness and ability to be a parent
Common changes for both	♦ Sexual desire and activity may change ♦ Pregnancy becomes more enjoyable	♦ Awareness of parenting styles increases

Calendar of Pregnancy: Third Trimester

	Twenty-eight weeks	*Thirty-two weeks*	*Thirty-six weeks*
Fetal growth	♦ Is 14 to 17 inches long and weighs 2½ to 3 pounds ♦ Is adding body fat ♦ Is very active ♦ Rudimentary breathing movements are present	♦ Is 16½ to 18 inches long and weighs 4 to 5 pounds ♦ Has periods of sleep and wakefulness ♦ Responds to sounds ♦ May assume birth position ♦ Bones of head are soft and flexible ♦ Iron is being stored in liver	♦ Is 19 inches long and weighs 6 pounds ♦ Skin is less wrinkled ♦ Vernix caseosa is thick ♦ Lanugo is mostly gone ♦ Is less active ♦ Is gaining immunities from mother
Placental and uterine changes	♦ Uterus is 3 finger-breadths above navel	♦ Uterus is 6 finger-breadths above navel ♦ Braxton-Hicks contractions are more noticeable	♦ Uterus is just below breast-bone and ribs ♦ Amniotic fluid volume is decreasing ♦ Efficiency of placenta is decreasing ♦ Hormone production is changing: progesterone levels are decreasing, estrogen levels are increasing ♦ Prostaglandin levels are increasing

Third Trimester

Common physical changes in mother	♦ May have backache ♦ May have heartburn ♦ May have shortness of breath ♦ May have hemorrhoids ♦ May have varicose veins ♦ May have anemia ♦ May have insomnia or light sleep ♦ Colostrum increases	♦ Pelvic ligaments relax ♦ Ankles may be swollen ♦ Stretch marks may appear ♦ Perspiration may increase ♦ Vascular spiders may appear ♦ Metabolism increases ♦ Urination may become even more frequent ♦ Total weight gain is usually 24 to 30 pounds
Common emotional changes in mother	♦ Is focused on birth, possibly apprehensive of labor, delivery, the unknown ♦ May have a variety of feelings about body image	♦ Dependency on others increases ♦ May desire protection ♦ May have decreased sexual interest ♦ Time is a burden
Common emotions of father/ partner	♦ Is protective of family ♦ Questions fathering role ♦ May long for independence	♦ May fear harming fetus during sexual intercourse
Common changes for both	♦ Changes in sexual relationship are still occurring; may try alternative positions or techniques	♦ Fears and concerns about pain of labor and birth, health of mother and baby, and responsibilities of being parents are felt

continued

Calendar of Pregnancy: Term	Post Partum
Forty weeks	*The first weeks after birth*
Fetal growth	♦ Is about 20 inches long; average weight is about 7 to 7½ pounds ♦ Fingernails protrude beyond fingers ♦ Arms and legs are in flexed position ♦ Body fat is ample ♦ Lungs are mature ♦ Fetus may be "engaged" in pelvis	♦ Newborn needs sleep (10 to 20 hours per day), milk, suckling, warmth, comfort (touching, cuddling), and auditory and visual stimulation
Placental and uterine changes	♦ Uterus returns to same height as at 34 weeks when fetus is engaged ♦ Placenta is 6 to 8 inches in diameter, 1 inch thick, and about 1 pound ♦ Umbilical cord is 12 to 39 inches (usually 20 to 22 inches); is moist, white, and twisted or spiral in appearance ♦ Uterine contractions are more frequent due to increased sensitivity to oxytocin ♦ Cervix is softening (ripening) and thinning (effacing)	♦ Uterus is at height of navel right after birth and almost back to prepregnant size by 10 to 20 days post partum
Common physical changes in mother	Signs of labor: ♦ *Possible:* vague backache causing restlessness, menstrual-like cramps, soft stools, unusual burst of energy ("nesting urge") ♦ *Preliminary:* blood-tinged, mucousy vaginal discharge ("bloody show"), continuing nonprogressing uterine contractions (do not become longer, stronger, or closer together), leaking of amniotic fluid ♦ *Positive:* progressing labor contractions (become longer, stronger, and closer together over time), rupture of membranes followed within hours by progressing contractions	♦ "Afterpains" (contractions of uterus) are common, especially in multiparas ♦ Increased urination and perspiration, lochia (vaginal flow) ♦ Breasts enlarge ♦ Fatigue from labor and lack of sleep ♦ Initial weight loss may be 10 to 15 pounds ♦ Ovulation may be delayed, but is possible within weeks
Common emotional changes in mother	♦ Imagines what labor and birth will be like ♦ Has a sense of anticipation, exhilaration, and apprehension—all at the same time ♦ May experience a "nesting urge"	♦ Emotional ups and downs exaggerated by fatigue ♦ May have a variety of feelings toward the baby (fascination, love, anxiety, frustration, anger) ♦ Time seems nonexistent
Common emotions of father/ partner	♦ May fear for health of mother and baby during childbirth ♦ May question ability to cope or perform during childbirth	♦ May feel strong attachment to and fascination with baby ♦ Fatigue and lack of sleep may cause impatience or depression ♦ Is protective of family ♦ May feel left out at this time ♦ May wonder about baby care
Common changes for both	♦ Are mentally prepared for birth ♦ Are excited, apprehensive, or both	♦ Baby requires almost constant care ♦ "Fall in love" with baby ♦ Trial and error period; need sense of humor ♦ Relationship with partner is changing, may be strained or strengthened ♦ Fatigue can make everything seem difficult ♦ Realize parenting responsibilities

Chapter 3
Prenatal Care

Thorough prenatal care helps ensure the birth of a healthy baby. Shortly after you become pregnant, you should begin seeing your physician or midwife on a regular basis. During these prenatal visits, you will undergo certain routine examinations, and you will have an opportunity to discuss with your caregiver any matters that concern either of you. This is also the time to introduce your ideas for a birth plan and begin to work with your physician or midwife in planning your birth experience. At some time during your pregnancy, your partner should accompany you to meet your caregiver and discuss the partner's role at the birth. You should also try to meet the other doctors or midwives in the practice, since one of them might be on call when you are in labor. If this is not possible, discuss with your caregiver any differences in philosophy or practice that exist among the other caregivers.

Prenatal Exams

At your first or second prenatal visit, your doctor or midwife performs a complete physical examination and a number of tests and asks you about your own and your family's medical history. At each prenatal appointment, your caregiver checks on your health and the growth and well-being of your baby. Through most of pregnancy your appointments are scheduled each month. Toward the end they are scheduled every two weeks and then every week.

Throughout pregnancy, routine screening tests and/or diagnostic tests are offered or performed to detect a variety of fetal or maternal problems. (See the charts on page 46 and page 60 for descriptions of the tests.) These tests are reassuring when the results indicate a normal pregnancy or a healthy fetus. But if the results are uncertain or if they indicate a problem, you may face some difficult choices and much anxiety. It helps to know the drawbacks as well as the purposes and potential benefits of these tests. The answers to the following questions will help you decide whether to have the test:

♦ What is the purpose of the test?

♦ How is it done?

♦ Are there risks or drawbacks for either mother or fetus?

♦ How reliable or accurate are its results?

Routine Pregnancy Tests

This table lists the tests you can expect during pregnancy. If a test indicates a possible problem, further testing and appropriate treatment will be started.

Test	Purpose	Comments
A pelvic (vaginal) examination	*First or second prenatal visit:* ♦ To confirm pregnancy ♦ To correlate size of uterus with date of last menstrual period ♦ To estimate size and shape of pelvis ♦ To obtain vaginal secretions to detect infection or cervical cancer (Pap smear) *Late pregnancy:* ♦ To assess condition of cervix and station of baby ♦ To obtain vaginal secretions to detect infection, if indicated	 ♦ Exam may cause dark brown or reddish vaginal discharge. ♦ Exam may increase risk of infection or premature rupture of membranes.[a]
Urine tests	*First prenatal visit:* ♦ To confirm pregnancy *Each prenatal visit:* ♦ To detect infection ♦ To check for sugar and acetone, which might indicate diabetes ♦ To check for protein, which might indicate preeclampsia or infection	♦ Urine tests may be less accurate than blood tests to confirm pregnancy. ♦ Urine tests are less accurate than blood tests to confirm diabetes.
Blood tests	*First or second prenatal visit:* ♦ To confirm pregnancy ♦ To determine blood type, Rh type ♦ To test for anemia (hematocrit and hemoglobin) ♦ To test for German measles immunity ♦ To test for syphilis ♦ To test for antibodies to human immunodeficiency virus (HIV), the AIDS virus ♦ To test for antibodies to hepatitis B virus	♦ Some tests will be repeated. ♦ Some caregivers do not perform all these tests. ♦ Anemia may be treated with iron supplements and/or diet changes. ♦ See page 54 for information about infections during pregnancy. ♦ See page 57 for a discussion of Rh incompatibility.

Test	Purpose	Comments
Blood pressure test	*Each prenatal visit:* ♦ To detect pregnancy-induced hypertension (PIH) or preeclampsia	♦ See page 56 for a discussion of PIH.
Maternal weight check	*Each prenatal visit:* ♦ To detect sudden weight gain that could be due to preeclampsia ♦ To help monitor mother's nutritional status	♦ See page 56 for information on preeclampsia. ♦ See page 71 for a discussion of normal weight gain in pregnancy.
Abdominal examination	*Each prenatal visit:* ♦ To measure the growth of the uterus (fundal height) which indicates fetal growth and gestational age *Last weeks of pregnancy:* ♦ To estimate size and position of the fetus (Leopold's maneuvers) ♦ To estimate amniotic fluid volume ♦ To detect breech presentation	♦ If a problem is suspected, ultrasound visualization (page 65) is usually recommended. ♦ If breech, mother may use self-help measures to turn fetus (page 178); a medical professional may perform external version.
Listening to fetal heart rate (FHR) The FHR is heard through the mother's abdomen with a fetal stethoscope or a Doppler, which uses ultrasound.	*Each prenatal visit after the FHR can be heard (about 12 weeks):* ♦ To assess the well-being of the fetus	♦ Hearing the FHR increases the expectant parents' feelings of attachment for their baby and makes the baby seem more real.
Breast exam	*Once or more during pregnancy:* ♦ To check for flat or inverted nipples ♦ To assess condition of breasts for ability to breastfeed ♦ To detect any breast abnormalities including screening for breast cancer	♦ If her nipples are flat or inverted, the mother can use methods to draw them out. See page 266 for a discussion of these measures. ♦ Breast self-exams should be performed regularly throughout pregnancy.

continued

Test	Purpose	Comments
Alpha-Fetoprotein (AFP) A blood test that measures the level of alpha-fetoprotein, a substance produced by the fetal liver that crosses to the maternal bloodstream in predictable amounts. Test results are usually available in one week.	*16 to 18 weeks gestation:* ♦ To screen for a baby with a neural tube defect (spina bifida, anencephaly), the presence of twins, or fetal death (high level of AFP) ♦ To screen for Down's syndrome (low level of AFP)	♦ If AFP test results are outside the normal range, then further testing includes a repeat blood test to confirm findings, ultrasound, genetic counseling, and possible amniocentesis. ♦ The test will not detect all cases of neural tube defects or Down's syndrome. ♦ There is a high rate of false positives (the test indicated a problem when there is none). ♦ The test's accuracy is questionable if the due date is unclear. ♦ The risk of neural tube defects is about 1 to 2 per 1,000 births. ♦ Insulin-dependent diabetics usually show an AFP level lower than others. ♦ The test helps parents plan management of pregnancy or birth (they could terminate the pregnancy, plan a cesarean if spina bifida is detected, or prepare for a child with a disability).
Prenatal risk profile (Triple Screen)[a] A blood test that measures levels of three substances: human chorionic gonadotrophin (hCG), a hormone produced by the chorionic villi; estriol, a by-product of estrogen metabolism; and maternal serum alpha-fetoprotein (AFP).	*15 to 18 weeks gestation:* ♦ To screen for Down's syndrome (low levels of estriol and AFP combined with high levels of hCG)	♦ Initial studies indicate that the Triple Screen is more accurate than AFP screening alone in detecting Down's syndrome (2 to 3 times more accurate in women under 35; 50 percent more accurate in women over 35).[b] ♦ It is useful for those who do not have amniocentesis, although it does not detect the hundreds of other possible inherited disorders that can be detected by amniocentesis or chorionic villus sampling. ♦ It is a screening procedure only; this test may miss 20 to 30 percent of Down's syndrome pregnancies in women over 35, and 40 percent in women under 35.

Test	Purpose	Comments
Glucose screening A blood sample is taken from the mother one hour after she drinks a sugary (glucose) drink or eats a special carbohydrate meal.	*24 to 30 weeks gestation (commonly 28 weeks):* ♦ To screen for gestational diabetes, which, if untreated, may cause problems for mother and baby	♦ If the mother's blood sugar is elevated, a longer and more sensitive glucose tolerance test (GTT) is planned. ♦ Approximately 85 percent of those with an elevated blood sugar in the screening test will be found to have normal blood sugar levels in the GTT. ♦ Detection of diabetes enables treatment to avoid problems for the mother or baby. ♦ See page 55 for a discussion of gestational diabetes.

[a]J.P. Lenihan, "Relationship of Antepartum Pelvic Examinations to Premature Rupture of the Membranes," *Obstetrics and Gynecology* 83 (January 1984): 33.

[b]M.L. McDonald et al., "Sensitivity and Specificity of Screening for Down Syndrome with Alpha-Fetoprotein, hCG, Unconjugated Estriol, and Maternal Age," *Obstetrics and Gynecology* 77 (January 1991): 63.

♦ How will the information gained influence the management of my pregnancy?

♦ What steps follow a negative or a positive result?

♦ How much does it cost? Is it covered by my insurance policy or HMO program?

♦ What are the consequences of not having it done?

♦ Are there other ways to get similar information?

Your caregiver can explain most tests thoroughly in a short time. With other tests (for example, amniocentesis and chorionic villus sampling), complete discussion is complex and requires the services of a genetic counselor or other expert.

With today's advancing medical technology, the ability to detect or diagnose prenatal problems is improving; however, the ability to treat or cure these problems is not nearly as advanced. Nevertheless, with good prenatal care, including screening and diagnostic tests, the chances of a good pregnancy and birth outcome are greatly increased.

Complications during Pregnancy

Unfortunately, not every pregnancy is free of complications. Early recognition and treatment, however, greatly improve the chances of a good outcome, and early recognition is more likely if you are knowledgeable and observant. Since your doctor or midwife sees you only periodically during pregnancy, keep him or her informed if any problems or adverse changes arise between visits. Optimal prenatal care depends on cooperation between the expectant parents and their caregiver.

Miscarriage

A *miscarriage*, or spontaneous abortion, is the unexpected and involuntary expulsion of the embryo or fetus before the twentieth week of pregnancy. Although doctors cannot determine the specific cause of most miscarriages, some are due to genetic abnormalities in the embryo that interfere with normal development, and others are caused by acute infection, uterine abnormalities, or a severe physical shock.

The signs of a possible miscarriage are vaginal bleeding and intermittent pain. The pain often begins in the lower back and is later felt as abdominal cramping. Only rarely can a miscarriage be stopped. However, if you suspect you are having a miscarriage, call your caregiver for advice on what to do, for confirmation of the miscarriage, and to help ensure physical and emotional healing afterward.

If you lose a baby from miscarriage, you will probably feel some degree of shock, grief, and depression, even when the pregnancy has not been visible to others. These feelings tend to be more pronounced if you carefully planned the pregnancy or if you have had more than one miscarriage. Support groups and books are available if you need understanding and help at this difficult time (see Recommended Resources). Most women who have one or more miscarriages go on to have normal and healthy pregnancies in the future.

Hyperemesis Gravidarum

Hyperemesis gravidarum is a rare condition characterized by persistent, excessive nausea and vomiting (far more than the "morning sickness" of early pregnancy, described on page 73). The condition may involve weight loss, dehydration, and changes in blood chemistry. Treatment, which is highly successful, includes medication to relieve nausea and vomiting and/or hospitalization to provide nourishment intravenously to restore the balance of body fluids.

Ectopic Pregnancy

Ectopic (extrauterine or tubal) pregnancy occurs when the fertilized ovum implants itself outside the uterus, usually in the wall of a fallopian tube. The most common symptom of an ectopic pregnancy is sudden, severe abdominal pain in early pregnancy. Treatment usually involves surgery and termination of the pregnancy.

High Body Temperature (Fever)

A *high body temperature* for a prolonged period, especially in early pregnancy, may harm your baby. Consult your doctor or midwife if your oral temperature is over 100.6 degrees Farenheit (38 degrees Celsius) and certainly before taking any medication, even aspirin. To lower a fever, drink plenty of liquids or take a lukewarm bath, sponge bath, or shower. Also be aware that hot tubs and saunas may raise your body temperature to a high level, which can be dangerous in early pregnancy (see page 87).

Placenta Previa

In *placenta previa*, a condition that occurs in about 1 out of every 200 pregnancies, the placenta is implanted over (or partially over) the cervix. The most characteristic symptom of the condition is vaginal bleeding, generally after the seventh month of pregnancy. The bleeding is usually intermittent and is not usually accompanied by pain. As with any bleeding from the vagina, you should notify your physician or midwife immediately. The caregiver often orders an ultrasound to determine the location of the placenta and the cause of bleeding. Treatment might involve bed rest, close medical observation of mother and fetus, and a cesarean birth.

Warning Signs during Pregnancy

During your pregnancy, report any of the following warning signs to your doctor or midwife. In addition, your caregiver may ask you to report other pertinent signs and symptoms and any pain that concerns you.

Warning signs	Possible problems
Vaginal bleeding (even a small quantity)	Miscarriage, placenta previa, placental abruption (separation), preterm labor
Abdominal pain	Ectopic pregnancy, miscarriage, placental abruption, preterm labor contractions
Continuing intermittent abdominal tightening (contractions) or cramping	Preterm labor
Constant painful firmness of the abdomen, with or without vaginal bleeding	Placental abruption
Leaking or gushing of fluid from the vagina	Rupture of the membranes
Sudden puffiness or swelling of the hands, feet, or face	Preeclampsia (toxemia)
Severe, persistent headache	Preeclampsia (toxemia)
Disturbance of vision — spots, flashes, blurring, or blind spots	Preeclampsia (toxemia)
Dizziness, light-headedness	Preeclampsia, supine hypotension
Noticeable reduction in fetal activity	Fetal distress
Painful, reddened area in leg	Thrombophlebitis (inflammation and blood clots in the vein)
Severe pain in pubic area and hips with impairment of leg movements	Strain or separation of pubic symphysis joint
Pain or burning sensation when urinating	Urinary tract infection, sexually transmitted disease
Irritating vaginal discharge, genital sores or itching	Vaginal infection, sexually transmitted disease
Fever—oral temperature over 100°F (38°C)	Infection
Persistent nausea or vomiting	Hyperemesis gravidarum, infection

Placental Abruption

Placental abruption, separation of the placenta from the uterus before birth, occurs in about 1 out of about 200 pregnancies, most often in the third trimester or during labor. Although it sometimes happens for no apparent reason, women at greater risk are those with high blood pressure and those who smoke, drink heavily, or use cocaine. Any or all of the following symptoms might appear: continuous abdominal pain, tenderness and rigidity of the uterus, and vaginal bleeding.

Besides the danger of hemorrhage to the mother, extensive separation of the placenta deprives the baby of adequate oxygen. Treatment of placental abruption depends on the amount of bleeding and how far labor has progressed. If bleeding is minor, labor is progressing, and the fetal heart rate remains normal, the caregiver usually allows the labor to continue. Otherwise, a cesarean delivery is performed.

Thrombophlebitis

Thrombophlebitis is a rare disorder of pregnancy or post partum characterized by inflammation of a vein with development of blood clots that adhere to the wall of the vein.

Because of the risk of the blood clots traveling to vital organs such as the lungs, signs of thrombophlebitis should be reported immediately: pain, tenderness, redness, and swelling, usually in the lower leg. Fever is present if the thrombophlebitis is caused by infection.

Treatment consists of bed rest, hot packs to the affected area, antibiotics, if indicated, and an anticoagulant (to prevent the formation of blood clots) such as Heparin.

Preterm Labor

Approximately 6 to 10 percent of births are *preterm*, that is, they occur before the thirty-seventh week of pregnancy. Preterm (or premature) babies tend to have more health problems because they are immature and underdeveloped (see page 254). Therefore, one of the major goals of maternity care is to prevent preterm labor by recognizing it early and stopping it. Current medical opinion holds that treatment before the cervix is two centimeters dilated can often stop preterm labor. This is controversial, however. Some experts suggest that such emphasis on very early detection results in overtreatment of cases of normal uterine activity. High rates of successful treatment may be due to overdiagnosis, a possibility supported by the fact that the rates of premature births in the United States have not dropped despite more aggressive diagnosis and treatment. While the medical profession continues its search for the most reliable and cost-effective approach to the prevention of preterm labor, most practitioners identify those at greater risk, teach all pregnant women the symptoms of preterm labor, and if necessary, provide treatment.

Risk Factors
If you have any of the following risk factors, you are more likely than others to go into preterm labor:

♦ Previous miscarriage or preterm labor

♦ Twins or overdistention of the uterus

♦ Abdominal surgery during the pregnancy

♦ Abnormally shaped uterus

♦ Being a DES daughter (meaning that your mother took diethylstilbestrol—DES—when she was pregnant with you)

♦ More than one previous induced abortion in the second trimester

♦ Genital or urinary tract infections during this pregnancy

♦ Infection of the membranes

- Heavy smoking or drug abuse

- Age under 18 or over 35 years

- Poor nutrition before or during pregnancy

- A high degree of physical or mental stress

Symptoms

Although women with the above risk factors are at increased risk of preterm labor, it is possible to go into preterm labor even if you don't have them. You should know the following symptoms. Since these symptoms are often similar to normal pregnancy sensations, you should watch for slight differences or changes. If you have these symptoms, call your doctor or midwife immediately.

- *Uterine contractions* that are frequent and regular (every 15 minutes or less for 1 hour or more). They do not have to be painful. Contractions come in waves as the uterus alternately tightens and softens. Place your fingertips gently but firmly on your abdomen to help tell if these are labor contractions. Time them (see page 139). If you have four or more in an hour, especially if combined with any of the other symptoms described below, be sure to call your caregiver.

- *Menstrual-like cramps* causing intermittent or continuous discomfort in lower abdomen.

- *Dull low backache* that is not influenced by position change.

- *Pelvic or thigh pressure* that may come and go.

- *Intestinal cramping* with or without diarrhea.

- *Sudden increase or change in vaginal discharge* (more mucousy, watery, or blood-tinged).

- *A general feeling that something is not right.*

Treatment

If your caregiver determines that you are having preterm contractions, the following measures will probably be used to stop them:

- Hospitalization to closely monitor your contractions and to start and evaluate the treatment, followed by continued treatment at home.

- Bed rest.

- Adequate fluid intake. (Initially you may be asked to drink several glasses of water and observe your contractions for an hour or two to see if they stop.) Sometimes an increased fluid volume can stop preterm labor contractions.

- Possible use of medications to stop or slow labor—tocolytic drugs (Ritodrine, Terbutaline), magnesium sulfate, Indomethacin, Motrin (see page 217).

- Possible amniocentesis to determine lung maturity (see page 60).

If the contractions stop, you may be sent home on a program including bed rest, tocolytics to take by mouth or continuous subcutaneous pump, and restriction of sexual activity, including nipple stimulation. Once you reach thirty-six to thirty-seven weeks, the treatment will probably be stopped and your pregnancy will be allowed to follow its own course. In some parts of North America, ambulatory tocodynamometry (a contraction monitor) is available to electronically monitor uterine activity for later telephone transmission to the hospital or clinic (see the discussion on page 65 for further information).

If the treatment is unsuccessful in stopping the contractions or in preventing dilation of the cervix, you may be transferred to a hospital with an intensive care nursery where you will deliver the baby and where the baby will be cared for. The decision to transfer you to such a hospital is based on the degree of fetal prematurity and the kind of care your caregiver thinks your baby will need after birth.

Infections

Infectious diseases, including sexually transmitted diseases and other common and uncommon illnesses, can complicate your pregnancy and endanger your baby. The percentage of babies who become infected and the seriousness of the infection depends on the particular organism (some organisms rarely harm the fetus; others are more serious), whether the mother has antibodies to the organism, whether the disease is treatable, and when during pregnancy you catch the illness. The infection can be passed to your baby in any of several ways. The chart below lists some infections and how they are transmitted to the fetus or newborn.

Infections during Pregnancy and Mode of Transmission	
Mode of Transmission	**Infections**
Transplacental The infecting organism crosses the placenta and infects the baby.	♦ Chicken pox ♦ Cytomegalovirus ♦ HIV (AIDS virus) ♦ Listeriosis ♦ Lyme disease ♦ Rubella ♦ Syphilis ♦ Toxoplasmosis
Ascending The infecting organism, which is present in the vagina, can migrate upward into the uterus to infect the membranes, amniotic fluid, or the baby. The baby is at greater risk after the membranes rupture.	♦ Gonorrhea ♦ Group B streptococcus ♦ Herpes (genital) ♦ Mycoplasma
At birth The baby comes in contact with the infecting organism while descending through the vagina. Cesarean delivery can prevent this exposure.	♦ Chicken pox ♦ Chlamydia ♦ Gonorrhea ♦ Group B streptococcus ♦ Hepatitis B ♦ Herpes (genital) ♦ HIV (AIDS virus) ♦ Venereal warts (condyloma) ♦ Yeast (candida, monilia, or thrush infection)
Post partum The baby acquires the infection through breast milk, physical contact with the mother, or from others who have the infection.	♦ Chicken pox ♦ Herpes ♦ HIV (AIDS virus) ♦ Yeast (candida, monilia, or thrush infection)

If you come down with rubella (German measles), listeriosis, toxoplasmosis, chicken pox, or cytomegalovirus in the first trimester, your baby is at risk for the same infection. The infecting organism can cross the placenta, infect the baby, and cause congenital problems such as deafness, blindness, heart defects, and mental and physical delays. Sometimes the infection can cause a miscarriage or neo-natal death. Even though many babies are not harmed by their infected mother, try to avoid exposure to these diseases. If you do have symptoms of these or other infections (fever, headache, body aches, rash, or respiratory flu), report them to your caregiver.

Lyme disease, human immunodeficiency virus (HIV, the AIDS virus), and syphilis can also harm the fetus in the first trimester and throughout pregnancy. About half of the babies born to mothers with AIDS will become infected with HIV (which could lead to AIDS, for which presently there is no cure). However, Lyme disease and syphilis in the mother and fetus can be treated with antibiotics.

Some infections, especially listeriosis and some sexually transmitted diseases, can cause serious problems toward the end of pregnancy and during the birth. Listeriosis is a rare illness with minor flu-like symptoms in the mother. It can cause preterm delivery, stillbirth, or meningitis and death in the newborn. Group B streptococcus and mycoplasma may infect the membranes, causing them to rupture prematurely, or they can infect the baby during pregnancy or during the birth process. Since Group B streptococcus and mycoplasma can cause serious disease or death, expectant mothers and babies are treated with antibiotics.

If you have had multiple sexual partners, or if you now have or ever have had symptoms of a sexually transmitted disease (STD) such as genital sores, abnormal vaginal discharge, or discomfort or difficulty with urination, tell your caregiver so you can be tested and treated if possible. Gonorrhea and chlamydia can cause serious eye damage in the newborn but may be prevented with antibiotic treatment. Babies at risk of infection with the hepatitis B virus are given immune globulin and a hepatitis B vaccine. A cesarean delivery is done to prevent the spread of the herpes virus to the newborn if the mother has a herpes sore or is shedding the virus at the time of birth. The mother who has had genital herpes for a long time is less likely to pass it to her baby than another who acquires herpes during the pregnancy. For babies who do get herpes in the newborn period, treatment with antiviral drugs may help reduce the severity of the infection. See Recommended Resources for more on herpes in pregnancy.

If you have a vaginal yeast infection (candidiasis or moniliasis) at the time of birth, your baby could become infected and develop thrush in the mouth or gastrointestinal tract. Though this is not a serious disease for mother or baby, it can cause severe breast pain for the nursing mother and a sore mouth or buttocks for the baby. Both mother and baby should be treated with medication for yeast.

Diabetes Mellitus and Gestational Diabetes

Diabetes mellitus, which affects the body's ability to use glucose (sugar) because of inadequate insulin production, presents special problems for the pregnant woman. During pregnancy, diabetes becomes more difficult to control and can affect the unborn baby. If you are pregnant and diabetic, you need the care of a specialist.

Gestational diabetes is a type of diabetes that develops in 3 to 12 percent of pregnant women during the second trimester. Gestational diabetes is not caused by diminished insulin production as is diabetes mellitus. Rather, it is related to normal changes in glucose metabolism that promote fetal growth. Human placental lactogen (HPL), a pregnancy hormone, suppresses the action of insulin, thus freeing up more glucose for fetal growth. In some women, HPL activity is out of balance, leading to excessively high blood glucose levels, which can cause complications, such as an overly large baby and newborn hypoglycemia (low blood sugar). Early detection and appropriate treatment can prevent these problems. A glucose screening test is usually performed at approximately twenty-eight weeks gestation (see page 49). If the screening and further testing indicate gestational diabetes, treatment usually consists of a special diet, and, in some cases, insulin injections. The mother is also taught how to check her own blood glucose levels regularly. Labor is sometimes induced near term to prevent excessive growth of the baby.

Pregnancy-Induced Hypertension (PIH) and Preeclampsia

Pregnancy-induced hypertension, also called PIH, affects approximately 6 to 8 percent of expectant mothers in the United States. This potentially serious condition can be divided into three categories:

1. *Hypertension* or *high blood pressure* is defined as blood pressure that exceeds 140/90 for at least two recordings, or as a sustained rise in systolic pressure (the top number) of more than 30 points, or a sustained rise in diastolic pressure (the lower number) of more than 15 points above the first trimester pressures.

2. *Preeclampsia,* sometimes called toxemia, is characterized by an elevated blood pressure accompanied by excessive retention of fluid (edema), especially in the hands and face; a rapid weight gain; and presence of protein in the urine. Edema and protein in the urine indicate possible kidney impairment. Preeclampsia occurs after the twentieth week of pregnancy and may be accompa-

nied by headaches, dizziness, and visual disturbances.

3. *Eclampsia* is an extension of preeclampsia and is characterized by convulsions, coma, and sometimes fetal and maternal death. Eclampsia is preventable and rarely occurs (1 in 1,000 to 1,500 deliveries).

Although the causes of pregnancy-induced hypertension and preeclampsia are not yet understood, studies indicate that it is more likely to occur in women who are first-time mothers, teenagers, women over thirty-five, those with twin pregnancies, and women with poor diets and highly stressful living conditions. In addition, expectant mothers with a personal or family history of renal or vascular disease, hypertension, diabetes mellitus, or a past pregnancy complicated by PIH are more likely to develop hypertension in pregnancy or preeclampsia.

The treatment for PIH includes bed rest (preferably on the left side) and close medical supervision to monitor blood pressure, to check for signs of preeclampsia, and to test the blood for signs of the HELLP (hemolysis, elevated liver enzymes, and low platelets) syndrome, which indicates liver and blood complications. Sometimes medications are given to lower blood pressure. With preeclampsia, drugs to decrease the risk of seizures are given if indicated (see page 218 for more on these medications).

If signs of preeclampsia persist after strict bed rest, labor may be induced or a cesarean birth planned. A return to normal blood pressure usually takes place soon after the birth of the baby.

Pregnancy-induced hypertension can cause serious complications, including reduced placental blood flow to the baby. If you notice any of the following, you should report them to your caregiver: sudden swelling, dizziness, blurred vision, or spots before your eyes. With early diagnosis and treatment, complications from PIH are minimal and a healthy pregnancy outcome can be expected.

Multiple Pregnancy

Any pregnancy in which the woman carries more than one baby is called a multiple pregnancy. Multiple pregnancies occur in about one in every eighty pregnancies. When compared with rates among people of European descent, multiple pregnancies are less frequent among people of Asian descent and more frequent among people of African descent. Older women, those with twins in the family, multiparas, and women using fertility drugs also have an increased likelihood of a multiple pregnancy. *Fraternal* twins are produced by the fertilization of two eggs by two sperm. *Identical* twins occur when one sperm fertilizes one egg, which later divides into two developing babies. One out of every three sets of twins is identical. Triplets, quadruplets, or quintuplets are even more rare.

A multiple pregnancy may be suspected if two or more fetal heartbeats are heard, if you have a family history of multiple births, if you have a rapid weight gain, or if your uterus grows faster than normal. If a multiple pregnancy is suspected, an ultrasound scan will probably be ordered to confirm it. Although ultrasound can detect more than 95 percent of multiple pregnancies by the early part of the second trimester, some remain undetected until birth.

Expecting twins can be both exciting and stressful. Supporting the growth of more than one baby places extra demands on your body. You may be encouraged to increase the number of calories in your diet, and you may need to rest more because of discomfort, fatigue, and the possibility of premature labor. Most problems for newborn twins are those associated with prematurity. Since multiple pregnancy births may be more complicated, you may need the care of an obstetrician instead of or in addition to your midwife or family physician. Besides the increased medical attention, you can also expect more attention from your friends and relatives.

Helpful books and support groups are available to help parents of twins cope with their unique emotional and practical problems. The National Organization of Mothers of Twins Clubs, Inc., P. O. Box 23188, Albuquerque, New Mexico 87192, (505) 275-0955, provides information, support, and the names of local twin groups. Your childbirth educator may be able to connect you with other mothers of twins from her or his classes.

Rh Incompatibility

Special care will be given to pregnant women with Rh (Rhesus) negative blood. About 85 percent of the population is Rh positive, which means they have a particular antigen, the Rh factor, in their blood. You will be tested for the presence of Rh factor early in your pregnancy. If you are Rh negative (that is if you have no Rh factor) and the baby's father is Rh positive, your baby may be Rh positive. If so, the chances are one in six (or less) that the Rh factor from the baby will cross the placenta into your bloodstream during pregnancy, or when the placenta separates from the uterus after birth. If the transfer takes place, you will produce antibodies against (become "sensitized to") the Rh factor. The problem comes with your next pregnancy with an Rh positive fetus who may be harmed when your antibodies cross the placenta and destroy some of your unborn baby's red blood cells.

Sensitization can almost always be prevented by giving an injection of Rh immune globulin (RhoGam) to the mother. Since 1968, RhoGam has been given to Rh negative mothers as soon as possible after delivery, miscarriage, abortion, or amniocentesis. This reduces the likelihood of sensitization to approximately 2 in 100. However, on rare occasions, transfer of Rh factor and sensitization take place earlier in pregnancy. If so, giving RhoGam at birth is too late. In an effort to prevent early sensitization,

RhoGam is now offered at about twenty-eight weeks gestation, as well as soon after birth. When RhoGam is given both at twenty-eight weeks and after birth, the sensitization rate is reduced to approximately 1 in 1,000.[1]

If you are Rh negative, the number of antibodies in your blood will be assessed throughout your pregnancy. If you have become sensitized to the Rh factor, the number of antibodies increases, warranting further studies such as amniocentesis, the removal of amniotic fluid from the uterus for the purpose of detecting destroyed fetal red blood cells. This indicates how seriously your fetus has been affected by your sensitization. Your fetus can have mild to severe jaundice, anemia, heart failure, or brain damage. Treatment possibilities include early delivery of the baby or, in selected cases, intrauterine blood transfusions utilizing the percutaneous umbilical blood sampling (PUBS) technique described on page 64. Newborn infants may also be given blood transfusions if they have been severely affected by Rh incompatibility.

Prenatal Tests

If your physician or midwife suspects a pregnancy complication, or if more information is needed on the size, age, or condition of the unborn baby, he or she will schedule additional tests. Because many of the diagnostic examinations described in the chart on page 60 involve greater risks than the routine prenatal tests described in the chart on page 46, carefully weigh the risks against the benefits as suggested earlier in this chapter on page 45. Two of these tests deserve extra discussion: fetal movement counting, because it is a test you can do yourself, and ultrasound, because it offers so much information that caregivers often perform it routinely.

Fetal Movement Counting

Keeping track of your baby's movements for a short time each day during late pregnancy gives you and your caregiver valuable information about the baby's health and well-being.

Babies who are doing well in the uterus have several active periods during the day. They also have sleeping periods characterized by a lack of activity. Even though healthy babies may reduce their activity slightly toward the end of pregnancy, they do not slow down markedly unless they have a problem. If your baby becomes less active, you should notify your caregiver, who can test further and take action (for example, early delivery), if necessary. Some caregivers ask only those women with high risk pregnancies to do fetal movement counting, while others ask all pregnant women to do it. Some studies have found that the likelihood of an unexpected stillbirth was markedly reduced for low-risk women who did fetal movement counting.[2] Other studies did not detect clear benefits from routine fetal movement counting.[3] Since this is a test that you do yourself, you can decide if you would like to do it or not. The following directions show you how.

The most accurate way to keep track of your baby's activity is to set aside a period of time each day to focus on the baby and actually count the number of times he moves. What is a movement? Fetal movements may be short (a kick or a wiggle) or long (a continuing squirming motion). Count it as one movement when it ends with a clear, if brief, pause. Hiccups should not be counted. Many methods of fetal movement counting have been proposed and found to be beneficial. A simple method is described here.

The Count to Ten Method
Beginning at thirty-two weeks of pregnancy or anytime thereafter, count fetal movements each day, during roughly the same

Fetal Movement Count

Date	Starting time	Record of movements	Time of 10th movement	Total time
8/24	7:30 pm	~~THL~~ ~~THL~~	7:53 pm	23 min
8/25	6:00 pm	~~THL~~ ~~THL~~	6:15 pm	15 Min
8/26	6:30 pm	~~THL~~ ~~THL~~	6:35 pm	5 Min
8/27	7:00 pm	~~THL~~ ~~THL~~	7:25 pm	25 Min
8/28	7:15 pm	~~THL~~ ~~THL~~	7:33 pm	18 Min
8/29	6:30 pm	~~THL~~ ~~THL~~	6:47 pm	17 Min
8/30	9:00 pm	~~THL~~ ~~THL~~	10:05 pm	65 Min

time period. Don't worry if you miss a day now and then. Pick a time when the baby is normally active. After the evening meal is a convenient time for most people. Find a comfortable position and avoid doing anything that might distract you. The method consists of timing how long it takes for the baby to move ten times. Record each day's fetal movements on a chart like the one above.

If your baby does not move at all during the time you set aside, he may be asleep. Try waking him with a loud noise, or wait until you feel him move and then begin timing how long it takes him to move ten times. Report to your caregiver if your baby clearly takes a longer time to reach ten movements or if the baby does not have an active period within twelve hours.

While the purpose of fetal movement counting is to detect a slowing in fetal activity, you should also notify your caregiver if your baby becomes strikingly more active for a longer period than a few hours. This might mean the baby's oxygen supply has suddenly declined (from pressure on the cord, for example), and the baby is trying to find a position to correct that.

Ultrasound

Few pregnant women go through pregnancy without being exposed to *diagnostic ultrasound* (testing done with the use of high frequency sound waves). Diagnostic ultrasound can be used in different ways for different purposes. *Doppler ultrasound* uses continuous transmission of sound waves to detect changes in blood flow and to monitor the fetal heartbeat. The *ultrasound scan* uses intermittent transmission to "see" inside the uterus. Sound waves are transmitted into the body less than 1 percent of the time. The rest of the time the equipment is receiving the sound waves echoing back. The echoes indicate differences in tissue density and are converted into a video image that shows the skeleton and organs of the fetus, umbilical cord, placenta, and other parts. See the charts on page 65 and page 185 for a more detailed description of the tests that use ultrasound.

How safe is obstetric ultrasound? Numerous small studies of the short- and long-term hazards of diagnostic ultrasound have found no evidence of harmful physical effects. These promising results have led researchers to conclude that the benefits of the prudent use of diagnostic ultrasound outweigh the possible risks.[4] (Note that diagnostic ultrasound is different from *therapeutic ultrasound,* which uses much higher doses to promote healing of deep tissue injuries.)

Through ultrasound, caregivers have gained extensive information about the fetus and the uterine environment, and they have come to rely heavily on it in clinical decision making. Many parents like ultrasound for other reasons. Seeing the baby inside is exciting — his face, fingers, and toes; his heart beating, his body wriggling. The use of ultrasound is here to stay, but because the possibility still exists that high exposure could cause harm, routine ultrasound scans (that is, scans done without a medical reason) are not recommended.[5]

Diagnostic Tests

The following tests evaluate either your well-being or your baby's. Rarely is any one test used alone. For example, if there is a question about fetal well-being in early pregnancy, an ultrasound and an amniocentesis might be recommended. If a question arises in later pregnancy, the doctor or midwife might ask you to count fetal movements daily and come in once or twice a week for a nonstress test, particular blood tests, and a biophysical profile. If fetal well-being is still in question, ultrasound examinations, amniocentesis, contraction stress tests, and others might be performed.

Amniocentesis

A local anesthetic may be given to numb the skin of your abdomen. Then a needle is passed through your abdomen and uterus into the amniotic sac, and fluid is withdrawn and sent to a laboratory for the appropriate examinations. Amniocentesis is performed with ultrasound to avoid puncturing the fetus, placenta, or umbilical cord. Amniocentesis can be performed whenever there is an adequate pocket of fluid, usually after 13 to 16 weeks gestation. The amniotic fluid is handled differently, depending on the test being performed. To identify chromosomal abnormalities, fetal cells are isolated from the amniotic fluid and given time (2 to 4 weeks) to multiply, which provides sufficient quantities to allow analysis. For other tests, the fluid can be analyzed immediately for the presence of various substances that reveal specific information about your baby.

Benefits/purposes

Amniocentesis in early pregnancy (done at 13 to 16 weeks gestation):

♦ Provides information on certain birth defects, metabolic disorders, or chromosomal abnormalities such as Down's syndrome, sickle cell anemia, neural tube defects, and many others; some of these may be suspected after routine screening tests

♦ Helps you make a decision about continuing or terminating a pregnancy

Risks/disadvantages

♦ Slightly increases risk of miscarriage; should be weighed against the fact that women aged 35 have a 0.5 percent risk of chromosomal abnormality

♦ Requires injection of RhoGam if mother is Rh negative

♦ Produces a small amount of discomfort

♦ Is invasive and carries a small additional risk of intrauterine infection

♦ Length of time required to obtain results (2 to 4 weeks) may be stressful

♦ Termination of pregnancy (abortion), if desired, might not be performed until 15 to 20 weeks gestation (later abortions are more risky and may be more stressful than earlier abortions)

♦ Is expensive, although health insurance covers costs for women over 35 and those at risk for genetic defects

Benefits/purposes	Risks/disadvantages

Amniocentesis in late pregnancy (often in the last trimester):

Benefits/purposes	Risks/disadvantages
◆ Provides vital information on fetal lung maturity when early delivery is being considered for the health of mother or baby	◆ May cause premature labor
	◆ May injure fetus, placenta, or cord, but this risk is greatly reduced if ultrasound is used
◆ Reveals severity of Rh disease or other suspected blood disorders and helps determine if treatment of baby will be necessary	◆ May cause intrauterine infection
	◆ Slight risk of hemorrhage or embolism

Chorionic Villus Sampling (CVS)

A slim catheter is inserted into the uterus through the opening in the cervix (transcervical CVS) or through the abdominal wall via a needle (transabdominal CVS). It is guided by ultrasound and placed on the chorionic membrane, which covers the fetus. Fragments of the chorionic villi are suctioned through the catheter into a syringe and then sent to a laboratory for analysis. The procedure takes about 15 to 20 minutes. Chorionic villus sampling is usually performed between 8 and 11 weeks gestation.

Benefits/purposes	Risks/disadvantages
◆ Provides information about genetic defects and chromosomal abnormalities (same as that obtained from midtrimester amniocentesis)	◆ May risk miscarriage, but not clear that it adds to miscarriage rate, which is normally rather high (as high as 4 percent) at this stage of pregnancy
◆ Performed at an earlier gestational age than amniocentesis; test results are available within 7 to 14 days, allowing for earlier decision about termination of pregnancy (early abortions are safer and simpler than those done after 16 to 18 weeks)	◆ May cause maternal bleeding and cramping or amniotic fluid leakage
	◆ Available in only a few perinatal centers
	◆ Is expensive and may not be covered by insurance
	◆ Requires injection of RhoGam if mother is Rh negative
	◆ Has not been used as long as amniocentesis; extensive long-term studies of full range of risks and benefits are still needed
◆ Provides a sample large enough to take advantage of molecular genetics technology such as DNA analysis	◆ Often requires mother to have a full bladder, which may be uncomfortable

continued

Contraction Stress Test (CST) or Oxytocin Challenge Test (OCT)

This test indicates how the fetal heart rate (FHR) responds to uterine contractions. The woman is either given intravenous Pitocin (a form of oxytocin) or she stimulates her nipples (causing a natural release of oxytocin) by stroking or rolling them until she has three contractions in ten minutes. Then, while the uterus continues contracting at that rate, an external electronic fetal monitor measures the FHR. Test results are "reassuring" if the heart rate remains normal during contractions. The test is "nonreassuring" or "ominous" if the FHR indicates fetal distress. It sometimes takes several hours to complete this test. It is considered reliable only during the last weeks of pregnancy.

Benefits/purposes

♦ Helps indicate how well fetus can withstand stress of labor contractions

♦ Helps determine if a high-risk pregnancy can continue, if labor should be induced, or if a cesarean birth is indicated

♦ Reflects placental function and fetal reserves

Risks/disadvantages

♦ May cause preterm labor

♦ Interpretation of results differs

♦ Produces occasional false results, which could lead to unnecessary intervention

♦ Is costly, since it is usually performed in a hospital or clinic

Doppler Blood Flow Studies (Velocimetry)

A Doppler ultrasound unit, placed on the woman's abdomen, obtains information about the rate of blood flow (velocity) in the umbilical artery of the fetus and/or the uterine artery of the mother. This information is recorded as velocity wave forms that show the differences in blood flow during and between heartbeats (reported as the "systolic/diastolic ratio"). These studies may be performed during the latter months of pregnancy or during labor.

Benefits/purposes

♦ Provides insight about condition of utero-placental and/or fetal circulation

♦ Helps identify a fetus at risk for an adverse outcome due to fetal-placental blood flow problems (intrauterine growth retardation, pregnancy-induced hypertension, and other problems)

♦ Helps evaluate effect of labor or obstetric intervention on fetal-placental circulation

♦ Is noninvasive

Risks/disadvantages

♦ A relatively new procedure; full range of applications still undetermined

♦ Possible inappropriate intervention because its ability to predict maternal and fetal outcome is unclear

Estriol Excretion Studies

Estriol, made jointly by the fetus and placenta, is a form of estrogen. The estriol content of a woman's 24-hour urine collection or a single sample of her blood is measured in several consecutive studies (usually weekly). If estriol levels drop, it is a possible sign that the fetus is not tolerating the pregnancy well. Estriol studies are performed in late pregnancy.

Benefits/purposes
♦ May indicate efficiency of placenta and status of fetus; used when deciding whether to induce labor or continue a pregnancy complicated by diabetes, maternal hypertension, or postmaturity

Risks/disadvantages
♦ Is no longer considered accurate enough to be used in deciding to induce labor or perform a cesarean because many factors other than fetal problems can cause low estriol excretion; other tests are considered to be far more reliable
♦ Produces variable results with multiple pregnancy, presence of a kidney infection, or use of certain drugs

Fetal Biophysical Profile (FBP or BPP)

This test evaluates fetal physical functions and has five components. It combines a nonstress test to check the fetal heart rate during movement with an ultrasound scan that allows assessment of fetal activity, muscle tone, breathing movements, and amniotic fluid volume. Each component is scored with 0, 1, or 2 points, so the highest possible total is 10 points. Fetal biophysical profiles are usually done in the latter weeks of pregnancy.

Benefits/purposes
♦ Is rapidly performed in office or clinic
♦ Is relatively risk-free
♦ Is a fairly good predictor of fetal condition when scores are high (6–10) or low (0–2)

Risks/disadvantages
♦ Experts may disagree on interpretation of results
♦ Intermediate scores (3–5) are difficult to interpret
♦ See Ultrasound and Nonstress Test for other possible disadvantages

Fetal Movement Counts

During late pregnancy, the woman counts and records her baby's movements during a brief period each day. See pages 58–59 for a description of fetal movement counting. Formal fetal movement counting is a more reliable predictor of outcome than reliance on the mother's informal impressions of fetal activity.

Benefits/purposes
♦ Helps assess well-being of fetus
♦ Is free and relatively simple
♦ Is noninvasive
♦ Can be done by the mother herself, at her convenience, in her own home
♦ Helps mother learn about her baby

Risks/disadvantages
♦ Requires more time and work by expectant mother
♦ May raise mother's anxiety over her baby's well-being

continued

Nonstress Test

This test indicates how the fetal heart rate responds when the fetus moves. The fetal heart rate (FHR) is recorded for 20 to 30 minutes with an external electronic fetal monitor, and the woman indicates each time she feels the fetus move. If there is no spontaneous fetal movement, the baby may be asleep. The examiner may push on the woman's abdomen or sound a loud noise near her abdomen to stimulate the baby to move. An increase in heart rate of approximately 15 beats above the baseline during fetal movement (a reactive test) is normal and a sign of fetal well-being. Nonstress tests are considered reliable only during the last weeks of pregnancy.

Benefits/purposes

♦ Helps predict fetal well-being

♦ Is done in caregiver's office, clinic, or hospital

♦ Is noninvasive

♦ Helps determine if a high-risk pregnancy can safely continue or if further testing is desirable

Risks/disadvantages

♦ Interpretation of results somewhat subjective; experts may differ over meaning

♦ Occasionally produces false results

Percutaneous Umbilical Blood Sampling (PUBS)

First described in 1983, this relatively new procedure is similar to amniocentesis except that blood from the baby's umbilical cord, rather than amniotic fluid, is withdrawn. During PUBS, also called cordocentesis, the doctor, guided by a high resolution image created by ultrasound, passes a needle through the mother's abdomen and uterus into the umbilical cord. The procedure takes about 10 minutes. Sometimes a similar technique is used to give a blood transfusion or drugs to a fetus with a serious blood disorder, anemia, or an infection. PUBS can be performed after 16 weeks gestation.

Benefits/purposes

♦ Provides same information as amniocentesis, but with quicker results (within 48 to 72 hours)

♦ Allows evaluation and treatment of a fetus with a blood disorder, like Rh incompatibility or sickle cell disease

♦ Enables diagnosis of suspected fetal infection, hemophilia, and other conditions

♦ Assesses fetal red blood cell count to detect anemia

♦ In future, may be used to monitor effectiveness of drug treatment of fetus

Risks/disadvantages

♦ Requires greater technical skill than amniocentesis on part of doctor and is only available at large prenatal diagnostic centers

♦ Is invasive

♦ Potential complications include infection, preterm labor, premature rupture of membranes, bleeding from umbilical cord, placental abruption, blood clot in cord, transient irregular fetal heart rate, and fetal death

Preterm Labor Detection (Tocodynamometry)

An electronic monitor, strapped to the mother's abdomen and connected to a recorder in a shoulder bag, measures uterine contractions and fetal movement. Information from ambulatory tocodynamometry can then be transmitted over the telephone from the mother's home to the doctor's office. The monitor is usually worn twice a day for 1 to 2 hours during late pregnancy.

Benefits/purposes

♦ Used for early detection and treatment of preterm labor

♦ Is noninvasive

♦ Helps determine effectiveness of medications given to prevent labor contractions

Risks/disadvantages

♦ Sometimes leads to an incorrect diagnosis of preterm labor and unnecessary treatment

♦ Is costly and inconvenient

♦ May give false sense of security because it sometimes misses preterm labor

♦ Scientific studies have not shown that tocodynamometry prevents preterm labor

Ultrasound

High-frequency sound waves are sent through a transmitter, called a transducer or probe, into the woman's uterus via the abdomen or, less commonly, the vagina. These waves echo back from various structures of the fetus, the placenta, and the mother's internal organs and are reproduced as a picture on a video screen. It usually takes 20 to 30 minutes to get an entire image of the fetus and other structures. Ultrasound can be performed at any time during the pregnancy. The timing depends on the reason for testing. Vaginal ultrasound may be better than abdominal ultrasound for detecting some problems, such as placenta previa and ectopic pregnancy.

Benefits/purposes

♦ Confirms pregnancy

♦ Can determine whether the pregnancy is uterine or ectopic

♦ Helps estimate the age of fetus (by providing measurements of various landmarks, such as the skull, femur, and abdomen)

♦ Helps locate fetal organs for inspection, measurement, diagnosis, or treatment

♦ Helps assess the position and condition of the placenta

♦ Detects how fetus is lying in uterus, showing presentation and position

♦ Confirms a multiple pregnancy

♦ Gives immediate results

♦ Helps assess amniotic fluid volume

♦ Helps estimate fetal growth or weight

♦ Appears safe when used judiciously and medically indicated

Risks/disadvantages

♦ Adds additional expense to prenatal care

♦ Accuracy varies, depending on quality of equipment, skill of person interpreting results, and gestational age of fetus

♦ Often requires that mother have a full bladder, which may be uncomfortable

continued

Vaginal/Cervical Smear

At any time during pregnancy, secretions from the mother's vagina or cervical area can be removed by a swab or suction bulb and examined under a microscope or cultured.

Benefits/purposes

♦ Detects organisms that cause infections (for example, trichomonas or yeast, bacteria, herpes virus)

♦ Determines if premature rupture of membranes has occurred by testing the acidity (pH) of fluid or by inspecting it with a microscope; amniotic fluid has a fern-like appearance under the microscope

♦ May be used to evaluate the lipid content of amniotic fluid with premature rupture of membranes to determine fetal lung maturity

Risks/disadvantages

♦ Carries very slight risk of infection

X ray

Ionizing radiation is used to take an internal picture of the mother and the fetus. X rays are rarely used in pregnant women today. Ultrasound is considered a safer, more reliable, and more useful alternative. When used, X ray should be done only after the first trimester.

Benefits/purposes

♦ Helps determine size and shape of mother's pelvis (pelvimetry)

♦ Helps discover position and number of baby or babies

♦ Helps determine if baby is a breech presentation

♦ Helps confirm fetal skeletal problems

Risks/disadvantages

♦ Early prenatal exposure to radiation has been associated with leukemia and genetic mutations in babies

♦ Is a poor predictor of course of labor and "fit" of baby when used for pelvimetry

Chapter 4
Nutrition in Pregnancy

Your eating habits before and during pregnancy affect your baby's health as much as or more than any other single factor. Since eating properly influences the future health of your baby, you should know how to provide the best nourishment for yourself and your unborn child.

It is never too late in pregnancy to improve your eating habits, since your baby will benefit whenever you make any needed improvements, even in late pregnancy. In fact, your baby's requirements for iron, protein, and calcium are greatest in the last eight to twelve weeks of pregnancy. Permanent improvements in your diet will have other long-term effects on your children since they will grow up with better eating habits and will feed their own families better.

Over the years there has been much misunderstanding of what constitutes good nutrition during pregnancy. Such matters as weight gain, calorie intake, the use of salt, what foods to eat and avoid, and vitamin supplementation were poorly understood, and as a result women were given erroneous information. Although there is still much to learn, nutritional information today is based

on more solid research and a better understanding of the physiology of pregnancy.

Good Nutrition during Pregnancy

During pregnancy, you supply all the nutrients for your developing baby, who will weigh an average of seven pounds at birth. The baby's life-support system, consisting of the placenta, uterus, membranes, fluid, and maternal blood supply, also grows during pregnancy, developing as necessary to meet her increasing needs. Your body also prepares for birth and the subsequent nourishment of the baby through breastfeeding. All these added demands require that you nourish yourself adequately; otherwise your pregnancy may deplete you and deprive your baby of important nutrients.

Which foods (and how much) should you eat to ensure the best possible outcome of pregnancy? Why are these foods important? How much weight should you gain while pregnant? What about salt, fluid retention, special diets, heartburn, nausea, and vomiting? This chapter provides discussion of these questions, along with some practical advice and an opportunity to evaluate your own diet.

In the last two trimesters of your pregnancy, you will need about 300 calories per day more than you did when you were not pregnant. For the average woman this amounts to approximately 2,500 calories per day. These added calories should be in the form of high-protein, high-calcium, and iron-rich foods. Three hundred calories are really not all that much—two tall glasses of milk, a bowl of hearty soup, a serving of meat, or three tablespoons of peanut butter. Try not to add lots of high-calorie, nonnutritious foods such as cake, cookies, candies, and soft drinks to your diet.

Sample Daily Menu during Pregnancy

Breakfast
- 1 slice of toast
- Butter or margarine
- 2 eggs
- Citrus fruit or juice
- Milk or water

Lunch
- 1 whole wheat roll
- Butter or margarine
- Chef's salad (meat, cheese, carrot, tomato, lettuce, reduced calorie or regular blue cheese dressing)
- Milk

Dinner
- Potatoes with butter, margarine, sour cream, or yogurt
- Fish
- Spinach salad (reduced calorie or oil and vinegar dressing)
- Melon slice
- Milk and water

Snack
- Options (1 to 2 per day): milk shake, bran muffin, apple or celery with peanut butter, carrot sticks, water, and juice

Basically, a good daily pregnancy diet is a varied diet—plenty of fresh fruits and vegetables, whole grains, dairy products, protein foods (such as meat, fish, nuts, eggs, and legumes), some fat (such as margarine, oil, or butterfat), and about two quarts of fluid a day.

Food Groups

Good nutrition has been explained by separating foods into four basic groups: (1) dairy products, (2) meat and protein foods, (3) fruits and vegetables, and (4) breads and cereals. However, it is possible to eat daily from these four food groups and not take in all the necessary nutrients. Therefore, foods should be further sorted into seven basic groups: (1) dairy products, (2) high protein foods, (3) green and yellow vegetables, (4) citrus fruits and vitamin C-rich foods, (5) potatoes, other vegetables, and fruits, (6) grain products, and (7) fats.

Two other food categories are important to nutrition-conscious people: (8) liquids and (9) sugar foods. You should drink about eight cups of liquid per day. The body has no requirement for sugar foods. If you eat many of these foods, they may become substitutes for more nourishing food, and they may cause excessive weight gain.

Nutrients

The chart that begins on page 76 presents a brief summary of nutrients and vitamins, their functions, and sources. Some nutrients, however, deserve special mention for their particular importance in pregnancy.

Protein

All cells are formed from protein. In this period of rapid growth—of baby, placenta, uterus, breasts, and the volume of blood and amniotic fluid—your protein require-

Basic Food Groups

A good diet consists of eating a variety of foods in the appropriate amounts. The lower number of servings is appropriate for a woman whose pregnancy is normal but who has a smaller appetite. A diet analysis form is provided for your use on page 80.

Food group	One serving equals	Recommended daily servings
Dairy products (calcium-rich foods)	♦ 1 cup milk or yogurt ♦ 1½ cup cottage cheese ♦ 2–3 scoops ice cream or ice milk ♦ 1-inch cube cheese	3–4
High-quality protein	♦ 3 ounces meat, fish, poultry ♦ 2 eggs ♦ 1 cup dried beans or lentils ♦ 4 tablespoons peanut butter ♦ 60 nuts	3–4
Green and yellow vegetables	♦ ½ cup dark green and deep yellow vegetables such as spinach, broccoli, green pepper, or squash	1–2
Citrus fruits and vitamin C foods	♦ 4 ounces citrus juice ♦ 1 orange ♦ ½ grapefruit ♦ 1 tomato or 8 ounces juice ♦ ⅔ cup strawberries ♦ ⅙ watermelon	2
Potatoes and other vegetables and fruits	♦ 1 potato, ear of corn, apple, banana ♦ ½ cup peaches, pineapple, apricots, beets, cauliflower, or lettuce	1
Bread, flour, and cereals	♦ 1 slice bread ♦ 1 ounce cold cereal ♦ ½–¾ cup cooked cereal, macaroni, or rice ♦ 1 cookie, muffin, slice of cake, doughnut, or pancake	2–4
Fats and oils	♦ 1 tablespoon butter, margarine, or oil	1–2
Liquids	♦ 1 cup	8+
Sugar foods	♦ 3 teaspoons sugar ♦ ½ ounce hard candy, marshmallows, or chocolate ♦ 1 tablespoon honey, jam, or syrup	0

ments increase by about sixteen grams over your normal requirements. Remember that prenatal vitamins and mineral supplements supply no protein. Food or protein supplements are your only sources. Be sure that any meats, poultry, or fish you eat are well cooked to avoid food-born illness.

Calcium

Calcium promotes the mineralization of the fetal skeleton and teeth. The fetus requires approximately 66 percent more calcium than normal during the last trimester, when the teeth are forming and skeletal growth is most rapid. Calcium is also stored in the mother's bones as a reserve for later milk production. High caffeine intake can interfere with one's ability to use calcium (see page 81).

Iron

Iron is required for the manufacture of *hemoglobin*, the oxygen-carrying protein in the blood. Your blood volume increases by 50 percent during pregnancy, so your need to provide hemoglobin and the other constituents of blood increases accordingly. In addition, during the last six weeks of pregnancy, the fetus stores enough iron in his liver to supplement his needs for the first three to six months of life. This is necessary because the main food during that period—breast milk or formula—only partially fulfills an infant's iron requirements. Since a healthy person absorbs only 10 to 20 percent of the iron ingested, the National Research Council's Committee on Maternal Nutrition recommends a daily supplement during pregnancy of thirty to sixty milligrams of iron to ensure absorption of the iron needed each day.[1]

Although it is necessary for good nutrition, iron upsets the digestive tract in many people. The side effects—nausea, heartburn, diarrhea, or constipation—are related to the amount of elemental iron given and individual reactions, not to the type of

preparation. In other words, whether you are taking ferrous sulfate, ferrous fumerate, or ferrous gluconate is less important than how much iron you take at a time. To relieve the unpleasant side effects, you may be advised to decrease each dose of iron or take food along with the tablets. Vitamin C-rich foods (citrus fruits, tomatoes) or calcium-rich nondairy foods (broccoli, almonds) enhance the absorption of iron. Some antacids interfere with iron absorption. Check with your caregiver.

Also remember that the easiest and most effective way to "take" iron is to eat a variety of foods rich in iron: liver and other organ meats, red meats, egg yolks, dried fruits, prune and apple juices, dried peas, beans, lentils, oysters, almonds, walnuts, and blackstrap molasses.

Vitamins

Vitamins are essential to most life functions (see the chart on pages 76–79). They are classified by their solubility: water-soluble—C and B complex; and fat-soluble—vitamins A, D, E, and K. The water-soluble vitamins can be lost in cooking. Vegetables high in these vitamins should be eaten raw or cooked briefly in small amounts of water, stir-fried, or steamed.

Folic acid is a water-soluble vitamin in the B complex. Because it is essential for the normal growth of all cells and is involved in RNA and DNA synthesis, the requirement for folic acid doubles during pregnancy. Since long storage and overcooking of food destroy folic acid, the National Research Council's Committee on Maternal Nutrition recommends a daily supplement of 400 micrograms during the last half of pregnancy.[2]

The only way to make sure you get all the vitamins and minerals you need is to eat a varied, high-quality diet. It is not a good idea to eat junk food (high in calories, low in nutritional value) while depending on vitamin or mineral supplements, since vitamin preparations contain only some of these essential nutrients. There are other nutrients present in food, about which we still know very little. They may be present only in trace amounts, and their functions are not yet fully understood. Because vitamin manufacturers do not include them in their preparations, food is your only source.

Weight Gain

How much weight should you gain during pregnancy? No single amount is appropriate for every pregnant woman. Proper weight gain depends on many variables: your prepregnancy weight and stature, the size of your baby and placenta, the quality of your diet before and during pregnancy, your ethnic background, and number of previous pregnancies.[3] Until the early 1970s, most North American obstetricians placed great emphasis on limiting weight gain to between fourteen and seventeen pounds, believing this range would result in easier labors and less postpartum obesity. It was assumed that the fetus always managed to extract the necessary nutrients from the mother. Recent research studies investigating the association between weight gain and the health of the baby have shown that a higher weight gain during pregnancy results in more full-term pregnancies and larger, healthier babies.

♦ If your prepregnancy weight was below normal, it may be wise for you to gain more weight than women who are of normal weight or overweight. If your baby is large (over eight pounds) the chances are that your placenta is also larger than average. It stands to reason that you will gain more weight than if your baby and placenta are of average or small size.

♦ If the quality of your diet is normally excellent and you and your baby are of average size, you will probably gain between twenty and thirty-five pounds.

♦ If, on the other hand, you are overweight or if you ate many high-calorie, low-quality foods before pregnancy, you may gain less weight while benefiting your baby by replacing the high-calorie, nonnutritious foods with better-quality foods.

The point to keep in mind is that your weight gain is of secondary importance to the quality of your diet. If you eat consistently well and in appropriate quantities, you can trust that the amount of weight you gain is right for you.

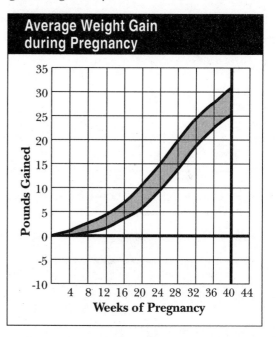

Average Weight Gain during Pregnancy

You will be weighed at each prenatal visit, and your weight will be recorded on a graph similar to the one shown on the next page. As you can see, weight gain is typically slow early in pregnancy, and it increases more rapidly as the baby grows and her support system develops to meet her requirements. An increase in maternal weight of two to four pounds by the end of the first trimester and approximately one pound per week thereafter is fairly typical. A sudden, excessive gain or drop in weight from one visit to the next can be a sign of illness or other problems. It may also be a sign that you went on a food binge or starved yourself between visits!

If you gain twenty-seven pounds and have a seven-and-a-half-pound baby, where does the rest of the weight go? The following list shows approximately how the weight is distributed during pregnancy.

Average Weight Gain Distribution during Pregnancy	
Baby	7½ lbs.
Placenta	1 lb.
Uterus	2 lbs.
Amniotic fluid	2 lbs.
Breasts	1 lb.
Blood volume	2½ lbs.
Fat	5 lbs.
Tissue fluid	6 lbs.
Total	**27 lbs.**

Most women accept the weight they put on during pregnancy, especially when they realize that most of it is lost either during birth or shortly thereafter. But what about that extra five pounds or more of fat? Since it may take weeks or months before that disappears, many weight-conscious women dislike putting on fat during pregnancy. Consider the following:

♦ It is not possible to gain only the weight necessary for the baby and the placenta and avoid adding the fat. The fat is not the last five pounds of weight you gain, so it cannot be avoided if you stop gaining weight at twenty-two pounds instead of twenty-seven. In fact, fat is produced gradually along with the other components of the weight gain. Trying to avoid the fat may deprive you or your baby of essential nutrients.

♦ Most women are able to lose their extra weight gradually over a period of several months after the baby is born—that is, if they maintain sensible eating habits. Breastfeeding promotes the loss of these extra pounds because calories are required for adequate milk production. The stored fat provides some of these calories; the rest comes from additional calories taken in by the breastfeeding mother. The usual recommendation during breastfeeding is to add 500 calories per day above the requirement for a nonpregnant woman. This should be individualized as described on page 269 in chapter 14.

The point is that pregnancy is not the time to lose weight; it is a time to concentrate on a high-quality diet.

Salt and Fluids

Salt

For years pregnant women were told to eliminate or restrict their use of salt. The rationale for this treatment was based on the tendency of the pregnant woman to retain fluid—which was assumed to cause preeclampsia. (See chapter 3 for a discussion of preeclampsia.) It is now known that gradual, moderate water retention in pregnancy is not only normal, it is necessary to ensure an adequate volume of blood and amniotic fluid. The abnormal, sudden increase in fluid retention seen in preeclampsia is not due to excessive salt intake but rather to the impaired functioning of the liver and kidneys, which normally regulate protein, electrolyte, and fluid balance. Adequate salt intake during pregnancy is now known to be important in maintaining fluid balance. The wise pregnant woman does as any well-nourished person does; she salts her food to taste.

By the same token, the use of diuretics, once prescribed almost routinely during pregnancy to wash away fluids and electrolytes, is now known to stress the system that controls blood pressure and fluid balance. Diuretics cause problems with fluid balance during pregnancy; they do not solve them.[4]

Fluids

As stated above, you normally retain fluid as part of the process that ensures the increase in blood and amniotic fluid necessary to a healthy pregnancy. You need to retain more fluid for two reasons:

♦ Your blood volume increases by 50 percent or more (from approximately two and one-half to three and three-fourths quarts).

♦ Toward the end of pregnancy, your baby is immersed in about one quart of amniotic fluid, which is replaced every three hours. Fluid is also retained in the tissues, shifting across blood vessel walls, helping maintain a healthy balance of fluids. It is estimated that tissue fluid increases by two to three quarts during pregnancy.

During pregnancy, try to drink at least two quarts of liquid a day (milk, fruit juices, and water). This is difficult if you are not in the habit of drinking enough fluids. It may be helpful to fill a one-quart pitcher with water, put it in the refrigerator at home or take it to work, and drink from it throughout the day, making sure it is empty by bedtime. In addition, plan to have a glass of milk or other liquid with each meal and a glass of fruit juice at snack times. You can easily develop this habit with a little conscientious effort.

In summary, by gaining an appropriate amount of weight, eating a well-balanced diet, using salt as desired, drinking a generous amount of liquids, supplementing your diet with iron and folic acid, and avoiding diuretics, you are following the nutritional guidelines most likely to produce a healthy baby and mother.

Common Concerns

Several nutrition-related problems commonly arise during pregnancy due to normal changes in hormone production and the increased size and weight of the uterus. The following pages discuss these problems, their causes, and their treatments.

Nausea and Vomiting

Nausea and vomiting are sometimes referred to as "morning sickness" (although for many women it is not restricted to the morning). Pregnant women frequently feel nauseated and may vomit when they have not eaten for several hours or when they smell certain odors, such as cigar smoke, a stuffy room, or certain foods being cooked. Although the "trigger" may vary from woman to woman, the problem is common.

With today's emphasis on good nutrition, you may worry about your baby's health if nausea and vomiting are a problem. You will be reassured to know, however, that recent studies indicate that women who are healthy at conception have sufficient reserves to supply the growing embryo and fetus, even if they are unable to eat well for the first several months.[5] Furthermore, another study indicates that nausea and vomiting are more likely to be associated with a healthy pregnancy outcome than is an absence of these symptoms.[6]

Be assured that nausea is neither abnormal nor a sign of unconscious rejection of the baby, as is sometimes suggested. The cause is probably related to the body's increased production of twenty-six hormones, plus the manufacture of at least four other hormones produced only during pregnancy. Some of these hormones, when present in large quantities, may be upsetting until the body adjusts.

Treatment

♦ Try modifying your eating habits. You may find it helpful to eat several (five or six) small meals a day to avoid an empty stomach and to help maintain a stable blood sugar level. Some protein should be included in each of these meals. Eating crackers, a bagel, or toast whenever you feel queasy is also helpful. To prevent morning sickness, try leaving bland food such as crackers by the bed at night and eating it before you get up.

♦ Try increasing your intake of foods rich in vitamin B_6 (pyridoxine) such as whole grains and cereals, wheat germ, nuts, seeds, legumes, and corn. Sometimes vitamin B_6 supplements are prescribed. Discuss this with your caregiver.

♦ Know that the condition will usually pass within three to four months.

♦ Try to maintain a sense of humor. For some women, throwing up becomes as much part of their morning routine as brushing their teeth and combing their hair. Their attitude has much to do with how well they cope with this and other annoyances.

♦ On very rare occasions, nausea and vomiting are severe and a woman actually becomes dehydrated, loses a great deal of weight, and is unable to retain any food. This condition is called hyperemesis gravidarum, and it may require medication or even hospitalization if the nausea and vomiting endanger either the mother or the baby's health. See page 50 in chapter 3 for further discussion.

♦ Medications are available to help control nausea and vomiting. They are prescribed either when the nausea and vomiting are severe and thought to be causing dehydration, or when the woman is upset or inconvenienced and requests medication. You should realize that these medications cross the placenta to the fetus and that neither their safety to the unborn baby nor their effectiveness has been established. Because they are used during the time of pregnancy when the fetus is most vul-

nerable, it is wise to try the nonmedical forms of treatment first and to think twice before requesting medication.

Heartburn

Heartburn, a feeling of fullness, with some burping up of acid from the stomach, is a common complaint in late pregnancy. It is caused by a combination of increased pressure from the growing uterus and hormonal effects that relax the muscular opening at the top of the stomach and cause the stomach to empty more slowly. Fatty foods, foods that produce gas, and large meals may also make the heartburn worse.

Treatment

♦ Avoid fatty food and foods that produce gas or heartburn.

♦ Eat several small meals (rather than a few large meals). Some women find that eating slowly and not eating just before bedtime also help reduce heartburn.

♦ Antacids or other drugs are sometimes used to control heartburn, but they should be used only if necessary. Consult your caregiver for recommendations for safe antacids and to learn about possible undesirable side effects.

Constipation

During pregnancy, the movement of food through the intestines is slowed. This allows for greater absorption of nutrients and water, but also sometimes causes constipation. Pressure from the growing uterus on the large intestine magnifies the problem.

Treatment

♦ Drink plenty of fluids and eat foods with high-fiber content, such as raw or dried fruits and vegetables, whole grains, bran, and prune juice, all of which encourage elimination.

♦ Exercise regularly. Exercise such as walking is an often neglected but effective aid to regularity.

♦ If proper diet and exercise are followed, laxatives can and should be avoided. Prevention of constipation also alleviates the discomfort of hemorrhoids, another common problem during pregnancy.

Special Circumstances

Good nutrition in pregnancy is always an important concern, but in some circumstances, you need to be even more conscientious about your diet. If your pregnancy is a "special pregnancy" or if you are on a special diet, your nutritional demands will be greater than normal.

In all the following special circumstances, seek nutritional counseling and be particularly conscientious about eating nutritious foods. Nutritional counseling is available from your midwife, your physician, or a nutritionist. These professionals can help you plan your diet in a practical and beneficial way.

Special Pregnancies

Multiple Pregnancy
If you are carrying two or more babies, you need to consume more calories and more nutrients. For further information on nutrition in multiple pregnancies, see the Recommended Resources.

Adolescent Pregnancy
If you are a teenager, you are still growing and have greater-than-adult requirements for most nutrients. You need to eat particularly well when pregnant to maintain your own growth while nourishing your fetus.

Pregnancies Close Together
Sometimes a pregnancy depletes your reserves of certain nutrients such as calcium and iron. If you have sufficient time between pregnancies to replenish those reserves, no nutritional deficiency occurs. If

you soon become pregnant again, however, your reserves may be depleted and you may need extra calories and nutrients. The length of time needed between pregnancies to correct deficiencies depends, of course, on your overall nutritional status and the quality of your diet.

Special Diets

A Vegetarian Diet
If you are a vegetarian, you can, with knowledge and careful planning, adequately nourish yourself and your unborn baby, especially if you include milk and eggs in your diet. Your major concerns are these: the need to take in sufficient calories, the (possible) need to supplement B_{12} found mostly in animal meats, and the need to combine protein-rich foods to obtain all the essential proteins. (See Recommended Resources for references on vegetarian diets.) The information in this chapter applies to both the vegetarian and the meat-eater.

Milk Intolerance
If you cannot tolerate milk, you may have a problem getting enough calcium. Try cultured forms of milk, such as acidophilus milk, yogurt, and cheese, which are often well tolerated by people who are upset by milk. Another option is to drink low-lactose milk, which contains lactase, an enzyme that helps to change lactose into a more digestible sugar. Otherwise, you should learn about and eat other foods high in calcium (see page 77). If you simply do not like the taste of milk, try cooking with dry powdered milk or eating cream soups and cheeses. These alternatives will give you the benefits of milk without its taste. If you are not meeting your needs through your diet, however, you may need calcium supplements. Consult your physician or midwife if this is a problem for you.

Food Allergies

If you have significant food allergies, you may need a nutritionist to help you plan a healthful pregnancy diet. Sometimes the elimination of problem foods leads to an inadequate diet, so you will need careful guidance.

Anorexia and Bulimia

If you have been anorexic or are struggling with bulimia it may be more difficult for you to accept the weight gain and body changes that occur with pregnancy. In addition, you may be at risk for a poor pregnancy outcome. Nutritional and psychological counseling may be beneficial for your well-being and your baby's. Many urban areas have anorexia and bulimia support groups that may be helpful as well.

Medical Problems

If you are pregnant and have a medical problem, such as diabetes, anemia, or heart or lung disease, you will need special nutritional guidance and close prenatal observation and management. It is beyond the scope of this book to deal with such problems, except to emphasize the necessity of thorough prenatal care. Be sure you understand and follow the instructions you are given for any medical problems.

Nutrients and Vitamins[a]

Key nutrient & RDA*	Important functions	Important sources	Comments
Calories N—2,200 P—2,200 (1st trimester) P—2,500 (2nd & 3rd trimesters) L—2,700	♦ Provide energy for tissue building and increased metabolic requirements	Carbohydrates, fats, and proteins	Calorie requirements vary according to the stage of your pregnancy, your size, activity level, prepregnant weight, and how well nourished you are.
Water or liquids N—4 cups P—8+ cups L—8+ cups	♦ Carries nutrients to cells ♦ Carries waste products away ♦ Provides fluid for increased blood, tissue, and amniotic fluid volume ♦ Helps regulate body temperature ♦ Aids digestion	Water, juices, and milk	Liquid is often neglected, but it is an important nutrient.

* N—nonpregnant
  P—pregnant
  L—lactating (first 6 months)

Key nutrient & RDA*	Important functions	Important sources	Comments
Protein N—46 g P—60 g L—65 g	♦ Builds and repairs tissues ♦ Helps build blood, amniotic fluid, and placenta ♦ Helps form antibodies ♦ Supplies energy	Meat, fish, poultry, eggs, milk, cheese, dried beans and peas, peanut butter, nuts, whole grains, and cereals	Fetal requirements increase by about one-third in late pregnancy as the baby grows.
Minerals			
Calcium N—800 mg P—1,200 mg L—1,200 mg	♦ Helps build bones and teeth ♦ Important in blood clotting ♦ Helps regulate use of other minerals in your body	Milk, cheese, whole grains, vegetables, egg yolk, whole canned fish, and ice cream	Fetal requirements increase in late pregnancy. Caffeine can decrease the amount of calcium available to the fetus.
Phosphorus N—800 mg P—1,200 mg L—1,200 mg	♦ Helps build bones and teeth	Milk, cheese, and lean meats	Calcium and phosphorus exist in a constant ratio in the blood. An excess of either limits the use of calcium.
Iron N—15 mg P—30 mg L—15 mg	♦ Combines with protein to make hemoglobin ♦ Provides iron for fetal storage	Liver, red meats, egg yolk, whole grains, leafy vegetables, nuts, legumes, dried fruits, prunes, and prune and apple juice	Fetal requirements increase tenfold in last 6 weeks of pregnancy. Supplement of 30 to 60 mg of iron daily is recommended by the National Research Council.
Zinc N—12 mg P—15 mg L—19 mg	♦ Component of insulin ♦ Important in growth of skeleton and nervous system	Meat, liver, eggs, and seafood—especially oysters	Deficiency can cause malformations of fetal skeleton and nervous system.
Iodine N—150 mcg P—175 mcg L—200 mcg	♦ Helps control the rate of body's energy use ♦ Important in thyroxine production	Seafoods, iodized salt	Deficiency may cause goiter in infant.

*N—nonpregnant
  P—pregnant
  L—lactating (first 6 months)

continued

Key nutrient & RDA*	Important functions	Important sources	Comments
Magnesium N—280 mg P—320 mg L—355 mg	♦ Helps energy, protein, and cell metabolism ♦ Enzyme activator ♦ Helps tissue growth and muscle action	Nuts, cocoa, green vegetables, whole grains, and dried beans and peas	Most is stored in bones. Deficiency may cause neuromuscular dysfunction.
Fat-soluble vitamins			
Vitamin A N—800 mcg RE P—800 mcg RE L—1,300 mcg RE	♦ Helps bone and tissue growth and development ♦ Essential in development of enamel-forming cells in gum tissue ♦ Helps maintain health of skin and mucous membranes	Butter, fortified margarine, green and yellow vegetables, and liver	In excessive amounts, it is toxic to the fetus. It loses its potency when exposed to light.
Vitamin D N—5 mcg P—10 mcg L—10 mcg	♦ Needed for absorption of calcium and phosphorus and mineralization of bones and teeth	Fortified milk, fortified margarine, fish liver oils, and sunlight on your skin	Toxic to the fetus in excessive amounts.
Vitamin E N—8 mg ∝-TE P—10 mg ∝-TE L—12 mg ∝-TE	♦ Needed for tissue growth, cell wall integrity, and red blood cell integrity	Vegetable oils, cereals, meat, eggs, milk, nuts, and seeds	Enhances absorption of vitamin A.
Vitamin K N—65 mcg P—65 mcg L—65 mcg	♦ Essential for the synthesis of blood clotting factors		Produced in the body by the intestinal flora
Water-soluble vitamins			
Folic acid N—180 mcg P—400 mcg L—280 mcg	♦ Essential in hemoglobin synthesis ♦ Involved in DNA and RNA synthesis ♦ Needed for synthesis of amino acids	Liver, leafy green vegetables, and yeast	Deficiency leads to anemia. Can be destroyed in cooking and storage. Supplement of 400 mcg per day is recommended by the National Research Council. Oral contraceptives may reduce blood level of folic acid.

*N—nonpregnant
 P—pregnant
 L—lactating (first 6 months)

Key nutrient & RDA*	Important functions	Important sources	Comments
Niacin N—15 mg P—17 mg L—20 mg	♦ Needed for energy and protein metabolism	Pork, organ meats, peanuts, beans, peas, and enriched grains	Stable; only small amounts are lost in food preparation.
Riboflavin N—1.3 mg P—1.6 mg L—1.8 mg	♦ Essential for energy and protein metabolism	Milk, lean meat, enriched grains, cheese, and leafy greens	Oral contraceptives may reduce serum concentration of riboflavin.
Thiamin (B$_1$) N—1.1 mg P—1.5 mg L—1.6 mg	♦ Important for energy metabolism	Pork, beef, liver, whole grains, and legumes	Essential for conversion of the carbohydrates into energy in the muscular and nervous systems.
Pyridoxine (B$_6$) N—1.6 mg P—2.2 mg L—2.1 mg	♦ Important in amino acid metabolism and protein synthesis ♦ Required for fetal growth	Unprocessed cereals, grains, wheat germ, nuts, seeds, legumes, and corn	Excessive amounts may reduce milk supply in lactating women. May help reduce nausea in early pregnancy.
Cobalamin (B$_{12}$) N—2.0 mcg P—2.2 mcg L—2.6 mcg	♦ Essential in protein metabolism ♦ Important in formation of red blood cells	Milk, eggs, meat, liver, and cheese	Deficiency leads to anemia and central nervous system damage. Is manufactured by micro-organisms in the intestinal tract. Oral contraceptives may reduce serum concentration.
Vitamin C N—60 mg P—70 mg L—95 mg	♦ Helps tissue formation and integrity ♦ Is the "cement" substance in connective and vascular tissue ♦ Increases iron absorption	Citrus fruits, berries, melons, tomatoes, chili peppers, green vegetables, and potatoes	Large supplemental doses in pregnancy may create a larger-than-normal need in infant. Benefits of large doses in preventing colds have not been confirmed.

* N—nonpregnant
P—pregnant
L—lactating (first 6 months)

[a] The main sources of information for this chart are B. Worthington-Roberts and S. Williams, eds., *Nutrition in Pregnancy and Lactation*, 4th ed. (St. Louis: C.V. Mosby Co., 1989); and National Research Council, Food and Nutrition Board, *Recommended Dietary Allowances*, rev. ed. (Washington, D.C.: National Academy of Sciences, 1989).

Diet Analysis

Photocopy this and use it to record the foods you eat. Then compare your diet with the recommendations. Try checking yourself several times during your pregnancy, especially if you found you needed to change some of your eating habits. Opposite each food group, indicate how many servings you eat on each day. If you eat the food at breakfast, use the letter *B*; if at lunch, *L*; if at dinner, *D*; and if as a snack, *S*. The lower number of servings is suggested for those whose pregnancies are normal but who have smaller appetites.

Food group	Number of daily servings	Sample day	Day 1	Day 2	Day 3	Changes to make
Dairy products (calcium-rich foods)	3–4	BLLD				
High-quality protein	3–4	BLDS				
Green and yellow vegetables	1–2	LD				
Citrus fruits and vitamin C foods	2	BLD				
Potatoes and other vegetables and fruits	1	LDS				
Bread, flour, and cereals	2–4	BLS				
Fats and oils	1–2	BLDD				
Liquids	8+	BB, SSS, L, DD				
Sugar foods	0	S				

Chapter 5

Drugs, Medications, and Environmental Hazards in Pregnancy

In recent years, studies have examined the effects of various drugs and environmental agents on the unborn baby. Until the 1960s, it was assumed that the placenta protected the fetus. Now we know that most drugs and other harmful substances cross the placenta freely. Some cause birth defects; some cause other harmful effects, like slow growth, mental or developmental retardation, or problems in organ development. Some medications may be harmless; others may be beneficial to the fetus. At the least, their effects on the fetus are similar to and possibly greater than their effect on the mother because of the fetus's small size and rapid growth and development.

Where does all this leave the pregnant woman? When should she take a drug? Are all drugs bad? What about the social or "recreational" drugs, tobacco and alcohol? What about the medicines she has been using? What about caffeine, artificial sweeteners, and herbs? What is an environmental hazard? This chapter reviews what is known about the answers to these questions, provides some guidelines on what to avoid, and suggests some substitutes for common social drugs and medications.

Drugs

Generally speaking, if you are pregnant, be very cautious about using any drug. No drug has been proven safe for all fetuses under all circumstances, though many drugs are thought to be safe or at least have not been proven to be harmful. The best course to follow when considering the use of a drug is to weigh the possible risks against the possible benefits. If the benefits clearly outweigh the risks, then use the drug or medication; if not, look for alternative treatments or pleasures.

Caffeine

Coffee, tea, colas and other soft drinks (read the labels), chocolate, and some over-the-counter drugs contain caffeine. How harmful is caffeine? Some early animal studies found a connection between caffeine consumption and certain birth defects.[1]

It is difficult to study the effects of injesting caffeine, since many women who take in large amounts of caffeine also smoke and use alcohol or other drugs, making it difficult to isolate caffeine's effect. Caffeine use by pregnant women has not been associated with malformations of the fetus, but some studies have associated caffeine use with miscarriages in the late first and second trimesters[2] and with low birth weight in term infants.[3] The effects increase with increased caffeine intake. More than a decade ago, the Food and Drug Administration (FDA) advised "prudent and protective" expectant mothers to limit caffeine use.[4]

Other effects besides birth defects and prematurity should concern you as an expectant parent. According to a National Academy of Sciences report, pregnant women take in an average of 200 milligrams of caffeine per day, the equivalent of about one and a half to three cups of coffee or two to four cups of tea.[5] Caffeine increases urinary excretion of calcium and decreases the amount available for you and your baby. Pregnant women eliminate caffeine from their bodies more slowly than nonpregnant women. This means that the effects on both mother and fetus last longer.[6] Caffeine also causes an increased production of "stress" hormones—epinephrine (adrenaline) and norepinephrine (noradrenaline). These hormones constrict peripheral blood vessels, including those in the uterus, and cause a temporary decrease in the amount of oxygen and other nutrients available to the fetus. The more caffeine you take in, the more the fetus is affected in this way.[7] Caffeine readily enters the fetal blood stream. If the baby has caffeine in his circulation at birth, it takes a much longer time to clear his system than it would take an adult.[8] Considering what we now know, it seems wise to eliminate or reduce caffeine intake during pregnancy.

Aspartame

Aspartame, marketed as NutraSweet or Equal, is present in numerous products including diet drinks, chewing gum, desserts, and vitamins. Aspartame is a combination of two amino acids, phenylalanine and aspartic acid, both of which are known to be toxic at high levels. Unlike other artificial sweeteners, aspartame has never been found to cause cancer. Even though the FDA has established a safe upper limit of aspartame for adults (3.5 grams of aspartame per day for a 150-pound adult), they have not addressed the issue of safe levels for pregnant women and their unborn babies. Furthermore, food companies do not list the amount of aspartame in food products Therefore, it is difficult to determine how much you take in and even more difficult to determine whether a safe level for the fetus has been exceeded. Probably the best advice is to limit or avoid aspartame since few people need artificial sweeteners.

Alcohol

Until the mid-1970s, alcohol, even in large amounts, was thought to be harmless to the fetus. Alcoholism was felt to be a problem because an alcoholic pregnant woman might not eat enough nutritious food, causing malnutrition in her fetus. We now know, however, that alcohol has a direct toxic effect on the developing fetus.[9] Alcohol quickly crosses the placenta and enters the fetus's blood in the same concentration as in the mother's blood. Babies born of alcoholic mothers are at substantial risk for suffering from fetal alcohol syndrome (FAS), a cluster of disabilities that includes mental and physical retardation, tremors, and peculiar facial characteristics. Lesser amounts of alcohol (about two drinks a day or a few occasions of heavy drinking) have been associated with some of the lasting harmful effects of FAS and with birth weights that are significantly lower (an average of five ounces) than the birth weights of babies born of nondrinking mothers. The babies who have fewer or less severe problems suffer from alcohol related birth defects.

If you are pregnant, you are wise to give up drinking—the earlier the better. While drinking in early pregnancy is more likely to be associated with birth defects, drinking later in pregnancy is more likely to be associated with smaller fetal size. Stopping at any time, therefore, will allow your baby the opportunity to catch up in growth before birth.

Questions about Alcohol

♦ *What if I drink only occasionally, and then only lightly or moderately?* At this time it has not been shown that this type of drinking has lasting or measurable effects. We do know, however, that the baby receives alcohol when you drink, and no one has yet been able to determine a "safe" dose. Beer and wine are not less harmful than hard liquor. A four-ounce glass of wine or a can of beer contains as much alcohol as a mixed drink.

♦ *What if I have drunk too much during my pregnancy because I either did not know the dangers of alcohol or that I was pregnant?* It would be difficult for you not to be concerned about the health of your baby. A few points may be helpful here. As stated above, whenever you stop drinking, it will probably be beneficial. Also, remember that the fetus is remarkably strong and resilient. Consider the very high percentage of healthy babies born to mothers who drank alcohol or took drugs or medicines, or had illnesses or other problems during their pregnancies. Of course, you should not depend on the strength of the fetus and deliberately abuse drugs. But if you have used drugs, it should be reassuring to know that the fetus has resources to help him combat their effects.

It has also been shown that pregnant women commonly develop an aversion to alcohol (as well as smoking and caffeine). Many women cut down on their use of alcohol simply because it loses its appeal. Perhaps our bodies are trying to tell us something! In any situation where you

might drink alcohol, substitute fruit juice, tomato juice, or mineral water with a twist of lemon.

Tobacco

Tobacco smoking has been widely studied for its effects on the unborn baby. The evidence strongly suggests that if you are pregnant and you smoke, you should stop or cut down as much as possible and as soon as possible—before pregnancy begins, if you can.

Cigarette smoke contains many substances—tars, nicotine, carbon monoxide, lead, and others—that are harmful to both you and your child if you smoke. Compared to nonsmokers, pregnant women who smoke give birth to babies of smaller average size and have a greater chance of premature rupture of the membranes, premature birth, perinatal death, placental abnormalities, and bleeding during pregnancy. These conditions are directly proportional to the amount of smoking: the more you smoke, the greater the chance you will have these complications.[10]

Smoking may also produce harmful, long-term effects on the child. The incidence of respiratory illness is higher in children from households where adults smoke. Children of smoking parents are also more likely to smoke than are the children of nonsmoking parents. In one very large study that compared the children of smokers and nonsmokers, the children of smokers were an average of one centimeter shorter and three to five months behind the children of nonsmokers in intellectual ability. (The study accounted for associated social and biological factors.)[11]

What if you do not smoke, but your friends, family, or coworkers smoke in your presence? Passive smoking (breathing in other people's smoke) can be uncomfortable to you and possibly harmful to your fetus, depending on how smoky the area is and how much time you spend in it. If you feel strongly about this and are assertive, you may choose to avoid smoky areas and ask friends, colleagues, and family members not to smoke near you.

Marijuana

Until recently we knew very little about the effects of marijuana on the unborn baby (or even on adults). It is clear, however, that marijuana affects the fetus at least as much as it does the mother. The amounts of tar and nicotine in marijuana are considerably greater than in tobacco cigarettes, because no effort is being made to reduce these substances in marijuana. Carbon monoxide, which is present in all smoke, including marijuana smoke, significantly reduces the blood's capacity to carry oxygen. Recent studies have shown an association between regular use of marijuana and preterm delivery, low birth weight, and small-for-gestational-age infants.[12] In summary, the regular use (two to three times per month or more) of marijuana during pregnancy certainly poses some health problems for both mother and infant.

Cocaine (Crack)

The reports of the effects of cocaine use during pregnancy are clearly alarming.[13] Its use during the third trimester is associated with the sudden onset of uterine contractions and placental abruption. Its use throughout pregnancy is associated with miscarriage, reduced birth weight, increased incidence of stillbirth, and a higher malformation rate. Newborns sometimes suffer withdrawal symptoms (constant crying, hyperactivity, poor suckling) that may last for weeks or months. Recent reports indicate a possible association between cocaine use during pregnancy and sudden infant death

syndrome (SIDS). It is clear that you should avoid using this dangerous drug during pregnancy and lactation.

Amphetamines (Crank, Speed, Ice)

Use of amphetamines by pregnant women is associated with intrauterine growth retardation (lowered birth weight, length, and head circumference) and prematurity. Newborn problems associated with amphetamines include rapid heart and respiratory rates and altered newborn behavioral patterns.[14]

Herbs (Tinctures, Teas, Capsules)

Hundreds of herbs are available commercially. Traditional healers use them for various curative or restorative purposes. It is not possible to comment on the safety or value of herbs for the fetus since there has been little scientific scrutiny and little is known about the active ingredients that produce the benefits. It is known, however, that some herbs can produce undesirable side effects in some adults.[15] For instance, teas made from juniper berries, buckthorn bark, senna leaves, duck roots, and aloe can irritate the stomach and intestinal tract, sometimes severely. People allergic to ragweed and related plants may develop unusual allergic symptoms after drinking chamomile tea. A popular ingredient of tea—licorice root—if used in large quantities, is associated with water retention and loss of potassium. Blue cohosh, sometimes used to start labor, has been associated with elevated blood pressure and irritation of mucous membranes.

Sassafras root contains safrole, known to cause liver cancer in rats. The Food and Drug Administration recently stated that safrole cannot be considered safe for human use. Ginseng contains small amounts of estrogen, and there have been reports of swollen and painful breasts after its use in large quantities. Various combinations of herbs are used during pregnancy to tone the uterus, and during labor to nourish the woman's body.[16] These ingredients almost certainly reach the fetus and affect the baby at least as much as they do the mother. Because dosages vary and little is known about the risks and benefits of most herbs, you should use them with caution, and only under the guidance of an expert, as you would any medication.

Medications

Medications such as pain relievers, sedatives and tranquilizers, antihistamines, antacids, and antiemetics (to control nausea and vomiting) are used by many women during pregnancy. Many are self-prescribed. These drugs do not treat or cure an illness; they relieve symptoms like pain, headache, nervousness, sleeplessness, runny nose, heartburn, and nausea. Other medications, such as antibiotics, insulin, and steroids, either cure or control an illness, and their benefits are surely greater than those drugs that merely relieve symptoms. Even so, medication should be used only when the benefits clearly outweigh the potential hazards.

Some conditions are in themselves risky enough to mother and child to require treatment. Conditions such as epilepsy, pneumonia, asthma, strep throat, high fever, arthritis, diabetes, and heart disease may require treatment with strong medications even during pregnancy. Under these circumstances, nontreatment would be far more harmful to mother and fetus than treatment. Therefore, in deciding whether to use medication, consider the seriousness of the condition, the benefit to be gained from the medication, other possible treatments and their benefits, and the risks of both condition and treatment.

Particular mention should be made of three widely used drugs that are generally considered harmless: aspirin (Anacin, Bayer, Bufferin, Empirin); acetaminophen (Datril,

Tempra, Tylenol); and ibuprofen (Advil, Mediprin, Motrin, Nuprin). These drugs reduce pain and fever but have potential side effects for both mother and baby. Should they be used during pregnancy?

Aspirin

Even one tablet of aspirin affects the body's ability to clot blood and prolongs bleeding time.[17] Two tablets, the usual adult dose, will double bleeding time, an effect that lasts from four to seven days after a single dose. There is greater concern over aspirin taken toward the end of pregnancy, because normal bleeding after birth may be increased and prolonged, but it is wise to avoid aspirin even earlier in pregnancy; using it could worsen any bleeding you have during your pregnancy. Continued use of aspirin also interferes with prostaglandin production and may postpone the onset of labor.

Aspirin present in the baby's circulation at birth prolongs bleeding time for the newborn, and it increases the likelihood of jaundice. Therefore, you are better off avoiding aspirin during pregnancy unless prescribed specifically by your doctor or midwife, who should explain to you why the benefits outweigh the risks described here.

Acetaminophen

Acetaminophen is less potentially harmful than aspirin. No adverse fetal effects have been reported with the moderate use of acetaminophen. However, if you consistently use more than the recommended amounts, there may be kidney damage in the fetus.[18] If you normally tolerate acetaminophen well, it is preferable to use it in moderation rather than aspirin if you really need a pain or fever medication during pregnancy. Generally speaking, it is wise to use nonmedical forms of treatment before resorting to medications (see Home Remedies on the next page).

Ibuprofen

Ibuprofen, a medication for relief of pain, fever, and inflammation has recently become available in nonprescription form. It, like aspirin, interferes with prostaglandin production and may postpone the onset of labor.[19] You are better off not using ibuprofen during pregnancy unless specifically prescribed by your caregiver, who has considered these concerns.

Home Remedies

Here are some suggested alternatives to the medical treatment of common ailments. If any of these discomforts persist or seem harmful to your well-being, however, consult your doctor or midwife for further treatment.

Headache

Instead of using aspirin, acetaminophen, ibuprofen, or combination drugs, try a warm, relaxing bath, a massage, tension-reducing exercises (such as shoulder circling), and relaxation routines. Hot packs or cold packs on the back of the neck or shoulders and cold packs on the forehead also help relieve headache for many people.

Cold, Hay Fever, Runny Nose, and Cough

A cool-mist vaporizer, saline nose drops (available from the drugstore or you can make your own: mix a cup of warm water, ⅛ teaspoon salt and a small pinch of soda), rest, liquids, and honey and lemon are safe and as effective at curing a cold as decongestants, aspirin, and cough syrups. All the drugs available treat only the symptoms and do nothing to cure or shorten the cold.

Nausea, Vomiting, and Heartburn

See the discussion of this subject on pages 73–74 in chapter 4.

Backaches

Backaches are a common problem for pregnant women. You can best alleviate a backache with rest, massage, hot or cold packs, and exercises to strengthen the abdominal muscles and to decrease the curve in the lower back. (See chapter 6 on comfort measures and posture.) Avoid aspirin and muscle relaxants unless the condition is severe, and check with your caregiver before taking these drugs.

Sleeplessness

This is especially common in late pregnancy. Instead of drinking alcohol or taking a sleeping pill, try these helpful sleep aids. Take a brisk walk each day; this will help release tension that might keep you from sleeping. Try a warm bath, a glass of warm milk, a massage, or soothing music. If you find yourself wide awake in the middle of the night, try reading (a dull book is more likely to help you get back to sleep) or using the relaxation techniques described in chapter 7.

Harmful Environmental Agents

Pregnant women (and young children) should avoid the following environmental agents or hazards.

Herbicides and Insecticides

Weed- and insect-killing sprays are widely used along roadsides, in farming areas, and in residential communities. Their presence in the atmosphere and on food has been associated with both miscarriage and birth defects. While numerous chemicals are used against weeds and insects, their safety for the unborn and young child has not been established. Some have already been banned because they are known to be harmful. While pregnant, avoid using pesticides.

Also, wash fruits and vegetables well to help remove pesticides and other chemicals.

Radiation

During your pregnancy, you should avoid X rays (or ionizing radiation) for medical and dental diagnosis and you should not work in areas where radiation levels may be high. This is especially important during your first trimester since radiation interferes with cell division and organ development. Fortunately, most X rays can be avoided or postponed until after the birth.

In the past, X rays were used in late pregnancy to assess the relationship between the size of the baby's head and the size of the mother's pelvis (X-ray pelvimetry), to find out if there were twins, and to determine fetal presentation. The benefits of the information gained were thought to outweigh the risks of exposure. Today X rays are rarely used, because ultrasound, which is safer, is used for the same purposes. If X rays are suggested, ask your physician or midwife what information he or she expects to gain and whether that information would alter clinical management of your pregnancy. Ask if ultrasound is available as a safer and equally reliable alternative. Generally speaking, as with any potentially risky procedure or medication, exposure to X rays should not be done routinely or if there is reasonable doubt about the benefits.

Video Display or Computer Terminals

Video display or computer terminals (VDTs) have been investigated as potential sources of radiation exposure, because of concerns that heavy VDT use may be a hazard to the unborn child. Ionizing radiation (or X ray), which carries the most harm to fetal cells and increases the chances of cancer and birth defects, is not emitted in any meaningful amount from VDTs.[20] Exposure to low frequency or nonionizing radiation (radio waves, microwaves, infrared, and visible light) is higher in women who sit at VDTs for their work than for women who do not. The safety of nonionizing radiation was questioned in the early 1980s when a possible association was found between VDT use for more than 20 hours a week and miscarriage. Several recent scientific studies have failed to confirm these findings.[21]

While an association between miscarriage and VDT use has not been established, there are some other possible side effects, unrelated to radiation exposure, resulting from prolonged time and repetitive activity at a computer terminal: fatigue, muscle strain, headache, carpal tunnel syndrome, and eyestrain. These side effects, of course, can also occur in nonpregnant women. It makes sense to vary your work responsibliies so that you are not constantly in front of a VDT, to take your breaks away from the VDT, and to request that your work station be as comfortable and free from glare and radiation exposure (even very low frequency radiation) as possible.

Saunas and Hot Tubs

Prolonged exposure to extreme heat during the first half of pregnancy such as that found in saunas or hot tubs may raise the mother's body temperature, creating a fever that impairs fetal development. The high temperature of a fever may interfere with cell division and may cause birth defects or even fetal death if fever occurs repeatedly, for extended periods, or at a crucial time in fetal development.[22] If you find saunas or hot tubs relaxing and beneficial, you would be wise to take your oral temperature while you are exposed to the heat. When your normal body temperature rises one degree or more, it is time to get out and cool down. If the water temperature is set at a comfortably warm (not hot) level, you can probably still enjoy a nice long bath. Ten minutes in a sauna or hot tub seems to be a reasonable limit since it does not seem to cause the body temperature to rise. If you become uncomfortably hot in a sauna or hot tub, get out, even if you have been there for a short time. You may also reduce the temperature of the sauna or bath water, or hold your shoulders and arms out of the water to promote heat loss and maintain a safe body temperature.

Toxoplasmosis

Toxoplasmosis is a mild infection that causes coldlike symptoms or no apparent illness at all in adults. It can be very serious, however, to the unborn baby, sometimes causing congenital malformations or fetal death. Cats are the common carriers of toxoplasmosis—especially outdoor cats who eat raw meat, such as rats and mice. The toxoplasmosis organism passes from the cat in its feces and lives for up to a year. You may be exposed to these organisms by handling cats or cat litter boxes or by working in soil where a cat has buried its feces. Eating raw or undercooked meat or eating unwashed root vegetables or potatoes are other ways of acquiring this disease. To avoid getting toxoplasmosis and passing it on to your unborn baby, be sure to cook your meat, wash vegetables thoroughly, wash your hands after handling cats, have someone else clean the cat litter box, and avoid soil where cats defecate.

Other Infectious Diseases

Lyme disease, German measles, chicken pox, fifth disease (parvovirus B_{19}), listeriosis, hepatitis, and sexually transmitted diseases are examples of infectious diseases that may harm the fetus or newborn. (See pages 54–55 or page 242 for a discussion of infections.)

Occupational Hazards

Scientific studies have shown that exposure to certain chemicals in the workplace can cause severe pregnancy problems, including spontaneous abortion, congenital malformations, or preterm birth. The agents associated with adverse pregnancy outcomes in human studies include anesthetic agents, cytotoxic drugs, ethylene oxide, lead, methyl mercury, organic solvents, polybrominated biphenyls (PBBs), and polychlorinated biphenyls (PCBs).[23]

Drugs, Environmental Hazards, and the Father

At this time there is little known about how drugs, environmental hazards, or other influences affect the reproductive capability of the male. Evidence is growing, however, that the man's health and well-being are more important than previously suspected in producing a healthy baby. For example:

◆ One report concluded that there was a decrease in sperm density and motility among smokers.[24] Another study of infertility found that men who smoke more than twenty cigarettes a day and drink more than four cups of coffee per day have a decrease in sperm motility and more dead sperm than nonsmoking, non-coffee-drinking males.[25]

◆ The age of the father seems to be important for normal fetal development. Just as the mother's age at conception has been found to be significant as a risk factor for Down's syndrome, the father's age is equally significant as a risk factor for other congenital disorders, such as dwarfism (achondroplasia). These disorders, termed "autosomal dominant mutations," are more likely in children born to fathers over forty. (They occur at a frequency of 0.3 to 0.5 percent.) It should be

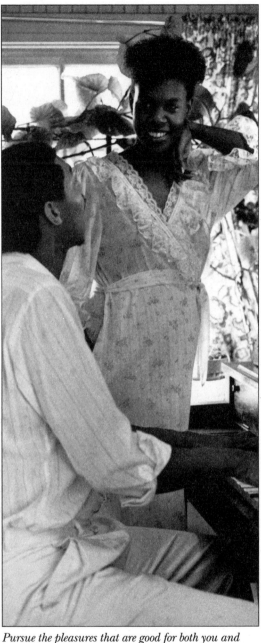

—photograph by Lise Alexander/Beginnings

Pursue the pleasures that are good for both you and the baby.

noted that, unlike Down's syndrome, these disorders cannot be diagnosed before birth.[26]

♦ Exposure to herbicides, pesticides, and solvents is suspected of causing genetic mutations and birth defects in the offspring of exposed men.[27]

Other than a few reports on how certain drugs may alter the reproductive potential of men, the direct contribution by the father to his unborn infant's health is poorly understood.

The indirect contribution of the partner, whether male or female, however, is of great significance. A woman is much more likely to control her use of drugs, tobacco, and alcohol if her partner also controls his or her use of these agents. If she is supported in her concern for a positive pregnancy outcome and joined in making any change she has to make, she is much more likely to be successful.

Conclusion

After reading this chapter, you may wonder if there are any pleasures left for the pregnant woman or expectant couple! Concentrate on the pleasures that have not been taken away: exercise, sports, dancing, outdoor recreation, good food, massage, love and sex, music, art, movies, reading, television, and, perhaps the best of all, the experience of "growing" a baby.

Chapter 6

Exercise, Posture, and Comfort in Pregnancy

Exercise is particularly important for you during pregnancy. As your body grows and you gain weight, regular exercise helps you remain healthy and comfortable. Exercise helps tone and strengthen the muscles most affected by pregnancy, including those in the pelvic floor, the abdomen, and the lower back; it also helps maintain good respiration, circulation, and posture. Although prenatal exercise and physical fitness do not guarantee an easy labor, they may give you more stamina to cope with a long, hard labor and more body awareness to help you work with your body during labor. One recent study found that women who exercised moderately and regularly during the last trimester perceived their labors as less painful than women who did not exercise. Furthermore, the exercising women had higher levels of endorphins; the body's natural pain relieving substances.[1] Regular exercise increases the body's production of endorphins. One of the major benefits of prenatal exercise comes after birth. Recovering your energy level, your strength, and your prepregnant size are unquestionably easier when you have maintained good physical condition during pregnancy.

This chapter suggests ways to improve your posture and to perform everyday tasks comfortably, provides specific exercises for the parts of your body most affected by pregnancy and birth, and includes a discussion of aerobic exercise. You will also find explanations for some common discomforts, along with techniques to relieve them.

Posture and Movement

Good posture and body mechanics—the safe and efficient performance of everyday tasks—are the cornerstones of a comfortable pregnancy. As you gain weight and your body changes shape, you must adjust your posture to maintain alignment and balance. By observing the following principles, you can perform everyday activities with the least strain and effort and can reduce fatigue and common aches and pains. In fact, these principles apply whether you are pregnant or not, and they are especially important in the first few months after your baby is born.

Posture

You can improve your posture by standing as tall as possible and by keeping your chin level. Imagine a string attached to the crown of your head, pulling it toward the ceiling. If you hold your head high, the rest of your body usually aligns itself properly.

Check the following list for signs of good posture. Watch yourself in windows and mirrors to increase your awareness of your posture, and ask your partner to observe you.

Good Posture

Stand tall with

Head: high

Chin: level, not jutting out

Shoulders: relaxed, down, and back

Abdominal muscles: firm, working to straighten spine

Back: slightly curved (avoid swayback)

Buttocks: tucked under

Hips: level

Knees: relaxed, not locked

Feet: supporting body weight evenly on both feet

Poor posture often causes backaches. When your posture is poor, your abdominal muscles are relaxed, the curve of your back is exaggerated, and the small muscles of your lower back shorten and tighten to maintain your balance and alignment. This continual shortening and tightening of the back muscles may cause low back pain.

During pregnancy, your center of gravity shifts as your baby and uterus grow, and it takes special efforts to maintain good posture. Flat or low-heel shoes help. Exercises to maintain abdominal muscle tone and strength are also beneficial. (See the pelvic tilt exercises on page 98.)

Standing

When possible, avoid standing for long periods of time during late pregnancy. Standing may slow the return of blood from your legs to your heart and head, which can make you feel light-headed. If you must stand for long periods, use your leg muscles to stimulate the blood flow from your legs to your heart. Shift your weight from leg to leg, rotate your ankles in small circles, and rock back and forth from your toes to your heels. Be fidgety; avoid standing still in one spot.

To help prevent backaches while standing, put one foot on a low stool or opened drawer. Alternate feet. This helps flatten your back and reduces the strain on your low back muscles.

Sitting

During late pregnancy, try to avoid prolonged sitting since this also impairs the return of blood from your legs. To improve the circulation in your legs while sitting, do not cross your legs at the knees for long periods, and frequently move and rotate your feet at the ankles. Sitting with your feet up and calves supported is also a restful and beneficial position.

On a long car trip, stop hourly to get out and move around. In the car, shift your position occasionally and move your legs about.

As your uterus enlarges, you will find a straight-back chair more comfortable (and easier to get out of!) than a low, deep one. A small, firm pillow in the small of your back and a low stool under your feet will provide additional comfort for your back. To avoid back strain when you get up, first move to the edge of the chair and use your leg muscles to raise your body.

Lifting

Joints and ligaments are softened and relaxed during pregnancy, so you are more likely to injure your back if you lift heavy objects. You can safely lift light objects if you do so properly.

To lift or pick up an object, use your strong thigh muscles instead of the short,

92

weaker muscles of your lower back. Remember to bend at the knees when lifting, not at the waist. Follow these guidelines for picking up anything, even a piece of paper:

1. Get as close to the object as possible.

2. With your feet wide apart, lower yourself by bending both knees (squatting), keeping your back upright.

3. Grasp the object and hold it close to your body. Try to avoid twisting at your waist.

4. To avoid strain on your perineum, contract your pelvic floor muscles and do not hold your breath as you rise.

5. Stand up by straightening your legs. Remember to keep your back upright.

Lying Down

As your pregnancy progresses, it becomes increasingly difficult to be comfortable while lying down. Pillows help. When you are lying on your side, put a pillow between your knees and puff a pillow under your head so it is well supported. You may need a small pillow or a wedge shaped pad to prop your uterus in late pregnancy.

It is a good idea to rest on your side for a while during the day, especially if you have pregnancy-induced hypertension (high blood pressure). It is preferable to lie on your left side, because placental circulation and heart function are most efficient in this position.

Some women find side-lying comfortable if they lie toward the front of their body. Try it. Put your lower arm behind you. Straighten your lower leg. Bend your upper leg and rest it on a firm, fat pillow. Bend your upper arm, bringing your hand toward your face. You will need only a flat pillow for your head.

Toward the end of pregnancy you may experience heartburn or shortness of breath when you are lying down. Propping yourself up with pillows to a semisitting position or raising the head of the bed a few inches by placing blocks under the feet may help alleviate these problems.

For some women, lying flat on their backs (the supine position) in late pregnancy makes them feel dizzy, short of breath, or light-headed. This condition, called *supine hypotension*, is caused by the weight of the uterus pressing on the large abdominal vein (the inferior vena cava) located between the spine and the uterus. Blood flow in the vein from the lower body to the heart is reduced, which causes a drop in blood pressure and the feelings of light-headedness. It also can cause a reduction in blood flow to the placenta and oxygen for the fetus if a woman with supine hypotension remains in that position for too long. If you feel these discomforts while lying on your back, simply roll over or sit up.

Getting Up

Getting up from the floor or out of bed becomes more difficult as pregnancy advances. The usual "jackknife" style of getting up (a sudden jerking sit-up) may strain your abdominal and low back muscles. To get up properly from lying down on the floor:

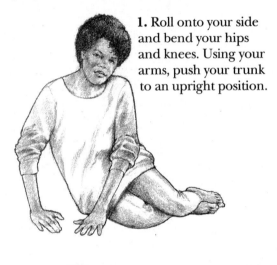

1. Roll onto your side and bend your hips and knees. Using your arms, push your trunk to an upright position.

2. Get onto your hands and knees. Place one foot on the floor in front of you, while keeping the other knee on the floor.

3. Stand up, using your leg muscles. Use your knee or another stable object for balance.

To get out of bed, roll onto your side, put your legs over the edge of the bed, then push yourself to a sitting position and stand up.

Exercise

The amount and type of exercise that is best for you during pregnancy depends on your general health, the course of your pregnancy, your fitness, and your usual activity level.[2] Physical changes during pregnancy directly affect your tolerance for exercise. Hormonal changes cause your ligaments to relax and your joints to become more mobile; your center of gravity shifts because of the enlargement of your abdomen; your heart rate speeds up because of changes in your cardiovascular system; your body temperature and metabolic rate are higher.

Regular, moderate exercise during pregnancy maintains muscle tone, strength, and endurance; it also protects against back pain, helps prevent excessive accumulation of body fat, and has a positive effect on your energy level, mood, and self-image. To ensure that a fitness program is appropriate for you, check with your doctor or midwife before starting or continuing to exercise during pregnancy.

Sports

Pregnancy is not a time to take up vigorous sports that require good balance or sudden jerky movements, such as softball, skating, or tennis. If you are already skilled in those or other demanding sports, however, you may continue playing them until you feel uncomfortable. In other words, as long as your pregnancy remains normal, you may safely continue a recreational sport or activity in which you feel competent, including tennis, swimming, cross-country skiing, jogging, or bicycling. Limit or avoid potentially dangerous activities such as skydiving, scuba diving, springboard diving, surfing, or rock climbing. Some caregivers restrict participation in downhill skiing, waterskiing, snowmobiling, and horseback riding. Talk with your caregiver if you have questions about a particular athletic activity during pregnancy.

General Guidelines for Safe, Effective Exercise

During exercise sessions, follow the guidelines below to avoid injury and to provide the most benefit to you.

♦ Exercise regularly, three or four times a week. Always include a "warm-up" and "cool-down."

♦ For land exercise, use a firm surface.

♦ Wear supportive footwear appropriate to the type of land exercise.

♦ Exercise with smooth movements; avoid bouncing or jerking, or high-impact exercises.

♦ While performing an exercise, do not hold your breath; it can increase pressure on the pelvic floor and abdominal muscles or make you feel dizzy.

♦ Keep track of your pulse rate (it should not exceed 140 beats per minute) or use the "talk test."

♦ Stop the exercise if you feel pain. Your body might be telling you that muscles, joints, or ligaments are being strained.

♦ To avoid strain and fatigue, start with the easiest position, then try others as your muscles strengthen. Start with a few repetitions, gradually increasing the number. Toward the end of pregnancy, you may need to decrease your level of exercise.

♦ Consider your calorie and liquid intake. Liquids should be taken before, during, and after exercise to replace body fluids lost through perspiration and respiration. You can take a water bottle along with you. You need to eat enough to meet the caloric needs of pregnancy.

♦ Avoid vigorous land exercise in hot, humid weather or when you are ill and have a fever. Your body temperature should not exceed 101°F (38°C).

♦ Check with your doctor or midwife if you have questions about exercising.

Aerobic Exercise

The goal of an aerobic exercise program is to improve heart and lung performance. Aerobic exercise programs for expectant mothers should include at least five minutes of "warm-up" including slow, smooth movements and stretching; a period of sustained, vigorous exercise lasting approximately fifteen minutes; and a "cool-down" consisting of mild activity while your heart rate returns to normal. Exercises for strength and flexibility are sometimes added.

The American College of Obstetricians and Gynecologists (ACOG) recommends that you take your pulse at times of peak activity and reduce your exercise intensity if your pulse rate exceeds 140 beats per minute.[3] At a pulse rate of 120 to 140, you can improve your fitness without risking overexertion, no matter how accustomed you are to regular exercise. If you exercise regularly, you will need more intense activity to raise your heart rate to 140; if you do not exercise regularly, mild exertion will elevate your heart rate to this level. In addition to taking your pulse, you will want to be sure that your activity passes the "talk test": it is too vigorous for you if you are gasping and are unable to continue a conversation. Slow your activity to a level that allows you to continue talking. Guidelines for aerobic exercise during pregnancy are based on your age, health, and fitness level. If you choose an aerobic program, start slowly and gently. Avoid exhausting exercise, which may adversely affect you or your baby. Stop exercising if you experience pain, headache, nausea, severe breathlessness, dizziness, vaginal bleeding, or loss of muscle control. You can let your body be your guide if you listen to it carefully.

What kind of aerobic exercise is best for pregnant women? Generally speaking, low-impact exercise (exercise that does not involve jumping, bouncing, or leaving the ground) is preferable because it is easier on your joints, which become more susceptible to injury or strain as pregnancy advances. Brisk walking, cross-country skiing, cycling, swimming, and low-impact aerobic classes (in or out of water) are examples of low-impact activities. Swimming and low-impact aerobic classes tend to provide more total body involvement than the others listed above. Swimming and water exercise offer still other advantages that make them superior to land exercise for pregnant women. They cause the lowest impact possible because of the bouyancy provided by the water. Vigorous land exercise sometimes causes a rise in your temperature and a drop in the baby's heart rate, which means that the baby's oxygen supply has dropped. Immersion in water prevents these potential problems. It has the added advantage of reducing swelling (edema) by moving tissue fluid back into your circulation and allowing you to excrete it through urination. In fact, this benefit has been found to last approximately forty-eight hours after one hour in water.[4]

Conditioning Exercises

Whether or not you participate in an organized exercise program, you can practice the following conditioning exercises along with an invigorating activity such as walking, stationary cycling, swimming, or modified dancing. The conditioning exercises described here are designed to keep the muscles most affected by pregnancy (the pelvic floor and abdominal muscles) in good condition during pregnancy, to help you to use your muscles effectively during birth, and to speed your postpartum recovery.

Conditioning the Pelvic Floor Muscles

The pelvic floor (or perineal) muscles are attached to the insides of the pelvic bones and act like a hammock to support your abdominal and pelvic organs. During pregnancy, these muscles may sag in response to the increased weight of your uterus and the relaxing effect of the hormones produced by your body. Regular exercise of the pelvic floor muscles maintains tone and improves

circulation, which can reduce the heavy, throbbing feeling that you might experience during pregnancy or post partum. Since the pelvic floor muscles are stretched during birth and their condition is of lifelong importance, regular exercise of the pelvic floor is essential during pregnancy and throughout your lifetime.

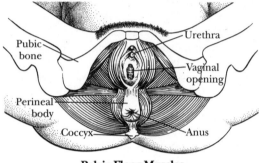

Pelvic Floor Muscles

The pelvic floor muscles form a figure-8 pattern around the urethra, vagina, and anus. During childbirth, the circle of muscles around the vagina stretches to allow the birth of the baby. When they are in good tone, they are elastic, which means they can stretch but also return to their original length. Birth is quicker, more comfortable, and easier if these muscles are in good tone and you relax them rather than tighten them. Pelvic floor exercises during pregnancy (along with perineal massage, described on page 126) will help you prepare for this process. Regular exercise of these muscles may also enhance sexual enjoyment for you and your partner. Problems such as leaking urine and the relaxation of the rectal wall may be prevented or reduced if the muscle tone of the pelvic floor is maintained.

To check the strength of your pelvic floor muscles, try to stop the flow of urine in midstream. If you cannot, it is a sign of weakness, but do not despair. These muscles respond quickly to exercise. You may also check by inserting one finger in the vagina and tightening your pelvic floor muscles around it. You should feel the grip of the muscles on your finger. (If you do not feel the gripping sensation, it is probably a sign of weakness.) During intercourse, check by tightening your pelvic floor muscles around your partner's penis; he can help evaluate your progress.

Pelvic Floor Contraction (also called perineal squeeze or Kegel exercise)
Aim: To maintain the tone of the pelvic floor muscles, improve circulation to the perineum, and provide better support for the uterus and other pelvic organs.

Starting position: Assume any position—sitting, standing, or lying down.

Exercise: Contract or tighten the pelvic floor muscles as you would to stop the flow of urine. You will feel tension and a slight lifting of the pelvic floor. Hold as tightly as you can for ten seconds or more. At first you will probably notice the contraction diminishing or fading, even though you have not deliberately let go. Simply tighten the muscles whenever you feel this letting go, again and again, until ten to twenty seconds or more have passed, then relax and rest.

Repetition: Do three to five pelvic floor contractions in a set. Try to do several of these sets each day. If at first you are unable to maintain the tightening effort for ten seconds, begin with three or five seconds and gradually work up to ten, then twenty.

Pelvic Floor Bulging
Aim: To practice and prepare for the second stage of labor—pushing the baby out. Bulging the pelvic floor (not contracting it) is what you should do as the baby is coming out.

Starting position: Get into the tailor-sitting position, squat, or any of the birthing positions (see chapter 8, pages 151–52). Make sure your bladder is empty when practicing this one!

Exercise: Consciously relax the pelvic floor muscles. Hold your breath and bear down or strain gently as you do when you are having a bowel movement, letting the perineal muscles relax further and bulge outward. Putting your hand on your perineum will help you to feel this bulge. Do not bear down hard or strain forcefully; hold for three to five seconds.

Stop bearing down. Breathe in, contract the pelvic floor, then relax and rest. Once you have learned to do this while holding your breath, try doing it while letting air out. You will find that you do not have to hold your breath to bulge your perineum.

Repetition: Repeat once a day.

Mobilizing the Pelvic Joints
Squatting
Aim: To increase the mobility of the pelvic joints, stretch the muscles of the inner thighs and the Achilles tendons or heel cords, and practice a position used to assist the birth of the baby.

Starting position: Stand with your feet comfortably apart (approximately two feet) and your heels on the floor. Squat with your weight evenly on your heels and toes to allow for greater stability, greater curve of the lower back, and better alignment of the birth canal. To maintain your balance, squat with support: hold onto your partner's hands, a stable piece of furniture, or the doorknobs on either side of a door, or you can lean your back against a wall and slide down. Your partner can also support you from behind by sitting on a chair as you squat and lean back between his or her knees with your arms over the knees.

If your feet roll inward or if you cannot squat with your heels flat, it is because of short or tight Achilles tendons. Try spreading your feet farther apart, wearing shoes with moderate heels, elevating each heel with a one- to two-inch book, or squatting with support. Many hospital birthing beds come equipped with squatting bars, which can be attached to the bed to give you something solid to hold onto while squatting. (See the illustration on page 123.)

Caution: If you have hip, knee, or ankle problems, consult your caregiver before trying this exercise. If the squatting position causes pain anywhere in your legs or pubic area, try squatting and leaning back with support. If support does not help, discontinue this exercise.

Exercise: Slowly squat with your weight on your heels and toes, not just your toes. Do not bounce. Stay down for at least thirty seconds, then rise slowly.

Repetition: Repeat five times daily. Progress to squatting for one and a half minutes at a time.

Conditioning the Abdominal Muscles

The abdominal muscles are the muscles most obviously stretched during pregnancy. Keeping them in good condition helps you maintain good posture, avoid backache, push the baby out more easily, and hasten the full recovery of your figure after the birth.

There are four layers of abdominal muscles that, like a corset, support the contents of the abdomen. These layers work together to bend the body forward or sideways, rotate the trunk, tilt the pelvis, and help with breathing. Many abdominal exercises done by nonpregnant women are potentially risky for pregnant women, especially in late pregnancy. To avoid back and abdominal muscle strain in late pregnancy, do not do double-leg lifts, straight sit-ups, or sitbacks. An exercise that conditions these muscles without causing excessive strain is described below.

Pelvic Tilt

Aim: To strengthen the abdominal muscles, improve posture, and relieve backaches.

Starting position: Lie on your back with your knees bent and your feet flat on the floor.

Exercise: Flatten the small of your back onto the floor by contracting your abdominal muscles. Hold the abdominal muscle contraction for a count of five as you exhale. Relax.

Note: To check that you are doing the exercise correctly, place your hand beneath the small of your back as you tilt your pelvis. You will press your back onto your hand. If you feel light-headed while lying on your back, perform only the variations of this exercise.

Repetition: Repeat this exercise and each variation five times daily.

Pelvic Tilt Variation A

Starting position: Get on your hands and knees. Keep your back straight—not hollowed, swayed, or arched—and your knees comfortably apart.

Relaxed (No Pelvic Tilt)

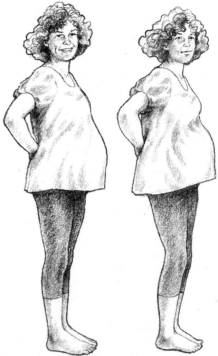

Relaxed (No Pelvic Tilt) **Contracted (Pelvic Tilt)**

Contracted (Pelvic Tilt)

Exercise: Tighten your abdominal muscles to arch your lower back. (Imagine a frightened dog who tucks her tail between her legs.) Hold for a count of five. Relax and return your back to the starting position—do not sag.

Pelvic Tilt Variation B

Starting position: Stand leaning against a wall. Have your buttocks and shoulders touching the wall, your feet apart and twelve to fifteen inches away from the wall, and your knees slightly bent.

Exercise: Breathe in. As you exhale, press your lower back against the wall by contracting the muscles of your abdomen. Imagine that your abdominal muscles are hugging your baby within your uterus. Hold for a count of five without holding your breath. Relax.

Note: To check yourself, put your hand between the wall and the small of your back.

As you tilt your pelvis, you should feel your back press against your hand. To progress in this exercise, move your feet closer to the wall until you can do it without leaning against a wall (see variation C below).

Pelvic Tilt Variation C

Starting position: After you have mastered the pelvic tilt leaning against a wall, try it while standing upright.

Exercise: By flattening your back and raising your pubic bone in front (as if you were tilting a basin), you can maintain good posture and help relieve or even prevent backaches. To check, put your hands on your hips. You will feel your hip bones move as your pubic bone tips up toward your chest.

Comfort Measures

Even if you stand and move properly, aches and pains are still common during pregnancy. The positions and exercises described below can help relieve some of these discomforts.

For Low Backache

Treatment of low back pain during pregnancy depends on the cause of the discomfort. Increased awareness of correct posture helps some women. Use of good body mechanics at work and at home decreases mechanical strain on joints, ligaments, and tendons that are softened and relaxed by hormonal changes. Positions and exercises that reduce lumbar lordosis (sway back) and/or increase abdominal muscle tone, described below, also may prevent or relieve low back pain. If your back pain is severe or if these measures do not help, ask your caregiver for a referral to a physical therapist, who can diagnose the problem and treat it with cold packs, heat, hydrotherapy, massage, other exercise, or techniques that mobilize joints and connective tissue. Your caregiver or therapist might recommend a special garment that provides additional support to the abdomen and lower back.

Tailor-Sitting

Tailor-sitting (or sitting cross-legged) is a comfortable way to keep the lower back rounded and relaxed.

Squatting

Many women find that squatting (described on page 97) helps relieve low backache.

Pelvic Tilt on Hands and Knees

This exercise (described on pages 98–99) relieves low back pain by stretching the low back muscles and strengthening the muscles of the abdomen.

Knee to Shoulder Exercise

Starting position: Lie on your back with your knees bent and your feet flat on the floor.

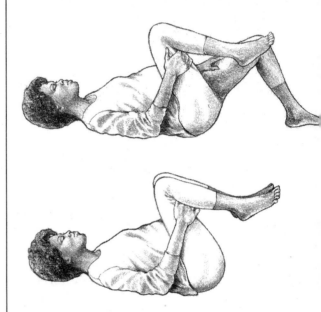

Exercise: Draw one knee up toward your chest and hold it behind the thigh with one hand. Bring the other knee up and hold it, letting your knees spread apart around your abdomen. Keep your head on the floor while gently pulling your knees toward your shoulders until you feel a slight stretch in the lower part of your back. Hold for a slow count of five. Release the pull without letting go of your knees. Repeat five times. Lower one foot; then the other.

Note: In late pregnancy, you may wish to raise and pull only one leg at a time. Roll onto your side as soon as you finish the exercise. If this exercise causes light-headedness, do not do it.

For Upper Backache

Shoulder Circling

Starting Position: Stand or sit with your back straight, your arms relaxed, and your chin level.

Exercise: Raise your shoulders toward your ears, then slowly roll them forward, down, back, and up again. Think of making large circles with your shoulders. Imagine that someone is rubbing your back as you slowly make circles with your shoulders. Feel the relaxation. Finish with your shoulders back and down in a relaxed position. Do five rotations, then repeat, reversing the direction.

Upper Body Stretch

Starting Position: Sit tailor fashion or stand with your arms straight and extended in front of you.

Exercise: Cross your arms at the elbows; feel your upper back stretch. While slowly breathing in, raise your hands toward the ceiling and gradually uncross your arms. Reach upward so you feel the stretch in your entire upper body.

Exhale as you lower your arms out to the sides and behind you with palms up. Feel the stretch across your chest and upper arms. With your arms down and behind you, stretch further by pressing your arms back with five gentle pulsing motions. Exhale with each stretch, making a "who" sound. Drop your arms to your sides and relax without slumping. Repeat five times.

For Aching Legs or Swollen Ankles

If you are bothered by aching legs, swollen feet and ankles, or varicose veins, do the following to promote better circulation:

♦ Walk, do not stand still.

♦ When you are sitting, rotate your feet at the ankles, and do not cross your legs at the knees.

♦ When you are resting during the day, lie on your side or elevate your feet (sit with your feet up, for example).

♦ Do the pelvic tilt exercise on hands and knees. This position reduces the weight of the uterus on the blood vessels in the pelvis and abdomen. The rocking movements promote blood flow.

♦ Exercise or simply rest in water (a large tub or pool is better than a regular bathroom tub) for an hour every other day. The hydrostatic pressure of the water reduces swelling and promotes diuresis (excretion of excess fluid by urination). The benefits last for approximately forty-eight hours.

To help prevent or reduce excessive swelling in the legs, try the following:

♦ Wear support stockings. Put them on before you get out of bed, since this is when there is the least amount of swelling.

♦ Raise the foot of your bed with two- to three-inch blocks. When you are lying down, your feet need be only a little higher than your heart to reduce the swelling in your legs, feet, and ankles. If this position causes more heartburn or shortness of breath, rely on the other measures described above.

♦ As stated above, exercise or rest in a pool or large tub of water.

For Leg and Foot Cramps

Cramps in the calves or feet commonly occur in late pregnancy when you are resting or asleep. Cramps are caused by fatigue in calf muscles, pressure on the nerves to the legs, impaired circulation, or a calcium-phosphorus imbalance in the blood. This imbalance can result from inadequate calcium intake or from eating large amounts of phosphorus, which is found in foods such as processed meats, snack foods, and soft drinks. Even with a good diet and careful attention to circulation in the legs, you may still get cramps, especially when you point your toes or when you stand or walk on your tiptoes. A muscle cramp disappears when the muscle is slowly stretched.

Relieving Leg Cramps

To relieve a cramp in the calf, straighten your knee and bend your foot up, bringing your toes toward your nose. Here are two ways of doing this:

♦ Stand with your weight on the cramped leg. Keep your knee straight and your heel on the floor, then lean forward to stretch the calf muscle.

♦ When a leg cramp is severe, you may need help. While sitting on a chair or bed, have your partner hold your knee straight with one hand and, while gripping your heel with the other, use his or her forearm to gently press your foot and toes toward your face. When the cramp is gone, do not point your toes, or it will return.

Relieving Foot Cramps

A cramp in the foot tightens the muscles of the arch and curls the toes. To relieve the cramp, stretch out your toes and foot with your hand. To prevent cramping, do not curl your toes.

For Sudden Groin Pain

A common discomfort of pregnancy is a sudden pain in the lower abdomen or groin, on one or both sides. This may occur when you stand up quickly, or when you sneeze, cough, or laugh with your hips extended (lying down or standing). The sudden stretching of one or both of the round ligaments that support the uterus causes the pain. These ligaments, which connect the front sides of the uterus to either side of the groin, contract and relax like muscles, yet much more slowly.

Any movement that suddenly stretches these ligaments, causing them to rapidly contract, causes pain. You can avoid this pain by moving slowly, allowing the ligaments to stretch gradually. If you anticipate a sneeze or expect to cough, bend or flex your hips to reduce the pull on these ligaments.

In labor, the round ligaments contract when the uterus contracts. This is beneficial, because they pull the uterus forward and align it and the baby with the birth canal for the most efficient and effective action.

Conclusion

Pregnancy brings rapid and profound changes in your body shape, size, and weight that can make you feel awkward and uncomfortable. This chapter has focused on physical fitness and comfort measures that will help you adjust as smoothly as possible to these changes and maintain or even improve your physical condition. Many women find pleasure in their pregnant bodies, especially when they can remain physically active and comfortable.

Chapter 7

Preparation for Childbirth:
Relaxation, Comfort, and
Breathing Techniques

During pregnancy you and your partner will want to prepare yourselves physically, emotionally, and intellectually for the extraordinary experience of having a baby. During labor you can help yourself immensely by using relaxation techniques, patterned breathing, and a variety of other comfort measures and body positions. This chapter includes complete descriptions of these techniques with guidelines for adapting them, and a practice guide—a step-by-step, week-by-week approach to childbirth preparation (pages 128–30).

Though these techniques cannot guarantee a completely pain-free childbirth, they can reduce pain and stress to manageable levels in most labors. They also promote labor progress and give you more control over the experience. Along with the support you will have from your partner and others, these techniques and your adaptations of them are your resources for coping with labor. You may use them instead of, or in conjunction with, medical interventions. When you use these techniques and participate fully, the birth of your child will be rewarding, exciting, and fulfilling—an experience to remember with satisfaction and joy.

Historical Overview

Over the last seventy years the efforts of many outstanding individuals have led to the development of the methods now used to enhance relaxation, reduce stress, relieve labor pain, promote labor progress, and strengthen early parent-infant bonds.

Grantly *Dick-Read,* a British physician, actively studied and promoted natural childbirth from the 1920s until the 1950s. He taught his obstetric patients that when a woman is afraid of labor, she becomes tense and thereby increases her pain. The more pain she feels, the more frightened she becomes, and the cycle is perpetuated and intensified. To interrupt this "vicious cycle," he advocated education, relaxation, and controlled abdominal breathing.

In the 1950s, Dr. Fernand *Lamaze,* a French physician, developed his psychoprophylactic method, which he adapted from methods used by Soviet physicians. It is based on the theories of conditioned response developed by Pavlov. *Psychoprophylaxis,* which literally means "mind prevention," involves the use of distraction techniques during contractions to decrease the perception of pain or discomfort. These techniques include various patterns of controlled chest breathing; a light massage of the abdomen, called *effleurage;* and visual concentration on an object called a *focal point.* Elisabeth Bing, a physical therapist, and Marjorie Karmel, an expectant mother, were trained by Dr. Lamaze and introduced and popularized the Lamaze method in the United States. They helped found the American Society for Psychoprophylaxis in Obstetrics (ASPO), which promotes the Lamaze method through teacher training and education of parents and professionals. The Lamaze method has evolved over the years to incorporate more flexibility; it now offers a greater variety of coping techniques.

In the 1950s and 1960s, Robert *Bradley,* an American physician, promoted and refined Dick-Read's methods. His major contribution, however, was to encourage husbands to participate as labor coaches. He founded the American Academy of Husband-Coached Childbirth (AAHCC) to train teachers and promote the Bradley method.

Since the 1960s, Sheila *Kitzinger,* British anthropologist and childbirth educator, has influenced childbirth preparation all over the world with her psychosexual approach. She sees childbirth as a highly personal, sexual, and social event. Kitzinger's methods emphasize body awareness, innovative relaxation techniques, and special breathing patterns.

During the 1960s the voice of the consumer in maternity care was given a great boost by the formation of the International Childbirth Education Association (ICEA), whose members continue to promote the concepts of family-centered maternity care and "freedom of choice based on knowledge of alternatives."

In the 1970s the childbirth movement began to examine and criticize conventional obstetrical practices and emphasize more "natural" physiological and psychological approaches. These included movement by the mother during labor and the use of the upright position to enhance the progress of labor (Roberto Caldeyro-Barcia and others); more spontaneous pushing techniques for birth (Kitzinger, Caldeyro-Barcia, Joyce Roberts, and Elizabeth Noble); greater contact between parents and newborn (Marshall Klaus and John Kennell); gentler handling of the newborn (Frederic Leboyer); and a recognition of the emotional impact of support during labor, a homelike environment, and freedom for the mother to behave spontaneously (Michel Odent, Gayle Peterson, Klaus and Kennell, Niles Newton, and many more).

An Individualized Approach to Childbirth Preparation

Expectant parents have benefited greatly from the insights and wisdom of the people mentioned above and many others, but it is really the woman herself, with the help of her partner, caregiver, and others, who develops her own personal method for handling labor. Each woman has her own learning style, her own belief system, her own way of dealing with change, stress, and pain. For example, some people have a highly academic approach to learning about birth, finding the information fascinating and essential to their ability to cope. Others learn better through experience, discussion, observation, and practice. Some find distraction from pain to be the most effective way to cope, others focus directly on the pain, still others transform the pain in their minds and imagine something more acceptable. Some women love to be touched, massaged, held, and talked to when they are in pain. Others must be left undisturbed to explore and utilize their inner resources. You will find that the relaxation, patterned breathing, and comfort techniques described here are presented within a broad framework with guidelines for modifying and adapting them to suit your personality, your preferences, and your particular labor.

The Gate Control Theory of Pain

The Gate Control Theory of Pain, first described in the 1960s by R. Melzack and P. D. Wall, provides a very useful explanation of how pain perception can be increased or decreased. The following is a brief description of the Gate Control Theory and how it applies to childbirth pain.

A painful stimulus feels more painful under some circumstances than others. A familiar example is the headache that seems to go away during an exciting movie but returns when the movie ends. Or the bruise, acquired during an athletic contest, that goes unnoticed until after the game is over. Or the backache that feels so much better with massage or hot packs. In all these examples, the pain is still there, but your awareness of it is decreased when your brain receives other nonpainful or pleasant stimuli.

The Gate Control Theory states that the severity of pain is determined by the balance of painful and nonpainful stimuli that reach your consciousness.

In childbirth, you can increase the nonpainful stimuli and decrease the painful stimuli in numerous ways, which are described in this chapter. These techniques are powerful enough to reduce (but not eliminate) your perception of pain. They may be all you need to keep your pain manageable. If not, you may choose to use pain medications along with them. Some of the techniques are more helpful if you practice and adapt them to suit yourself before you go into labor. Others, such as hot packs,

cold packs, baths, and showers, require no prior practice.

Relaxation

Relaxation—the art of releasing muscle tension—is the cornerstone of comfort during labor. The ability to relax comes more easily to some than to others. With concentration and practice, however, everyone can learn to relax. Many approaches to relaxation are presented in this chapter. Try them all, but concentrate on those that appeal to and work best for you. During labor, relaxation will help you do the following:

Conserve energy and reduce fatigue. If you are not consciously relaxing your muscles, you will most likely tense them during contractions. This increases your pain, wastes energy, decreases the oxygen available for the uterus and baby, and tires you.

Calm your mind and reduce stress. A relaxed body leads to a relaxed state of mind, which in turn helps reduce your stress response. There is evidence that distress in the laboring woman caused by anxiety, anger, fear, or illness produces an excessive amount of catecholamines (stress hormones) such as epinephrine (also called adrenalin) and norepinephrine (also called noradrenalin). High blood levels of catecholamines can prolong labor by decreasing the efficiency of uterine contractions and can affect the fetus by decreasing the blood flow to the uterus and placenta.[1]

Reduce pain. Relaxation decreases the tension and fatigue that intensifies the pain you feel during labor and birth. It also allows maximum availability of oxygen for your uterus, which may decrease pain, since a working muscle (like the uterus) causes pain if it is deprived of oxygen. In addition, the mental concentration involved in consciously relaxing your muscles helps focus your attention away from the pain of contractions and thereby reduces your awareness of pain.

Learning to Relax

The first step in learning to relax is to become aware of how your mind and body feel when you are resting or falling asleep. Since your mind and body influence each other, you probably will notice a simultaneous release of muscle and mental tension when you relax. Your breathing pattern will be slow and even, with a slight pause between each inhalation and exhalation. This type of breathing will aid you in the relaxation exercises and during labor.

When you practice relaxation, lie down on your side with plenty of pillows to make yourself comfortable, or sit in a comfortable chair with your head and arms supported. After you have learned to relax in these positions, practice relaxing while sitting up, standing, and walking, since you will need to relax in a variety of positions during labor.

When you are learning relaxation skills, begin in a quiet, calm atmosphere and progress to noisier, more active surroundings. Remember, hospitals are busy places, so you will need to be able to relax in the midst of activity. At the end of a practice session, lazily stretch all your muscles and get up slowly to avoid becoming light-headed or dizzy.

The next important step is to increase your body awareness by learning to recognize muscle tension. The following techniques will help you to detect and reduce the unnecessary tension that may develop during labor.

Body Awareness Techniques

Tensing and Releasing Muscles
Starting position: Sit in a chair or on the floor. Try to relax all the muscles you do not need to keep yourself upright.

Exercise: Make a tight fist with your right hand. Pay attention to how the muscles in your forearm feel. They are hard when they are tense. Touch those muscles with the fingers of your left hand. Now let go. Notice how soft the muscles feel when you release the tension.

Next, raise your shoulders toward your ears. Notice how you feel when your shoulders are tense. Relax and lower your shoulders. Now release even more. Really relax. Did you notice a change? Often you can release residual muscle tension when you become aware of it.

Tensing and Releasing the Whole Body
Starting position: Lie down in a comfortable position.

Exercise: Tighten the muscles of your entire body—stiffen your abdomen, hips, and legs, then your back, neck, and arms. Keep the muscles contracted for about five seconds. Pay attention to how you feel—tense, tight, cramped, or uncomfortable.

Then let your body go limp, releasing the tension all over. You may start by relaxing your abdomen and releasing outward toward your arms, legs, and head. Think of the tension flowing out of your limbs. Breathe slowly. Sigh, relaxing even more. Feel yourself relaxing.

Discovering the Effect of Mind on Body
Your state of mind has a great influence on how relaxed or tense your body is. If you are anxious or frightened, your body will reflect these feelings by tensing. If you are confident and positive, your body will remain relaxed. When in pain you can focus on these confident, positive feelings to help you release tension that might otherwise accompany and worsen your pain.

Exercise: Use the following visualizations to help you imagine contrasting reactions to labor contractions. Notice how they can affect the tension in your body. One can make you feel tense and afraid; the other can help you relax.

1. As your contraction begins, you feel tension, first in your back. . . . Oh-oh. Here it comes. This tight grip comes around to your front. . . . It's building. "Oh no!" It's getting stronger and stronger. It hurts! You want to say, "Owww. Make it stop. I can't do it! I can't!" You clench your fists. You stiffen your back. You grit your teeth and squint hard in an anguished expression of pain. "Please! Make it stop!" The grip tightens around your middle. You feel weak. You feel helpless. You hold your breath. Won't it ever stop? The grip begins to fade. It's leaving, but you're afraid to let go. Is it really gone? Is it coming back? "Ohhhhh."

How do you feel after reading the above visualization or hearing it read to you? Are you tense, upset? For contrast, try the following visualization of a labor contraction.

2. Your contraction comes like a wave, starting deep within you as a small swell. Vague at first, it grows larger and larger, stronger and stronger. You wonder, "What shall I do?" It's building to a peak of strength, power, and pain. *Your* strength, *your* power, *your* pain. You can ride the crest of this wave, letting it carry you along. As the power sweeps through you, your uterus works—to open your cervix and to bring your baby closer. You do not fight the wave, you go limp, and in doing so you feel safe, supported, and strong. Your face is still and peaceful; your arms and legs are floating—limp and relaxed. You are not afraid. You are open to this power. You are opening to this power. And now the wave eases; it ebbs; it flows back deep within you. You are at rest.

How do you feel as you visualize a contraction in this way? Do you find it less threatening? Does it help you interpret the contraction more positively than the first visualization? If so, you may wish to use such visualizations as you prepare for birth.

As you can see, your way of interpreting the pain of contractions can influence your physical response to them. It helps if you can visualize the pain as healthy pain with a positive purpose. Through knowledge and practice, you will be able to do this, and your labor will be far more fulfilling for you.

Practicing with Your Partner

While you are developing an awareness of tension and relaxation, your birth partner should also learn to recognize when you are tense or relaxed. He or she can detect signs of tension in several ways:

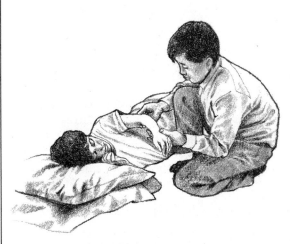

♦ By observing you when you are tense and when you are relaxed. How do you look when you are anxious, uncomfortable, calm, content, or asleep?

♦ By touching or feeling various parts of your body—arms, legs, neck, face. How do your muscles feel—hard or soft?

♦ By lifting one of your arms or legs, supporting it well, and moving the joints of the limb, feeling for the looseness and heaviness that accompanies relaxation. How does it feel to your partner when your limb is being moved? A relaxed arm or leg should neither help nor resist movement.

The way your partner checks you has a lot to do with your ability to relax. If he or she touches or moves you in a gentle manner—not dropping, shaking, or pinching your limbs—you will develop a sense of confidence and security. This trusting relationship carries over beautifully into labor. As you practice together, you will learn which parts of your body you have the most difficulty relaxing. For instance, you may have a particular "tension spot." Many people under stress tighten their shoulders. Some reflect tension with a frown or anxious brow; others clench their jaws or fists. Your tension spots should receive special attention, both as you learn relaxation and during labor. Find out what eases tension in these areas: touch, massage, verbal reminders, warmth? After exploring the possibilities together, you will both know what works best in helping you to relax and stay relaxed.

Once you both are skilled in relaxation and spotting tension, you can practice by deliberately tightening a limb and having your partner try to detect the part you have tensed. Try contracting the muscles most likely to be tense during labor—the buttocks, thighs, back, shoulders, face, or fists. Once your partner has found the tension, have him or her help you relax.

Relaxation Techniques

Passive Relaxation

Once you can recognize tension in your muscles, the next step is to master the art of releasing tension. By focusing on different parts of your body and by releasing tension in each part, you can achieve a state of deep relaxation of both body and mind. This takes some concentration and conscious effort. When you start passive relaxation, have your partner read the following exercise in a calm, relaxed voice. He or she should read slowly, allowing you time to focus on and release each part of your body. Pleasant, relaxing music may also help. Once you have selected some appealing music, use the same music each time you practice and then use it during labor to create a familiar and relaxing environment.

Practicing Passive Relaxation

Find a comfortable position lying on your side or semisitting, with your head and all your limbs supported by the floor or bed and pillows. Take plenty of time getting as comfortable as you can so you do not need to use any muscle effort to hold yourself in that position. Depending on the position you choose, you may want to put pillows under one or both knees, behind your head, or under your abdomen to help you feel comfortable and relaxed.

1. Take a long sigh, or yawn.

2. Now focus way down to your *toes* and *feet*. Just let go. Think how warm and relaxed they feel.

3. Think about your *ankles*—floppy and loose. Your ankles are very relaxed and comfortable.

4. And now your *calves*. Let the muscles go loose and soft. Good.

5. Now focus on your *knees*. They are supported and relaxed—not holding your legs in any position. They are very comfortable and loose.

6. Think of your *thighs*. The large, strong muscles of your thighs have let go. They are soft and heavy, and your thighs are totally supported. Good.

7. And now your *buttocks* and *perineum*. This area needs to be especially relaxed during labor and birth. Just let go. Think soft and yielding. When the time is right, your baby will make the journey down the birth canal, the tissues of your perineum will open and let the baby slide out. You will release, allowing the perineum to give and open for the baby.

8. And now your *lower back*. Imagine that someone with strong, warm hands is giving you a lovely rub. It feels so good. Your muscles relax to the imagined touch, and your lower back is comfortable. Feel the warmth. Feel the tension leaving.

9. And now let your thoughts flow to your *abdomen*. Let those muscles go. Let your abdomen swell as you breathe in and collapse as you breathe out. Your abdomen is free. Focus on how it moves as you breathe. Good. Focus on your baby within your abdomen. Your baby is floating or wiggling inside, free, warm, content, and secure within you.

10. And now your *chest*. Your chest is free. As you breathe in, bringing air into your lungs, your chest swells easily, making room for the air. As you breathe out, your chest relaxes to help the air flow out. Breathe easily and slowly, letting the air flow in and flow out, almost like sleep breathing. Ease the air into your chest, ease it out. This easy breathing helps you relax more. The relaxation helps you breathe even more easily and slowly. Good.

Now try breathing in through your nose and out through your mouth—slowly and easily, letting the air flow in and flow out. At the top of the in-breath, you notice just a little tension in your chest, which is released with your out-breath. Listen as you breathe out. It sounds relaxed and calm, almost as if you were asleep. Every out-breath is a relaxing breath. Use your out-breaths to breathe away any tension. This is very much like the slow breathing you will be using during labor. Good.

11. And now your *shoulders*. Imagine you have just had a lovely massage over your shoulders and upper back. Let go. Release. Feel the warmth. Feel the tension slip away.

12. Focus on your *arms*. With your out-breath, let your arms go limp—from your shoulders all the way down your arms, to your wrists, hands, and fingers. Heavy, loose, and relaxed.

13. And now your *neck*. All the muscles in your neck are soft because they do not have to hold your head in any position. Your head is heavy and completely supported, so your neck can just let go and relax. Good.

14. Focus on your *lips* and *jaw*. They are slack and relaxed. You do not have to hold your mouth closed or open. It is comfortable. No tension there.

15. And now your *eyes* and *eyelids*. You are not holding your eyes open or closed. They are the way they want to be. Your eyes are unfocused and still beneath your eyelids. Your eyelids are relaxed and heavy.

16. Focus on your *brow* and *scalp*. Think how warm and relaxed they are. Just let go. You have a calm, peaceful expression on your face, reflecting a calm, peaceful feeling inside.

17. Take a few moments to note and enjoy this feeling of calm and well-being. You can relax this way anytime—before sleep, during an afternoon rest, or during a quiet break. This is the feeling to have in labor. During labor you will not lie down all the time. You will be walking, sitting up, showering, and changing positions; but whenever a contraction comes, you will allow yourself to relax all the muscles you do not need to hold your position, and you will let your mind relax, giving you a feeling of peace and confidence. It is this feeling that helps you focus on the positive accomplishment of each contraction, yielding to these contractions and letting them guide you in breathing and comfort.

18. Now it is time to end this relaxation session. No need to rush. Gradually open your eyes, stretch, tune in to your surroundings, and get up slowly.

Touch Relaxation

With touch relaxation, you respond to your partner's touch by relaxing or releasing tense muscles. During pregnancy, touch relaxation is a pleasurable way to practice relaxation. During labor, you use your companion's touching, stroking, or massaging as a nonverbal cue to relax.

Starting position: Lie down on your side or sit in a comfortable position.

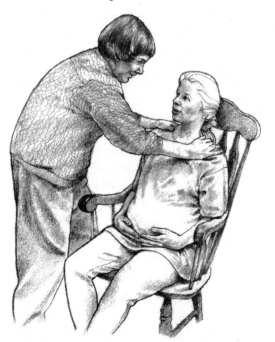

Exercise: Contract a set of muscles and have your partner touch those muscles with a firm, relaxed hand, molding his or her hand to the shape of the part of your body being tensed. Release the muscle tension and relax toward your partner's hand. Imagine the tension flowing out of your body.

Your partner can use several types of touch (listed below). Find out which you

prefer, but practice all methods, since your preference could change during labor.

Still touch. Your partner holds his or her hand(s) firmly in place until he or she feels you release your tension.

Firm pressure. Your partner applies pressure with fingertips or the whole hand on the tense area. Your partner gradually releases the pressure; you respond by releasing tension as you feel your partner's gradual release.

Stroking. Your partner lightly or firmly strokes the tense area. When stroking your arms or legs, he or she strokes away from the center of your body.

Massage. Your partner firmly rubs or kneads tense muscles. This is commonly used for neck and back rubs, but any muscle group can be massaged.

Practicing Touch Relaxation
Practice tensing the following muscle groups, then releasing to your partner's touch; learn to release to still touch, firm pressure, stroking, and massage:

- Scalp
- Face
- Neck
- Shoulders
- Arms and hands
- Abdomen
- Buttocks
- Legs and feet

Active Relaxation

If you practice relaxing in many positions and during physical activity, you can prepare more realistically for labor, because in labor you will probably use many positions and be physically active. Your goal is to achieve the same relaxed feeling and mental state while active that you had with passive relaxation, when your entire body was being supported by pillows, the bed, or the floor.

Practicing Active Relaxation

Practice relaxing in many positions—standing (upright or leaning against a wall or your partner), sitting, semisitting, on your hands and knees, kneeling with head and shoulders resting on the seat of a chair, squatting, and lying on your side. Different positions require that some muscle groups work, but they allow release of tension in others. Only by practicing in various positions will you be able to relax most effectively during labor. Imagine that you are having labor contractions while you practice relaxation and breathing patterns. By visualizing the intense sensations of labor contractions while relaxing, you can make each practice session a labor rehearsal.

The Roving Body Check

Sometimes you may think you are entirely relaxed, but when you focus on a particular body part (such as your arm, leg, or abdomen), you become aware that there is some tension there. The following exercise helps you release tension throughout your body, part by part. It combines the built-in tension-releasing properties of the out-breath with your own conscious release.

Practicing the Roving Body Check

Find a comfortable position. While breathing slowly and easily in through your nose and out through your mouth, focus on your right leg. As you breathe in, detect any tension in your leg. As you breathe out, deliberately release any tension from your leg. Take two breaths for this, if necessary. Then, with the next breath or two, focus on your left leg. Find any tension and release it as you breathe out. Repeat this exercise, dividing your body into about eight parts, as follows:

1. Right leg

2. Left leg

3. Buttocks and perineum

4. Chest and abdomen

5. Back

6. Right arm

7. Left arm

8. Head, face, and neck

By systematically releasing tension in each part as you release your breath, your entire body will be more relaxed at the end of the exercise than it was at the beginning.

You can use this technique during labor contractions. Your partner can help by telling you which part to relax with each breath, or by touching or stroking a different part for each breath.

Relaxation Countdown

After you have become aware of body tension and have mastered relaxation, learn the following technique to quickly release extra muscle tension. This is particularly helpful when you are trying to relax during labor. At the beginning of each contraction in labor, your "organizing breath" (see page 117) can be used as your relaxation countdown.

Practicing the Relaxation Countdown

Start by sitting in a comfortable position and progress to any position you might use

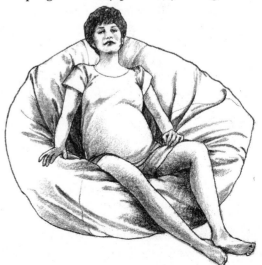

in labor—standing, on hands and knees, or lying down (see pages 144–45 for more on labor positions).

Breathe in through your nose. As you breathe out through your mouth, release the muscle tension throughout your body from head to foot. Count down from five to one to total body relaxation. At first use five slow breaths to accomplish this. With practice, you should be able to relax on the slow exhalation of one breath. Think of this countdown as a wave of relaxation that passes down through your body, from head to toe:

5. Head, neck, and shoulders

4. Arms, hands, and fingers

3. Chest and abdomen

2. Back, buttocks, and perineum

1. Legs, feet, and toes

Control in Labor

For many women, the prospect of "losing control" in labor is the most upsetting part of the whole thing. They worry that the pain will be so intense that they will panic or do or say things they will regret later. To prevent this, some plan to use anesthesia to reduce the pain. Others work on mastering prescribed self-help techniques like those described in this chapter to lessen the pain or to keep themselves from acknowledging or reacting negatively to it.

One of the undeniable facts about labor is that you cannot consciously control your labor or your contractions. You can, however, control how you respond to them. In a sense, then, control in labor is a matter of controlling how you will respond to your labor, not controlling the labor itself. As you know, the emphasis of this book is on helping you to understand and work in harmony with the powerful forces of labor rather than resisting or fighting them.

Women also lose control when everything is done for them. Many women want to participate in decisions about their care during labor. Feeling left out makes them feel out of control. In family-centered care, the mother is consulted and her wishes are followed. She does not give up control.

Comfort Measures for Labor

Women respond differently to labor, depending on the nature of their labors, their sense of readiness, their coping styles, and their goals and expectations. As you prepare and rehearse for labor, learn the various comfort measures and then adapt them to suit you. Analyze yourself and use this knowledge to develop your own style for labor. Think about what helps you relax: music, massage, soothing voices, a bath or shower, meditation, prayer, chanting or humming, or thinking about or visualizing pleasant places and pleasing activities. Plan to use these familiar comfort measures to help you relax in labor as well.

Unlike most pain, which is associated with injury, illness, or stress, the pain of labor is associated with a normal healthy body function. By recognizing your labor pain as productive and positive—a part of the process that brings the baby—you can help reduce the pain to a more manageable level. To cope with your pain, you may find it most helpful to "tune into it"—focus on it, accept it, and tailor your response to it. Or you may prefer distraction techniques, concentrating on outside stimuli, to keep yourself from focusing on your pain.

Many women successfully use both tuning in and distraction. For instance, in early labor they relax, breathe slowly and easily throughout their contractions, close their eyes, and visualize either something soothing and pleasant or the uterine contractions opening the cervix and pressing the baby downward. As labor intensifies, some continue in this way; others lighten and speed up their breathing. Then, during late labor (transition), when contractions are very intense and close, many women find that they cannot continue as before. They find they must open their eyes, focus outside (perhaps on their partner's face), and follow outside directions (their partner guiding their breathing with verbal directions, with hand signals, or by breathing with them). Sometimes more complex breathing patterns are helpful.

The following comfort measures are based on relaxation, the key to pain control in labor. Learn and adapt them to suit yourself.

Attention-Focusing

During labor contractions, your attention should be focused on something. Many women prefer an *internal focus*. They might visualize exactly what is happening—contractions of the uterine muscle pulling the cervix open, the baby pressing down and opening the cervix. Others prefer to visualize something calming and pleasant—the beach, a mountain top, a happy memory, or they visualize themselves as above their contractions, like a gull above a stormy sea, soaring over, but very much in touch with the contractions. Still others visualize each contraction as a hurdle to be overcome, for example, a steep hill to be climbed, a footrace, a wave to ride.

You might also find it helpful to look at something. This *visual focus* is often called an *external focal point*. You may wish to look at your partner's face, a picture on the wall, a reminder of the baby (perhaps a toy), an object in the room, a flower, or even a crack in the plaster. Some women focus on the same thing for many contractions; others change focal points often. Others focus on a line, such as the edge of a window, and follow that line visually during the contraction.

Many women find it helpful to focus on touch in the form of a particular rhythmic massage stroke or pressure on one area or a tight embrace. This is called a *tactile focus*.

Still other women focus on sounds, an *auditory focus*—taped music, the soothing voice of the birth partner, a tape recording of various environmental sounds (surf, rain, a babbling brook), repeating rhythms, or other sounds.

Some women focus on a particular *mental activity* (a song, a poem, a chant, a mantra, Bible verses, a repeated saying, counting backward), breathing in a complex pattern, or the roving body check (page 111). Others focus on a *physical activity,* performing a series of particular movements (pelvic rocking, swaying, walking, dancing, effleurage, or others).

As you and your partner practice breathing and relaxing together through mock (pretend) contractions, try the attention-focusing techniques described above. You will probably discover a preference for some over others. Be ready to try more than one if a particular focus loses its appeal in labor.

Massage and Touch

Effleurage is a light, rhythmic stroking of the abdomen, back, or thighs. It can help with relaxation and pain relief when done on bare skin by you or your partner.

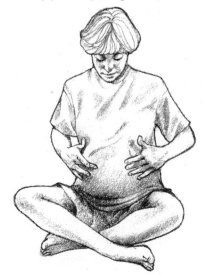

Some women prefer an extremely light, even "tickly" stroking, while others find a firmer touch more soothing. As you and your partner prepare for labor, try varying the pressure and rhythm of effleurage until you find the most appealing stroke. Then practice it as part of your labor preparation. Effleurage over the lower abdomen, following the lower curve of the uterus, is most popular. Some people think of it as stroking the baby's head. Others like to stroke the abdomen in circles with both hands.

Many women use effleurage during contractions in labor. Use cornstarch or powder to make your hands slide more easily. Keep the massage rhythmic, pacing it with the slow breathing. If you find that your skin is becoming sensitive as the contractions intensify, you might try effleurage in a different area or discontinue it.

Other types of *massage,* such as firm stroking, rubbing, or kneading (squeezing and releasing), are soothing and relaxing during both pregnancy and labor. Massage of the neck, shoulders, back, thighs, feet, and hands can be very comforting. Work together in pregnancy and find out how and where massage is most helpful and plan to use it in labor.

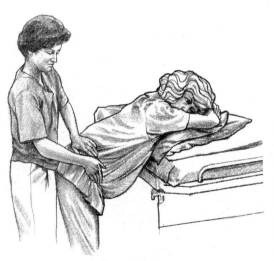

Counterpressure

Another helpful form of massage for labor is firm pressure, used particularly over the lower back or sacrum during contractions. One technique is called *counterpressure* and is especially helpful for back pain during contractions. Your partner presses a fist or the heel of a hand on a particular area of your lower back or sacrum. During labor you may want your partner to press with considerable force, so he or she should hold the front of your hipbone with his or her other hand to help you keep your balance. The exact spot for applying pressure varies from woman to woman and changes during labor, so it is difficult to know in advance which spot will be best. As long as you know the technique, you and your partner will be able to apply it during labor. You may need a surprising amount of pressure, which may be very tiring for your partner after a few hours. It is worth the effort, however, because of the relief and comfort it brings. Your partner can take turns with another support person or the nurse to allow him or her to take a break.

Another helpful technique for alleviating back pain, the double hip squeeze, is described on page 176.

Transcutaneous Electrical Nerve Stimulation (TENS)

TENS is a pain-relieving technique that has, until the past decade, been used primarily for chronic and post-surgical pain. More recently, TENS has also been used for labor pain (particularly back pain during labor). Its use for labor is not widespread, though most physical therapy departments or clinics have TENS units available. Your caregiver must prescribe it for use in labor.

TENS uses low-voltage electrical current to create a tingling or prickling sensation in a small area of skin. A TENS unit consists of a hand-held generator (powered by a nine-volt battery—the same type used to power many electronic toys) connected by wires to four Band-Aid-size stimulating pads (or electrodes), which are usually placed on your back on either side of your spine.

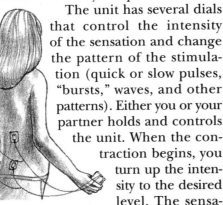

The unit has several dials that control the intensity of the sensation and change the pattern of the stimulation (quick or slow pulses, "bursts," waves, and other patterns). Either you or your partner holds and controls the unit. When the contraction begins, you turn up the intensity to the desired level. The sensations reduce your awareness of the pain. When the contraction ends, you turn it down. Many women have found TENS to be very helpful, while others have not.[2] The following conditions seem to improve the effectiveness of TENS:

1. Instruction in its use before labor.

2. Application before labor becomes painful.

3. Trying different stimulation patterns and having your partner work the controls so that you can focus on other coping techniques.

Baths and Showers

Warm water—in the form of a lingering bath, whirlpool bath, or shower—is a marvelous comfort measure for most laboring women. Contractions are usually less painful if you are in water. You are able to relax better because of the warmth and buoyancy of the bath water or the gentle massage provided by the shower. Find out if you will have access to a bath or shower during labor. In the shower, lean against the wall or sit on a towel-covered stool so you can rest. Direct the spray where it helps most. In the tub, lean back against a bath pillow or folded towels and relax. Some caregivers ask you not to take a bath if your membranes have ruptured. If so, you may use a shower. Sometimes the partner can accompany the

laboring woman into the shower. You may be in the shower for a long time. Because the nurse will check on you frequently, your partner may wish to wear a swimsuit. Besides relieving pain, baths and showers sometimes lower elevated blood pressure and speed up slow labors.[3] Sometimes the baby is born in the water because the mother is reluctant to get out of the tub, or because mother and caregiver have planned a water birth. For more information on water birth, see Recommended Resources.

Heat and Cold

Heat, applied to the low abdomen, back, groin, or perineum, is very soothing. An electric heating pad, hot water bottle, or hot compresses are good sources of heat. Hot compresses are simply washcloths or small towels soaked in hot water, wrung out, and quickly applied wherever you need them. As they cool, they are replaced. Covering them with plastic retains their heat longer.

A cold pack—such as an ice bag, frozen wet wash cloths, a rubber glove filled with crushed ice, a bag of frozen peas, a hollow plastic rolling pin filled with ice, "instant" cold packs, or frozen gel packs (camper's "ice" or the cold packs used for athletic injuries)—can provide a great deal of relief. Placed on the lower back for back pain during labor or on the perineum immediately after birth to reduce pain and swelling, a cold pack feels wonderful. For cold packs to bring comfort, however, you must be comfortably warm. If you are feeling chilled, the cold pack may make you uncomfortable.

Use common sense in deciding how hot or cold the compresses should be. When in labor you might easily tolerate compresses so hot or cold that they could damage your skin. Cover the cold pack with a towel to protect your skin.

Movement

Moving around during labor is another extremely useful comfort measure. Changing position frequently (every thirty minutes or so)—sitting, kneeling, standing, lying down, getting on hands and knees, and walking—helps relieve pain and may speed up labor by adding the benefits of gravity and changes in the shape of the pelvis. Swaying from side to side, rocking, or other rhythmic movements may be comforting. If labor is progressing slowly, walking may speed it up again. The upright position may give you a greater sense of control and active involvement than lying down. See pages 144–45 in chapter 8 for a further description of positions for labor.

Beverages

Most laboring women lose their appetites when they begin active labor, but their need and desire for liquids continues throughout labor. You should therefore take in liquids, either by drinking or, if that is not allowed (as might be the case if a cesarean or general anesthetic is anticipated), by an intravenous drip (IV). In a normal labor, you can drink water, tea, or juice, or suck on popsicles between contractions. By quenching your thirst you are also meeting your body's requirements for fluids. If your caregiver does not allow fluids by mouth, if your labor is prolonged, or if you are nauseated, you probably will receive fluids intravenously. You can still move around and walk when receiving intravenous fluids, if the IV unit is placed on a rolling stand. Hourly trips to the bathroom to urinate will increase your comfort during contractions. If oral fluids are restricted, you may have a very dry mouth, so suck on ice chips, a wet washcloth, or a sour lollipop. You may also refresh your mouth and teeth with cold water, a toothbrush, or mouthwash.

Patterned Breathing

In this section, you will learn a variety of breathing techniques to use during the *first stage of labor,* while the cervix dilates completely, and pushing techniques for the *second stage,* when the baby is born.

All activities involving physical coordination and mental discipline—swimming, running, singing, playing a musical instrument, public speaking, yoga, and meditation—require that you regulate your breathing for effective and efficient performance. Labor is no different. Along with relaxation and other comfort measures, *patterned breathing* is used during labor and birth to relieve pain. Patterned breathing simply means breathing at any of a number of possible rates and depths. The pattern you choose depends on the nature and intensity of your contractions, your preferences, and your need for oxygen. By learning and adapting breathing patterns before labor, you can use them to help calm and relax you during labor. Each method of childbirth preparation—Lamaze, Bradley, Kitzinger, Dick-Read, and others—relies on some form of patterned breathing.

In keeping with our individualized approach, no single method is promoted here; broad guidelines are offered, which will help you develop the breathing techniques that will fit your preferences and needs. Some women find abdominal breathing more comfortable than chest breathing; other women find just the opposite. The important thing is not where you breathe, but that the breathing calms and relaxes you. Through practice, experimentation, and adaptation, you and your partner will find your own best way to use the breathing patterns in labor.

Avoiding Hyperventilation

Hyperventilation occurs when the balance of oxygen and carbon dioxide in your blood is altered, causing a light-headed or dizzy feeling, or a tingling sensation in your fingers, feet, or around your mouth. It may be caused by breathing too deeply, too fast, or both. Tension also seems to contribute to hyperventilation. While rarely serious, hyperventilation is uncomfortable and unnecessary because it can be prevented or easily corrected. If you have practiced and mastered the relaxation and breathing techniques before labor begins, it is unlikely that you will hyperventilate during labor.

If hyperventilation does occur, it can be corrected by these measures:

♦ Rebreathing your own air (to restore your carbon dioxide to a normal level) by breathing into cupped hands, a paper bag, or a surgical mask (available in the hospital).

♦ Holding your breath after a contraction until you feel the need to take a breath. This also allows carbon dioxide levels in the blood to normalize. Do not hold your breath during a contraction.

♦ Relaxing and reducing tension. A shower, bath, massage, touch relaxation, or music may help here.

♦ Setting a slower breathing rate or making breathing more shallow. Your partner can help by "conducting"—setting a rhythm with hand movements—or breathing along with you.

Note: If your partner hyperventilates when breathing along with you, he or she should use the above measures, too.

Three Basic Breathing Patterns (First Stage)

There are three basic patterns of breathing for labor: *slow, light (accelerated),* and *variable (transition).* You will use these breathing patterns during your contractions to assist relaxation and ensure adequate oxygenation and to enable you to respond appropriately to the intensity of the contractions. It is most restful to begin using slow breathing in early labor and use it for as long in labor as it is helpful. Then you may want to switch to either the light or the variable pattern, depending on which is most comfortable for you. Reserve the third pattern to use last. Some women use only the slow breathing throughout labor. Others use

only slow and light or slow and variable breathing, while still others use all three. What you wind up doing will depend on your preferences and the intensity of your labor. We advise learning all three patterns and using them as you need them in labor.

How to Use Breathing Patterns and Comfort Measures during Labor

Once the contraction begins, you

1. Greet it with an organizing breath, releasing all tension as you breathe out (as in the relaxation countdown, page 111).

2. Focus your attention, either internally or externally.

3. Begin patterned breathing—slow, light, or variable—depending on the intensity of the contraction, your perception of the pain, and which pattern seems to be working best.

4. Use other comfort measures (massage, movement, heat or cold, bath or shower) if desired.

5. Continue the breathing, relaxation, and comfort measures through the contraction.

When the contraction ends, you

1. Take a finishing breath, as if to blow that contraction away forever.

2. Relax, move around, and sip liquids until the next contraction; then repeat the above.

Practice the following breathing patterns in all the body positions shown on the next page. Turn to the chart on pages 144–45 for a discussion of each position's advantages and disadvantages.

Slow Breathing

Use slow breathing, the first level of patterned breathing, when you reach a point in your labor when it feels better to use it than not to use it. A good rule is to begin slow breathing when the contractions are intense enough that you can no longer walk or talk through them without pausing. Use slow breathing for as long as you find it helps you in labor—at least until you are well along in the first stage of labor. Shift to

Positions for First Stage

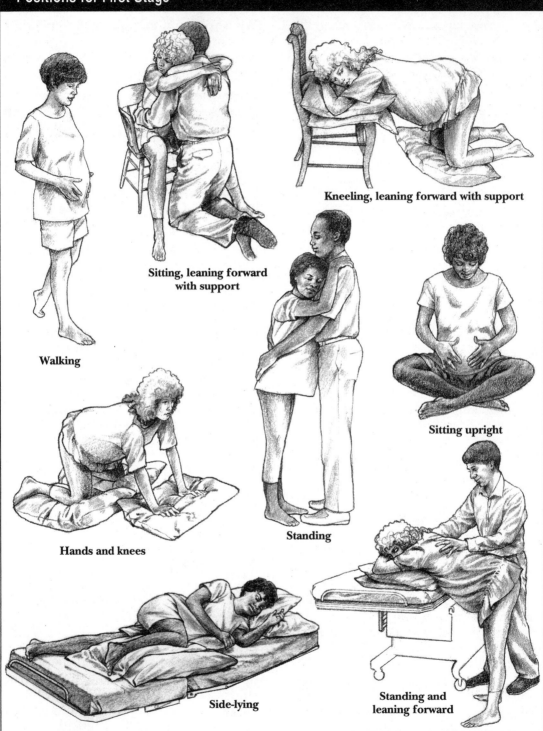

Kneeling, leaning forward with support

Sitting, leaning forward with support

Walking

Sitting upright

Hands and knees

Standing

Side-lying

Standing and leaning forward

another pattern if you become tense and can no longer relax during contractions. Some women use only slow breathing throughout the entire first stage; others use all the patterns described here.

Slow breathing may be chest breathing or abdominal breathing. More important than whether you breathe with your chest or abdomen is that the breathing helps you relax.

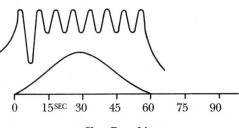

Slow Breathing

How to Use Slow Breathing in Labor

1. Take an organizing breath—a big sigh as soon as the contraction begins. Release all tension (go limp all over—head to foot) as you breathe out.

2. Focus your attention (page 113).

3. Slowly inhale through your nose (or if your nose is congested, through your mouth), and exhale through your mouth, allowing all the air to flow out. Pause until the air seems to "want" to come in again. Breathe about six to ten times per minute (about half your normal breathing rate).

4. Inhale quietly but make your exhalation audible to those close by, keeping your mouth slightly open and relaxed. The audible breath out sounds like a relaxing sigh.

5. Keep your shoulders down and relaxed. Relax your chest and abdomen so they can swell (rise) as you inhale and collapse (fall) as you exhale.

6. When the contraction ends, take a final deep relaxing breath. Exhale as if sighing. Sometimes a yawn is a good finishing breath.

7. Relax all over, change positions, take sips of liquids, and so on.

Note: After learning and practicing this pattern, a few women find it uncomfortable to breathe in through the nose and out through the mouth. If that is true for you, modify the pattern to all-nose or all-mouth breathing. The most important thing is that it is comfortable and relaxing for you.

How to Rehearse
Slow Breathing for Labor

Rehearse the technique described above until you become completely comfortable and consistent with it. Then you will be confident and able to use the slow breathing to relax deeply. In labor you will need to use this pattern for sixty to ninety seconds at a time. Practice in different positions—sitting up, lying on your side, standing, on hands and knees, and even in the car. With each breath out, focus on relaxing a different part of the body (the roving body check, page 111) so that you relax all parts of your body that are not necessary in maintaining your position.

Light (Accelerated) Breathing

Light (accelerated) breathing is the second pattern of breathing. Begin using it only if and when you find that slow breathing is no longer relaxing. If your partner notices that you are breathing more rapidly than six to ten times per minute or that you tense, grimace, clench your fists, or cry out at the peak of the contraction, he or she might suggest that you switch. Most women, though not all, feel the need to switch to light breathing at some time during the active phase of labor. Let the intensity of your contractions guide you in deciding if and when to use light breathing.

To do light breathing, breathe in and out rapidly through your mouth—about one breath per second. Keep your breathing shallow and light. Your inhalations should be quiet, your exhalations clearly audible.

If your contractions peak slowly, you may combine light breathing with slow breathing as follows: You begin breathing slowly when the contraction begins. Then your breathing accelerates and lightens as the contraction increases in intensity, remaining light and rapid over the peak. As the contraction subsides, your breathing gradually slows and deepens. As with slow breathing, it helps to think of each out-breath as a relaxing breath.

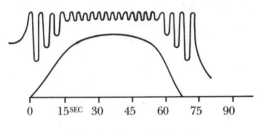

Light (Accelerated) Breathing

How to Use Light (Accelerated) Breathing in Labor

1. Take an organizing breath as soon as the contraction begins. Release all tension (go limp all over) as you breathe out.

2. Focus your attention.

3. Inhale slowly through your nose and exhale through your mouth, accelerating and lightening your breathing as the contraction increases in intensity. If the contraction peaks early, then you will have to accelerate early in the contraction. If it peaks more gradually, you will work up to peak speed more slowly. Keep your mouth and shoulders relaxed.

4. As your breathing rate increases toward the peak of your contraction, breathe in and out lightly through your mouth. Keep your breathing shallow and light—at a rate of about one breath per second.

5. As the contraction decreases in intensity, gradually slow your breathing rate, switching back to breathing in through your nose and out through your mouth.

6. When the contraction ends, take your finishing breath—exhale as if sighing.

7. Completely relax, change position, take sips of liquids, and so on.

How to Rehearse Light (Accelerated) Breathing for Labor

This pattern is not as easy to master as is the slow breathing. Be patient and give yourself enough time to learn it gradually. Begin learning the light breathing pattern by practicing only the peak rate, which is about one breath per second, but can range between two breaths per second and one breath every two seconds. Try breathing at different rates until you are comfortable. The best way to calculate your rate is to count your breaths for ten seconds. If you count between five and twenty breaths, you are in this range. When you are able to do the light breathing effortlessly, comfortably, and consistently for about one to two minutes, you are ready to practice combining it with slow breathing (see the above description). Start the practice contraction by breathing slowly, gradually lighten and speed your breathing to the peak rate, stay at that rate for thirty to sixty seconds, and then slow it down as the practice contraction subsides.

At first you may feel tense or as if you cannot get enough air. With practice it becomes easier and more comfortable. Mastering this breathing technique is like learning to breathe when you do the crawl stroke in swimming. Once you learn it, it becomes almost second nature and you swim much more easily and efficiently. During labor this pattern will seem more natural because your rate of breathing will be dictated by the pain and intensity of your contractions.

Breathing lightly through an open mouth may cause dryness, so use the following suggestions.

♦ Touch the tip of your tongue to the roof of your mouth just behind your teeth as you breathe. This slightly moistens the air that you breathe.

♦ With your fingers spread, loosely cover your nose and mouth so that your palm reflects the moisture from your breath.

♦ Sip water or other fluids or suck on a popsicle between contractions.

♦ Brush your teeth or rinse your mouth occasionally.

Variable (Transition) Breathing

Variable (transition) breathing, the third pattern, is really a variation of light breathing. It is sometimes referred to as "pant-pant-blow" or "hee-hee-who" breathing, because it combines light, shallow breathing with a periodic longer or more pronounced exhalation. Variable (transition) breathing is used in the first stage if you feel the need to try something different from slow or light breathing. If you feel overwhelmed, unable to relax, in despair, or exhausted, a switch to this variation may help.

The variable breathing pattern begins with a quick organizing breath, followed by light, quick breathing at a speed ranging from two breaths per second to one breath every two seconds (just like the light breathing). After every two to five of these quick, light breaths, blow out a longer, slower, relaxed breath. This blow helps steady your rhythm; it can also help if you need to keep from bearing down with a premature urge to push (discussed on page 122).

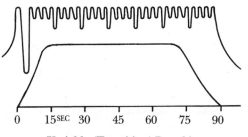

Variable (Transition) Breathing

How to Use Variable (Transition) Breathing in Labor

1. Take a quick organizing breath as soon as the contraction begins. Release all tension (go limp all over) as you breathe out.

2. Focus your attention. Your partner's face may be a reassuring focal point at this time in labor.

3. Breathe through your mouth in light, shallow breaths, at a rate of five to twenty breaths in ten seconds, throughout the contraction.

4. After every second, third, fourth, or fifth breath, blow out a longer breath. You do not need to take in a bigger breath for this. Keep the in-breath about the same as for all the others. Some women emphasize this blowing breath by making a "who" or "puh" sound as they exhale. Find the pattern you are comfortable with, then keep it constant throughout the contraction. Your partner might count for you ("one, two, three, four, blow"), or you might count to yourself for added concentration.

5. When the contraction ends, take one or two deep relaxing breaths.

6. Completely relax, sip liquids, move around, and so on.

Variation

Scramble breathing is another form of variable (transition) breathing, where you vary the number of pants per blow throughout each contraction. Your partner tells you or holds up a number of fingers to indicate the number of pants per blow. The number changes after each blow. Thus you might breathe as follows: one, two, blow; one, two, three, four, blow; one, two, three, four, five, blow; one, two, blow; and so on. If you prefer, you can choose your own scramble pattern (one woman breathed her own phone number). These variations add a significant element of distraction, which may be a help during the most difficult part of the first stage.

How to Rehearse Variable (Transition) Breathing for Labor

Add this breathing pattern to your practice sessions. Late first stage (transition) contractions might last two minutes, or they might "piggyback," that is, come in pairs, so you need to be able to use this pattern for up to three minutes. Practice in various positions. Relax for only thirty seconds or so between practice contractions to prepare yourself for the brief rest period between contractions in late first stage.

Working with the Urge to Push in Labor

The urge to push is an instinctive reaction to the pressure of the baby on the pelvic floor. It is characterized by a feeling of pressure and movement of the baby deep in the pelvis, which causes an irresistible need to bear down or strain. When you get an urge to push in labor, you will either hold your breath, make grunting sounds as you breathe, or have a catch in every breath. Ask your nurse or midwife to check for dilation at this time. If your cervix is fully dilated, you generally can begin bearing down and pushing when you feel the urge. If your cervix is not quite fully dilated but is very thin, soft, and stretchy, you should bear down only enough to satisfy the urge. If your cervix still has a thickened area (sometimes called a lip or an "anterior lip"), you may need to avoid bearing down altogether until the cervix dilates all the way; otherwise it may become bruised or swollen. Your birth attendant will guide you at this time. Although it is sometimes very difficult and uncomfortable to keep from pushing when you have a strong urge, it is not harmful to postpone bearing down until the cervix has dilated completely.

How to Avoid Pushing When Necessary

If you get a premature urge to push, lift your chin and blow lightly until the urge subsides. It may be helpful for you to vocalize at this time, actually saying or singing "puh, puh, puh" or "who, who, who." Then use your chosen breathing pattern for the rest of the contraction. This technique does not stop you from feeling the strong urge to push, nor does it keep your uterus from pushing. All it can do is keep you from adding your voluntary strength to the pushing effort.

How to Rehearse Avoiding Pushing in Labor

When you are rehearsing variable (transition) breathing, occasionally incorporate an imagined urge to push. When your partner says, "Urge to push," lift your chin and blow, blow, blow until he or she says, "Urge passes." As a variation, and to keep your partner alert, try occasionally holding your breath or grunting in the middle of a practice contraction. This should signal your partner to tell you to "blow, blow, blow."

Expulsion Breathing (Second Stage)

Once the cervix is fully dilated, the second stage of labor has begun. You may or may not feel an immediate urge to bear down (or push) with your contractions. The amount and speed of your baby's descent, her station and position within your pelvis, your body position, and other factors will determine whether the urge comes immediately or after a brief rest. Usually, with time or with a change to an upright or squatting position, this resting phase of the second stage subsides and the urge to push increases.

Your responses to second-stage contractions depend on the sensations you feel. You will probably feel several *surges*—strong, irresistible urges to push—within each contraction. Each lasts a few seconds. You simply breathe in whatever pattern suits you best—slow, light, or variable—until you have an urge to push and your body begins

Positions for Second Stage

Semi-sitting

Hands and knees

Lying on your back

Supported squat
"Dangle"

Squatting

Side-lying

Supported squat

bearing down. Join in with this urge to push, bearing down for as long as you feel the urge. Then breathe lightly until either another urge comes or the contraction is over. You will probably bear down three to five times per contraction, with each effort lasting about five to seven seconds. Between contractions take advantage of the opportunity to rest and relax.

This reaction is called "spontaneous bearing down," (meaning that you react spontaneously to your urge to push). It is recommended when labor is progressing normally and without medication. It is less effective when anesthesia is used, because anesthesia sometimes diminishes the pushing sensations and your ability to bear down effectively. When you have had anesthesia, your birth attendant or nurse will tell you how and when to push. This is called "directed pushing."

When practicing bearing-down techniques for the second stage, try to imagine what will be happening when you use them in actual labor. By visualizing the baby descending and rotating, you will be reminded of the importance of relaxing and bulging the pelvic floor. (See the exercise on page 97)

Positions for the Second Stage

Just as movement and position changes are helpful for both comfort and progress in the first stage, they may be equally beneficial in the second stage. Rehearse bearing down or expulsion breathing in the positions shown on the previous page. Turn to the chart on pages 151–52 for a discussion of each position's advantages and disadvantages.

The positions you use will depend on a number of factors: the speed and ease of delivery (you may not have time to change positions if the baby is coming rapidly, but if second stage is slow, you will have a chance to try them all); your willingness to move about; your mobility (electronic fetal monitors, catheters, anesthetics, intravenous equipment, and narrow beds discourage mobility); and your birth attendant's preferences. When you prepare your birth plan, discuss delivery positions. Although many doctors and midwives are most familiar with the semisitting position (often with your feet in stirrups) on the edge of the delivery table or bed, they may be willing to try other positions if you ask, at least until a few contractions before the actual birth. Then your attendant may ask you to change to the position of his or her choice.

Spontaneous Bearing Down (Expulsion Breathing)

How to Use Spontaneous Bearing Down in Labor

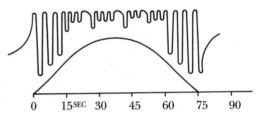

Spontaneous Bearing Down

1. Take an organizing breath as soon as the contraction begins. Release all unnecessary tension as you breathe out.

2. Focus on the baby moving down and out, or on another positive image.

3. Breathe slowly, letting the contraction guide you in accelerating and lightening your breathing as necessary for comfort. When you cannot resist the urge to push (when it "demands" that you join in), take a big breath, curl your body, and lean forward. Then bear down, while holding your breath or slowly releasing air by grunting or straining, whichever feels best at the time. Tighten your abdominal muscles. Most important of all, relax the pelvic floor. Help the baby come down by releasing any tension in the perineum.

4. After five to six seconds, release your breath and breathe in and out until, once again, the urge to push takes over and you join in by bearing down. How hard you push is dictated by your sensations. (In practice, never push hard.) You will continue in this way until the contraction subsides. The urge to push comes and goes in waves during the contraction, giving you time in between to "breathe for your baby"—to oxygenate your blood to provide sufficient oxygen for the baby.

5. When the contraction ends, slowly lie or sit back or stand up from a squat and take one or two relaxing breaths.

Avoiding Pushing as the Head Is Born

The breathing and bearing down described above continues for each contraction until much of the baby's head can be seen (crowning), at which time you will feel the skin of your vagina stretch and burn. At this point you may need to stop bearing down to allow the vagina and perineum to stretch gradually and reduce the likelihood of tearing or a too-rapid delivery. While the stretching, burning sensation is a clear signal to stop your bearing-down effort, your doctor or midwife will also give you directions at this point, telling you when to push and when to blow to stop pushing. To keep from pushing, continue blowing, as you do when avoiding the urge to push (page 122), until the urge to push goes away or until you are told to bear down again.

Directed Pushing

The previous description of the second-stage bearing-down technique is based on the assumption that you will feel a spontaneous urge to push, which will guide your response to your contractions. If, however, you do not feel your contractions because of anesthesia, or if you have no urge to push

even after letting fifteen or twenty minutes pass and trying gravity-enhancing positions (squatting, sitting, "dangling," or standing upright), then you may need to follow a routine of directed pushing.

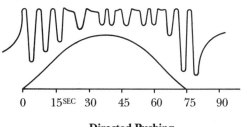

Directed Pushing

How to Use Directed Pushing in Labor

In this technique, your birth attendant, nurse, or partner tells you when, how long, and how hard to push.

1. When the contraction begins, take two or three breaths, and when you are told to push, take a breath in, hold it, tuck your chin on your chest and bear down, tightening your abdominal muscles.

2. Relax your pelvic floor muscles. Bear down for five to seven seconds. Quickly release your air, take another breath or two, and repeat the routine until the contraction eases off.

3. When the contraction ends, slowly lie or sit back and take two relaxing breaths.

Note: This routine continues for each contraction until the baby's head is almost out. At this point the doctor or midwife will tell you to stop pushing to allow the baby to pass slowly through the vaginal opening. At the attendant's direction, immediately relax and let all the air out of your lungs. Pant, or blow quickly, if necessary, to keep from bearing down.

How to Rehearse Spontaneous Bearing Down and Directed Pushing for Labor

Use the practice sessions as rehearsals, going through the contractions as described for spontaneous bearing down. Remember the importance of relaxing the perineum while bearing down. In practice, bear down only enough to allow yourself to feel bulging of the pelvic floor. In actual labor, your body guides you in how hard to bear down. Some women find it helpful to rehearse these bearing-down techniques during perineal massage.

In addition, occasionally rehearse directed pushing, with your partner counting to five or seven while you hold your breath.

Prolonged Pushing

Prolonged breath-holding and pushing was once taught for all births, whether the mother could feel her urge to push or not. It is still more familiar to many birth attendants than other methods, and it is more widely advocated by them.

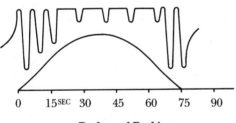

Prolonged Pushing

Prolonged pushing differs from directed pushing in the length of time the woman is expected to hold her breath and bear down—ten seconds or more instead of five to seven seconds. Although prolonged pushing may be beneficial under some circumstances (such as a very long second stage, inability to use a gravity-assisted position, or a large baby), it is not a good idea to use prolonged pushing when progress is good. This kind of pushing, especially in the supine (back-lying) position, is associated with a decrease in the oxygen available to the fetus, a drop in the mother's blood pressure, and too-rapid stretching of the vaginal

tissues, increasing the possibility of a tear and the need for an episiotomy.

Spontaneous bearing down and directed pushing efforts with breathing in between result in better oxygenation of the fetus[4] and more gradual distention of the vagina. Unless the woman uses upright positions that promote fetal descent, the second stage may last longer with spontaneous or directed pushing than with prolonged pushing, but the fetus usually remains in good condition throughout.

Under some circumstances the advantages of prolonged pushing may outweigh the disadvantages. These are discussed in chapter 9; they involve situations when there is a need to speed the second stage. Your caregiver is the best judge of this. Since you will be using this technique only under the guidance of your caregiver, there is no need to practice it before labor.

Preparation of the Perineum (Perineal Massage)

Perineal massage teaches you to respond to pressure in your vagina by relaxing your pelvic floor—a useful rehearsal for birth. It also is thought to increase the elasticity of the vagina and perineum, enhancing the hormonal changes that soften connective tissue in late pregnancy. You are more likely to avoid an episiotomy or serious tear if you practice perineal massage.[5] (Episiotomy is discussed further in chapters 8 and 9.)

If you are interested in avoiding an episiotomy, you may find it very helpful to massage the perineum five to seven times a week during the last six weeks of your pregnancy. Be sure your caregiver knows what you are doing and why. Because perineal massage is somewhat unconventional and outside mainstream obstetrical care, some caregivers are not familiar with it. Some women or couples find it distasteful and do not want to do it. Others feel it is worthwhile if it can reduce the chances of having an episiotomy or a serious tear. Some find it enjoyable, especially after doing it for a while and learning to relax.

If you have vaginitis, a herpes sore, or other vaginal problems, you should wait until you are healed before beginning perineal massage, as it could worsen the condition.

What to Do

Either you or your partner can do the massage. The first few times, take a mirror and look at your perineum so you know what you are doing. Be sure your hands are clean and your fingernails are short. If you or your partner has rough skin, it might be more comfortable to wear disposable rubber gloves.

Make yourself comfortable, in a semisitting position (if your partner is doing it) or standing with one foot up on the side of the tub or a chair (if you are doing it yourself).

1. Lubricate your fingers well with oil or water-soluble jelly by squirting it onto your fingers from a squeeze bottle or tube. This method is preferable to dipping your fingers into the oil, since repeated dipping will contaminate the oil. Some people recommend wheat germ oil, available at health food stores, because of its high vitamin E content, but other vegetable oils or water-based lubricants such as K-Y Jelly can also be used. Do not use baby oil, mineral oil, petroleum jelly, or hand lotion, as these are believed to be less well absorbed by the body than are vegetable or water-based products.

2. Rub enough oil or jelly into the perineum to allow your fingers to move smoothly.

3. If you are doing the massage yourself, use your thumb. Your partner can use the index fingers (one at first, both when you are more used to it). Place the fingers or thumb well inside the vagina (up to the second knuckle), then do a Kegel (pelvic floor con-

traction) so that you can feel the muscle tense on your or your partner's fingers. Then relax the pelvic floor muscles and move thumb or fingers within the vagina in a rhythmic U movement while gently pulling outward and down toward the anus. Do this for about three minutes. This stretching increases the suppleness of your vaginal tissue (mucosa), the muscles surrounding your vagina, and the skin of your perineum. Then massage briefly by rubbing the skin of the perineum between the thumb and forefinger (thumb on the in-side, finger on the outside or vice versa) for about one minute. In the beginning, your vaginal wall will feel tight, but with time and practice, the tissue will relax and stretch more easily.

4. Concentrate on relaxing your muscles as you feel the pressure and stretching. As you become comfortable with the massaging, increase the pressure just enough to make the perineum begin to sting or burn slightly from the stretching. (This same stinging sensation occurs as the baby's head is being born.)

5. If you have any questions after trying the massage, ask your caregiver or someone who teaches or has used this technique.

Practice Time— Rehearsals for Labor

Try to use practice time for more than simply going through a number of techniques. Use this time as a rehearsal for labor. Think about and discuss when you might use the techniques and why. Review what you have learned about the emotional and physical events of labor. Use the Labor and Birth Guide, pages 162–64, to help you review. Most of all, use this time together to explore the basic techniques you have learned, to adapt them to fit your needs, and to learn how to work together.

Practicing with Your Partner

Here are some suggestions for how your partner might work with you during practice. Many of these same suggestions will be useful in labor as well.

♦ To signal the beginning of a contraction, your partner says, "Contraction begins," "Here we go," or something similar. It might be in response to your organizing breath or whenever he or she wants to start a practice contraction. It is a good idea for you to take turns in "starting" the contractions. You both will get used to responding whether you are ready or not. (This is more like a true labor situation.) When the contraction ends, your partner acknowledges it by saying, "Contraction ends," "Blow it away," "It's gone," or something similar.

♦ Timing contractions and calling off fifteen-second intervals may be helpful ("fifteen seconds. . .thirty seconds. . .forty-five seconds," and so on). This counting helps you know where you are in a contraction and about how much longer it will last. It is often helpful in labor as well.

♦ To help simulate the pattern of intensity of labor contractions, your partner might use physical pressure—squeezing your inner thigh or upper arm. He or she should increase and decrease the intensity of pressure (sometimes gradually, sometimes rapidly) to follow a contraction pattern, varying the length of practice contractions between 45 and 120 seconds. After you have mastered the breathing patterns and relaxation techniques in a nonpainful situation, your partner might occasionally increase the pressure to painful levels so you can practice using the techniques as pain-relievers. It will be reassuring to both of you to discover how these skills reduce your awareness of pain.

♦ While practicing the techniques, your partner should be able to detect any tension and help you regain a relaxed state. Touching, massaging, talking, breathing with you, steadying your rhythm by conducting—using his or her hand to set a pace for breathing—and reminding you to move around are all ways your partner can help you during practice and during actual labor.

♦ Your partner's facial expression, tone of voice, and the way he or she touches you can affect how you respond. A loud or anxious tone of voice, a troubled expression, or tense or nervous rubbing send negative messages. On the other hand, a soothing voice, a confident facial expression, and a relaxed calming touch communicate positive messages. Help your partner become aware of the nonverbal messages he or she is sending.

How Much Should You Practice?

It is probably not necessary to practice daily to master these techniques, especially if you are attending childbirth classes together. Spend enough time practicing to become completely comfortable with each breathing pattern and relaxation technique and to figure out any adaptations you want to make. Then review them often enough that they remain very familiar and comfortable for you. Some people need or want to practice more than others.

Suggested Guide for Practice

The following learning sequence, which is based on an eight-week preparation period, will help you master the techniques discussed in this chapter and in chapter 6 in a careful, organized way. Try to begin about ten weeks before your due date to ensure that you finish even if the baby is born early. You will have to condense the sequence, of course, if your preparations begin later in your pregnancy.

Week 1

1. Do all the conditioning exercises described on pages 96–99, except the variations.

2. Practice body awareness (see pages 106–7).

3. Practice passive relaxation with slow breathing, ten to fifteen minutes (see pages 108–10).

Week 2

1. Continue the conditioning exercises, adding the variations.

2. Continue passive relaxation for shorter periods (about five minutes) with your partner checking and providing feedback (see pages 107–8).

3. Practice slow breathing in a contraction pattern (page 119), using many positions—side-lying, sitting, standing, leaning against a wall, on hands and knees, and squatting (see pages 144–45). Once mastered, practice three one-minute contractions with time between for feedback, changing position, and so on. Have your partner observe and assist you in maximum relaxation in all positions; he or she should watch for consistency in your breathing pattern.

4. Learn light (accelerated) breathing, (see pages 119–21). This may take several days. Experiment with depth and rate to find the best way for you. Have your partner observe for relaxation. You may need to practice five to ten one-minute contractions each day for a few days. Once you have mastered the technique—when you can relax and do it consistently—reduce the number of practice contractions.

5. Incorporate the use of attention-focusing (see page 113) with all breathing patterns.

Week 3

1. Continue your conditioning exercises.

2. Learn touch relaxation, page 110.

3. Continue practicing three slow-breathing contractions using different positions, with your partner observing for relaxation and consistency and providing feedback, suggestions, and encouragement.

4. Continue practicing light breathing for three ninety-second contractions in different positions.

Week 4

1. Continue your conditioning exercises.

2. Continue touch relaxation.

3. Learn effleurage and other massage techniques (see pages 113–14).

4. Continue practicing slow-breathing contractions, adding the roving body check (see page 111).

5. Continue using light breathing as before, with your partner conducting.

Week 5

1. Continue your conditioning exercises.

2. Continue touch relaxation and massage techniques with breathing patterns.

3. Learn the relaxation countdown.

4. Continue practicing slow breathing, using the roving body check (see page 111) each time.

5. Continue practicing light breathing.

6. Learn variable (transition) breathing (see pages 121–22).

7. Learn counterpressure, the double hip squeeze, and other techniques for back pain (see pages 175–76).

Week 6

1. Continue your conditioning exercises.

2. Practice active relaxation (see pages 110–11).

3. Incorporate relaxation countdown into your organizing and final relaxing breaths.

4. Continue practicing slow breathing, incorporating the roving body check.

5. Continue practicing light breathing, adding the roving body check. Think of "blowing out" tension with each out-breath.

6. Continue practicing variable breathing.

7. Learn ways to avoid pushing (see page 122).

8. Learn scramble breathing (see pages 121–22).

Week 7

1. Continue your conditioning exercises, particularly the pelvic floor bulging (see page 97).

2. Practice relaxation with each of the breathing patterns.

3. Continue practicing slow breathing.

4. Continue practicing light breathing.

5. Continue practicing variable breathing, along with "scramble" breathing.

6. Learn spontaneous bearing down in many positions. Have your partner help you by describing how you should be pushing (see pages 122–25).

7. Learn directed pushing in many positions, with your partner telling you when and how long to bear down (see pages 125–26).

8. Practice bearing down and suddenly blowing to avoid pushing during the same pushing contraction.

Week 8

1. Continue your conditioning exercises.

2. Rehearse for labor. Discuss the physical and emotional characteristics of each phase of labor, as well as the support and comfort measures likely to be useful. Practice several contractions for each phase, incorporating relaxation techniques, breathing patterns, and comfort measures. Use the Labor and Birth Guide on pages 162–64 as a review sheet.

Chapter 8

Labor and Birth

During labor, your uterus contracts, your cervix thins (effaces) and opens (dilates), your baby rotates and moves down the birth canal, and you give birth to your baby, placenta, umbilical cord, and amniotic sac. The entire process, which usually takes from a few hours to a day or more, is the transition to parenthood for you and the transition to an independent existence for your baby. Labor is the climax of pregnancy, when many seemingly separate systems work in harmony to bring about birth.

The onset of labor seems to be under the joint control of the endocrine (hormonal) systems of mother and baby. These systems function in synchrony so that most of the time the baby is ready to be born at about the same time that the mother is physically and emotionally ready to give birth. In late pregnancy the fetus begins producing labor-stimulating substances called oxytocin and prostaglandins. These pass from the fetus to the mother's circulation, increasing the level of oxytocin and prostaglandin she is already producing. The fetus thus plays a part in the onset of labor contractions.[1] In the meantime, the aging placenta begins producing a higher proportion of estrogen and a lower proportion of progesterone (the hormone that keeps the uterus from contracting). The higher ratio of estrogen to progesterone causes the following changes:

1. Increased sensitivity of the uterine muscle to oxytocin (the hormone that causes the uterus to contract).

2. Increased maternal production of prostaglandins (substances that ripen or soften the cervix).

3. Increased uterine activity and more noticeable contractions.

Although this physiological interaction between mother, placenta, and fetus is complex and not yet fully understood, recent research indicates that the maturity of the fetus is of great importance in triggering the mechanisms that begin labor. In the 1960s and 1970s, doctors frequently induced labor for the mother's or doctor's convenience—for instance, to take advantage of daytime hours or to meet a deadline such as a vacation date, anniversary, or time when a relative was available to help. Under these circumstances, many babies were born before they were ready. It was recognized in the early 1980s that much prematurity could be prevented if induction of labor was reserved for medical reasons only. Today caregivers generally recognize the advantages of spontaneous labor to the baby. See chapter 9 for further discussion of induction of labor.

As you approach the end of your pregnancy, you may wish you could have the baby sooner. You may feel awkward, tired, fat, hot, and uncomfortable. Try to remember, even if you pass your due date, that labor has probably not begun because the baby is not yet ready to be born.

The Last Weeks of Pregnancy

During the last weeks of pregnancy, your body goes through changes to prepare you to give birth and to nourish your baby. Your breasts produce more colostrum, which is the baby's first food after birth.

The Events of Late Pregnancy

During the last six or eight weeks of pregnancy, numerous complex interrelated events take place, as shown below. Birth is the climax. Each component of the fetal-maternal-placental unit contributes by triggering changes in other components, and

thereby continues the process that results in the birth of a mature and capable baby to a mother who is ready to nourish and nurture her. The timing is usually perfect, although in 10 to 12 percent of births, the timing is off and a premature or postmature baby is born.

Developed by Penny Simkin

Your uterus becomes more irritable, contracting more frequently, both spontaneously and in response to minor disturbances such as sneezing and bumping the abdomen. These contractions, usually mild, contribute to cervical changes such as ripening (softening) and effacement (thinning). Before labor begins, your cervix may have dilated one or two centimeters (or even more if you have given birth before). The ligaments and cartilage in your pelvis relax, allowing greater mobility in the joints, making it possible for the pelvic bones to spread during labor and birth and give your baby a bit more room in the birth canal. At the same time, vaginal secretions increase, and the tissues of the vaginal wall become more elastic. All these changes ease the baby's passage.

Fetal development late in pregnancy not only sets in motion some of the mechanisms that initiate labor, but also prepares the baby for life outside the uterus. He stores iron at a rapid rate in the last weeks of pregnancy, taking in enough to supplement the small amounts in breast milk and meet his needs for the next four to six months. The baby adds fat and develops the mechanism to maintain his own body temperature. He gains weight and strength. As the fetal adrenal glands mature, they begin secreting hormones that play a crucial role in lung maturation. As the placenta ages, the membrane that separates the fetal from the maternal circulation becomes more permeable to large molecules. This permits antibodies and immunoglobulins to cross from you to your baby, providing months of protection for the baby against diseases to which you are immune.

Thus, your baby's readiness for survival outside your body coincides with his production of certain substances, which feed back to your circulation and seem to play a key role in triggering at least some of the changes that start labor. Your own physical and psychological readiness for labor is the

other key. Usually, when the time is right for both you and the baby, labor begins.

Things to Do Before a Hospital Birth

The following lists will help you get ready for a hospital birth. If you are planning a home birth, much from these lists will still be relevant. In addition, ask your midwife or doctor what preparations to make in your home and what supplies to have on hand.

Early Preparation

1. Write a birth plan and go over it with your doctor or midwife. Your childbirth educator can help you write it if you have questions, but do make sure that the birth plan reflects your wishes, no one else's.

2. Tour your hospital, or backup hospital for a planned home birth.

3. Preregister at the hospital.

Pack Your Bags for the Hospital

For Use during Labor
Pack these in a separate bag from your suitcase, which may not be handy during labor:

♦ Chapstick or lip gloss

♦ Toothbrushes (for you and your partner)

♦ Warm socks in case your feet get cold

♦ Cornstarch or powder in shaker for massage

♦ This book

♦ A watch with a second hand to time contractions

♦ Tennis balls, rolling pin, or blue icepack for pressure on back

♦ Favorite juice, tea, or popsicles if not provided

♦ Partner's snack (if hospital does not provide food in the labor room)

♦ Shower cap

♦ Partner's swimsuit (so partner can accompany you in the shower)

♦ Phone numbers of people to call after the birth (money if needed)

♦ Camera and film, tape recorder and blank tapes, video recorder and blank videotapes (check with caregiver regarding any policies on these)

♦ Personalized focal point (a picture, design, or figure)

♦ Tapes of relaxing music

For Postpartum Stay
♦ Nightgowns or pajamas for nursing (you may prefer hospital gowns)

♦ Robe and slippers

♦ Usual cosmetic and grooming aids

♦ Shower cap

♦ Nursing bras (2)

♦ Reading and writing materials

♦ Money for newspaper, etc.

♦ Going-home clothes (a comfortable size, as you probably will not be back to your prepregnant size yet)

♦ Other personal items

For the Baby
♦ Diapers (2) and diaper pins (hospital may put a disposable diaper on baby)

♦ Undershirt

♦ Nightgown or stretch suit

♦ Waterproof pad or pants

♦ Receiving blanket

♦ Outside blanket, bunting, booties, and cap

♦ Car seat for ride home

Key Concepts for Understanding Labor

Descent

At some time during late pregnancy or early labor the baby begins moving down into the pelvis. This process is called *descent.* If the baby is said to be "floating," his lowest or *presenting part* is still above the level of the pubic bone. For *primigravidas* (women pregnant for the first time), some descent—either gradual or sudden—usually takes place several weeks before the onset of labor. For *multigravidas* (women who have been pregnant more than once), it is not unusual for labor to begin with the baby still floating or rather high in the pelvis. Most descent, for both primigravidas and multigravidas, takes place during late labor.

As the baby descends, his progress is measured in terms of *station,* which refers to the location of the presenting part (the body part that comes first—usually the baby's head) in relation to the ischial spines (the bones marking the middle of the true pelvis). For example, if the top of the head is at 0 station, it means that it has descended to the middle of the pelvis. When the head is floating, it is at a -4 (minus four) station (four centimeters above the midpelvis). If it is at a -1 or -2 station, the top of the head is one or two centimeters above the midpelvis. If the head is at a +1 (plus one) or a +2 (plus two) station, it is one or two centimeters below the midpelvis. When the head is at the vagina and on its way out, it is at a +4 station. In other words, descent means that the baby moves from the highest station (-4) down to the lowest station (+4) and is then born. Many women begin labor at a -1 or 0 station, meaning that some descent has already taken place.

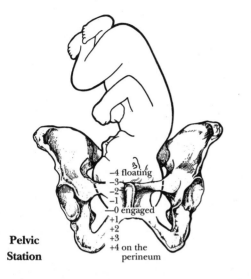

Pelvic Station

Other terms used to describe the descent that takes place in late pregnancy include "lightening" and "dropping," which refer to the relief of pressure in the woman's chest and upper abdomen, and to a noticeable change in her contour (carrying the baby lower). "Engagement," which can be determined only with a vaginal exam, means that the presenting part is "engaged," or at 0 station, and fixed in the pelvis.

Presentation and Position

The doctor or midwife uses these terms to describe how your baby is lying within your uterus. *Presentation* describes the part of the baby that is lying over the cervix. For example, the most favorable and most common presentation (occurring 95 percent of the time) is the *vertex* presentation, in which the crown or top of the baby's head is down over the cervix. Other, more rare presentations are the *frank breech* (buttocks), *footling breech* (feet), *complete breech* (buttocks and feet), *shoulder, face,* and *brow* presentations. (These rarer presentations, which may cause difficulties in labor, are discussed in chapter 9.) *Position* refers to the direction toward which the baby lies within your body. The possible positions are *anterior,* referring

to your front; *posterior,* referring to your back; and *transverse,* referring to your side.

If your doctor or midwife tells you the baby is *occiput anterior,* it means that the back of the baby's head (the occiput) is pointing toward your anterior (front). Here are some other common descriptions of the baby's presentation and position:

Left (or Right) Occiput Anterior (LOA or ROA). The back of the baby's head toward your left (or right) front.

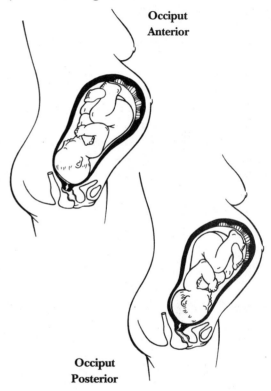

Occiput Anterior

Occiput Posterior

Occiput Posterior (OP). The back of the baby's head is directly toward your back. See page 175 for information on what you can do in labor.

Right or Left Occiput Posterior (ROP or LOP). The back of the baby's head is toward your right (or left) back.

Right or Left Occiput Transverse (ROT or LOT). The back of the baby's head is toward your right (or left) side.

Right or Left Sacrum Anterior (RSA or LSA). The baby's tailbone or buttocks (sacrum) is toward your right (or left) front. This is how a breech presentation is described.

Cervical Changes

The following changes in the cervix take place gradually, beginning before labor and ending when the baby is about to be born. The caregiver assesses these changes in evaluating your readiness for labor or your progress in labor. Because the assessments are subjective, they may vary from one caregiver to another. It may be confusing or discouraging if you are examined within a short period of time by two people whose assessments differ.

♦ The cervix *ripens* or softens, beginning in late pregnancy. Before ripening takes place, the cervix is firm.

♦ The cervix *moves forward*. Usually, weeks before labor, the cervix is high and posterior (pointing toward your back); it gradually moves down and forward, to an anterior position.

♦ The cervix *effaces* or thins. For a primigravida, a substantial degree of effacement usually occurs before significant dilation (opening) takes place. The multigravida's cervix usually effaces and dilates at the same time. Effacement is determined during a vaginal exam and is measured in percentages. "Zero percent effacement" means the cervix has not begun to thin; "50 percent effacement" means the cervix has thinned about halfway; "100 percent effacement" means the cervix has thinned completely.

♦ The cervix *dilates* or opens. Although it is usual for the cervix to dilate slightly before the onset of labor, most dilation takes place during labor. Dilation is estimated during a vaginal exam and is measured in centime-

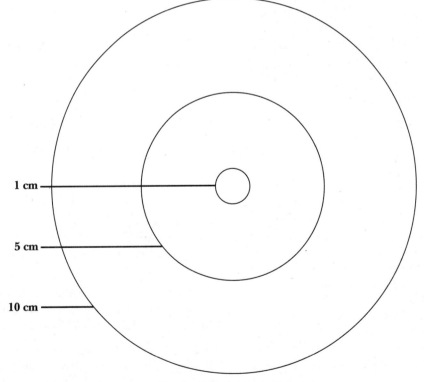

Cervical Dilation (actual size)

ters. When the cervix is opened only a finger-tip, it is one centimeter dilated; at the halfway point, it is five centimeters; and when fully dilated, it is about ten centimeters.

Labor—The Physiologic Process

The rest of this chapter contains a description of the physiologic process of a normal and healthy labor, along with what you can expect physically and emotionally and what you can do to help the process and make it more comfortable. The next chapter deals with labor situations that are more difficult or complicated, along with the interventions you and your doctor or midwife might use to correct the difficulties.

The Four Stages of Labor

Labor is divided into four distinct stages, according to the physiologic changes that take place.

First Stage—Dilation begins with progressing contractions and ends when the cervix is completely open.

Second Stage—Descent and Birth begins when the cervix is fully dilated and ends when the baby is born.

Third Stage—Delivery of the Placenta begins with the birth of the baby and ends with the delivery of the placenta.

Fourth Stage—Recovery begins after the placenta is born and ends one to several hours later when the mother's condition stabilizes.

The First Stage of Labor— Dilation

At some point in your pregnancy (usually within two weeks before or after your due date), you will recognize that you are in labor. You will probably miss the exact

moment labor begins; the process starts gradually and most of the early signs are subtle. Usually it takes a period of time (a few hours to a few days) for the signs to become clear enough for you to recognize labor.

Signs of Labor

By familiarizing yourself with the following signs, you will probably recognize labor and not be caught by surprise. You will also be more able to recognize when you are not in labor. The signs are not listed in order of occurrence because there is no consistent pattern. Some women do not experience all of these signs of labor. Some signs are more important than others—that is, they are more likely to indicate that your cervix is actually dilating, whereas others indicate that earlier changes are taking place, such as the moving forward of the cervix, ripening, or effacement.

Backache that comes and goes. This backache is often accompanied by a feeling of uneasiness or restlessness—an inability to feel comfortable in any position for very long. It differs from the "postural" backache most women have in late pregnancy after standing or sitting for a while. It may resemble the backache often experienced before a menstrual period. This subtle sign of labor may occur for days before or along with other signs of labor.

Frequent soft bowel movements. Often mistaken for an intestinal upset, this is probably a prostaglandin-induced change, which clears the lower digestive tract and makes more room for the baby to move down. Diarrhea-like symptoms on or near your due date *may* be a subtle sign of labor.

Passage of slippery mucus mixed with some blood ("bloody show"). Throughout pregnancy, the cervix contains thick mucus, which may be loosened and released in late pregnancy when the cervix begins thinning

Signs of Labor

In this chart, the signs of labor are categorized as Possible Signs, Preliminary Signs, and Positive Signs. These categories will help you decide when you are truly in labor. Please note that you may not experience all these signs and that they do not necessarily occur in a particular order. If you are unsure, call your caregiver or the hospital's labor and delivery nursing station. Usually women do not experience the preliminary or positive signs of labor until they are close to forty weeks of pregnancy. Occasionally, however, women go into preterm labor; that is, they begin having signs of labor before thirty-seven weeks of pregnancy. See page 53 for signs of preterm labor.

	Signs	*Comments*
Possible signs of labor. These may or may not be early signs of labor; time will tell.	◆ **Backache.** Vague, low, nagging; may cause restlessness	Different, less defined than posture-related backache from prolonged standing or sitting; may be caused by early contractions
	◆ **Menstrual-like cramps.** May be accompanied by discomfort in thighs	May be intermittent or continuous
	◆ **Soft bowel movements.** May be accompanied by intestinal cramps or digestive upset	May be related to increase in circulating prostaglandins, which ripen your cervix while causing these other symptoms
	◆ **Nesting urge.** An unusual burst of energy resulting in great activity and a desire to complete preparations for baby	Think of this extra energy as a sign that you will have strength and stamina to handle labor; try to avoid exhausting activity
Preliminary signs of labor. These are signs of progress, but are still associated with very early labor or prelabor.	◆ **Bloody show.** Passage of blood-tinged mucus from vagina	Associated with thinning (effacement) and early opening (dilation) of cervix; may occur days before other signs or not until progressing labor contractions have begun; continues throughout labor
	◆ **Leaking of amniotic fluid from the vagina.** Caused by a small rupture of membranes (ROM)	Sometimes stops when membranes seal or continues on and off for hours or days; see page 139 for precautions
	◆ **Nonprogressing contractions.** Tend to stay about the same length, strength, and frequency; prelabor contractions that may last for a short time or continue for hours before they go away	Accomplish softening and thinning (effacement) of cervix, although most dilation does not occur until you have positive signs
Positive signs of labor. These are the clearest signs of true labor.	◆ **Progressing contractions.** Become longer, stronger, and closer together with time; are usually described as "painful" or "very strong" and are felt in abdomen, back, or both	Dilate cervix; are not reduced by mother's activity and will not subside because of a change in activity
	◆ **Gush of amniotic fluid from the vagina.** Caused by a large rupture of membranes (ROM)	Often accompanied or followed by progressing contractions

and opening. On rare occasions this appears as a mucus "plug." More often the mucus is thinner and may be tinged with blood because small blood vessels in the cervix break as it thins and opens. This bloody show can appear days before any other signs of labor or may not appear until hours after contractions have begun. Bloody show continues as labor progresses. (*Note:* if there is a steady flow of blood, this is probably not show and should be immediately reported to your caregiver.)

In late pregnancy, women often pass some brownish, bloody discharge within twenty-four hours after a vaginal exam because the exam often causes some cervical bleeding. It is easy to mistake this discharge for the show. If you are not sure whether it is show or a post-exam discharge, note the appearance of the blood. If it is show, it is pink or bright red and mixed with mucus; after an exam, it is usually brownish, like old blood.

Progressing contractions of the uterus. Contractions that become longer, stronger, and closer together as time passes are a sign of labor. In early labor, contractions are usually felt as a tightening with some backache. Contractions usually become painful as labor advances. Uterine contractions shorten the muscle fibers in the body of the uterus, pull open the cervix, and push the fetus down and out of the uterus. Nonprogressing contractions (that is, contractions that do not become longer, stronger, and closer together as time passes) may come and go over a period of days before labor actually begins.

To determine if your contractions are progressing or not, time them and keep a written record, because it is easy to forget after a few contractions (see the Early Labor Record on page 140). To time contractions you need a watch or clock with a second hand. When the contraction begins, write down the time in the *Time* column. When the contraction ends, figure out how many seconds it lasted. *Duration* refers to the number of seconds the contraction lasted. *Interval* refers to the length of time between the beginning of one contraction and the beginning of the next. You use the interval to determine the *frequency,* which refers to how often the contractions are coming; for instance, every five minutes.

Rupture of the membranes (ROM). Also called breaking of the bag of waters, rupture of the membranes occurs before labor in only about 10 to 12 percent of pregnancies. In such cases, progressing contractions usually begin soon or within twenty-four hours. In most pregnancies, the membranes do not rupture until late in labor. When the membranes break, there may be a sudden "pop" followed by a gush of amniotic fluid, or there may be a slow, uncontrollable leak of fluid. ROM may feel like urination; sometimes women believe they have lost bladder control. When ROM occurs and labor does not begin, the risk of infection increases as time passes. If your membranes rupture before labor, follow these guidelines:

1. Note the time, color, odor, and describe the amount of fluid (a trickle or a gush). If normal, the fluid is clear and practically odorless.

2. Notify your doctor or midwife. Know his or her plan for your care. Some birth attendants induce labor soon after ROM if it occurs at term. If it occurs before term, they may try to prevent labor. Some caregivers are comfortable waiting to see if you will go into labor spontaneously or if you can get labor started by yourself. See What You Can Do to Start or Stimulate Labor on pages 167–69, for suggestions.

3. Do not put anything into your vagina (no tampon to control the flow, no fingers, and do not have intercourse), because it could increase the possibility of infection. Caregivers disagree on the advisability of taking a tub bath after ROM. Discuss this issue with your caregiver at a prenatal exam or when informing him or her of your leaking membranes. Most caregivers limit the number of vaginal exams they do to reduce the chance of infection, since the caregiver's fingers in the vagina and cervix (even when clean and gloved) can increase the chance of infection.

One further caution on rupture of the membranes: on rare occasions the cord prolapses (slips into the vagina) as the membranes rupture. This is a true emergency because the baby may press against the cord and cut off his oxygen supply. Refer to page 177 in chapter 9 for further information on prolapsed cord.

Changes in the cervix confirmed by vaginal exam. Your caregiver performs this exam to determine what changes have taken place in the position, ripening, effacement, or dilation of your cervix.

Early Labor Record

To help you decide if you are truly in labor, keep track of what is happening by using an Early Labor Record form like the one below.

You may find this form helpful in deciding when to call your caregiver or go to the hospital. Time five or six contractions in a row; if there is no progression in your contractions (if they do not become longer, stronger, and closer together), stop timing. Resume timing later if there seems to be a change. If the contractions have not clearly progressed, then you are probably still in prelabor.

When you call your caregiver, be prepared to furnish the following information: how long your contractions are lasting (duration); how many minutes apart they are (interval); how strong contractions seem (intensity); how long your contractions have been like this; status of membranes (have they ruptured?); presence of show; and any other pertinent information.

In Labor

When labor is established, your contractions are progressing and your cervix is dilating; you are in the first stage of labor, which normally lasts from two to twenty-four hours. The average length of the first stage for a primigravida is twelve and one-half hours; for a multigravida, seven and one-third hours. Prepare yourself for a short, average,

Sample Early Labor Record

Contractions

Date_____

Time	Duration	Interval or Frequency	Comments
Starting time	How many seconds long?	How many minutes since the beginning of the last one?	Intensity of contractions, food eaten, breathing level, bloody show, status of membranes, other events
1:46 am	25 sec	—	Bloody Show at 6pm
2:03 am	35 sec	17 min	Can't sleep
2:18 am	28 sec	15 min	Loose BM ¿ backache
2:31 am	55 sec	13 min	STRONGER !

and long first stage, since it is impossible to predict just how long it will take.

Contractions continue intermittently throughout labor, shortening the muscle fibers in the body of the uterus and pulling the cervix open. Each contraction follows a wavelike pattern: it builds to a peak, then gradually goes away, allowing the uterus to rest for a time. Early in labor, contractions may feel like a dull, low backache or menstrual cramps. These early contractions are usually (though not always) short and mild, lasting thirty to forty seconds, and the interval between them may be as long as fifteen or twenty minutes. Some labors, however, begin with contractions closer together and rather intense. As labor advances, you will feel the contractions more in your abdomen or in both your abdomen and lower back, and the backache may persist even between contractions. By the end of the first stage, contractions are usually very intense and last as long as 90 to 120 seconds, and the interval between them may be as short as two to three minutes.

By the end of pregnancy your uterus has become the largest and strongest muscle in your body. When your uterus contracts, it hardens and bulges like any other muscle. It is capable of powerful contractions, which become increasingly stronger and longer as labor progresses. Usually these stronger contractions are more powerful and more effective both in dilating the cervix and pressing the baby downward. Labor contractions, under the control of various hormonal and other physiological factors, are involuntary. Once the process begins, it does not usually stop until the baby and placenta are born. Then you can rest and rejoice in your baby.

The first stage of labor is subdivided into three phases: *latent, active,* and *transition.* The phases become shorter and more intense as labor progresses. Each phase is distinguished by its own physiological and emotional characteristics. If you and your partner understand the process, you will be better prepared to recognize each phase and cope with your labor.

The Latent Phase

The latent phase is usually the longest phase of the first stage, and the contractions are farther apart, shorter, and less intense than during the later phases. During this phase, your cervix will efface and dilate to three, four, or possibly five centimeters. You will probably spend most of this phase at or near home, doing whatever activity is appropriate for the time of day—resting if it is nighttime, keeping busy if it is daytime. You and your partner will also probably spend a good portion of this phase uncertain whether you are in labor. Keeping an Early Labor Record will help you decide.

—photograph by Harriette Hartigan/Artemis

You will probably feel excited and a bit nervous in early labor.

During this phase, it is best for you not to be alone and to keep your mind active so that you do not become preoccupied with the labor. You will probably feel excited and a bit nervous. Try to do things that are calming or distracting, not exhausting. Pack your bag (see suggestions on pages 133–34) for the hospital, or prepare your home if you're planning a home birth. Focus on relaxing your muscles and your mind during your contractions. Have a massage. Take a long bath or shower; do not underestimate the soothing, pain-relieving properties of water. Eat and drink easy-to-digest, appealing foods such as soup, broth, fruit, juice, pasta, and toast. Pass the time with pleasant, distracting activities; go for a walk, visit friends, listen to music, dance, watch television, or play games. Such activities can keep you from becoming preoccupied with your contractions too soon. You will reach a point where you can no longer be distracted from the contractions—you cannot continue walking or talking through them without pausing during the peak. Then it is time to begin the first level of patterned breathing, slow breathing.

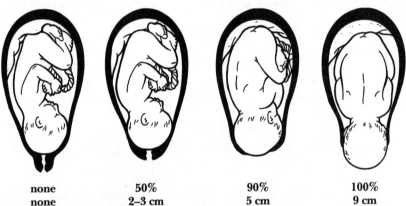

Effacement	none	50%	90%	100%
Dilation	none	2–3 cm	5 cm	9 cm

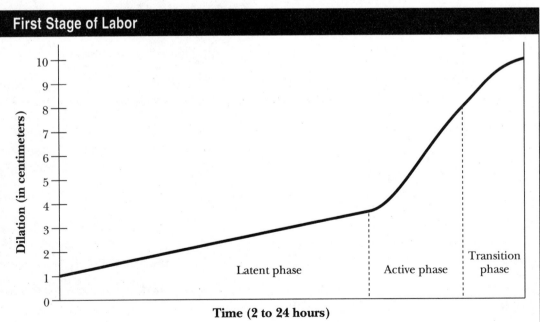

First Stage of Labor

Dilation (in centimeters)

Latent phase   Active phase   Transition phase

Time (2 to 24 hours)

When to Call Your Caregiver

When should you call your doctor, midwife, or hospital? During the last month of your pregnancy, ask your caregiver when and whom to call. Unless you live far away or have received other instructions, a primigravida should call when her membranes rupture or when the contractions are very strong, requiring total concentration and breathing. By this time, contractions may be about five minutes apart. The multigravida should call when her membranes rupture or when she has experienced several of the signs of labor. Be ready to report the information on show, membranes, and contractions that you recorded in your Early Labor Record. Of course, if you are anxious or have questions even without evidence of true labor, call to allay your fears. If you have a condition that will benefit from being in the hospital in very early labor, go in whenever you suspect labor. Your caregiver should be sure to tell you if you have such a condition (for example, a low-lying placenta, a herpes sore, high blood pressure, or others).

The Active Phase

As the latent phase draws to a close, your labor pattern changes. Your contractions may be painful, though manageable, each lasting a minute or more and coming close together—three to five minutes apart. This is the time when most people go to the hospital or birth center, or when the midwife or doctor arrives for a home birth. You may feel as if this now-intense labor has gone on for a long time without much progress. As you look back on how long it took to get to four or five centimeters you may feel discouraged if you think it will take that much more time to get to ten centimeters! You may wish you could call it quits for the day. You may feel trapped in the labor as you realize that there is no way out but to go on and complete the process. We sometimes refer to this realization as the "moment of truth."

These are typical reactions to the more demanding and more productive active phase of labor. In the latent phase, your spirits were high; in the active phase, you become serious, quiet, and preoccupied with the contractions. Earlier your partner's jokes were funny and the conversation entertaining; now you cannot listen. You may even feel resentful of any "small talk" around you. As you become more centered on your labor, your partner should move in closer, focus more on your labor, and share your serious, quiet mood. He or she should help you to relax, find comfortable positions, and maintain your focus and breathing. Most importantly, your partner can help you interpret what is going on. You may be discouraged because you seem to be progressing as slowly as before, yet the contractions are demanding so much more of you. The truth is, when you enter the active phase, labor is speeding up and you are accomplishing more with each of these intense, painful contractions. It is the knowledge that you are finally getting somewhere that renews your confidence and optimism.

Arrival at the Hospital

Once you decide to go to the hospital, call the maternity floor and anyone else you want to tell, get your bag and your birth plan, gather any last-minute items (a pillow and blanket, and a towel if your bag of waters is leaking), and go. Do not drive yourself. If your partner is not available, have a backup plan for someone else to take you. Be sure you know which hospital entrance to use. In the middle of the night, the emergency room may be the only open entrance.

When you arrive, go first to the admitting office if it is open. Admitting procedures do not take long if you have preregistered. Otherwise it might take a while. If you are having painful contractions or are in active labor, the hospital staff can take care of the admitting procedures later. You or your

Positions for First Stage

Position	Advantages	Disadvantages
Standing	◆ Takes advantage of gravity during and between contractions ◆ Contractions less painful and more productive ◆ Fetus well aligned with angle of pelvis ◆ Relieves backache ◆ May speed labor	◆ Tiring for long periods ◆ May be impossible with anesthesia
Standing and leaning forward	◆ Same as with standing ◆ May be more restful than standing	◆ Same as with standing
Walking	◆ Same as with standing ◆ Movement in pelvis encourages descent	◆ Tiring for long periods ◆ Difficult or impossible with anesthesia, analgesia, or electronic fetal monitoring
Sitting upright	◆ Good resting position ◆ Some gravity advantage ◆ Can be used with electronic fetal monitor	◆ May slow labor progress if used for long periods
Semisitting	◆ Same as with sitting upright ◆ Vaginal exams possible	◆ Same as with sitting upright ◆ Increases back pain
Sitting, leaning forward with support	◆ Same as with sitting upright ◆ Relieves back pain ◆ Good position for back rub	◆ Same as with sitting upright
Hands and knees	◆ Helps relieve backache ◆ Assists rotation of baby from OP position ◆ Allows for pelvic rocking ◆ May be used when other positions cause a drop in fetal heart rate	◆ Vaginal exams inconvenient for most caregivers ◆ Hands and knees may go to sleep or hurt after a while ◆ May interfere with external fetal monitor tracing ◆ May be tiring for long periods
Kneeling, leaning forward with support	◆ Same as on hands and knees ◆ Less strain on wrists and hands than in hands and knees position	◆ May interfere with external fetal monitor tracing ◆ May be tiring for long periods

Position	Advantages	Disadvantages
Side-lying	♦ Very good resting position ♦ Convenient for many interventions ♦ Helps lower elevated blood pressure ♦ May promote progress of labor when alternated with walking ♦ Safe if pain medications have been used	♦ Contractions may be less effective and longer ♦ May be inconvenient for vaginal exams
Squatting	♦ Takes advantage of gravity ♦ May be comfortable and relieve backache ♦ May enhance fetal alignment and descent within pelvis	♦ May not enhance descent of baby if station is high ♦ Tiring for long periods ♦ Legs can go to sleep if used for long periods
Back-lying (supine)	♦ Convenient for caregiver for procedures and vaginal exam ♦ May be restful ♦ Convenient for electronic fetal monitoring	♦ May cause supine hypotension and fetal distress ♦ May increase backache ♦ Psychologically vulnerable ♦ Labor contractions found to be longest, most painful, and least productive

partner will sign admission forms, including a general consent form. Most general consent forms are intimidating and make it seem as if you are giving the hospital permission to do whatever they want to you. Try to read this form before labor, and ask for clarification of any items you are uncomfortable with. Some patients simply cross out or reword the items that concern them and initial those changes before signing the form. Some add a statement that they want to be informed of reasons, risks, benefits, and alternatives before any treatment or procedure is done. It might be helpful to know that the general consent form may not be the only one you will sign. If you or your baby develops a problem requiring major procedures (such as cesarean section, other surgery, a septic workup, or in some hospitals, epidural anesthesia), you will probably be asked to sign another consent form.

You can take a wheelchair or walk to the maternity floor. A nurse usually greets you, assesses your condition, your labor, and your baby's well-being, and then calls your caregiver. The nurse checks the same things that are checked at your prenatal exam: She or he will ask questions about what is happening and about your medical history, and will check your weight, pulse, blood pressure, temperature, the baby's heart rate and position, your contractions, and the dilation of your cervix. The nurse will also get urine and blood samples. If you are making progress in labor, you will put on a gown (you may wear a hospital gown or bring your own) and proceed with the usual care during labor. If it appears that you are still in very early labor (or prelabor), the nurse might suggest that you leave the hospital for a while, until the labor pattern changes. This is usually a good idea, because if you get to the hospital too early, labor can seem awfully long and discouraging.

Initial Procedures for a Home Birth

Once you call your midwife or doctor for a home birth, she or he will arrive and make similar assessments to those described for hospital admission. If you are progressing in labor, the caregiver will bring in the essential implements, medications, an oxygen tank, and other equipment. She or he may remain with you from then on or, if labor is still quite early and you are comfortable on your own, may leave for a while. Your caregiver may work with an assistant, who may remain with you.

Working with Your Labor

After these initial procedures, make yourself comfortable. Try pressure and cold packs on your back or hot compresses on your lower abdomen, groin, and back. Go to the bathroom once an hour, because a full bladder is uncomfortable and can slow labor. Change position frequently unless you are very tired and need to rest or unless the contractions are coming so fast you cannot move; try to walk and sit rather than lie in bed. Some laboring women make the mistake of staying immobile in bed throughout labor. Lying down may increase the pain of contractions and slow the progress of labor.[2] Take advantage of gravity by standing and walking for at least part of the time. (See the photos on page 118 and the chart on pages 144–45 for a discussion of positions.) You may want to alternate activity with rest. It is important to get fluids, so drink something after each contraction or suck on a popsicle or ice chips. To gauge your progress, at each vaginal exam find out the effacement and dilation, as well as the station and position of the baby.

Continue your relaxation and breathing

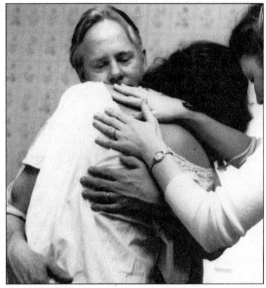

—photograph by Harriette Hartigan/Artemis

In active labor, your partner should move in close and share your serious, quiet mood.

techniques. This is a good time for lots of encouragement from your partner, who can praise your efforts, rub your back and legs, count off every fifteen seconds in the contraction, and remind you to move around, drink fluids, and go to the bathroom. Relaxation is the key at this time. Make a special effort to keep from tensing during contractions.

You will want to continue slow breathing (see page 117) for as long as it helps you relax. If your breathing begins to sound tense or labored, if you are unable to keep the rate slow, or if you find you cannot maintain your focus and remain relaxed, even after renewed efforts and more active encourgement from your partner, switch to light (accelerated) breathing (see page 119). This may give you just the boost you need. Light breathing follows the pattern of your contractions, lightening and quickening as the contraction intensifies, then slowing and deepening as the contraction subsides. Used in this way, the breathing pattern can help you tune in to your labor contractions and calm you with its rhythm.

The Transition Phase

The transition phase represents the peak of difficulty in most labors, not necessarily because the pain is greater, but because the contractions are longer and closer together, there is more pressure in the pelvis, and the accompanying physical and emotional signs are intense. The cervix dilates the last one or two centimeters, the baby's head leaves the uterus and presses down lower in the birth canal, and your body prepares for the expulsion stage. Relatively short, the transition phase usually lasts from five to twenty contractions. These contractions, the longest of your labor, will give you the shortest rest in between. You will probably be tired, restless, and irritable, totally consumed by your efforts to cope. The intensity of transition is almost overwhelming and you will need much reassurance and help to get through.

During this phase you are truly in a transition—from first to second stage. Not only is your cervix dilating the last couple of centimeters, but the baby is beginning to descend. The head slips through your cervix and into your vagina. Your body shows some of the signs of the second stage, although labor is still technically in the first stage. You will probably have some very intense new feelings to cope with. For example, your diaphragm may be irritated by the involuntary spasms that are the precursors of bearing down. As a result you may begin hiccuping, grunting, or belching. You may find yourself holding your breath and straining at times during each contraction. This is what is known as "the urge to push." Nausea and vomiting are common. The baby's head, pressing through your vaginal wall against your rectum, feels like a bowel movement and may cause a backache or aching thighs. Trembling of the legs, which may spread throughout the body, and a heavy discharge of bloody mucus from the vagina reflect the increased downward pressure. Contractions may be irregular, with double peaks, and may last 90 to 120 seconds with only 30-second rests between. Despite the intensity and pain of the contractions of transition, you may doze off during the short rests between contractions, as if your body is conserving every bit of energy for the work of contractions. Dozing is helpful, but the moment the next contraction begins, your partner should wake you and help you focus and begin breathing so the contraction does not get ahead of you.

During transition, you become very focused on your labor; nothing else matters. You may worry that something is wrong. You may feel frightened by the intensity of labor and very dependent on those around you. You may feel transition will last forever, that you cannot take any more. But as one woman said, "When you can't take any more, there's no more to take." Transition pushes you to your limits, but with good support and the knowledge of where you are and what you need to do, you will meet the challenge because transition is short.

Getting through Transition

Recognition is one of the keys to coping with transition. If you are experiencing the extreme sensations of transition and believe you are only five or six centimeters dilated, you will probably become discouraged. Remember that labor is a progressive process. "You are not where you were at the last vaginal exam. You are beyond that point," is a guideline to remember after you have passed the latent phase, especially if your sensations and emotional responses change during contractions. Know the signs of transition described above and be ready for them any time after you enter the active phase of labor. When a woman and her partner know where they are, they are heartened by their progress and see the pain and difficulties of transition in a more positive light—transition is bringing the baby closer.

—photograph by Harriette Hartigan/Artemis

During transition you become totally focused on your labor.

Understanding the normal feelings, reactions, and events of transition is another key. Pain, nausea, trembling, despair, dependence, crying, an urge to push, and an inability to relax and breathe "perfectly" are normal responses during transition. They do not mean anything is wrong. It is when you think that your labor is worse than it is supposed to be that you begin to worry and seek relief with pain medications or anesthesia. Pain medications, of course, are an option, but do not take them because you fear your transition is abnormal. The medication can only reduce pain, it does not remove the other symptoms.

Reassurance and kindness from your partner and caregiver are essential. You need to know that you and your baby are all right, that your sensations are normal, that you are coping well, and that this difficult time will be short.

Finally, more active support and direction from your partner and caregiver may help you through transition. Your partner might "take charge" by getting you to look at him or her, pacing or conducting your breathing with hand movements or by breathing with you. Your partner gets very close to you, helps you focus, and encourages your every breath. Switch to a variable breathing pattern if light or slow breathing seem ineffective. If you have a premature urge to push, blow or pant to keep from pushing. (The breathing patterns for transition are described on page 121) Many women like being held close at this time; others do not want to be touched but find visual and verbal contact very helpful. Hot, moist towels on the lower back, lower abdomen, and perineum can be soothing. Changing positions between contractions sometimes brings relief.

Women often worry that transition will be too much for them, that they will lose control, panic, and behave in a way they will later regret. They have heard of women who lost control, struggled, screamed, or begged for relief from the pain. These impressions of childbirth probably came from women who were unprepared, frightened, and groggy or confused from medication.

You can get through a normal transition without pain medications, especially if you prepare in advance, have good support, know what is happening, and use relaxation, breathing, and comfort techniques. Be assured that you will not change character or lose the ability to respond to clear, simple directions. Your labor partner should not mistake moans, groans, or other sounds during transition for cries of agony. Many women find transition easier to manage if they vocalize or make noise during the contractions. If so, they should be encouraged in making these sounds. Some women, on the other hand, go into a state of deep relaxation and remain very still and quiet during their contractions. There is no single correct way to handle transition; responses to childbirth pain are very individual.

The Second Stage of Labor—Birth of the Baby

After dilation is complete, transition ends and the second stage of labor begins. A new series of physiological events begins; your baby gradually leaves the uterus, rotates within your pelvis and descends through the vagina, and is born.

Signs of Second Stage

The urge to push. This urge—the most significant sign—coincides roughly with full dilation, although many women experience it before full dilation, others experience it sometime later, and a few not at all. (See page 122 on how to handle a premature urge to push.) The urge to push is a combination of powerful sensations and reflex actions caused by the pressure of the baby in the vagina during contractions. As difficult to describe as labor contractions, the urge to push is a strongly felt need to grunt or hold your breath and bear down. It occurs several times within a contraction, and is responsible for your pressing the baby downward. It is as compelling and difficult to control as a sneeze, an orgasm, or vomiting. For many women, joining in with the urge to push is one of the most satisfying aspects of the entire birth experience. For others it is disturbing and painful.

Relief from sensations of transition. This is another sign of second stage. The pain lessens, you calm down and cheer up, and you become less focused on your labor and more aware of those around you. Now you can collect yourself for pushing your baby out of your body. During the first stage, you cooperate with your labor contractions by relaxing as much as possible and using positions and movement to enhance the process. During the second stage you cooperate with your labor by voluntarily bearing down and assuming appropriate positions.

Key Concepts

Two key concepts should guide you and the staff during the second stage:

The importance of not rushing. Although both you and the staff are anxious to get that baby out, do not rush. Follow your body's signals; bear down or "push" spontaneously as the urge demands and allow time for your vagina to open. By not rushing, your vagina can stretch open gently, decreasing the likelihood of damage.[3] You will also use your energy more efficiently. By joining in, holding your breath, and bearing down only when you cannot resist the urge to push, you will be working in harmony with your uterus and not wasting your effort.

By bearing down for five to six seconds at a time and taking several breaths between bearing-down efforts, you take in more oxygen and make more oxygen available to your baby than if you hold your breath and strain as long as possible. Although there is very little exchange of oxygen across the placenta during contractions, when the uterus relaxes, exchange resumes and the fetus benefits.[4]

It often seems as though the staff is in a rush to get your baby out, imploring you to push as long and hard as you can, without regard for your urge to push. Prolonged maximal bearing down in a normal labor, with or without anesthesia, is usually not necessary and sometimes causes problems (fetal distress, failure of the baby to rotate, arrest of descent, possible perineal tears) that would not have occurred with spontaneous bearing down.[5] Prolonged maximal pushing is best reserved for times when progress is inadequate or the baby is already in distress and other interventions (forceps, vacuum extractor, or cesearean) are being considered. Discuss this with your caregiver in advance and with the nurses when you arrive at the hospital. Include your wishes in your birth plan.

The importance of different positions. Progress and comfort should guide your choice of position. Feel free during the second stage to use positions that are comfortable, that alter progress, either by enhancing slow progress or slowing too rapid progress, or that provide other advantages.

Positions for Second Stage

The chart on pages 151–52 lists a variety of possible positions for second stage and their advantages and disadvantages. (Also, see the illustrations on page 123.) The most common position in North America is semisitting, with legs raised in stirrups or with feet either in footrests or resting on the bed. Although this is convenient for the birth attendant, it is not always the best for the mother's comfort or labor progress. It is a good idea to know all of the positions and their advantages and disadvantages, and be prepared and willing to try them all. Sometimes switching to a new position makes medical intervention (such as a vacuum extractor or forceps) unnecessary. If one position is very uncomfortable, or you make no progress in that position, try another. Positions that take advantage of gravity are an asset and may aid progress and descent.

When the second stage is progressing at a reasonable pace—not too fast or slow—use whatever positions seem most comfortable. If the second stage is going very fast, try a gravity-neutral position such as side-lying to slow it down. Sometimes, even if it hurts, you may have to get into another position, especially if descent is not taking place or if the baby's heart is adversely affected by your position. When birth is imminent, assume the position favored by your doctor or midwife.

The second stage lasts from fifteen minutes to over three hours. The multigravida's second stage is usually faster than it was with her first birth. As with the first stage, the second stage can be divided into three phases:

latent, active, and transition. The three phases share similar characteristics with the three phases of the first stage. The latent phase of both stages is characterized by high spirits, little pain, and slow progress. Both active phases are characterized by total mental absorption, rapid progress, and intense contractions. Both transition phases bridge into the next stage, and are characterized by intense pain and confusion over what to do.

The Latent (Resting) Phase

The latent or resting phase of the second stage is characterized by a lull in uterine activity, a brief rest for you, a pause after the intensity and confusion of transition, and excitement over your baby's imminent arrival. Contractions may be weak and farther apart for ten or twenty minutes, descent may slow or stop temporarily, and your urge to push may be nonexistent or easily satisfied with slight bearing-down efforts. This resting phase takes place because your baby's head has slipped through the cervix, causing your uterus, which had been stretched tightly around your baby, to become a bit slack. It needs time to tighten down around the rest of your baby's body. Then strong contractions resume and your urge to push becomes powerful. This temporary lull is normal and very welcome as a chance to rest and recuperate after transition; it is no cause for alarm.

If your baby is at a very low station when the second stage begins, or if she is descending very fast, you may skip this resting phase, or it may be very brief. You will move right into the active phase as soon as your cervix is fully dilated. If the latent phase lasts for more than fifteen or twenty minutes, your caregiver may ask you to try a gravity-enhancing position, such as squatting, to encourage rotation, descent, and an urge to push.

Positions for Second Stage

Position	Advantages	Disadvantages
Semi-sitting	♦ Convenient for birth attendant ♦ Some gravity advantage when compared with lying flat ♦ Easy to get into on bed or on delivery table	♦ May aggravate hemorrhoids ♦ May restrict free movement of sacrum when more room is needed in pelvis ♦ May slow passage of head under pubic bone
Side-lying	♦ Gravity-neutral ♦ Useful to slow a very rapid second stage ♦ Favorable if mother has high blood pressure ♦ May improve chances of an intact perineum ♦ Takes pressure off hemorrhoids ♦ May reduce backache ♦ Easier to relax between pushing efforts	♦ May not be familiar to birth attendant, who may need to adjust his or her technique for delivery ♦ Is unfavorable if you need to speed second stage
Hands and knees	♦ Gravity-neutral ♦ Helps assist rotation of an OP baby ♦ May improve chances of intact perineum ♦ Takes pressure off hemorrhoids ♦ Allows for free movement, rocking back and forth, tilting pelvis ♦ May reduce backache	♦ Same as for side-lying ♦ Tiring for long periods
Lying on your back with legs pulled back, raising head to push	♦ Pulling legs back and apart helps widen pelvic outlet ♦ Sometimes helps press baby's head beneath pubic bone	♦ Supine hypotension ♦ Maintaining position exhausts mother and may work against gravity
Squatting (with or without sideways movement or kneeling on one knee)	♦ Takes advantage of gravity ♦ Widens pelvic outlet ♦ Requires less bearing-down effort ♦ May enhance rotation and descent in a difficult birth ♦ Helpful if mother does not feel urge to push	♦ Difficult to get into on an ordinary bed (a birthing bed with squatting bar helps) ♦ Difficult for birth attendant to see perineum ♦ May promote too rapid expulsion, leading to perineal tears ♦ May be uncomfortable
Sitting on toilet or commode	♦ Helps mother relax tense perineum for effective bearing-down ♦ Takes advantage of gravity	♦ Toilet may not be available nearby ♦ Mother must move for birth

Position	Advantages	Disadvantages
Supported squat or "dangle" (in an upright position, mother "dangles," supported under her arms by her partner, who may stand and support her with his or her arms, or sit high on bed or counter and support her with his or her thighs)	♦ Enhances descent in difficult birth ♦ Permits relaxation of pelvis, allowing baby to spread pelvic bones ♦ May improve chances of an intact perineum ♦ Eliminates external pressures on pelvis from bed, chair, stretched muscles, etc. ♦ Takes advantage of gravity	♦ May be hard work for support person, if standing ♦ If support person is sitting, may require woman and partner trading places in bed ♦ Awkward for caregiver who may require mother to change position for birth
Semilithotomy (back-lying with head and shoulders elevated, legs in stirrups, and hips on edge of delivery table)	♦ Slight gravity advantage over lying flat ♦ Mother able to view birth ♦ Mother can see birth attendant, which is reassuring ♦ Convenient for attendant ♦ May be necessary for interventions (forceps, episiotomy, etc.) ♦ Stirrups support legs when anesthesia causes loss of mother's muscle control	♦ Leg cramps common ♦ May be frightening to give birth over edge of table ♦ Restricts sacral movement ♦ Possible supine hypotension ♦ Restricts mother's efforts, which could prolong delivery
Lithotomy (lying on back with legs raised in stirrups and hips on edge of delivery table)	♦ Convenient for attendant ♦ May be necessary for interventions (forceps, episiotomy, etc.)	♦ Works against gravity ♦ May be frightening to give birth over edge of table ♦ Leg cramps common ♦ Difficult to view birth or birth attendant ♦ Supine hypotension ♦ Restricts mother's efforts, which could prolong delivery

The Active (Descent) Phase

During the active phase of the second stage, your baby descends and you will feel powerful contractions and an irresistible urge to push. You may find bearing down with all your strength extremely rewarding. You can feel progress. The baby's head distends your vagina and presses on your rectal wall. You may feel alarmed by the full, bulging feeling. You may be afraid to let the baby come down and may tense your pelvic floor against it, while raising your hips as if to escape from it. This will increase pain and slow progress. The most important thing for you to do during pushing efforts is to relax your pelvic floor and bulge your perineum (as in the pelvic floor bulging exercise on page 97). Prenatal perineal massage, in which you relax your perineum while it is being stretched, is excellent preparation for second stage.

Your partner's reminders to "relax," "let the baby out," "open up," "bulge your bottom," or "ease the baby out" are very important at this time, certainly more important than directions to "push, push, push." Your caregiver or partner might press hot, moist towels against your perineum to help you relax and appropriately direct your bearing-down efforts. Clenching your jaw and clamping your lips together is a sign that you are probably tensing the muscles in your vagina. By relaxing your face, particularly your mouth, you may be more able to let go below. Sometimes, even though it hurts, you have to push anyway. If you allow yourself to let go and push despite the pain, you will find it feels better than holding back.

As the active phase progresses, your perineum begins to bulge, your labia part, and your vagina opens as your baby's head descends with each bearing-down effort. Between efforts, your vagina partially closes and your baby's head retreats. Soon, your baby moves further down and her head becomes clearly visible. The joy and anticipation you now feel will give you renewed strength. You may be able to see the baby's head in a mirror. You may want to reach down and touch it. These concrete reminders will help you bear down more efficiently. During this phase, your baby descends and usually completes rotation to the occiput anterior position. Sometimes, for a few contractions during this phase, your baby's head looks and feels strange—soft, slimy, wrinkled, and blue. This may be alarming to you or your partner. The wrinkles are caused by the normal squeezing of the head by the vagina; the loose skin of the baby's scalp forms wrinkles until the baby's head moves

down a little further. The blue color of the skin is normal. The entire baby is blue while inside the uterus, but she pinks up within seconds after birth.

The Transition (Crowning) Phase

The third phase of the second stage is the transition or crowning phase, when your baby passes from inside your body to outside. It begins when your baby's head crowns (that is, it no longer recedes between bearing-down efforts). This phase represents the maximum stretching of your vaginal opening and is characterized by a stinging, burning sensation sometimes

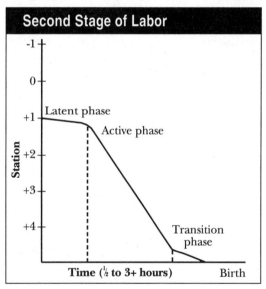

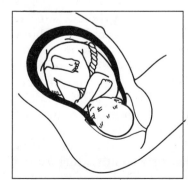
Latent (Resting)

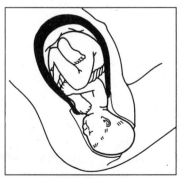
Active (Descent)

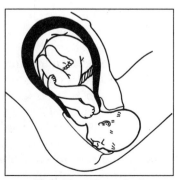
Transition (Crowning)

called the "rim of fire." Strong bearing down at this time increases the pain and the likelihood of a serious tear of your vagina or perineum. Think of the "rim of fire" as your body's signal to stop your bearing-down efforts. Breathe with a light panting or blowing pattern—do not hold your breath—and relax your vagina as the head crowns and emerges. Some birth attendants support the perineum with hot compresses, or massage it with oil or K-Y jelly to assist gradual stretching, or maintain steady pressure on the baby's head to keep it from coming too rapidly. Many caregivers perform an *episiotomy* at this point. This surgical incision of the perineum enlarges the vaginal outlet as the perineum is stretching.

Episiotomy

The use of episiotomy, once a standard practice, has become controversial in recent years. Some caregivers' episiotomy rates are as high as 80 or 90 percent, while others' are as low as 10 to 20 percent. Recent scientific studies have found little benefit to routine episiotomy, and some real risks.[6] As shown in the chart on the next page, many of the long-held beliefs about the advantages of routine episiotomy simply could not be confirmed by these studies.

As a result of the accumulated evidence against routine episiotomy, many caregivers now use techniques to protect the perineum from tearing and to avoid episiotomy, except when the fetus is in distress or when the perineum is unable to stretch. Others are not convinced that avoiding an episiotomy is a good idea and have more confidence in their skills in performing and repairing episiotomies than in avoiding them.

If this matter is important to you, discuss it with your caregiver at a prenatal visit. Rather than asking if he or she does routine episiotomies, ask his or her opinion on episiotomy and how often women need one. Those caregivers with high episiotomy rates tend to believe that a tear is always worse than an episiotomy, and that an intact perineum has probably been overstretched. Those with low rates believe an intact perineum, which can be expected about half the time, is the best result. They point out that most spontaneous tears are smaller than the average episiotomy and that serious large tears are more likely with an episiotomy than without one.

If you wish to avoid an episiotomy, you should realize that you have a 50 percent chance of a tear, but that most of these tears are smaller or about the same as the average episiotomy. The more experienced your caregiver is in avoiding episiotomies, the better your chances are for an intact perineum or a minor tear. Besides choosing the right caregiver, you can do other things to help safely avoid an episiotomy. During pregnancy, eat a balanced diet to promote healthy tissues and do perineal massage (described on page 126). During the second stage, use appropriate positions and bear down spontaneously without excessive straining. At the time of birth, follow your caregiver's instructions and pant as the baby's head crowns and is born.

Further discussion on the advantages and disadvantages of episiotomies can be found in the chart on page 187.

Birth

Your baby emerges, first the top of the head to the ears, then her face—bluish-gray and soaking wet. After her head is out, it rotates to the side. This allows her shoulders to slip more easily through the pelvis. One shoulder (the one near your pubic bone) emerges, and then the rest of the baby comes rather quickly. You or your partner may want to help lift the baby out. The entire baby appears bluish at first and may be streaked with blood. She also will be partially covered with the white, lotionlike vernix. With her first breath, which comes within seconds, her skin begins to turn to more normal flesh tones. All babies,

Research Findings on Common Beliefs about Episiotomy

The findings below come from comparative studies of routine versus selective episiotomy.

Many caregivers base their practice of routine episiotomy on these beliefs.[a]

Belief	Finding
Shortens second stage	True, by 5 to 15 minutes. An early episiotomy can cause hemorrhage in the mother, so caregivers must do an episiotomy when most of the second stage has passed.
Spares baby from brain damage or other harm	Apgar scores and newborn problems were the same. With fetal heart rate monitoring, those babies who need to be delivered quickly are identified and an episiotomy is performed.
Prevents tears	Approximately one half of all women who have no episiotomy will have no tear and need no stitches. Smaller tears (first or second degree) are prevented, but larger (third and fourth degree) tears are far more likely with episiotomy. There may be more tears toward the front of the vagina when an episiotomy is not performed. Caregiver skills and techniques may be a factor here.
Preserves strength of pelvic floor	No differences were found up to 3 years after birth.
Prevents stretching of pelvic floor	The pelvic floor has already stretched considerably before the episiotomy is performed.
Reduces likelihood of future pelvic floor problems: leaking of urine (incontinence), uterine prolapse ("fallen uterus"), cystocele (protrusion of bladder into vagina), rectocele (protrusion of rectum into vagina), sexual difficulties	Incontinence was the same three year later. Sexual difficulties were no different. No differences in the other problems, although there have been no studies that have followed women for more than 3 years after birth.
Is easier to repair	Debatable, since approximately half of the women in the selective episiotomy group need no repair, and since the very extensive tears are far more likely to occur when episiotomies are performed.

[a] J. Sleep et al., "Care during the Second Stage of Labour," *Effective Care in Pregnancy and Childbirth,* Vol. 2 (New York: Oxford University Press, 1989); P. Shiono et al., "Midline Episiotomies—More Harm than Good," *Obstetrics and Gynecology* 75 (May 1990): 765-70; D. Banta and S. Thacker, "Benefits and Risks of Episiotomy: An Interpretative Review of the English Language Literature, 1860-1980," *Obstetric and Gynecologic Survey* 38 (November 1983): 322-38.

whether dark- or light-skinned, go through these color changes in the first minute or two of life. Some are quite ruddy until their respiration and circulation adjust to normal. To assist respiration by clearing your baby's airway of mucus, blood, meconium, or amniotic fluid, your doctor or midwife may suction your baby's nose and mouth as soon as her head is out and again later. Your baby may be placed on your abdomen or in your arms to await the delivery of your placenta. (See chapter 13 for more information about the advantages and disadvantages of routine suctioning and the appearance of a newborn.)

How do you feel, now that the baby is born? Women's reactions vary. You may first feel disbelieving, then grateful and relieved that the baby is out and that the contractions are over, or nearly so. These feelings may predominate over your interest in the baby at first, especially if it has been a long, tiring labor. Or you may focus immediately on the baby. Many women are surprised, awed, or full of wonder at their baby's appearance. The first moments, waiting for

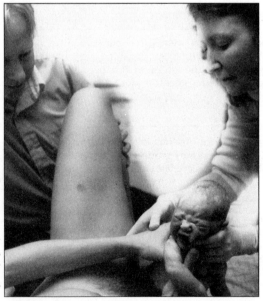

After the head and shoulders appear, the baby quickly emerges.

—photograph by Harriette Hartigan/Artemis

the baby to begin breathing and crying, are suspenseful. Everyone's attention is on the baby, intently awaiting the gurgling, grimacing, and crying as the first breath is taken. Smiles of relief and joy greet the baby's first cry. Then you await the birth of the placenta. You may find yourself unable to focus entirely on your baby because your caregiver is inspecting your perineum and checking for separation of your placenta, which may be painful and distracting. The full impact—the feelings of fulfillment and of love for your baby and your partner—may not come until after your placenta is born and your caregiver has finished the afterbirth tasks. Then you can devote yourself completely to your baby.

Your partner may be overwhelmed with emotion at this time—deep joy and love for you and the baby, giddiness, exhaustion, relief. Tears may flow. The baby becomes the focus of attention.

The Third Stage of Labor— Delivery of the Placenta

The third stage, the shortest of all, begins with the birth of your baby and ends when your placenta is born. It lasts about ten to thirty minutes. After your baby is born, there is a brief lull, then your uterus resumes contractions and separates itself from the placenta. You might need to continue relaxation and patterned breathing because the uterus sometimes cramps vigorously. You might, on the other hand, be so engrossed in your baby that you hardly notice the third stage. Some parents enjoy seeing the placenta after it is delivered.

Immediately after the birth, your baby will receive close medical attention. As soon as his breathing is established and the baby is dried off, your caregiver performs a routine examination. Your baby's overall condition is

Birth

The head shows (1), gradually emerges (2), crowns (3), and is born (4). The baby then rotates to one side, allowing the shoulders to fit through the pelvis (5 and 6).

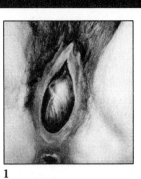

1

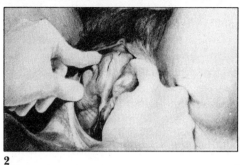

2

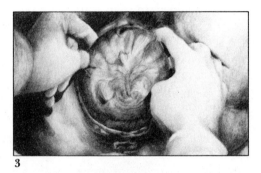

3

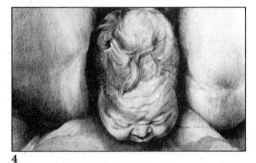

4

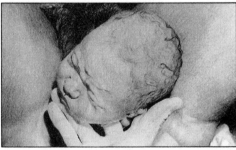

5

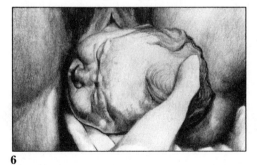

6

Then–suddenly–the baby slips out, wet, warm, blinking, and crying. The caregiver clamps the cord and may suction the baby's nose and mouth (7).

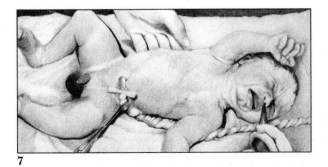

7

evaluated twice—at one minute and again at five minutes—using the Apgar score, a grading system devised by Dr. Virginia Apgar. Five areas are graded, each with a maximum of two points, making ten the highest possible score. The chart below illustrates how newborns are evaluated.

The baby receives a total score each time the test is done. A first (one-minute) score of seven to ten indicates a normal baby (babies seldom receive a "ten"; most babies' hands and feet are bluish for a while, lowering their Apgar score); four to six indicates mild to moderate depression; zero to three indicates severe depression. A score of six or less means that the baby needs extra medical attention and more observation. The second (five-minute) score is usually higher than the first, indicating improvement with time and/or medical assistance. While Apgar scores are helpful, especially in detecting babies who need extra immediate medical attention, they are not perfect indicators of the baby's overall health. A physician or midwife will perform a thorough newborn exam within a few hours of birth to provide a more accurate assessment of your baby's condition.

Clamping and Cutting the Cord

The umbilical cord is cut soon after the birth. It is first clamped in two places and then cut with scissors between the two clamps. Sometimes the father or partner makes the cut. The exact timing of cord clamping and cutting is a subject of some disagreement.

Some people believe that by delaying the clamping of the cord, the baby receives more oxygen. This is not true, because even though blood continues to flow back and forth between placenta and baby, it does not contain oxygen. The placenta ceases transferring oxygen as soon as the baby is out, even before it separates from the wall of the uterus.

The amount of blood passing to the baby is influenced by the timing of cord clamping and the position of the baby in relation to the placenta. When the uterus contracts, it squeezes blood out of the placenta into the baby's body. If the cord is clamped then, the baby will have a higher blood volume. Between contractions, the baby's heart pumps blood back to the placenta (it is the baby's heartbeat that causes the cord to pulsate). If the cord is clamped between con-

Apgar Scoring

Sign	0 points	1 point	2 points
Heart rate	Absent	Below 100/minute	Above 100/minute
Respiratory effort	Absent	Slow, irregular	Good, crying
Muscle tone	Limp	Arms and legs flexed	Active movement
Reflex irritability (reaction to baby's nose being suctioned)	No response	Grimace	Sneeze, cough, pulls away
Skin color	Blue-gray, pale all over	Normal skin color, except bluish hands and feet	Normal skin color all over

tractions, the baby's blood volume is lower. The shift of blood between the placenta and baby can also be affected by gravity. If the baby is held high above the level of the placenta, more blood flows from baby to placenta. If the baby is held below the placenta, blood flows from placenta to baby. Within a few minutes, exposure of the cord to the air causes expansion of Wharton's jelly (a substance contained within the cord) and compression of the blood vessels in the cord. From then on, there is no movement of blood in either direction.

Timing of cord clamping and cutting, then, does not affect the baby's oxygen levels but does influence the blood volume. Whether clamping takes place between contractions, during a contraction, or after the cord stops pulsating will influence the volume of blood within the baby's circulatory system. A low blood volume can lead to anemia; excessive blood volume can overload the baby's circulatory system and increase the chances of newborn jaundice. To achieve the optimal blood volume, the caregiver places the baby at the level of the placenta (on the mother's abdomen) until the cord stops pulsating.

Discuss the timing of cord clamping with your doctor or midwife and be sure to include your preferences in your birth plan. There are some circumstances when immediate cord cutting is necessary—for example, with a short cord or a cord wrapped tightly around the neck.

The Fourth Stage of Labor—Recovery

The fourth stage begins when the placenta is born and lasts until your condition is stable, as indicated by your blood pressure, pulse, *lochia* (the normal vaginal discharge of blood from the uterus), and uterine tone. This usually takes about one or two hours. If anesthesia was used, if labor was difficult or prolonged, or if delivery was by cesarean, the fourth stage may last longer.

After birth the uterus immediately begins the process of *involution* (returning to its nonpregnant state). By continuing to contract, the uterus shuts off the open blood vessels at the site of the placenta, preventing excessive blood loss, and sloughs off the extra lining that built up during the pregnancy. You will begin passing lochia immediately and will need to wear a sanitary pad.

Your nurse or midwife will check your uterus frequently to make sure that the fundus (the top of the uterus) remains firm after the birth. If it is relaxed, she or he will massage it firmly to cause it to contract, which can be very painful. You might check your fundus yourself and, if it seems soft, massage it yourself. This way you can keep your uterus firm with less discomfort. This fundal massage cannot be ignored, because the uterus can bleed excessively if it is not firm.

To Massage Your Uterus

Lie flat on your back and check your fundus by pressing several areas of your abdomen above your pubic bone. If you feel your uterus as firm as a grapefruit, you do not need to massage it. If you cannot feel your uterus, massage as follows:

With one hand slightly cupped, massage your lower abdomen firmly with small circular movements until you feel your uterus contract and become firm. It may be painful. If you cannot make your uterus contract, tell your nurse or midwife.

During the first minutes after birth, you may experience trembling in your legs, pain as your uterus contracts (*afterpains,* a common occurrence, especially in multigravidas), and swelling and discomfort in your perineum from the stretching or stitches. A warm blanket helps relieve trembling, and an ice pack on your perineum reduces discomfort and may control swelling. Use slow breathing if necessary for the afterpains.

You may feel hungry and thirsty—not at all surprising, since you have been working hard and have probably missed some meals.

You will probably hold your baby and let her nuzzle at your breast. Many babies are ready to suckle at this time. (See page 271 for advice on the first feeding.)

Your New Family

While your body is settling down after the birth, your family is settling down also. You, your partner, and any other family members or close friends will savor these first moments with the baby. The labor stimulates a state of wakefulness and alertness in the baby that may last for several hours. During this time, your baby is likely to become calm and alert, and she will begin observing and sensing the new sounds, smells, sights, touches, and tastes around her. If the light is not too bright, she stares, particularly at faces. You can ask to dim the lights or use your hand to shield your baby's eyes from the bright light. As your baby cuddles with you, gazes into your face, or suckles at your breast, you will probably find her fascinating and irresistible. This is a time of falling in love and is a significant step in attachment, or bonding. Your partner also will want to hold her close, perhaps skin-to-skin, and enjoy these first moments together.

In most hospitals, routine care of the healthy newborn includes time for the baby and her family to be together. Check your hospital's policies; if you wish to be together in privacy for an hour or more after birth, discuss the possibility with your doctor or midwife and the nursing administration. If necessary, include this wish in your birth plan, or get a doctor's order for delaying the baby's admission to the nursery. Some family-centered hospitals do not admit healthy babies to the nursery. The babies stay with their mothers and go to the nursery only if they develop problems. Routine observations or procedures can be performed on the normal newborn in the presence and even in the arms of the mother or partner. See chapter 13 for a description of procedures in newborn care.

After one to several hours, the baby usually falls deeply asleep. The initial exhilaration that you feel after the birth may give way to fatigue, the aftermath of labor. At this time, someone who is awake and alert should observe your and your baby's vital signs. In the hospital, a nurse will do the job. After a home birth, the observations are made by the midwife, a birth assistant, or an informed and rested friend or relative. Your partner may be as tired as you and may be unable to take on these responsibilities until he or she gets some sleep.

The fourth stage begins your adjustments to your nonpregnant state and the new state of parenthood. The "real" baby replaces the "imagined" baby; your body begins the process of involution; and you begin the important work of reviewing, understanding, and gaining perspective on your labor and birth experiences.

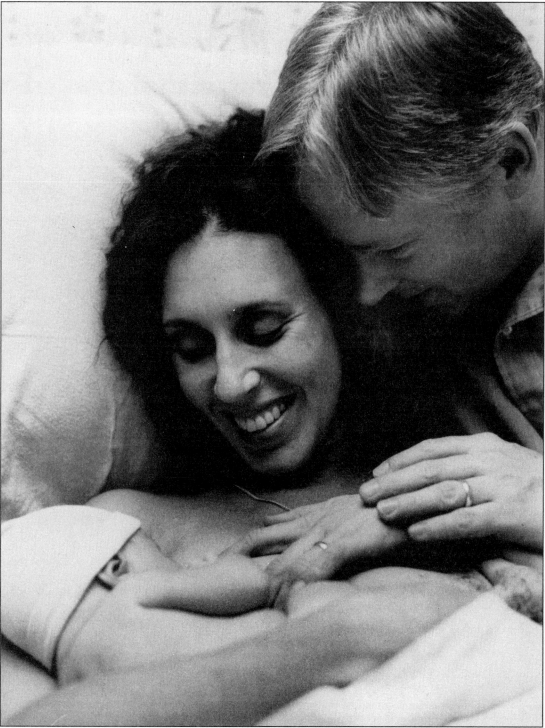

Smiles of relief and joy greet the baby.

—photograph by Harriette Hartigan/Artemis

Labor and Birth Guide

	Prelabor (late pregnancy)	Stage I: Effacement and dilation of cervix		
		Latent phase	Active phase	Transition
		2 cm 3 cm 4 cm	5 cm 6 cm 7 cm	8 cm 9 cm 10 cm
Cervical changes	◆ Some forward movement, ripening, partial efface-ment, possible dilation to 1 or 2 cm			
Breathing pattern	◆ No breathing pattern needed, usually; if needed, slow breathing	◆ Slow breathing; begin when unable to walk or talk through contractions; use for as long as possible	◆ Light (accelerated) breathing; begin when slow breathing no longer keeps you relaxed or becomes difficult	◆ Variable (transition) breathing pattern, begin if necessary to change breath-ing pattern
Contraction pattern	0 15 SEC 30 45 60 75 90 **Prelabor Contraction**	0 15 SEC 30 45 60 75 90 **Slow Breathing**	0 15 SEC 30 45 60 75 90 **Light (Accelerated) Breathing**	0 15 SEC 30 45 60 75 90 **Variable (Transition) Breathing**
Possible physical signs	◆ Nonprogressing contrac-tions (lasting a short time or continuing, may go away with change in activity) ◆ Menstrual-like cramps ◆ "Restless" backache ◆ Increased energy (nesting urge) ◆ Small chance of rupture of membranes (leaking or gush of fluid from vagina) ◆ Bloody show ◆ Loose bowel movements	◆ Same as prelabor, except that contractions begin to progress ◆ Progressing contractions (becoming longer, strong-er, and more frequent)	◆ Contractions very intense, closer together, (less than 5 minutes apart), longer (more than 1 minute) ◆ Contractions continue progressing ◆ Rupture of membranes, if it has not already occurred	◆ Very strong, long contrac-tions; may have double peaks ◆ Very little rest between contractions (30 seconds to 3 minutes) ◆ Pressure on vagina and rectum ◆ Possible urge to push ◆ Nausea, vomiting ◆ Leg cramps ◆ Uncontrollable shaking ◆ Sensitivity to touch ◆ Drowsiness ◆ Hiccups ◆ Cold feet ◆ Flushed face ◆ Rupture of membranes, if has not already occurred

| | Prelabor (late pregnancy) | Stage 1: Effacement and dilation of cervix | | |
		Latent phase	Active phase	Transition
Possible emotional signs	◆ Premonitions ◆ Exhilaration, excitement ◆ Anticipation ◆ Confusion whether this is labor or not ◆ Distractible during contractions	◆ Uncertain whether in labor ◆ Excited ◆ Confident ◆ Talkative ◆ Apprehensive ◆ Possibly distractible during contractions	◆ Feel trapped, discouraged, and tired ◆ Serious; uninterested in anything but labor ◆ Cannot tolerate small talk or distracting conversation	◆ Restless ◆ Irritable ◆ Forgetful ◆ Fearful ◆ Have difficulty with relaxation and breathing pattern ◆ Overwhelmed, want to give up
What to do: mother	◆ Prepare and pack bag ◆ Alternate pleasant, mild, distracting activity with rest or nap ◆ Walk ◆ Sleep (at night) ◆ Bathe or shower ◆ Eat and drink normally	◆ Alternate rest and activity (appropriate to time of day) ◆ Empty bladder every hour ◆ Time and record contractions ◆ Eat and drink sensibly, according to desire ◆ Bathe or shower for comfort and cleanliness ◆ Relax ◆ Begin slow breathing when you are unable to walk or talk through a contraction ◆ Call doctor or midwife (with membrane rupture, progressing contractions, or other concerns)	◆ Go to the hospital or birth center (or caregiver arrives at home) ◆ Settle in, go over birth plan with nurse ◆ Use relaxation, comfort, and breathing techniques (light), attention-focusing (visualization, massage ◆ Alternate rest and activity ◆ Use positions of comfort ◆ Drink liquids, suck ice chips or popsicles ◆ Empty bladder ◆ Relieve backache (pelvic tilt, change positions every 30 minutes)	◆ Take contractions one at a time ◆ Remember—transition is intense, but short ◆ Use relaxation and breathing patterns (variable), pant to control urge to push, if necessary ◆ Use focal point and massage as desired ◆ Change position as needed for comfort
What to do: partner	◆ Help pack ◆ Rest or sleep (at night) ◆ Give moral support ◆ Encourage mild activity (during day) ◆ Make sure you can be reached while away	◆ Help pass the time with walking, talking, music, TV, meal preparation for after birth, games, and so on ◆ Time contractions ◆ Help her relax as necessary ◆ Suggest comfort measures as indicated (massage, back rub, food, fluids) ◆ Help her prepare to go to hospital or get ready for home birth ◆ Follow her lead	◆ Remain calm ◆ Help her relax and use breathing pattern ◆ Give her your undivided attention with every contraction ◆ Use touch, stroking, massage, counterpressure, cold or hot pack ◆ Use verbal encouragement, soothing voice ◆ Offer ice, liquids ◆ Remind her to urinate ◆ Help her move in bed, stand, or walk ◆ Match her mood	◆ Know signs of transition ◆ Encourage and reassure her; give clear directions ◆ Remind her that transition is short ◆ Compliment her; avoid criticizing her ◆ Stay with her ◆ Help with relaxation and breathing pattern; maintain eye contact if she begins to fight contractions ◆ Comfort her (back rubs, warm or cold packs, ice chips) ◆ Hold her tight

continued

	Stage 2: Birth of baby	Stage 3: Delivery of placenta	Stage 4: Recovery—first hours after birth
Breathing pattern	• Bearing down or pushing, (spontaneous, directed, or prolonged)	• Slow or light breathing • May push to expel placenta	• Slow breathing if necessary for afterpains or perineal discomfort
Possible physical signs	• Possible lull in contractions at first • Urge to push becomes stronger with descent of baby • Pressure of baby stretches vagina • Crowning ("rim of fire") • Birth of baby's head, then body	• Mild to moderate contractions • Uncontrolled shaking • Pain with inspection of vagina or administration of local anesthetic and possible stitches	• Possible shaking • Afterpains—painful uterine contractions, especially with multigravidas who are breastfeeding • Perineal discomfort, swelling • Difficulty with urination • Hunger
Possible emotional signs	• Cheerful • Anxious to get the baby out • Excitement and optimism • Fatigue • Amazement at effort required • Relief	• Excitement • Fatigue • Relief • Engrossment with baby • Surprise, if contractions are painful	• Excitement, elation • Fatigue, exhaustion • Surprise, disappointment at pain of vaginal inspection, repair • Relief • "Empty" feeling • Desire to talk and review labor and birth • Surprise or fascination with appearance of baby • Desire to see and hold baby
What to do: mother	• Relax perineum, buttocks, and legs • Bear down with the urge to push during contractions • Change position for comfort or to aid descent as necessary • Pant as necessary during crowning, keeping chin up • Keep eyes open; listen to doctor or midwife • Touch baby's head if desired and allowed	• Use breathing patterns as necessary • Push placenta out as directed • Hold baby (skin to skin) • Relax and enjoy baby • Watch initial examination and care of baby • Ask to see placenta, if desired	• Rest, relax • Interact with baby (cuddle, stroke, kiss, breastfeed, talk to) • Drink or eat • Massage fundus • Ask for ice pack for perineum to decrease discomfort and swelling
What to do: partner	• Help her change positions • Support her in her chosen position • Remind her of the baby • Remind her to relax her perineum and keep her eyes open • Give her encouragement, approval • Help with panting or pushing as necessary • Watch and, if desired, record birth	• Help with breathing pattern if needed • Cut cord if allowed and desired • Hold baby or help mother hold baby • Watch initial examination and care of baby	• Hold, touch, talk to baby; family time • Comfort mother as necessary (change positions, fluids, back rubs) • Discuss the birth experience with mother, caregiver • May go to nursery with baby, if baby is taken there • Call family and friends

Chapter 9

Labor Variations, Complications, and Interventions

Each birth experience is unique. Some labors and births are very short, some are taxingly long, and some require surgical intervention (episiotomy, cesarean birth) or instrumental delivery (forceps, vacuum extraction). You can expect that your experience will be different from your mother's, your sister's, or even your own prior experiences. Because no one can predict what kind of labor and birth you will have, you will want to prepare for all possibilities and include your ideas and wishes in your birth plan. This chapter discusses variations and complications in labor and birth and how they can be handled both by you with special effort and by your caregiver with medical or surgical interventions.

A labor *variation* presents additional problems and challenges beyond the typical labor but is still within the wide range of normal. A variation in itself does not pose dangers to either the mother or the baby, but it does pose problems that require the mother and her partner to draw more deeply on their resources.

A labor *complication* presents problems to the mother or baby that cannot be solved by the extra efforts of the mother and her partner. Such labors require medical assistance and intervention to ensure an optimal outcome. Sometimes a variation becomes a complication when, despite all the mother's efforts, the problem remains unsolved. Other complications are emergencies that pose immediate problems for the mother or baby and require prompt medical attention.

Monitoring Techniques

By monitoring your condition and your baby's during labor, your doctor or midwife becomes aware of labor variations and can detect most complications. The monitoring techniques described below help identify variations and complications, and they help your caregiver decide how to manage your labor, especially if it is a difficult one.

Monitoring the Mother

Periodic vaginal exams by the nurse or caregiver determine the dilation of your cervix, and the station, presentation, and position of your fetus. They are recorded on a time chart or labor graph to show how your labor is progressing. The frequency and intensity of your contractions will be observed by the nurse or midwife, who will assess them either by feeling your contractions with her hand or by using an electronic monitor (see pages 185–86). Throughout labor, your nurse or midwife will assess your blood pressure, temperature, pulse, urine output, and fluid intake.

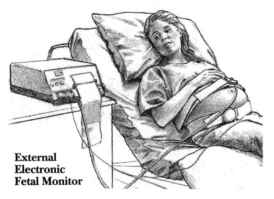

External Electronic Fetal Monitor

Monitoring the Fetus

Fetal Heart Rate

The fetal heart rate responds to changes in the availability of oxygen or to other stresses; it is one indicator of fetal well-being. Your caregivers will evaluate the baby's heart rate, noting any changes and the relationship of these changes to uterine contractions, fetal movements, the administration of medications, your position, or other factors. They monitor the fetal heart rate in two ways: *auscultation* (listening and counting the heartbeats) with a special fetal stethoscope or with a hand-held ultrasound stethoscope called "the Doppler"; or with an *electronic fetal monitor* (EFM), a machine that detects and prints out a graph of fetal heartbeats. The machine receives impulses from either an ultrasound device placed on your abdomen or a scalp electrode attached to your baby's head (or other presenting part). The mother's uterine contractions are detected and graphed on the printout at the same time. (See pages 184–86 for more information.)

Amniotic Fluid

The appearance of the amniotic fluid gives useful information about the baby's condition. A strong odor may indicate an infection. A pink or red color may indicate bleeding from the placenta. A green or dark color means the baby has expelled meconium from her bowels, which is a warning sign that she has been stressed. If meconium is present, your caregiver will check the fetal heart tones frequently to determine the degree of fetal distress. At delivery, your caregiver will probably suction the baby's nose and mouth as soon as the head is out, and then suction again more deeply as soon as the baby's entire body is born. This is done in hopes of removing meconium from the baby's airway before she breathes it into her lungs, which can create breathing problems or pneumonia.

Fetal Stimulation Test

If fetal distress is suspected because of observed fetal heart rate changes, your caregiver may seek to confirm the diagnosis by pressing or scratching your fetus's scalp during a vaginal exam (the fetal scalp stimulation test) or by making a loud buzzing, clapping, or clanging noise near the uterus (the fetal acoustic stimulation test). If the fetal heart rate speeds up, it is a good sign that your baby is all right. If not, it may indicate fetal distress.

Fetal Scalp Blood Sample

If your caregiver suspects fetal complications, he or she may take a sample of scalp blood from a small cut in the fetus's head. The blood sample is analyzed for changes in the blood due to a lack of oxygen.

The Need to Start Labor

Sometimes problems arise for either the mother or the fetus in late pregnancy, and the doctor or midwife and the parents agree that the best way to handle the problem is to start labor. The decision is usually made after examining the mother, running lab tests, and testing for fetal well-being and maturity (see chapter 3).

Some of the most common reasons for starting labor are a clearly prolonged pregnancy, membranes that have been ruptured for a long time, pregnancy-induced hypertension (PIH), preeclampsia, a fetus who is no longer growing or thriving in the uterus, and particular illnesses in the mother (diabetes, heart disease, and so on). When any of these conditions is suspected or known, the mother and fetus are watched closely. If it appears that one or the other might be harmed if the pregnancy continues, labor is started.

If you are in such a situation, there may be time for you to try some ways to start your own labor. If you are successful, you may avoid a medical induction of labor, a procedure that has some disadvantages, or you may cause enough cervical changes to make a medical induction easier and more likely to succeed. If, because of medical problems, you do not have time to use these techniques, or if they do not start your labor, then your caregiver has several methods available for inducing labor. These are described on page 169 and in the chart on pages 183–84.

What You Can Do to Start or Stimulate Labor

When it is important that labor start, or when labor is progressing too slowly, you might try these measures. *Consult your caregiver before trying any of these techniques,* because they carry some risks, as do the medical methods of inducing labor.

Walking

Long walks (thirty minutes or several hours) may help start labor, but are more effective in keeping labor going than in starting it. If it is important for you to go into labor soon, you may want to use the other more effective and less tiring methods listed below.

Acupressure

Firm finger or thumb pressure over particular acupuncture points sometimes starts contractions or makes them stronger. One such point (called "Spleen 6") is located four

fingerbreadths above the inner anklebone. You press the inside of your shin bone, angling forward and in. This is a painful spot. Try pressing three times for ten to fifteen seconds each time, resting for a few seconds in between.

Caution: Because pressure on Spleen 6 can cause contractions, you should not do it to yourself until it is appropriate for you to go into labor. To practice finding the acupuncture point, try it on a nonpregnant friend or your partner.

Another method of ripening the cervix or causing contractions involves stimulation of particular acupressure points with TENS (transcutaneous electrical nerve stimulation).[1] (See pages 114–15 for a description of TENS.) The points used are Spleen 6, located above the inner ankle bone, and Liver 3, located on the top of the foot. (Exact locations should be determined by your caregiver.)

Bowel Stimulation

You can sometimes start labor by stimulating your bowels to contract and empty. This may increase the production of prostaglandins, which cause the cervix to ripen.

♦ Sometimes an *enema* will start labor by causing enough bowel action to initiate uterine activity. You can buy complete, disposable enema units at your drugstore and give yourself the enema at home. You might also be able to get an enema in the hospital. Enemas that use a larger volume of liquid are more effective (but also more unpleasant) than the small-volume ones designed for home use.

♦ *Castor oil* causes powerful contractions of the bowel and is a strong laxative. Castor oil induction has been used with some success for years.[2] It may cause contractions soon after taking it, or it may be a matter of hours before you notice contractions. Ask your caregiver for specific instructions. Castor oil may cause painful intestinal cramping and diarrhea and could aggravate hemorrhoids. It is sometimes used in combination with an enema.

Orgasm, Clitoral Stimulation, Intercourse

Sexual excitement, particularly orgasm, causes contractions of the uterus. Prostaglandins are released into your bloodstream under these circumstances and act on the uterus and cervix. Prostaglandins are also present in semen, and after intercourse they act directly on the cervix. Manual or oral stimulation of the clitoris, even without orgasm, may also be effective in starting labor. Intercourse, manual stimulation, and oral-genital stimulation can be done as long as the membranes are intact and it is comfortable for you and your partner. If your membranes have broken, only clitoral stimulation should be done, as nothing should enter the vagina. Blowing into the vagina is dangerous and should never be done. If you choose these techniques, make them as pleasant as possible. Try to forget your goal of starting labor, and enjoy the sexual experience.

Nipple Stimulation

Stimulating your nipples causes the release of your own oxytocin, which contracts your uterus and often succeeds in either ripening the cervix or starting labor. You may have to repeat this measure after a few hours or for half a day.

Caution: Occasionally, nipple stimulation causes contractions that last too long (more than sixty seconds) or are too strong (painful), and the baby may not tolerate them. To protect against these potential problems, you might do nipple stimulation first in the hospital or clinic while your contractions are measured by an electronic fetal monitor. This is actually how a test of fetal well-being (the contraction stress test) is carried out. Then, if all is well, you can go home and continue nipple stimulation. Some caregivers are more comfortable with nipple stimulation if such a test is done first. Another way to protect against too long or too strong contractions is to time the contractions caused by the nipple stimulation. If they are painful or if they last longer than one minute, decrease the nipple stimulation (from both breasts to one; from continuous to intermittent).

♦ *Use self-stimulation.* Lightly stroke or brush one nipple with your fingertips or wash cloth, or roll it between your fingers. Begin with one nipple. Within a few minutes you will probably feel contractions. If not, stimulate both nipples. Because contractions may stop when you stop nipple stimulation, you may have to continue stroking or nipple rolling on and off for hours, especially if you are trying to start labor soon. If your goal is to ripen your cervix, and you are not under pressure to go right into labor (for example, if an induction is scheduled within a few days), you might stimulate or gently massage your breasts with warm, moist towels for an hour, three times a day, for several days.[3]

♦ *Use an electric or manual breast pump* for ten to twenty minutes per breast. (Electric pumps are often available in the hospital.)[4]

♦ *Caressing and oral stimulation by your partner* may cause contractions. Try this for as long as you find it effective and pleasant, or until contractions become strong.

♦ *Try nursing a borrowed baby.* Suckling by a three- to twelve-week-old baby is the most effective form of nipple stimulation. At this age, babies are usually efficient nursers but are not too fussy to suckle from the breast of someone other than their mother. The baby needs to be awake and not very hungry; a sleepy baby will not suck, and a hungry baby gets frustrated. The baby's fussy period is a good time, because the baby often wants simply to suck, not to eat. Suckling for at least ten minutes on each side seems to be effective. Sit on a waterproof pad, because your membranes might rupture. Your breasts and hands should be clean. Both you and the borrowed baby should be free of infection and disease.

Herbal Tea and Tinctures

Some caregivers recommend teas or various tinctures to induce labor. They should be used only with the knowledge and guidance of your caregiver, since they contain active ingredients that enter the bloodstream, have potential undesired side effects, and therefore represent a medical approach to inducing labor. For example, one of the most common, blue cohosh tea, causes your uterus to contract, but can also cause your blood pressure to rise to unsafe levels.[5]

Medical Induction of Labor

There are several methods used by physicians and midwives to start labor: stripping the membranes, artificial rupture of membranes (AROM), prostaglandin gel, and intravenous Pitocin. For a description of these methods, see the chart on page 183.

The choice of method depends on the state of your cervix and the philosophy of your caregiver and hospital. If you are scheduled for an induction, find out which method will be used so you will know what to expect.

♦ *Stripping the membranes* is a relatively non-invasive procedure, but it has a low success rate. Your caregiver might want to try it if you are at or beyond your due date and your cervix is very ripe and dilated enough to allow insertion of your caregiver's finger.

♦ *Artificial rupture of the membranes (AROM)* is rarely successful if your cervix is firm (unripe), thick, and posterior. AROM is sometimes tried before or along with Pitocin if your cervix is found to be "favorable" for the procedure, that is, ripe, anterior, and partially effaced and dilated.

♦ *Prostaglandin gel* is less invasive and more effective than AROM when the cervix is unfavorable, but it is not available everywhere in the United States. Many hospitals do not use prostaglandin gel because the U.S. Food and Drug Administration (FDA) has not approved it for the purpose of ripening the cervix. The reason that it has not been approved is not that the FDA believes it unsafe, but simply because no drug manufacturer is asking the FDA to consider it. Prostaglandin gel has been widely studied in Canada and Europe and is a standard method of induction there. In America, after evaluating the research on prostaglandin gel for ripening the cervix, many physicians feel that the value and reasonable safety of prostaglandins have been established and use it with confidence.

♦ *Pitocin infusion* is the most common type of medical induction in the United States. Because it is less likely to succeed when the cervix is thicker, posterior, and unripe, a combined approach using prostaglandin gel followed by Pitocin is becoming more popular. With this method, prostaglandin gel is inserted in or around the cervix once or twice or more within a period of a day or two. Then, for the next day or two, intravenous Pitocin is given. Often the Pitocin is discontinued at night to allow the mother to eat and sleep. This gradual approach, though most successful, can be emotionally and physically draining for the mother and her partner.

Short, Fast (Precipitate) Labor

A *precipitate labor* lasts less than three hours. Though a short labor probably sounds appealing, a precipitate labor presents its own special problems and challenges. The latent phase of a precipitate labor passes unnoticed or so quietly and uneventfully that you miss the early signs of labor. Suddenly, you find yourself in active, hard labor without time to prepare psychologically. The first noticeable contractions can be long and very painful. You may feel panicked and confused, unprepared and discouraged. You may lose faith in your ability to handle labor.

If you are planning a hospital birth, you hurry off to the hospital while trying to cope with these strong, almost continuous labor contractions, all the time thinking that this is early labor and feeling overwhelmed by the thought of what is yet to come! At the hospital, you may be met with a flurry of activity and an unfamiliar doctor or midwife. You may feel anxious if your partner was unable to accompany you. As a result, you may experience feelings of loneliness, a lack of direction, and panic. In fact, you may feel like giving up and taking all the medication available to you to make the pain go away. Your partner is caught off guard, too, and may be shocked by the sudden intensity of your labor and surprised by your reaction to what he or she believes is early labor.

What You Can Do

Do not give up on yourself. Trust your ability to get through this. Try not to tense with your contractions. Try each level of breathing, starting with slow breathing, to find the level that helps you cope. Have a vaginal exam before you make any decision about pain medication. You may have dilated to eight or ten centimeters. If labor has pro-

gressed this rapidly, birth will soon follow and anesthesia may be unnecessary or may take effect too late to help you. What you need more than anything is reassurance that this labor is normal and is progressing very rapidly. You also need help in handling the painful contractions.

Because your contractions will be intense and very effective, you may have the urge to push before the hospital staff is ready. When the second stage begins, lie on your side and pant or gently bear down, rather than using an upright position. This will give your birth canal and perineum more time to stretch, decrease the likelihood of tearing, and protect your baby's head from being pressed through the vagina too rapidly.

After the birth, you will probably feel relieved that you and the baby are safe, but stunned that it is over so quickly. You may need to review what happened. Talk with the staff and your partner to put the pieces together. You may also experience disappointment because your labor passed so quickly you were not able to savor it, use all the breathing and relaxation techniques, or share it with your partner as you had planned.

Rapid Birth without Medical Help

Sometimes labor progresses too rapidly for you to get to the hospital in time. Babies are occasionally born in cars or at home under these circumstances. What if you are alone or with only your partner when the baby starts to come? Initially, you may panic and temporarily forget all you know about labor, birth, and coping techniques.

If the baby is truly about to be born, it is far better to stay home, where it is warm and comfortable, than to attempt to rush to the hospital. If the baby starts to come during your ride to the hospital, you'll have to pull over to the side of the road, deliver your baby, and then continue to the hospital. Usually, babies born under these circumstances are in excellent condition, but the following guidelines will help you and your partner during such an emergency and ensure the best possible outcome.

Signs of an Imminent Birth

♦ You feel a strong urge to bear down.

♦ You see the baby's head or presenting part at the vagina.

♦ You feel the baby coming.

Getting Help

♦ If you are alone when you have the above signs that birth is imminent, try to get help from someone nearby. Do not drive your car yourself.

♦ If you are riding in the car, pull over and do as many of the following as possible. If at home, the time you have will dictate how much you can do before the birth.

♦ You or your partner should call the emergency care number (usually 911) and request an aid car. Tell them your baby is being born. Do not sound too calm or they may not realize how important it is that they come quickly. Paramedics are trained to handle emergency childbirth.

♦ You or your partner should call your caregiver's office or the labor and delivery unit of your hospital. Ask for help or emergency instructions.

♦ Call for someone to help you at home— your partner, a relative, a neighbor, or a friend. Even children can help if they know specifically what to do.

Before the Birth

Follow as many of these suggestions as time allows:

♦ Remove your clothing from the lower half of your body.

♦ Lie on your side or in a semisitting position in as warm and comfortable a place as possible (in bed or on the seat of your car) with clean towels under your buttocks. Be sure you are positioned so that there is a safe, clean place for the baby to land as he is born. Then there will be no problem if the baby comes out too fast for an inexperienced person to "catch" him.

♦ Remain as relaxed as possible. Let your uterus do the work. Try not to push or bear down with the contractions; pant or blow through them.

♦ Your partner or attendant should quickly but calmly gather a clean cloth handkerchief, tissues, clean towels, and receiving blankets. Keep these supplies nearby. If possible, put the receiving blankets in a clothes dryer or warm oven so they will be warm when the baby arrives.

♦ Your partner should thoroughly wash his or her hands and arms up to the elbows.

During the Birth

When you and your partner first see the baby's scalp at the vagina, it will be wet and somewhat wrinkled, and it may be streaked with blood and vernix in places. The pressure of the baby's head bulges your perineum and opens your anus. With the contractions, you will see more and more of the baby's head. With labor progressing so rapidly, try not to bear down. Instead, raise your chin and pant or "puh, puh" as lightly and rapidly as you can. Sometimes, as your baby's head descends, you will pass some stool (bowel movement). If this happens, your partner or attendant should wipe it away with tissues or toilet paper to keep the area clean. He or she should remind you to keep your thighs and pelvic floor relaxed.

As the head emerges from the vagina and as "crowning" begins, make extra efforts to relax, pant, and keep from pushing. If the head is delivered slowly, it lessens the risk of injury to the perineum.

Once the head has fully emerged, your partner or attendant should use the clean handkerchief or tissues to wipe away excess mucus from around the baby's nose and mouth. If the membranes cover the baby's face, he or she should break them with a fingernail and peel them away. Wipe the baby's face. Most babies are quite blue at first but turn pink quickly after birth.

A baby's head is usually born facing your back. After the head is born, the baby will turn ninety degrees to face your thigh so the shoulders can be born. At this time your partner or attendant can gently support the baby's head but should not pull on it. He or she should feel the baby's neck to see if the umbilical cord is around it. If so, the cord may slow the birth. Your partner or attendant should gently slip the cord over the baby's head.

With the next contractions, you can bear down smoothly to deliver the shoulders and the rest of the baby's body. You or your partner can support the body; remember that the baby will be wet and slippery.

After the Birth

Care of the Baby

Usually the baby begins breathing and crying immediately. Place the baby on his side or stomach on your bare abdomen, with his head slightly lower than his body to drain any mucus remaining in his nose and mouth. Be sure his nose and mouth are clear so that he can breathe. Wipe away any mucus, and dry the baby completely, especially his head, to help keep him warm. Cover his head with a hat to prevent further heat loss. He will stay warmest with his skin next to yours (no blanket in between) and a warm blanket or any available cover over both of you.

Do not cut the cord. It is safer to wait until a doctor or midwife can clamp it properly and cut it with proper equipment. There is no rush because the blood vessels within the cord begin to close when the cord is exposed to air, automatically stopping the blood flow. You will know the blood flow has stopped when the cord stops pulsating.

Care of the Mother

Your contractions will resume after a slight lull and they will cause the placenta to separate from the uterine wall and slide down into the vagina. Bear down to deliver it. You can kneel or squat if it does not come out easily. Wrap the placenta in a towel or newspapers and place it on the bed. Place a sanitary pad, folded diaper, or small towel on your perineum to absorb the heavy vaginal flow.

You can start breastfeeding right away. It makes your uterus contract and reduces the bleeding. Even if the baby does not suck, his nuzzling at your breast may cause your uterus to contract. Your uterus will be at the level of your navel, and should feel firm like a large grapefruit. If your uterus is not firm, and the baby is not nursing, stroke your nipples or have your partner do it. In addition, massage your lower abdomen firmly until your uterus contracts. Do not continue the massage if your uterus is firm, but check it from time to time and massage again if necessary.

You should get medical attention after all this. The baby's cord needs to be clamped and cut, the baby should be checked, and you should be checked to be sure the entire placenta was born, the uterus remains contracted, and there are no vaginal injuries. Have someone call the emergency aid number (usually 911) if it has not already been called, while you tend to the baby.

Possible Problems

Baby does not breathe spontaneously. Place the baby's head lower than his body and rub his back or chest briskly but gently. If he does not respond within thirty seconds, hold his feet together and smack his soles sharply. If he still does not respond, repeat the procedure. If the baby still does not breathe, check his mouth with your finger for mucus, then place the baby on his back and tilt his head back to straighten his airway from face to chest. Place your mouth over his nose and mouth and your fingers on his chest. *Blow gently* until you feel or see his chest rise a little. *Do not blow hard.* Remove your mouth. Continue this sequence, one blow every three seconds, until the baby responds or medical help arrives. This is mouth-to-mouth resuscitation, one of the techniques used in infant CPR (cardiopulmonary resuscitation). Every parent should learn how to do CPR. Check with your hospital, fire department, or Red Cross office to find a course.

Excessive bleeding from the birth canal. Some bleeding normally occurs after labor and delivery, during the third stage. However, if you lose more than two cups of blood, you may be hemorrhaging. Hemorrhage is characterized by a steady flow of blood and symptoms of shock (rapid pulse, pale skin, trembling, faintness, cold, sweating). If you or your partner suspects hemorrhage, firmly massage the top of your uterus until it contracts, and encourage the baby to nurse (or stroke your nipples). To avoid shock, elevate the lower half of your body.

If the bleeding appears to come from tears at the vaginal opening, press an ice pack and towels firmly against the perineum. Apply firm pressure. Call the hospital or 911 for assistance or go in to a hospital where the staff will assess you and give the appropriate medical assistance.

Placenta does not come. If the placenta does not come within thirty minutes be sure to stand or kneel to get the help of gravity. If it still does not come and no help has arrived, you or your partner will need to call the hospital for guidance.

In an emergency situation, your options are limited. Luckily, in most areas aid cars and experienced paramedics are only minutes away. If an emergency home birth becomes necessary, remember what you have learned about relaxation, breathing techniques, and the birth process. An emergency birth can be hectic, but if you respond calmly and wisely, the experience will always be precious to you, despite its unconventionality.

Prolonged Labor (First Stage)

A labor that lasts longer than twenty-four hours after progressing contractions begin (see page 139) is considered a prolonged labor. More important than the length of labor is the phase of labor in which the progress slows. A long prelabor (a long period of time with continuous non-progressing contractions) or a long latent phase can discourage, exhaust, and emotionally drain you, but it is unlikely to be due to an obstetrical problem. On the other hand, a labor that slows or stops in the active phase or later is more likely to turn into a complication.

Prolonged Latent Phase

If your labor is slow in starting or you are experiencing a long latent phase, do not assume that your entire labor will be prolonged. In most cases, labor will progress normally once you reach the active phase. A slow beginning or a long latent phase may simply mean that your cervix has not moved forward, ripened, or effaced before labor and that your early contractions are having to accomplish these things before they can effectively open the cervix. Your cervix needs time, and you need patience and the reassurance that a slow early labor is not a complication.

What You Can Do

Try not to become discouraged or depressed. Visualize the contractions bringing your cervix forward, ripening and effacing it. Try to accept your slow progress as temporary and appropriate under the circumstances. Alternate among distracting, restful, and labor stimulating activities. Nurture yourself with food or drink, back rubs, or long baths or showers. You may find you can get more rest in a tub (filled high with warm water) than anywhere else. Baths also sometimes temporarily slow a nonproductive labor pattern, thus giving you more rest. Try the various methods of stimulating labor (see pages 167–69). Try distractions, such as a movie, a walk in the park or on the beach, food preparation, a shopping trip, or a visit with friends or relatives. Think of something to do that helps keep your mind off the contractions. You do not need to time every contraction; it is too depressing. Time four or five contractions in a row; then wait a few hours or until the labor has changed before timing another series of contractions.

Medical Care

If your contractions become exhausting or go on for more than twenty-four hours despite your efforts, you and your caregiver may turn to medical interventions. There are two major approaches: attempting to stop contractions and help you rest by using medications (such as tranquilizers, uterine relaxants, sedatives, alcoholic beverages, or morphine); or stimulating more effective contractions by using procedures such as stripping the membranes, breaking the bag of waters, giving prostaglandins to ripen your cervix, or inducing labor with Pitocin.

Prolonged Active Phase

Labor that slows or stops once the active phase has begun may be a more serious problem than a prolonged latent phase. A prolonged active phase can result from inefficient uterine contractions, an unfavorable presentation or position of the baby, a small pelvis, or a combination of these factors. Immobility, restriction to bed, a full bladder, drugs that slow or stop labor, fear, anxiety, and stress can all contribute to a prolonged active phase.

What You Can Do

The solution will depend on the problem. For instance, a full bladder can prevent the baby's descent, so empty your bladder every hour. If you have received drugs that may have slowed your labor, allow time for them to wear off. It may be possible to speed excretion of the drug by drinking liquids. If you have been lying still in one position, try walking or standing (positions that make use of gravity), or try shifting positions in bed from lying on one side or another to sitting or to resting on your hands and knees. You can use these positions even if you are attached to an intravenous line and an electronic fetal monitor. To enhance contraction effectiveness, try nipple stimulation, walking, and standing.

If you are discouraged, tired, anxious, or fearful, you will need reassurance, encouragement, help with relaxation, and other comfort measures such as a bath, massage, or shower. Ask for help, not only from your partner, but also from the staff caring for you. Do not neglect these resources—they can sustain you.

Medical Care

During a prolonged active phase, you can expect your caregivers to closely evaluate the progress of your labor and the well-being of your baby. Nurses will give you more vaginal exams, checking for progress in dilation, descent, or rotation. They will monitor the fetal heart rate more, probably with the electronic fetal monitor. Intravenous fluids to prevent dehydration and medications for relaxation and pain relief become more likely and more welcome if your labor is unduly long. Eventually the doctor or midwife may rupture the membranes in an attempt to speed the labor or administer Pitocin to increase the frequency and intensity of your contractions.

If the baby is under stress, as indicated by the fetal heart rate in response to contractions, or if labor continues to lag, even with Pitocin, you and your doctor may decide a cesarean birth is necessary.

The Occiput Posterior

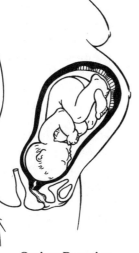

One of the most common reasons for a prolonged active phase is the occiput posterior (OP) position, where the back of the baby's head is toward the mother's back. Approximately one woman in four begins labor with the baby in the OP position, which is associated with longer labors

Occiput Posterior

because the baby must rotate further to get to the anterior position. Dilation and descent may not take place as efficiently when the baby is OP. By transition, however, most babies in the OP position have turned to an occiput anterior position (OA), though some turn even later. Other "persistent" occiput posterior babies are born in that position with their faces toward their mother's front (sometimes called a "sunny side up" delivery).

If your baby is OP, you may have considerable back pain during and sometimes between contractions, because the hard round part of your baby's head (the occiput) presses on your sacrum (lower back), straining the sacroiliac joints and causing pain in the entire low back area.

What You Can Do
Rotation of the baby. To encourage the baby to rotate, change position every twenty to thirty minutes to take advantage of gravity and movement:

♦ Stand and walk. This helps to align the baby's body with the pelvis and enhances pelvic mobility.

♦ Get into the hands and knees position, kneeling and leaning forward with your head and arms resting on a low bed or chair seat. In this position gravity assists rotation. (In the hands and knees position, gravity encourages the OP baby's trunk to drop toward your abdomen.)

♦ Do the pelvic tilt while on your hands and knees (page 99) to provide movement that may free the baby's head from the pelvis and allow it to turn to an anterior position.

Relief of back pain. To help relieve the accompanying back pain, use these measures:

♦ Use positions that prevent the baby's head from pressing on your back. (See the chart on pages 144–45.)

♦ Ask your partner or nurse to use counterpressure (see page 114) on the painful area. To apply counterpressure yourself, press your fists into your lower back or lean back on your fists or another hard object such as a tennis ball.

♦ Ask your partner for a massage.

♦ Use cold or hot packs on your lower back during or between contractions.

♦ Stand or sit in the shower and let the water spray on the painful area.

♦ If a tub or whirlpool bath is available, get in and fill it above the level of your pregnant abdomen.

♦ Ask your partner to do the double hip squeeze during contractions by placing his or her hands on either side of your buttocks and pressing your hips together as illustrated. You can guide your partner on exact placement of his or her hands and how hard to press.

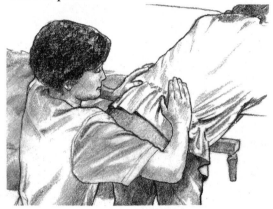

Double Hip Squeeze

♦ Try transcutaneous electrical nerve stimulation (TENS). This method of pain relief utilizes four stimulating pads placed on your back and a small hand-held generator that produces buzzing or prickly sensations over your back. These reduce your awareness of back pain. If your caregiver is unfamiliar with TENS, a physical therapist can advise you on its use during labor. (See pages 114–15 for more on TENS.)

♦ Continue using relaxation and breathing techniques.

♦ If necessary, use pain medications.

Prolonged Labor (Second Stage)

Sometimes labor slows or stops after the cervix is fully dilated for many of the same reasons that cause a prolonged active phase. In those cases, the prolonged second stage may be handled with the same measures. In addition, there are other possible problems that can arise only in second stage. A delay in second stage can occur when the pelvic inlet (upper part) is large enough for the baby to enter, but the pelvic outlet (lower part) is not large enough for the baby to rotate and descend. If this is the case, problems do not arise until the baby is quite low in the pelvis. Another possible, but rare, problem is a short cord, which limits the descent of the baby or causes the fetal heart rate to slow during contractions. A third, also rare, problem occurs if the birth of the baby's shoulders is delayed after the birth of the head—*shoulder dystocia*. This serious complication arises when the shoulders are so broad or in such a position that they do not fit through the pelvis. It is not possible to do a cesarean section after the head is out. Instead, skilled maneuvers by the doctor or midwife, with the cooperation of the mother, are used to rotate the baby and deliver the shoulders. Time is of the essence, since the baby's oxygen supply from the cord may be reduced.

What You Can Do

If you have a problem with descent during the second stage, you should change to gravity-enhancing positions (pages 151–52). If there is no apparent progress after twenty to thirty minutes in one position, change again. Do not continue doing something if it is not effective. Squatting and the supported squat (or "dangle") are perhaps the best aids to descent, since they not only use gravity but also allow maximum enlargement of the pelvic outlet.[6] These positions might provide enough room for a baby in the occiput posterior position to rotate, or they might enlarge a relatively small pelvic outlet enough for the baby to pass through. You might also try the standing, semisitting, and hands and knees positions.

If tension in your perineum seems to interfere with effective bearing-down, even with hot compresses and reminders to relax, sitting on the toilet may encourage release of the perineum.

If using various positions does not enhance progress, you may need to use prolonged pushing with more forceful bearing-down to get the baby moving. At this time the advantages of prolonged pushing may outweigh the disadvantages described in the discussion of expulsion breathing in chapter 7. Your birth attendant directs your pushing at this time.

Medical Care

Close medical observation is necessary if the second stage is prolonged. Your caregiver will carefully monitor the fetal heart rate. If the fetus seems to be tolerating the contractions and positions, the caregiver will encourage you to continue your efforts. (Remember that lying on your back often causes a drop in the fetal heart rate). But if your attempts are unsuccessful, if you are exhausted and unable to push effectively, if you have received medications that inhibit your efforts and slow your labor, or if your fetus is responding poorly, procedures such as vacuum extraction, episiotomy, forceps delivery, and cesarean section may be used. (See the chart on pages 187–88 and chapter 10 for information on cesarean birth.)

Prolapsed Cord

Prolapsed Cord

Though rare, a *pro-lapsed ·cord* is an extremely serious complication. If the umbilical cord slips through the cervix into the vagina before the baby is born, it can be pinched between the baby and the partly opened cervix or the mother's bony pelvis. Especially during contractions, this compression of the cord can drastically reduce oxygen to the fetus, which can be a life-threatening emergency for the baby.

A prolapsed cord is most likely (though still rare) if your membranes suddenly rupture *and* your baby is in a breech or transverse presentation or her head is "floating" and not engaged in your pelvis. At your prenatal checkups in late pregnancy, find out if your baby is breech, transverse, or high. If you know that your baby is high, breech, or transverse, and your membranes break with a gush, you should take the following precautions until medical care is available: Get into a knee-chest position in which gravity can move the baby away from your cervix and off the cord, which may have prolapsed. You may or may not be able to feel the cord in your vagina. Someone needs to arrange for immediate transportation to the hospital, and you should remain in the knee-chest position in the car or ambulance. Once you arrive at the hospital, a nurse will check for a prolapsed cord, and if necessary put her or his hand in your vagina to hold the baby off the cord. A cesarean delivery will be performed as soon as possible.

Difficult Presentations

About 5 percent of the time, the baby is in a presentation other than vertex. Face and brow presentations occur less than 0.5 percent of the time and usually prolong labor. The shoulder presentation (transverse lie) occurs rarely, in about one in five hundred births. Because a baby in this position only occasionally turns to a head-down presentation, a cesarean delivery is usually necessary.

Finally, the breech presentation (with buttocks, legs, or feet over the cervix) occurs 3 to 4 percent of the time. (The incidence rises with prematurity or twins.) This is the most common of the difficult presentations.

Breech Presentation

There are three types of breech presentations: *frank*—buttocks down and legs straight up toward the face; *complete*—sitting cross-legged; and *footling*—one or both feet down. The frank breech is the most common. Although breech deliveries usually turn out

Complete Breech

well, they are riskier to the baby than the vertex presentation. A breech presentation increases the chances of a prolapsed cord, because the baby's buttocks or feet do not cover the cervix and thus do not prevent the descent of the umbilical cord into the vagina. This is most likely to occur when the membranes rupture with a gush.

Because the baby's feet and body are delivered before his head in a breech birth, the baby's head can compress the cord at the cervix or within the birth canal, reducing the oxygen available from the placenta to the baby. Another added risk exists because the baby's feet and buttocks are small enough that they can be born before the cervix dilates enough for the birth of the head. This may result in a delay in the birth of the head and in fetal distress. Another risk is spinal cord injury, if the head of the fetus is hyperextended (bent back).

What You Can Do

Try to keep informed about your baby's presentation and position, which are checked at each prenatal visit during late pregnancy. Most babies assume their birth position by thirty-four to thirty-six weeks. Others turn later, even during labor. If your baby is breech at thirty-six weeks, you may try the "breech-tilt" position to encourage your baby to turn.

This position involves tilting your body so your hips are higher than your head. Lie on your back with your knees bent and your feet flat on the floor. Raise your pelvis, and slide enough firm cushions beneath your buttocks to raise them ten to fifteen inches above your head. You may also lie head down on an ironing board or a similar flat board tilted with one end on a chair, the other on the floor. Lie in this position for about ten minutes three times a day when the baby is active. For your comfort, make sure your stomach and bladder are empty. Try to relax your abdominal muscles. Your baby will probably squirm as his head presses into the fundus, and he may seek a more comfortable position. This technique does not always work, but since it is harmless, it is worth trying.

Another technique utilizes sound to turn a breech baby. This harmless technique is not uncomfortable, as is the breech tilt position. It involves placing earphones from a tape player just above your pubic bone and playing music for the baby during his active periods. Or your partner can talk to the baby with his or her head in your lap. The music or voice should be at a volume that is comfortable for you to listen to. You can do it for as long as you like. The rationale is this: We know that the fetus can hear very well and responds to sound coming from outside the womb. We think that if the fetus hears pleasing sounds coming from low in the uterus, he might move his head down to hear it better. While not always successful, numerous women who have tried this technique have reported that their babies turned. While it is possible that the babies would have turned spontaneously, this harmless and enjoyable technique may be useful.

Medical Care

There are several medical approaches to breech presentation: external version, vaginal birth, and cesarean birth.

External version. This procedure, done at about thirty-seven to thirty-eight weeks, involves turning the baby from a breech to a head-down presentation. Before the version is performed, ultrasound is used to confirm that the baby is still breech and to visualize the site of placental attachment. Also, a nonstress test is usually done before and after the version to determine that the baby is doing well. A *tocolytic* drug (for example, terbutaline) is given to you to relax your uterus and decrease your risk of preterm labor contractions. Then, using ultrasound for guidance and to observe the fetal heart rate, your caregiver presses and pushes on the baby through your abdomen, turning him to a head-down position. If the baby shows signs of fetal distress (as indicated by his heart rate), the procedure is stopped. In the unlikely event that the placenta begins to separate during the version or that the baby is in distress after the procedure is stopped, a cesarean section might have to be performed. Sometimes the version is unsuccessful, that is, the baby does not turn. Sometimes after a successful version, the baby turns back later. Studies of external version indicate that it is a safe and quite successful procedure, and it lowers the cesarean rate for breech presentations.[7]

Vaginal or cesarean birth of the breech. Many physicians evaluate each breech presentation individually and weigh the risks carefully before deciding whether a vaginal or cesarean birth is best. Doctors who are skilled in vaginal breech deliveries consider the size and gestational age of the baby, the type of breech presentation, the size of the pelvis, and other factors. Some doctors require that a woman have had a previous vaginal birth. The best candidate for a vaginal breech birth is a term baby estimated to weigh less than eight pounds who is in a frank breech presentation with a well-flexed head (chin on chest) within a roomy pelvis. Careful monitoring and medical interventions during labor are likely in this situation. When these conditions are met and the caregiver has been trained to manage vagi-

nal breech births, outcomes have been shown to be better with vaginal than with cesarean delivery.[8]

Some women are not candidates for a vaginal breech birth because of obstetrical factors or because their physicians prefer to deliver all breech babies by cesarean. In addition, some women attempting a vaginal breech birth develop problems in labor that require a cesarean birth. For these reasons, the cesarean birth rate for breeches is very high.

Preterm (Premature) Birth

A *preterm birth*, by definition, occurs before the thirty-seventh week of gestation. If you experience any of the signs of preterm labor (page 53), call your caregiver. After evaluating your condition, your baby's health, and the progress of labor, your caregiver may decide to try to stop labor. The methods used to prevent premature labor (described on page 53) are more likely to succeed if preterm contractions are detected early, before two centimeters of dilation.

When labor and birth appear inevitable or desirable, the focus of care shifts to managing your labor for the best possible outcome and providing necessary special care for your baby after the birth. Your baby's heart rate will be assessed very frequently or by continuous monitoring. Systemic pain medications that affect fetal heart rate and depress newborn respirations will probably be discouraged. Therefore, in early labor you should plan to use relaxation and breathing patterns for pain relief. In active labor or during birth, you may continue these techniques or you may request regional anesthesia. Episiotomy and forceps are sometimes used in an attempt to protect the premature baby's head.

Since the health of the baby is paramount and she may be in need of medical attention, you may not be able to hold her immediately after birth. Most premature infants are taken to a special nursery. Depending on how small and immature the baby is, her care may involve prolonged hospitalization and possibly long periods of separation from you. In most hospitals, parents are encouraged to visit and care for their babies. Participating in the care of your baby benefits both of you. (For more information on care of the premature infant, see page 254.)

Twins

The birth of twins is more complicated than the birth of a single baby. The added stretching of the uterus and the combined weights of the babies and one or two placentas often cause premature labor. Early rupture of the membranes is more common with twins and is another cause for prematurity. Generally, labor with twins progresses normally, but sometimes the overstretched uterus cannot work as efficiently, and labor progress is slow. Because of the high incidence of prematurity and increased chances of postpartum hemorrhage, you should expect more medical supervision and more interventions than are usual with the birth of a single baby at term.

The most common and favorable presentation for the birth of twins is with both babies head down (vertex). Ultrasound during labor might be indicated to identify the positions of the babies. The results help your caregiver determine the best type of birth—vaginal or cesarean. If the first baby is head down and the other one is breech, the second baby might be turned after the birth of the first baby. The second twin is usually born within thirty minutes of the first, and the delivery of the placenta(s) will occur after both twins are born. The probability of cesarean birth is higher in twin or multiple pregnancies due to the increased likelihood of complications such as preeclampsia, prematurity, breech presentation, prolonged labor, and prolapsed cord.

Third Stage Variations and Complications

Postpartum hemorrhage is the most common problem of the third stage of labor. It is defined as a loss of at least five hundred milliliters (about two cups) of blood during the first twenty-four hours after birth.

The three major causes of postpartum hemorrhage are *uterine atony* (poor uterine muscle tone), *lacerations* or tears of the cervix or vagina, and *retention of the placenta* or placental fragments. Of these, uterine atony is the most common cause of hemorrhage. The treatment of postpartum hemorrhage depends on the cause. If bleeding is serious, you may need intravenous fluids or a blood transfusion.

Uterine Atony

To encourage your uterus to contract, you or your caregiver can massage your uterus. Nursing your baby also helps the uterus to contract by stimulating the release of your body's oxytocin. If these measures do not control bleeding, your doctor or midwife may give you medications such as Pitocin to promote uterine contractions (see pages 218–19).

Lacerations

Lacerations or tears of the cervix, vagina, or perineum sometimes occur with or without an episiotomy. They will be sutured to control bleeding. Occasionally, packing the vagina with sterile gauze is also required to stop bleeding.

Retention of the Placenta

If the placenta or fragments of it are retained in the uterus, they interfere with postpartum uterine contractions, allowing the blood vessels at the placental site to bleed freely. Your caregiver will manually remove the placenta, clots, or fragments, administer Pitocin, and massage your uterus. You can help by massaging your uterus yourself, and by breastfeeding your baby. Very rarely the placenta cannot be separated from the uterine wall (*placenta accreta*), and the only safe treatment for this rare but serious complication may be a hysterectomy (removal of the uterus).

When a Baby Dies or Has a Birth Defect

Birth defects, stillbirth, and death resulting from birth trauma, infection, and disabilities are relatively uncommon but do occasionally occur. If you are faced with a birth defect or the death of your baby, your agony, sadness, and loneliness are deep and long-lasting. Being prepared by deciding what you would do if your baby dies or is deformed can help you in the first painful days.

If your baby dies before you go into labor, you have to consider how you want the labor managed. Will labor be induced, and if so, when? Do you want to write a special birth plan? Do you want to be awake and participate in the birth? Would an additional support person be helpful? If you have a stillbirth or your baby dies soon after birth, you will also have these options to consider. Would you prefer to recover on the postpartum floor where other mothers and babies are, or somewhere else in the hospital, or would you prefer to take an early discharge? Do you want an autopsy to help find a cause for the baby's death?

What might make your memories of the baby more meaningful? Many counselors recommend that parents see and hold their dead or dying baby. Naming or baptizing the baby, taking photographs, footprints, or a lock of hair are ways to acknowledge the

baby's life and provide memories. A funeral or memorial service provides an opportunity for family and friends to come together to grieve, say good-bye to the baby, and express their concern and love for you. Later, you may want to join a support group of parents who have experienced a similar loss. They are there for as long as you need them. While nothing takes away the pain of losing a baby, this support can help you emotionally at a very difficult time.

If the baby has a birth defect, is premature, or is very ill, you have other decisions to make. In most cases, you or your partner can spend time with your baby, even if he is in a special care nursery. If the baby is transferred to a hospital that specializes in seriously ill babies, your partner may have to divide his or her time between visiting you and the baby. You may be able to have an early discharge from your hospital so that you may visit. You may want to provide your baby with the special nourishment of your colostrum and breast milk, either by breastfeeding or by pumping your milk to be fed to your baby.

You will have many questions about your baby's condition, the treatment, and what to expect now and in the future. Your baby's doctors and nurses can help you get the information you need and show you how you can best help your baby. Parent support groups exist for those whose babies are premature or disabled. They are immensely helpful with emotional support and practical help.

If your baby dies or has health problems, you will need time to review and reflect on the birth experience. Recalling the events with your partner, childbirth educator, the attending nurse, or your caregiver and writing a birth report can help you put the pieces together. A counselor, therapist, the hospital chaplain, or your priest, rabbi, or minister can help you work through your emotions. Friends and family can help you with the numerous practical details that must be attended to: care of other children; transportation; food preparation; notification of business associates, friends, and relatives; answering the phone; and more. Helpful books are listed in Recommended Resources.

If your baby dies or has health problems, you will need time to grieve. Grieving is painful and exhausting, but it must be experienced. You and your partner will experience and reexperience many feelings—shock, disbelief, fear, anger, guilt. Eventually, after months or even years, you will reach a level of acceptance, although the sorrow will linger. Be gentle with yourself. Give yourself time to heal emotionally and physically. Lean on the people and the community resources that are most supportive.

There are good memories as well as painful ones. Allow yourself to acknowledge your baby's life and savor the good memories from pregnancy, the birth, and the time you had with your baby. Your baby is a special part of you and will always exist in your memories as an important person in your life.

Medical Interventions in Labor and Birth

Medical interventions in labor are procedures carried out by your caregiver or nurse to alter the course of labor, provide diagnostic information, or prevent complications. All medical interventions carry some disadvantages (just as medications do), and they should not be used unless they are necessary. There is disagreement within the obstetrical community over how routine some of these interventions should be. You will want to know what your caregiver considers a desirable routine intervention (and why). Ask if your caregiver will give you a chance to solve problems in labor and birth by using your own techniques, such as changing positions, comfort measures, relaxation, breathing patterns, and time. Your birth plan should include your preferences regarding the use of interventions. The following chart describes and outlines the benefits and risks of various interventions.

Interventions

Intervention	Description	Benefits/purposes	Risks/disadvantages
Intravenous (IV) fluids	Fluids are administered through a small plastic tube or needle inserted into a vein in the back of the hand or forearm. The fluid drips continuously from an IV bag or bottle. (Sometimes a heparin lock, a tube containing an anticoagulant, is used to keep the vein open if a need for IV fluids is anticipated.)	◆ Maintains hydration (adequate fluid intake) when you are unable to drink liquids ◆ Helps maintain blood pressure if regional anesthesia is used or if you bleed too much ◆ Allows immediate access to a vein if medications or a blood transfusion are necessary ◆ Needed for administration of Pitocin (to augment or induce labor) ◆ Provides some calories for energy	◆ Restricts easy movement during labor; walking is more difficult (unless a heparin lock is used) ◆ Unnecessary if you are drinking sufficient fluids, receiving no medication or anesthesia, and labor is progressing normally ◆ May result in infiltration (fluids leaking into tissues surrounding vein near puncture site), causing tenderness and swelling
Induction (starting) and augmentation (speeding) of labor A. "Stripping" the membranes	The caregiver inserts a finger between the membranes and your cervix and loosens the membranes from the lower part of the uterus. The procedure is usually performed in the doctor's or midwife's office before labor begins.	◆ May start labor by stimulating prostaglandin action in cervix or by allowing amniotic sac to slip down into cervix, further dilating it ◆ If unsuccessful, pregnancy can continue without danger of infection	◆ May not induce labor ◆ Causes small amount of bloody or brownish vaginal discharge, often mistaken for bloody show ◆ Some caregivers do this during a vaginal exam without client's knowledge ◆ May rupture membranes
B. Prostaglandin gel	Prostaglandin gel is placed within or near the cervix. The application may be repeated. The gel is sometimes used before Pitocin induction.	◆ May ripen and soften cervix ◆ May start labor by causing uterine contractions	◆ May not induce labor ◆ Not universally available in United States
C. Synthetic oxytocin (Pitocin)	Pitocin is given intravenously when you are in the hospital. The IV drip is usually electronically regulated by a special infusion pump.	◆ Causes uterine contractions ◆ Used to induce labor when membranes have ruptured and contractions have not begun or when there is a medical reason to deliver baby before labor has begun (preeclampsia, maternal diabetes, postmaturity) ◆ Used to increase intensity and frequency of contractions when labor progress is stopped or slowed due to inadequate uterine activity	◆ Requires close observation of you and baby to avoid undesirable effects ◆ Increases intensity of contractions, requiring greater concentration and use of relaxation and breathing techniques or pain medication ◆ May be associated with an increased incidence of newborn jaundice ◆ May result in a premature birth if performed without knowledge of fetal maturity

continued

Intervention	Description	Benefits/purposes	Risks/disadvantages
D. Artificial rupture of membranes (AROM)	Either before or during labor, the caregiver makes a small tear in the membranes using a specially designed instrument called an "amnihook." AROM is done during a vaginal examination. There is no pain during this procedure other than the discomfort of a vaginal exam.	◆ May start labor ◆ May speed labor progress by allowing presenting part to fit snugly against cervix, stimulating contractions and enhancing dilation ◆ Enables caregiver or nurse to see consistency and color of amniotic fluid to help assess fetal well-being ◆ Necessary for application of fetal scalp electrode or intrauterine pressure catheter used for internal electronic fetal monitoring	◆ Does not always start labor, and subsequent risk of infection requires use of other interventions (usually Pitocin); caregivers usually want birth to occur or labor to be well underway within 24 hours of ROM ◆ May increase discomfort of uterine contractions ◆ Associated with greater umbilical cord compression, molding of fetal head, and drops in fetal heart rate during contractions ◆ If presenting part is high, AROM may cause prolapse of cord
Fetal heart rate monitoring A. Fetal stethoscope	Caregiver (usually a nurse) listens to the baby's heartbeat through your abdominal wall using a fetal stethoscope. The fetal heart rate (FHR) is usually counted before, during, and after a contraction, about every 15 to 30 minutes during the first stage of labor and more frequently during the second stage.	◆ Noninvasive ◆ Allows you to be mobile and active ◆ Encourages frequent attention from your caregiver	◆ Assessing relationship between the FHR and contraction is difficult ◆ Heart tones may be difficult to hear ◆ May require you to lie supine (flat) in bed in order to hear heart tones ◆ Does not provide continuous printed record of FHR and contraction pattern, requiring staff to record FHR on your chart ◆ Pressure of stethoscope against your abdomen may be uncomfortable
B. Hand-held ultrasonic fetal stethoscope	Often called the Doppler, this device is placed on your abdomen and audibly and/or visually transmits the fetal heart tone.	◆ Is most comfortable method of FHR monitoring ◆ Encourages frequent attention from your caregiver or nurse ◆ Allows you to be mobile and active ◆ Is more sensitive in picking up fetal heart tones than fetal stethoscope ◆ Volume can be increased so others in room may hear	◆ Assessing relationship between the FHR and contraction is difficult ◆ Does not provide a continuous record of FHR and contraction pattern, requiring staff to record FHR on your chart ◆ Exposes fetus to ultrasound

Intervention	Description	Benefits/purposes	Risks/disadvantages
C. External electronic fetal monitor (EFM) (fetal heart rate and contraction monitors)	An ultrasound device, held in place by a belt around your abdomen, sends and receives soundwaves to detect fetal heart rate. Another belt holds a pressure-sensitive device (a *tocodynamometer*) in place over your fundus to detect uterine contractions. These devices are attached by wires to a table-top monitor that displays and permanently records the FHR and uterine contractions. Monitoring can be intermittent (10 to 20 minutes every hour) or continuous.	◆ Enables assessment of how contractions affect FHR ◆ Enables assessment of fetal well-being when complications arise or when Pitocin or other medical interventions are used ◆ Provides information needed to determine whether more sophisticated monitoring is warranted ◆ Provides information on frequency of uterine contractions ◆ Provides a continuous printed record of FHR and contraction pattern ◆ Helps labor partner know when contractions begin so he or she can help you start a breathing pattern ◆ Does not require artificial rupture of membranes	◆ Not always accurate, requiring further assessments with more accurate techniques before changing medical management ◆ Needs frequent readjustment when you or baby move ◆ May be uncomfortable and restrict your movement and your ability to use effleurage or back massage (immobility may slow labor) ◆ Has not been associated with better outcomes than the fetal stethoscope[a] ◆ May tempt your labor partner to watch monitor instead of you ◆ Exposes fetus to ultrasound
D. External monitoring telemetry unit	The recording devices are the same as described above, but they are connected to a tiny wireless transmitter (a telemetry unit), which you carry. It transmits data to a monitor located in your labor room or in the nurses' station.	◆ Same as with external electronic monitoring described above ◆ In addition, allows you more movement, including walking around maternity area	◆ Same as with external electronic fetal monitoring, except that it allows mobility ◆ Very delicate machine more subject to breakdown than other monitors; high likelihood that you will have to use other system; improvements in technology may increase reliability

continued

185

Intervention	Description	Benefits/purposes	Risks/disadvantages
E. Internal electronic fetal monitor (EFM)	The fetal heart rate (FHR) is measured by a scalp electrode attached to the fetal head (or other presenting part). Wires from the electrode transmit the baby's heart rate to the monitor, which displays and records it. Uterine contractions are measured by placing an intrauterine pressure catheter (IUPC) into the uterus. During contractions, the increase in intrauterine pressure is measured, displayed visually, and recorded on the printout. Sometimes a combination of internal and external electronic monitoring is used; for example, the internal fetal scalp electrode and the external uterine pressure device.	♦ Enables accurate assessment of how contractions affect FHR ♦ Enables assessment of fetal well-being when complications arise or when Pitocin or other medical interventions are used ♦ Provides information needed to determine if further medical intervention or further testing is warranted ♦ Provides information on quality and frequency of uterine contractions ♦ Provides a permanent record of FHR and contraction pattern ♦ Helps labor partner know when contractions begin so he or she can help you start a breathing pattern ♦ Is more accurate than external monitor ♦ Is less restrictive of your movements in bed than external monitor	♦ Requires rupture of membranes ♦ Restricts free movement, especially walking during labor ♦ May cause infection of uterus and/or infection of baby's scalp ♦ Interpretation of FHR patterns varies among practitioners; fetal distress could be diagnosed when not actually present ♦ Pressure catheter may need frequent adjustment ♦ Has not been associated with better outcomes than fetal stethoscopes[b]
Fetal stimulation test	This test is used when EFM indicates possible fetal distress. A loud noise is created near your abdomen to startle the fetus (the fetal acoustic stimulation test), or, during a vaginal exam, the caregiver presses on or scratches the fetal scalp (the fetal scalp stimulation test). The fetal heart rate response to such stimulation is observed. A reactive heart rate (rises 15 beats per minute for 15 seconds) is a reliable sign that the fetus is compensating well for a shortage in oxygen. If the heart rate is not reactive, the fetus is in distress.	♦ Enables further assessment of fetal well-being if EFM indicates problems ♦ Sometimes prevents an unnecessary cesarean birth if test indicates fetal well-being ♦ Noninvasive ♦ More rapid than fetal scalp blood sampling, and as reliable[c] ♦ No cost	♦ No disadvantages

Intervention	Description	Benefits/purposes	Risks/disadvantages
Fetal scalp blood sampling	A small cut is made in the baby's scalp and a sample of the baby's blood is removed and tested for its oxygen and carbon dioxide levels, acid-base balance (pH), and other factors.	♦ Enables further assessment of fetal well-being if EFM indicates problems ♦ Prevents an unnecessary cesarean birth if fetal blood values are shown to be normal	♦ Time-consuming procedure ♦ Uncomfortable for mother and possibly for baby ♦ Invasive ♦ May cause scalp infection in baby ♦ Results take from 2 to 30 minutes to obtain ♦ Not all hospitals have necessary facilities to perform tests 24 hours a day
Amnioinfusion	When amniotic fluid volume is low (from ruptured membranes or from diminished production of fluid by placenta and membranes), sterile saline solution may be injected into an intrauterine pressure catheter (like the one used to measure contraction strength with internal EFM). This may be done if the umbilical cord is being compressed during contractions and causing fetal distress or if meconium is present in the amniotic fluid. The fluid cushions and protects the cord against compression.[d]	♦ Reduces fetal distress ♦ Allows labor to continue when a cesarean might otherwise be the only solution 	♦ Requires that mother remain in bed ♦ Invasive ♦ Requires artificial rupture of membranes ♦ Risks and benefits are still being investigated
Episiotomy	A surgical incision is made into the perineum from the vagina toward the rectum (midline or mediolateral) just before the birth of the baby's head. midline mediolateral	♦ Enlarges birth canal ♦ May speed delivery of baby by a few minutes ♦ Provides a straight incision, which is easier to repair than some large tears ♦ Provides more space for application of forceps or vacuum extractor ♦ Reduces compression from vaginal tissues on head of a premature baby	♦ Causes discomfort in early postpartum period ♦ Sometimes performed routinely when not necessary ♦ May delay mother-infant interaction (holding or nursing) as episiotomy is repaired ♦ Site of incision may become infected or bleed ♦ May cause pain with intercourse for several months after birth ♦ More likely to extend and seriously tear perineum than if an episiotomy is not performed[e]

continued

Intervention	Description	Benefits/purposes	Risks/disadvantages
Forceps	Two spoonlike instruments are inserted into the vagina and applied to each side of the baby's head. The caregiver turns and/or pulls on the handles to aid rotation and descent. Used only when the baby is at a low station.	♦ Helps rotate baby's head to an anterior position ♦ Helps bring baby down when anesthesia is used or bearing-down efforts are insufficient ♦ Helps protect premature baby's head from prolonged pressure in birth canal ♦ May be used to facilitate birth of head with a breech vaginal birth ♦ Allows a rapid delivery if necessary	♦ Usually requires an episiotomy ♦ May bruise soft tissues of baby's head or face ♦ Usually requires regional anesthesia ♦ May bruise vaginal tissues
Vacuum extractor	A caplike device is applied to the baby's head. A rubber tube extends from the cap to a vacuum pump that creates suction on the baby's head. During contractions the caregiver pulls on a handle attached to the cap to assist the baby's descent.	♦ Helps descent of baby's head ♦ Can be applied when fetus is at a higher station than is safe for use of forceps ♦ Requires less space in vagina than forceps	♦ May cause bruising or swelling of baby's soft scalp tissues ♦ Not as helpful with rotation as forceps

[a] K.K. Shy et al., "Evaluating a New Technology: The Effectiveness of Electronic Fetal Heart Rate Monitoring," *Annual Review of Public Health* 8 (1987):165; American College of Obstetricians and Gynecologists, "Intrapartum Fetal Heart Rate Monitoring," *ACOG Technical Bulletin* No. 132 (Washington, DC: American College of Obstetricians and Gynecologists, September 1989).

[b] Ibid.

[c] S.L. Clark et al., "The Scalp Stimulation Test: A Clinical Alternative to Fetal Scalp Blood Sampling," *American Journal of Obstetrics and Gynecology* 148 (1 February 1984): 274; C.V. Smith et al., "Intrapartum Assessment of Fetal Well-Being: A Comparison of Fetal Acoustic Stimulation with Acid-Base Determinations," *American Journal of Obstetrics and Gynecology* 155 (October 1986): 726; C.V. Smith et al., "Fetal Acoustic Stimulation Testing II: A Randomized Clinical Comparison with the Non-Stress Test," *American Journal of Obstetrics and Gynecology* 155 (July 1986): 131.

[d] B.J. Galvan et al., "Using Amnioinfusion for the Relief of Repetitive Variable Decelerations during Labor," *Journal of Obstetric, Gynecologic and Neonatal Nursing* (May/June 1989): 222.

[e] P. Shiono et al., "Midline Episiotomies: More Harm Than Good?" *Obstetrics and Gynecology* 75 (May 1990): 765.

Chapter 10

Cesarean Birth and Vaginal Birth after a Previous Cesarean

A cesarean section (also called C-section or cesarean birth) is a surgical procedure used to deliver your baby through an incision in the abdomen and uterus if labor or a vaginal birth is considered too difficult or dangerous for either you or the baby. Although it is major abdominal surgery, a cesarean is sometimes preferable to a vaginal birth. Under most circumstances, however, a vaginal birth is safer for both mother and baby, even if the mother has already had one or more cesareans. This chapter provides a description of reasons for cesarean birth, the surgical procedure, and the physical and emotional recovery. It is followed by a discussion of vaginal births after cesareans (VBACs)—benefits, concerns, and preparations.

Cesarean Birth

The cesarean rate has risen steadily in the United States and Canada since 1970, when approximately one woman in twenty had a cesarean birth. Today, the rate is approximately one in four in the United States and one in five in Canada. It has reached a level that has alarmed many experts, because the high cesarean rate has not resulted in the expected improvements in infant and maternal outcomes.

Leading public and professional organizations such as the International Childbirth Education Association, the Cesarean Prevention Movement, C/SEC (Cesareans/Support, Education and Concern), the American College of Obsetricians and Gynecologists, and the Society of Obstetricians and Gynaecologists of Canada have called for greater efforts by physicians, midwives, nurses, childbirth educators, hospital review boards, and parents to use our existing knowledge to lower the cesarean section rate.[1] They point out that there are numerous published reports in medical journals indicating that the cesarean rate can safely be lowered to 12 to 15 percent.[2] They ask for more patience from both caregivers and parents with long labors, more vaginal breech deliveries, more vaginal births for women who have had previous cesareans, more careful diagnosis of fetal distress, better education of parents on the benefits and risks of cesareans, and other measures.

Weighing the Benefits and Risks of Cesareans

Why the concern over a high cesarean rate? At first glance, it appears that the cesarean section is a quick and easy way to deliver a baby. Compared with other major surgery, it

189

is very safe. It is more convenient, faster, and more predictable than vaginal birth. The procedure itself is usually not painful because it is done under anesthesia. The doctor also receives a higher fee for a cesarean. These facts make the cesarean attractive to both parents and caregivers.

A closer look, however, reveals major disadvantages and risks that make it appropriate to limit cesareans to cases when a vaginal birth is either unsafe or impossible. Cesareans increase your risk of serious problems with anesthesia, infection, and hemorrhage. You have a longer hospitalization. You have pain for weeks afterward and more difficulty caring for your baby and any other children. You also need more pain medications and are more likely to require antibiotics and blood transfusions than you are if you have a vaginal birth. You may not feel ready to resume household responsibilities or to return to employment as soon. Furthermore, the financial costs greatly exceed the costs of a vaginal birth.

Babies born by cesarean are more likely to have breathing and temperature problems, especially if there has been no labor. Even when compared to long or difficult vaginal births, these added risks still exist.

In making a decision about a cesarean, you and your doctor should weigh these benefits and risks. The risks of a cesarean are worth taking only in situations where a vaginal birth might incur other even greater risks to mother or baby.

Improving Your Chances for a Vaginal Birth

There are a number of things you can do to improve your chances for a vaginal birth:

♦ Take good care of yourself (good nutrition, moderate exercise, stress management, avoidance of drugs and tobacco) so that you enter labor in the best possible health.

♦ Find a hospital and caregiver whom you trust, who have low cesarean rates, and who encourage you to use self-help techniques (such as those described in chapters 6, 7, and 8) in labor.

♦ If you have had a cesarean in the past, consider joining a support group that promotes vaginal births after cesareans (VBACs) and assists you with psychological preparation and practical information.

♦ Take childbirth preparation classes that emphasize your participation in decision making and the use of nonpharmacologic methods to relieve pain and stress and to promote labor progress.

♦ Prepare a birth plan with your caregiver to help ensure that you both are working toward the same priorities.

♦ Plan to utilize medications and interventions only when clearly necessary, since these tend to alter the course of normal labor.

♦ Consider having a support person (besides your partner) with you in labor, one who knows and shares your priorities. She or he should be well trained. Childbirth educators or experienced professional labor support people (sometimes called doulas, monitrices, or birth assistants) may be available in your area. They can be of great help to both you and your partner.

There are times when all the above measures have been employed but, even so, it becomes clear that a cesarean is necessary for a safe outcome. You and your partner should know what to expect with a cesarean and what choices you have.

Reasons for a Cesarean Birth

A cesarean section may be performed for any of the following reasons:

Cephalo-pelvic disproportion (CPD). The baby's head is too large, the pelvic structure too small, or a combination of the two. CPD can rarely be diagnosed (although it can be suspected) before labor, because, even if the baby is large or the mother's pelvis is somewhat small, the baby's head molds and the pelvic joints spread during labor, both of which create more room. If plenty of time has been allowed, contractions have been of good quality, and there is still no progress, then a diagnosis of CPD can be made. Sometimes it is difficult to distinguish CPD from a malposition.

Malpresentation or malposition. The baby's placement in the uterus is unfavorable for a vaginal birth. Examples of malpresentations and malpositions include the transverse lie (baby lying horizontally), certain breech presentations (bottom or feet first), face or brow presentations, the persistent occiput posterior position (see page 175), or asynclitism (the baby's head tilted so that it does not fit).

Failure to progress (or prolonged labor). Contractions are of poor quality, or dilation and descent are not progressing, or both, even after attempts to rest the uterus or to stimulate stronger contractions. This diagnosis cannot be made reliably until the active phase of labor (after five centimeters dilation), since a normal latent phase (zero to four or five centimeters) can often be very slow.

Fetal distress. Particular changes in the fetal heart rate detected by listening with a stethoscope or Doppler or by reading fetal monitor tracings can indicate problems for the baby. These changes mean the baby is conserving oxygen when the oxygen supply is reduced, as with cord compression or decreased blood flow to the placenta. Fur-

ther tests—scalp stimulation, or fetal scalp blood sampling (pages 186–87)—tell whether the baby is compensating well or is beginning to suffer from the lack of oxygen. If the baby is no longer able to compensate, a cesarean is necessary.

The major concern with a lack of oxygen is that it may cause brain damage (cerebral palsy, mental retardation, epilepsy) in the baby. While it is possible for brain damage to occur during birth, numerous recent studies have found that in most cases of brain damage, the damage actually takes place during pregnancy before labor begins.[3] These conditions are not detectable in the protected environment of the uterus. Everything appears fine until the stress of labor, when abnormal fetal heart rate patterns appear, or after birth, when abnormal neurological signs develop. Cesareans cannot prevent or cure these preexisting problems, although they can spare these babies from stresses in labor that they are not equipped to handle.

Prolapsed cord. When the umbilical cord descends through the cervix before the baby, the baby's body may pinch the cord, drastically reducing his oxygen supply, necessitating immediate cesarean delivery. See page 177 for more on prolapsed cord.

Placenta previa. The placenta covers or partially covers the cervix. As the cervix dilates, the placenta separates from the uterus, causing painless bleeding in the mother and depriving the fetus of oxygen.

Placental abruption. The placenta prematurely separates from the uterine wall. This may cause vaginal bleeding or hidden bleeding with constant abdominal pain. The separation decreases the fetus's oxygen supply, and depending on how much of the placenta has come away, a cesarean may be necessary.

Maternal disease. If you have diabetes, high blood pressure, preeclampsia, heart disease, or certain other conditions, you or the baby may not be able to withstand the stress of labor and vaginal birth. The presence of a herpes sore in or near the vagina is also an indication for a cesarean birth since the baby may acquire the infection when passing through the birth canal.

Repeat cesarean. Another cesarean may be performed because the reason for the first cesarean still exists or because the doctor or patient prefers a cesarean birth. Vaginal delivery is usually possible and is recommended by the ACOG (American College of Obstetricians and Gynecologists) and other professional organizations for subsequent births. Health insurers and state and federal Medicaid programs are pressuring physicians not to do repeat cesareans without medical indication. This is a recent departure from the long-standing policy that once you have had a cesarean, all your future births will be by cesarean. As this new approach is adopted, there will be fewer repeat cesareans. A discussion of vaginal birth after cesarean (VBAC) appears at the end of this chapter.

The Planned (Elective) Cesarean Birth

Sometimes a cesarean birth is planned in advance for an existing medical reason. Your doctor may wait until you go into labor and then perform the surgery. By waiting for labor to begin spontaneously, your baby is more likely to be full-term. The footling breech is an example of a problem that might be managed this way. Or, after considering your due date, the fetal size and maturity, and the urgency of need, your doctor may schedule the surgery before your due date. If there are any doubts about the maturity of your baby's lungs, fetal maturity tests are done. (See pages 60–66.) Placenta previa is an example of a problem that is usually managed this way.

With a scheduled cesarean, you check into the hospital for routine blood and urine tests. The anesthesiologist discusses the type of anesthesia and preoperative and postoperative medications he or she will use and asks about your allergies or sensitivities to drugs. The thought of surgery may make you feel nervous and afraid. It helps to have your partner with you at this time. Calm yourself by using slow breathing and relaxation techniques. Envision yourself a few hours in the future when you will be holding your baby. Feel free to ask questions and make requests. Review these pages describing the procedure. Discuss your birth plan for cesarean birth and your partner's role with your physician, the nurses, and the anesthesiologist. All this can make your cesarean birth experience more positive and less frightening.

The Unplanned or Emergency Cesarean Birth

Most cesareans are unplanned, that is, they are decided upon when difficulties arise during labor. Hospitals are equipped and staffed to perform cesareans within minutes or hours, day or night, so the fact that it is unplanned does not mean the hospital is unprepared. On rare occasions, an emergency arises (for example, a prolapsed cord or serious hemorrhage), and the mother's or baby's survival depends on a cesarean delivery within minutes. Under such rare circumstances, the hospital's ability to respond very quickly is crucial. Ask your caregiver about your hospital's response time. Most unplanned cesareans are done for failure to progress or fetal distress. These problems do not usually arise suddenly. They develop gradually, and there is time to try other measures to speed labor or get more oxygen to the baby. Only when these measures fail is a cesarean done. A quick response time is not critical under these circumstances.

Before the Cesarean Birth

Whether the cesarean is planned or unplanned, a nurse usually asks you to sign a consent form stating that you understand the reasons for and the risks and benefits of the cesarean, and you give your permission to the staff to do it.

The nurse then shaves your abdomen and the upper portion of your pubic hair. She may also give you an enema. The nurse starts an intravenous drip in a hand or arm vein; this will remain in place for a few to twenty-four hours after the delivery. She will insert a thin, flexible tube (a catheter) through your urethra into your bladder to keep it empty. The catheter will be removed within twenty-four hours after the surgery. Because it may be uncomfortable, you may prefer to wait until the anesthetic has taken effect before the catheter is inserted.

You might be surprised by the large number of people in the delivery room. Besides you and your partner, there are two doctors performing the surgery, an anesthesiologist or nurse anesthetist, a scrub nurse, a circulating nurse, a nurse for the baby, and possibly a doctor for the baby. They all have jobs to do. You may be impressed by the rapid and precise teamwork of this group of professionals.

Your partner is seated at the head of the delivery table where he or she can hold your hand, talk to you, and remind you to use relaxation and slow breathing to calm yourself.

Most doctors use regional anesthesia (a spinal or epidural), which allows you to be awake without feeling pain. A *spinal* numbs you from your lower chest to your toes, and you cannot move your legs. An *epidural* numbs you in the same area, but you may be aware of pressure or pulling during the surgery. Nausea, burning sensations, shoul-

der pain, trembling, and shortness of breath are all common reactions to regional anesthesia. To relieve these discomforts, the anesthesiologist can give you other medications, although they may make you drowsy and unable to enjoy your baby for the first few hours.

In those extremely rare cases of life-threatening emergencies where immediate intervention is required, a *general anesthesia* is used because it acts quickly. General anesthesia might also be used if a regional block is unsuccessful or if you are allergic to the medication used for regional blocks. Small or rural hospitals sometimes use general anesthesia because it does not require personnel with as much training as regional anesthesia requires. (See pages 210–15 for further information on anesthesia.)

The Surgery

During the surgery you will lie on your back, possibly with a wedge under one hip to move the uterus off the large blood vessels and reduce the likelihood of supine hypotension (see page 93). The nurse washes your abdomen with an antiseptic, drapes a sterile sheet over your body, and places a screen between your head and abdomen to prevent you from viewing the surgery or reaching down and touching the surgical area. If you ask, the attendant might lower the screen for the moment of birth. Cesareans take about one hour, but the baby is usually born ten to fifteen minutes after surgery begins.

During a cesarean, the doctor makes two incisions: one through the abdominal wall—the skin, fat, and connective tissue—and the other through the uterus. (Your abdominal muscles are not cut; they are spread apart, which allows them to heal better. Both incisions may be vertical or transverse (horizontal), or one may be vertical and one transverse. For example, you may have a transverse skin incision with a vertical uterine incision. It is important for future births that you know which type of uterine incision you have had, so ask the doctor to write it down for you.

Skin Incisions

There are two types of skin incisions for a cesarean. The *transverse skin incision* (or bikini cut) is the more common of the two; it is made horizontally just above the pubic bone. The *midline incision* is made vertically between your navel and pubic bone. It allows for a quick delivery in an emergency or may be preferable under some other circumstances (for example, some cases of maternal obesity).

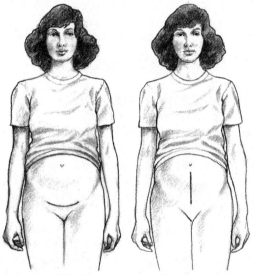

Transverse Skin Incision   **Midline Incision**

Uterine Incisions

There are three types of uterine incisions. The *classical incision* is made vertically in the upper part of the uterus. It is rarely done today except for fetal emergencies, placenta previa, and transverse lie. Vaginal delivery for future births is usually not recommended if you have a classical incision.

The most common uterine incision is the *low transverse incision*. Associated with less blood loss and reduced postpartum infection, this incision requires a little more time

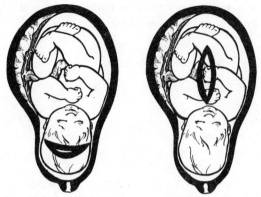

Low Transverse Incision   **Classical Incision**

to perform than the classical. After a low transverse incision, future vaginal births are encouraged, because the incision heals very well and leaves a strong scar.

The *lower segment vertical incision* is not commonly performed except when the lower part of the uterus has not developed or thinned enough to allow a transverse incision (as is the case in some premature births).

To control bleeding from the incisions, the doctor ties off or cauterizes (seals by burning) the ends of the cut blood vessels. Your doctor then suctions out the amniotic fluid from your uterus, removes your baby, shows her to you briefly, and hands her to the baby's nurse. The doctor then separates and removes your placenta by hand. You may feel some pressure or tugging at this time. The nurse suctions the baby's nose and mouth just as after a vaginal birth to remove the fluid and mucus. The baby is dried off, evaluated with the Apgar score (page 158), examined, and given any necessary medical care.

After the Cesarean Birth

After the baby and placenta are removed, the doctor inspects your uterus and begins the repair. The incisions in your uterus and abdomen are sutured with absorbable thread. The skin is closed with absorbable or nonabsorbable thread, or clamps or clips that are removed before you go home. The

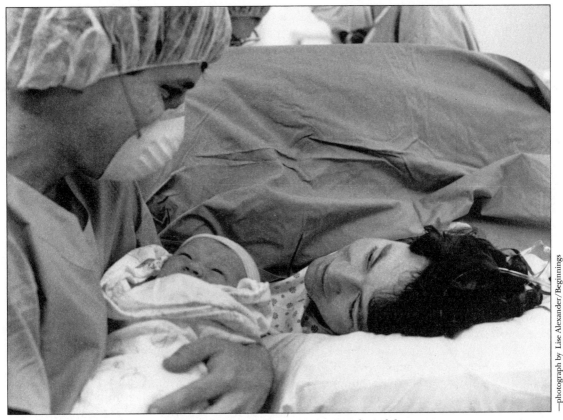

After a cesarean delivery, your partner may hold the baby so you can see and touch her.

—photograph by Lise Alexander/Beginnings

repair procedure usually takes about 30 to 45 minutes. A bandage is placed over the incision. Pitocin will be put into your IV to contract your uterus. If you had regional anesthesia, you will probably feel queasy or nauseated now. You may tremble all over. It is not clear why these reactions occur, but they usually pass within an hour or so. You may be given medication that will make you drowsy or put you to sleep through this period, but be aware that you may miss the baby's calm, alert period and be unable to nurse for a few hours. Ask in advance about these medications. You may refuse them if you wish. Warm blankets may help reduce trembling. If you have had general anesthesia, you remain unconscious through the repair and for an hour or so afterward.

If your partner is in the delivery room and the baby's condition is good, he or she can hold the baby and both of you can see and touch her. Otherwise, the baby will probably be taken to the nursery and you will see her later. As long as the baby is breathing well and is generally healthy, she can be brought to the recovery area for you to hold, admire, and breastfeed. (See pages 271–73 for help with the initial breastfeeding.) The nurses will observe the baby quite closely for the next hours and days, especially for breathing problems or a drop in body temperature, or for any other suspected problems.

In recovery (either in your labor room or in a special "recovery room"), the nurse will check your blood pressure, your incision, the firmness of your uterus, and the flow of lochia on your pad. They will observe you until the anesthesia wears off (two to four hours). Then you will be taken to your postpartum room where you will stay until you go home.

If you have had a spinal anesthetic, you may have a spinal headache when you raise your head. In that case, you will probably be told to lie flat for eight to twelve hours or you may be given a blood patch (see page 215). If you had general anesthesia, your throat and neck may be sore for a few days from the insertion of the airway tube used to administer the anesthetic.

Pain Medication after a Cesarean Birth

Pain in your incision will bother you quite a lot at first, but it gradually goes away. You will probably need pain medications for several days to a week. You might feel you should use as little as possible, but if pain keeps you from moving around and caring for your baby, you might be wiser to use enough medication to make you comfortable. If you are concerned that the medication will get to the baby via your breastmilk, you should know that only very low concentrations reach the baby.

Pain medications come in a variety of forms: pills, injections, self-administered intravenous doses, and epidural narcotics (given in the delivery room). See page 216 for a complete discussion of postcesarean pain medications.

Recovery from a Cesarean Birth

The first few days after a cesarean are the most difficult. Even little things like rolling over, coughing, breathing deeply, and reaching for the bedside telephone are difficult at first. Following are a few hints to make you more comfortable during your early recovery.

Rolling over. Here is a trick that makes rolling from your back to your side easier: Bend your knees and hips so that your feet are flat on the bed. Press your feet into the bed and lift your hips so that your body is straight from shoulders to knees. Twist your hips to one side and lower them. Then roll the upper part of your body to the same side. Now you are lying on your side. This way of rolling over keeps your incision from hurting too much and spares your elbows from painful rubbing on the sheets.

Coughing or "huffing." Coughing is painful, but it should be done if you had general anesthesia to clear the mucus that accumulates in your chest and sometimes causes infection. Use the following technique, called "huffing," to help you cough with the least pain: Support your incision gently and firmly with your hands, a small pillow, or a folded towel. Take in a deep breath, filling your lungs completely. Breathe out completely—forcefully and quickly, but evenly—pulling your abdomen in rather than pushing it out. Make a "huff" sound. Repeat several times an hour, especially if you feel a bubbly or rattling feeling in your chest. When your chest is clear and you are getting out of bed frequently, you do not need to do it so often. It helps if you try "huffing" a few times before the surgery to get the idea and make it easier to do afterward.

Standing and walking. Your first venture out of bed will take place a few to twenty-four hours after the birth. Your nurse or an aide will help you sit up, then stand. You will probably feel weak, dizzy, and light-headed the first few times you get up. You can reduce the dizziness if you do some ankle circling and leg bends to improve your circulation before getting up. Take your time. Give yourself a few moments to get used to each new position as you go from lying down to standing.

Here is how to go from lying in bed to standing up: After rolling to your side, let your legs dangle over the edge of the bed and push yourself up to a sitting position. Stay there a while and do some more ankle circling. When you are ready, place your feet on the floor and stand (with someone helping you). Stand as tall and straight as you can. It will not harm your incision even though it feels as if it is stretching and it hurts. Once you are used to the standing position, take a short walk. Each time you get out of bed you will find it a little easier. Try to increase the distance you walk each time.

Abdominal gas. Abdominal gas is sometimes a real problem after a cesarean or any abdominal surgery. You become bloated and may have sharp abdominal pains until you pass the gas. The accumulation of gas is caused by a slow-down of intestinal activity that occurs because of the surgery. Physical movement in and out of bed, deep breathing, and rocking in a chair may help prevent or alleviate gas buildup. You may also wish to avoid foods and beverages that cause gas for you. The nurse can use a rectal tube or a return flow enema to help you release gas if you are unable to.

Urination. You may have difficulty urinating after having had a urinary catheter, anesthesia, and abdominal surgery. Your nurse will suggest ways to help you urinate (see pages 227–28). If you are unable to urinate within a reasonable length of time, you will need to be recatheterized.

Breastfeeding. It is possible and desirable to breastfeed after a cesarean, but finding a comfortable position can be a problem. To protect your incision from the weight and wiggling of the baby, use the "football hold," laying the baby at your side supported by pillows, or lie on your side, or place a pillow over your incision before holding your baby on your lap for feeding. (See chapter 14.)

If your hospital has a family-centered philosophy, your partner may stay in a private room with you. If so, your baby can remain with you night and day. If your partner cannot stay, your baby may be kept in the nursery much of the time and brought to you for feedings and for cuddling.

If you share a room with another new mother, it may be comforting and reassuring if you have a roommate who also had a cesarean. You might find it difficult to watch another new mother who had an uncomplicated vaginal birth moving with ease and energy and eating normal food. Give yourself time; you will soon feel energetic and pain-free.

You will probably stay in the hospital three or four days (longer if you live in Canada). Your recovery will not be complete by then. You will still be sore, weak, and tired. If possible, arrange to have help at home for the first few weeks. You will recover much more quickly if you have help with meals, baby care, and household tasks.

When your physical condition permits, probably within one or two weeks, you may begin the postpartum exercises described on pages 230–34. Check with your caregiver as to when to begin.

Emotional Reactions to Cesareans

If you had desired and planned a vaginal birth, you have to adjust emotionally to the change in plans. If the cesarean is planned in advance, you have days or weeks beforehand to get used to the idea. If a problem develops gradually in labor, you may have hours during which you realize that the vaginal birth may not be possible. If an emergency requires an immediate cesarean, you may be shocked and completely unprepared emotionally. Everything happens so fast that you and your partner are simply swept along without enough explanation or time for questions.

After it is all over, you will think and wonder about your cesarean. There may be gaps or missing pieces, especially if labor was exhausting beforehand or if the cesarean was done suddenly. If the outcome was not good—if your baby died or is ill or if your recovery is impaired by infection or poor healing—you will have little time at first to reflect on the cesarean. Shock, grief, illness, and the numerous decisions to be made will occupy your immediate attention completely. (See pages 181–82 for further discussion of the poor outcome.) If it all turned out well, your gratefulness to be alive with a healthy baby will probably be your predominant feeling for a while. Later, although you may feel relieved and thankful for your baby, you may also find yourself depressed, disappointed in yourself or your partner, or angry with your doctor or the nursing staff. You may feel an emptiness when you recall the birth, where you had hoped and expected to feel a sense of fulfillment and joy.

This lonely, let-down feeling may persist for both you and your partner, or you may adjust to it at different rates. If possible, talk honestly and openly about the birth and your feelings—it can help. Mixed feelings about the birth may make it difficult to relate to your baby. Caring for the baby soon after birth, talking about your feelings, and getting help with baby care will help you gain perspective and adjust to your new role as a mother.

It takes time to let go of a vision, more time for some than for others. It is easier to adjust if you knew in advance that a cesarean was likely or planned; if you have confidence in the doctor who made the decision; if you had time to try measures to solve the problem and to realize that they were not succeeding; if you are treated kindly and respectfully by the staff; and if you have the opportunity afterward to review the labor and the cesarean with your caregiver or nurse.

Besides reviewing the reasons for the cesarean and filling in any gaps in your understanding or your memory of the events that took place, you should ask your caregiver two questions that will be important for future births:

1. *What type of uterine incision do I have?* Lower segment transverse or a vertical "classical" incision? The transverse incision is safer for future vaginal births since it does not weaken the body of the uterus.

2. *What about future births? Am I a good candidate for a vaginal birth?* Be sure you know the reason for your cesarean and whether it is likely to be a problem again next time. Most women can have vaginal births in the future. You should find out right away so that you do not go home assuming that you are unable to give birth vaginally. Such a belief is difficult for some to reverse suddenly in a future pregnancy.

Later, if you still have doubts or feelings of disappointment, your childbirth educator and other women who have had similar experiences (in some places there are cesarean support groups) may be able to help you and your partner review and come to terms with persistent negative feelings of sadness, anger, or disappointment.

Vaginal Birth after a Previous Cesarean (VBAC)

Most women who have had cesareans can and should, for safety reasons, have vaginal births with future pregnancies. The cesarean surgery, as it is now performed, almost always leaves a strong, healthy uterus with a scar that heals well without a weak spot. In fact, now that doctors and midwives have gained experience managing VBAC labors, they have found little or no added risk for most women. Their experience agrees with the numerous reports in the medical literature that document the safety and benefits of VBACs over repeat cesareans. These include lower maternal and newborn death rates, elimination of postoperative complications, shortened hospital stay and other economic benefits, ability to resume normal activity more quickly, and psychological benefits.[4]

There are a few situations where a VBAC may be impossible or unwise, for example, if the reason for the first cesarean still exists. If you have a chronic illness or a physical condition that makes a vaginal birth unsafe or impossible, you should probably have another cesarean. In most cases, however, the reasons for the first cesarean do not recur. The most common indications for the first cesarean—failure to progress (even CPD), fetal distress, malposition, or malpresentation—rarely come up again in future pregnancies. If the incision in the uterus was high and vertical (a classical incision), there is a slightly higher risk that the scar will separate during labor than if the incision was low and transverse. Most physicians support VBACs only with a low transverse scar, although if a woman with a classical incision is highly motivated and well-informed, some physicians will support her in a VBAC.

What if you have had more than one cesarean? The American College of Obstetricians and Gynecologists considers that more than one previous cesarean with low transverse uterine incisions is not a reason for another cesarean. The reports published in the medical literature of vaginal births after two or more previous cesareans show excellent outcomes.[5] Most caregivers do not try to persuade a woman with more than one previous cesarean to try for a vaginal delivery, but many would respect that desire if the woman is well-informed and highly motivated for a VBAC. They would either take her case themselves or refer her to a caregiver who could offer safe care.

Both caregivers and parents fear scar separation, sometimes called *uterine rupture*. This fear is the main reason that VBACs are not yet routine in the United States and Canada. To a great extent this fear is a holdover from the past, when different methods, including classical incisions and less effective suturing techniques, were used.

It is true that the likelihood of uterine rupture is somewhat higher (about two per one thousand births[6]) with VBACs than when there is no scar on the uterus. If the scar separates during labor, you will have another cesarean delivery and the separation will be repaired. Under these circumstances, the cesarean may have to be performed quite suddenly because of possible fetal distress and excessive bleeding from the uterus.

It was after comparing the risk of scar separation with the risks of a routine repeat cesarean that many leading professional medical organizations, the U.S. and Canadian national governments, many health insurers, and consumer groups endorsed VBAC as the safer choice.

VBAC Preparation

You may need to prepare differently for a VBAC than you would for another vaginal birth. Besides the recommendations on page 190 (Improving Your Chances for a Vaginal Birth) you may find it helpful to address any negative feelings left over from your cesarean that could interfere with your self-confidence and optimism for a VBAC.

Many communities have cesarean and VBAC support groups where women meet, share their stories and concerns, and support each other with the emotional issues surrounding cesareans and VBACs. If you feel no one understands what it is like to have an unexpected cesarean or that everyone feels you should be "over it" by now, or if you would like to meet other women who are preparing for a VBAC, seek out one of these groups. (If there is no such group in your area, you may be able to start one with the help of your childbirth educator and caregiver, who can help you contact others who have had cesareans. That is how most of these groups begin.)

Some communities also have special childbirth preparation classes for women and couples planning VBACs. These classes address the emotional aspects of VBACs and possible differences in medical management of the labor, along with the knowledge and skills necessary to prepare for childbirth.

As you review the circumstances of your cesarean, you might explore any deep-seated feelings in yourself that might have influenced the course of your labor. Sometimes the nature of labor itself evokes emotional responses (fear, a need to protect yourself) that you may have felt before in other painful or uncontrollable situations (sexual abuse, violence, or force). These feelings make it difficult to "yield," or to "open up." If becoming a mother evokes unpleasant associations with your own mother, neglectful parents, or an unhappy childhood, you may feel a desire to hold back, or a reluctance to allow the action that will make you a mother—birth.

Anyone who has experienced difficulties like these in the past may find them cropping up unexpectedly in the psychologically stressful circumstances of pregnancy or labor. If, as you read this, you feel that you have had some experiences in the past that have left you with unresolved or disturbing psychological issues, it might help to address them and deal with them. Good books are available that explore the psychological aspects of pregnancy and birth. (See Recommended Resources.) A counselor or psychotherapist may also be able to facilitate your resolution of these issues. Ask your childbirth educator, public health nurse, or caregiver for referrals.

The greatest challenge for the VBAC woman in labor seems to be emotional rather than physical. The following emotional challenges have been described by women as they look ahead to and go through a VBAC. You may or may not experience these yourself. These are perfectly normal reactions, but you will need to understand how to deal with them.

Fears. You may have fears of pain, of a long

labor, of a scar separation, of complications, of another cesarean, of "failure," of "the unknown." The list goes on and on, and sometimes, when comparing these fears with the familiar, if unpleasant, memories of your cesarean, it may seem easier to plan another cesarean. If you disclose any such fears to your caregiver, childbirth educator, or support group, you will probably receive much reassurance and extra support. A labor support person who has had a VBAC herself, or one who can spend extra time with you before labor, can help you overcome such fears.

Lack of confidence. You may doubt your ability to give birth vaginally. You may hesitate to invest much time and effort in a VBAC because you do not want to be disappointed again. Because you did not give birth vaginally before, you may lack hope or confidence that you can this time. It helps to review the differences between last time and this; this is a different pregnancy, a different birth. Get to know people who have had VBACs, be sure you know what to expect and ways to cope with labor pain, and surround yourself with people who can give you confidence. An experienced labor support person or your childbirth educator can encourage both you and your partner if you begin doubting your abilities. She or he can also suggest comfort measures and labor promoting measures and help you deal with medical decisions if they arise.

Stress in labor. In addition to the emotional hurdles that come up in most labors (see chapter 8), there are particular times in a VBAC labor that may raise your anxiety level.

♦ *Getting into labor* may be your "moment of truth." As you really get going, you may suddenly wonder if a VBAC is such a good idea after all. One study reported that it was in the first five hours of labor when most of the women who tried but did not have a VBAC gave up.[7] Be prepared for this, and

Your partner or a trained labor support person can provide encouragement and help you overcome your fears.

have ideas for dealing with it. You may find yourself tensing and overreacting to early labor contractions, which will increase your pain. Review chapters 7 and 8 for suggestions for ways to handle the discomforts and emotional hurdles of early labor.

♦ *Flashbacks to your previous labor* may be triggered by particular events that remind you of your last labor. They may bring back unpleasant associations or memories. Do not suppress these flashbacks. Acknowledge them openly and figure out how the circumstances are different this time from last. If your partner has similar flashbacks, it is better that he or she not bring them up with you. He or she should discuss them with your labor support person, the nurse, or caregiver.

♦ *Approaching the point in labor where you had a cesarean last time* (in hours of labor or centimeters of dilation) may loom ahead as a large hurdle for you, and until you pass that point you may still question your ability to have a VBAC. Once passed you may heave a sigh of relief and feel a boost of optimism.

As a woman who has had a cesarean, you know that you could have another. Preparing psychologically for both—a vaginal birth and a cesarean birth—is a challenge. Your preparation should be realistic and include the following: learning the reasons for the previous cesarean; changing caregivers and hospitals if their policies led to your first cesarean or if they are not supportive of VBACs; improving your eating and health habits if they contributed to your need for the cesarean; exploring any negative or destructive emotions that may have contributed to or resulted from the cesarean; taking good childbirth classes; planning to use medications and interventions only if necessary; and inviting caring, supportive people to help during labor. Then you have done all you can to ensure a vaginal birth.

The other essential—a reasonably normal labor with a baby and mother who remain healthy throughout—cannot be guaranteed. For that reason you have to keep the cesarean option open. It is a good solution when serious problems arise.

Feelings of fulfillment and joy are there when you know you did a good job—no matter how you gave birth.

Chapter 11
Medications during Labor, Birth, and Post Partum

Every culture throughout history has had its experts on childbirth—midwives, priests, shamans, medicine men, doctors—who established dietary, spiritual, and behavioral guidelines to ease the birth process and improve outcomes. These experts also used drugs during childbirth for various purposes, most commonly to ease labor pain or to bring on strong labor contractions. In earlier times and other cultures, these "drugs" were extracts from plants, such as poppies (opium and laudanum), fruits (wine and brandy), willow bark (aspirin), rye fungus (ergot, which caused uterine contractions), and many others.

In contemporary western culture, the emphasis is greater than ever on development, perfection, and wide utilization of drugs for every health care need. This is also true for pregnancy, birth, and breast-feeding, although these conditions pose a unique challenge in the search for safe, effective drugs: There are two "patients," each with very different responses to drugs. Your caregiver must consider both when selecting drugs.

Today drugs are used for numerous purposes in labor and afterward, for example:

♦ To induce sleep

♦ To reduce anxiety

♦ To reduce labor pain

♦ To stop contractions or reduce their intensity

♦ To ripen the cervix

♦ To start or strengthen contractions

♦ To raise or lower blood pressure or to control the effects of high blood pressure

♦ To stop bleeding

♦ To prevent seizures associated with eclampsia

♦ To treat nausea and vomiting

♦ To counter undesired side effects on mother or baby of medications, especially narcotics and general anesthetics

♦ To prevent production of breast milk

♦ To reduce pain after childbirth

Medications act by altering your body's responses in a way that will solve a particular problem. They may have other effects on you and your baby as well, some undesirable, some potentially serious. Your caregiver should evaluate all the possible effects of a drug when considering how to treat a particular problem. You need to know the possible disadvantages and risks as well as the benefits of the medications that may be used. It also helps to know if there are other acceptable ways to address the problem.

It helps to learn about medications before labor. Then, when the choice arises in labor, you already have some background. This chapter will provide general information.

Ideally, whenever considering medications, you and your caregiver should discuss the following questions (if you are in great pain or if there is an emergency, however, calm discussion may be impossible):

1. What are the benefits or purposes of the medications?

2. Is this medication the only treatment? Are there other options? What happens if you choose not to take it?

3. Have you ever had an adverse reaction to this or a similar drug? Have you told your caregiver and the anesthesiologist about any drug reactions you have and any other medications you are taking?

4. What are the risks or undesirable side effects of the drug on the mother, fetus/ newborn, or labor progress?

Once you have the answers to all these questions, you will be able to make an informed decision, one that contributes positively to your health and to the well-being of your baby.

Pain in Childbirth

When asked to describe labor contractions and the sensations of birth, women say the experience is exhilarating, uncomfortable, frightening, powerful, over-whelming, beautiful, and painful. The pain of childbirth, which is in the forefront of most women's minds when they think about labor and delivery, has been attributed to several factors:[1]

♦ Reduced oxygen supply to the uterine muscle (this pain is more intense if the interval between contractions is short, preventing full replenishment of oxygen to the uterine muscle)

♦ The stretching of the cervix (effacement and dilation)

♦ Pressure by the baby on the nerves in and near the cervix and vagina

♦ Tension on and stretching of the supporting ligaments of the uterus and pelvic joints during contractions and descent of the baby

♦ Pressure on the urethra, bladder, and rectum

♦ Stretching of the pelvic floor muscles

♦ Fear and anxiety, which can cause the release of excessive stress hormones (epinephrine, norepinephrine, and others), resulting in a longer labor[2]

The perception of pain in labor varies greatly from one woman to another. It may be increased by many factors: the length of prelabor, fatigue, fear and anxiety, feeling alone, lack of mobility, or a full bladder. At the same time, the perception of pain during labor can be reduced by the presence of one of more supportive persons, the upright position, immersion in water, and other comfort measures.

The pain of childbirth will be influenced by your past experiences, your cultural background, your beliefs about birth, and your expectations for the whole experience. Simply knowing the reason for the pain may help you cope better with it. Also, it helps to know that when childbirth is normal, the pain is not a sign of injury; it is, as Sheila Kitzinger, a well-known British childbirth educator, says, "pain with a purpose."[3] If you acknowledge the pain, work with your body during childbirth, and remember that the pain will soon end, you will be able to put it into perspective and keep it from overwhelming you.

This book emphasizes coping techniques and comfort measures that, whether used exclusively or in combination with medication, help reduce the pain of labor and birth. (See chapter 7 for a discussion of these techniques and comfort measures.)

The Use of Medication for Pain Relief in Childbirth

Some women want very much to have a natural childbirth (that is, to give birth without using medications), while others cannot imagine themselves going without medications. Most women's desires, however, fall somewhere between these two. While they would like to minimize their use of strong pain medications, they do not want to suffer. The information in this chapter will help you form your own opinions and preferences regarding your use of pain medications.

Clarifying Your Preferences

First of all, what factors should be present in order for you to have an unmedicated birth or to minimize your use of pain medications? There are four important factors:

1. *Your own desire.* The stronger your preference for a natural birth, the more likely you are to have one. How do you feel and how strongly? Make sure your partner and caregiver are aware of your preferences. Describe them in your birth plan.

2. *Childbirth preparation.* If you know what to expect and can use the pain-relieving and labor-enhancing techniques described in this book, you will not need to rely solely on pain medications. Childbirth preparation

classes provide not only information, but demonstration, practice, and personal guidance in these techniques. Take the best classes available. (See pages 6–7 for more on choosing childbirth classes.)

3. *Support and help from one or more partners, your caregiver, and nurse.* When everyone shares your desire and knows how to help you, it reduces your need for pain medications. In addition to a loved one or friend, you may invite or hire a trained, experienced labor support person who remains with you throughout labor and helps you cope with the pain and unpredictability of labor. Ask your childbirth educator for referrals.

Choose a doctor or midwife who supports you in your feelings about pain medications. Select a setting (hospital, birth center, or home) where the staff is most likely to help you accomplish your desires regarding pain medications. (See pages 3 and 5 for a discussion of these choices.)

4. *A reasonably normal labor pattern.* This is largely beyond your control. A very prolonged or complicated labor may require medications, even if all the other factors are present. Your classes and this book should help you understand when medications may be required, even if you had not wanted to use them.

Laboring without Pain Medication

If you prefer to avoid or minimize your use of pain medications, the following suggestions will help:

♦ Be sure the staff knows your wishes. Ask them to help you have an unmedicated childbirth. Ask them not to offer you medication, even if you appear to be in pain. Ask them instead to offer you encouragement, advice about your labor progress, and ideas for comfort measures. This does not mean that you cannot receive medication if you decide you need it.

♦ When you reach six centimeters, assess how you are coping. If you are able to relax *between* contractions (if not during) and are able to use patterned breathing or some other coping activity consistently during the contractions, you are doing very well. Do not expect to feel peaceful and relaxed during contractions. Remember that as labor intensifies, it also speeds up. (See the graph on page 142.) Labor's intensity is an encouraging sign of progress. By about six centimeters, your contractions are about as painful as they will become (though they will come closer together). If you are able to handle the contractions at six centimeters, and if labor continues to follow a normal course, you will probably be able to manage the rest of your labor without pain medications.

♦ If difficulties arise or if you become exhausted and discouraged during labor and start to think about pain medication, ask these questions: How far are you dilated? How is labor progressing? Is it likely to last much longer? Would other coping techniques and comfort measures help? Have you changed breathing patterns? (See chapter 7.) Can you postpone medication for three to five more contractions? The answers will help you make the best decision.

General Considerations

As you consider the pros and cons of laboring with or without pain medications, keep these factors in mind:

♦ Medications can relieve some or all of your labor pain.

♦ Labor often hurts more than you may have anticipated.

♦ Although many new techniques and medications are available today, a perfect method for abolishing the pain of childbirth has still not been achieved. Therefore, you should not expect total absence of pain from the beginning to the end of your labor even if you use pain medications.

♦ Drugs and anesthetics may affect your labor. For instance, while drugs sometimes promote relaxation and hasten the progress of labor, they often do just the opposite— impede labor progress and increase your need for other medical interventions.

♦ When you request pain medication, there may be a delay before the staff can respond. Once administered, it will take time before the medication takes effect.

♦ Since "no drug has been proven safe for the unborn child,"[4] most physicians and midwives discourage heavy or unlimited use of pain medications throughout labor and during childbirth.

♦ The fetus will be directly or indirectly affected by any medication you receive.

♦ The specific effects of medication depend on the particular drug, the amount received, how and when in labor it is given, individual reactions to the drug, and other factors. When you receive medication, the medical staff watches for negative effects and initiates corrective measures if necessary.

♦ Because the immature liver and kidneys of the newborn are unable to rapidly detoxify, metabolize, or excrete medications, the effects of some drugs last longer for the baby than they do for the mother.

♦ Pain medications or anesthetics are often used when birth requires painful interventions or surgical assistance (such as forceps, or an episiotomy) and are always used for cesarean births.

Weighing the Benefits and Risks

In most labors, if medications are used judiciously with up-to-date methods, the risks are slight, subtle, and probably temporary. In some cases, even with excellent care, medications cause more serious and longer

Benefits and Risks of Pain Medications

	Possible benefits	Possible risks
Effects on mother	Medications may reduce labor pain and the pain of surgical or medical intervention. They may promote relaxation, reduce anxiety, or increase comfort.	Medications inhibit your mobility. They may affect your blood pressure and cause nausea, dizziness, disorientation, or loss of control. They may have little effect on pain.
Effects on labor and birth	Although pain medications are not used for this purpose, they sometimes enhance the progress of labor.	Medications may slow progress by interfering with uterine activity or diminishing the urge to push. This may increase your need for further intervention.
Effects on fetus and baby	Medications may indirectly benefit a distressed fetus by hastening the progress of labor.	Medications may cause an abnormal fetal heart rate, interfere with normal newborn reflexes, inhibit sucking responses, cause difficulty with breathing, or produce drowsiness.

direct or indirect effects. Caregivers should be aware of the potential risks and be prepared to deal with them if they occur.

The choice is not always an easy one. With the help of your caregiver, you must weigh the expected physical or psychological benefits of a particular medication against its possible risks.

One factor that really cannot be predicted or controlled is the nature of the labor itself. It is wise to remain flexible when considering the use of medication. Most labors are uncomplicated and, depending on your desire, can be handled without pain medications. Other labors are far more difficult—some are very long and exhausting and some may require medical or surgical procedures that increase pain. In such cases the benefits of medication more clearly outweigh the risks. Since you may have a difficult labor that requires pain medications, your birth preparations should include an understanding of medications and the circumstances under which they might be used. Then, if you need medication, you can choose wisely and appropriately. Later, when you look back on your labor, you will feel satisfied that you handled a difficult situation well.

Pain Medications Used in Labor and Birth

Each drug and anesthetic has specific characteristics that make it appropriate only during a particular phase or stage of labor. Some medications should not be given too early because they will interfere with the progress of labor. Others should only be given early because they can have harmful effects on the newborn. With such drugs, if there's enough time, most of the drug is excreted from the baby's system before birth. Because of the different drug effects, you may be offered one medication during the latent phase of labor and a different medication during the transition phase or birth. When used appropriately, medications can relieve some or all of your pain while not seriously compromising the well-being of your baby or the progress of labor.

Medications that are used for pain relief in labor and birth cause either *analgesia* (pain relief) or *anesthesia* (loss of sensation). These medications can be classified as *systemic medications* and as *regional* and *local* anesthetics.

Systemic Medications

"Systemic" means "affecting your whole body." Systemic medications come in many forms (pills, liquids, injections, suppositories, or gases). All are absorbed into your blood stream, and because they go wherever your blood goes, they exert effects throughout your body, or whole system (thus the name, systemic). The desired effect is to

Systemic Medications

Systemic medications are listed here with their *generic* (chemical) names first and their *brand* names in parentheses. Effects and side effects vary, depending on total dosage, timing, fetal condition, and the mother's individual response.[a]

Type	Drug names	Benefits/purposes	Risks/disadvantages
Sedatives and hypnotics	*Barbiturates:* ♦ pentobarbital (Nembutal) ♦ secobarbital (Seconal) ♦ amobarbital (Amytal) ♦ phenobarbital (Luminal)	Sedatives (which allay anxiety, irritability, and excitement) or hypnotics (which induce rest, relaxation, or sleep) are usually administered early in labor. Sedatives are smaller doses and hypnotics larger doses of the same drugs. They may be given to decrease contractions in a slow, painful prelabor.	♦ *To the mother:* Hypnotic doses may cause dizziness and disorientation and can prolong labor by impairing uterine activity. ♦ *To the baby:* Barbiturates may accumulate in fetal tissue and cause respiratory depression, decreased responsiveness, and impaired sucking ability in the newborn.
Amnesics (anticholinergics)	♦ scopolamine	Amnesics are rarely used today. Years ago they were combined with narcotics to sedate the mother and keep her from remembering (called twilight sleep). Scopolamine alone is given before surgery to reduce saliva and bronchial secretions.	♦ *To the mother:* This drug causes dry mouth, blurred vision, heart palpitations, dizziness, disorientation, hallucinations, thrashing, suppression of lactation and, later, amnesia of the whole experience. ♦ *To the baby:* This drug changes the fetal heart rate, may cause newborn respiratory depression and sleepiness, and may contribute to newborn hemorrhage.
Tranquilizers	*Phenothiazines:* ♦ promethazine (Phenergan) ♦ prochlorperazine (Compazine) ♦ chlorpromazine (Thorazine) ♦ promazine (Sparine) ♦ propiomazine (Largon)	Tranquilizers are used to reduce tension, apprehension, and anxiety. If used in labor, the dosage is timed to wear off before birth. The phenothiazines and hydroxyzine are also used to reduce nausea and vomiting. They are sometimes combined with narcotics to increase the effects of lower doses of narcotics.	♦ *To the mother:* Tranquilizers may cause drowsiness, dizziness, blurred vision, confusion, dry mouth, and changes in blood pressure and heart rate. When given with barbiturates or narcotics, tranquilizers may increase their sedative and depressant effects.

Type	Drug names	Benefits/purposes	Risks/disadvantages
Tranquilizers (continued)	*Benzodiazepines:* ♦ midazolam (Versed) ♦ diazepam (Valium) ♦ chlordiazepoxide (Librium) ♦ alprazolam (Xanax) ♦ oxazepam (Serax) ♦ prazepam (Centrax) ♦ lorazepam (Ativan) *Miscellaneous:* ♦ hydroxyzine (Vistaril or Atarax)	The benzodiazepines are usually given only after birth because of potential serious side effects for the baby.	♦ *To the baby:* Use of the benzodiazepines in labor sometimes causes fetal heart rate alterations, the "floppy infant" syndrome (poor muscle tone, sleepiness, and sucking difficulties), and a drop in body temperature. The use of phenothiazines near term can inhibit newborn reflexes and cause jaundice.
Narcotic analgesics	♦ meperidine (Demerol) ♦ morphine ♦ fentanyl (Sublimaze) ♦ butorphanol (Stadol) ♦ nalbuphine (Nubain) ♦ pentazocine (Talwin) ♦ hydromorphone (Dilaudid) ♦ codeine	Narcotic analgesics, usually given during active labor, reduce pain and promote relaxation between contractions. Some (for example, Demerol) may speed a labor that has been slowed by tension and stress. Large doses of narcotics (especially morphine) are sometimes used in a prolonged prelabor in hopes of stopping contractions and giving the mother a rest. They may also be used post partum. Stadol, Nubain, and Talwin are combination drugs—a narcotic plus a narcotic antagonist (see below), which reduces some of the narcotic's undesired side effects.	♦ *To the mother:* Narcotic analgesics may cause drowsiness, hallucinations, dizziness, euphoria, respiratory depression, nausea, vomiting, and slowing of digestion. They may lower blood pressure. They often interfere with mental activity and use of breathing patterns. Narcotics may slow labor progress; this effect is more pronounced if the medication is given before the active phase of labor. ♦ *To the baby:* Narcotic analgesics may make the fetal heart rate less reactive to stimuli, depress the newborn's respiration, and alter the infant's behavioral responses (for example, breastfeeding) for several days or weeks.
Narcotic antagonists	♦ naloxone (Narcan)	Narcotic antagonists reduce or reverse the effects of narcotics including hallucinations, respiratory depression, sedation, and hypotension (low blood pressure). Narcan is given by injection to the laboring woman if there is narcotic toxicity, or to the newborn when there is respiratory depression caused by narcotics.	♦ *To mother and baby:* Abrupt reversal of narcotic depression may result in rapid heart rate, increased blood pressure, nausea, vomiting, sweating, trembling, and the return of pain to the mother. If she is addicted to narcotics, a narcotic antagonist may cause withdrawal symptoms in the mother or baby. The effects of narcotics may return if the narcotic antagonist wears off before the narcotic.

a *1990 Physician's Desk Reference,* 44th ed. (Oradell, NJ: Medical Economics Co., 1990).

reduce your pain, but there may be other undesirable effects as well.

Because systemic medications are carried throughout your body, including your placenta, they cross over to your baby and can cause side effects. The magnitude of these effects depends on the amount of medication used, the number of doses, and the amount of time that elapses between the last dose of medication and the delivery of the baby. Another important determinant is the baby's maturity, health, and response during labor. With the same amount of medication,

a healthy, full-term baby will probably show fewer effects than a premature, ill, or distressed baby. The medication or its metabolic by-products do not completely disappear from the baby's blood stream for days after birth,[5] and subtle neurobehavioral changes (described in the previous chart) are present during the first few days after birth. These changes may be so subtle that they are obvious only to professionals who examine your baby with very sensitive tests, such as the Brazelton Neonatal Neurobehavioral Assessment Scale.[6]

General Analgesics and Anesthetics

Type	Drug names	Benefits/purposes	Risks/disadvantages
Induction agents	♦ thiopental sodium (Pentothal) ♦ methohexital sodium (Brevital) ♦ thiamylal sodium (Surital)	Induction agents are usually very short-acting barbiturates that produce drowsiness and semiconsciousness. They are given intravenously to ease the administration of the inhalation agents.	♦ *To the mother:* Induction agents cause respiratory depression, lower the blood pressure, and may change her heart rate. Large doses may reduce uterine activity. ♦ *To the baby:* Large doses may result in respiratory depression and poor muscle tone.
Inhalation agents	♦ isoflurane (Forane) ♦ nitrous oxide ♦ enflurane (Ethrane) ♦ halothane (Fluothane)	Inhalation agents rapidly provide analgesia or anesthesia with loss of sensation and consciousness. May be used for cesarean birth when speed is important. Nitrous oxide in an analgesic concentration can be self-administered by the mother with a hand-held mask.	♦ *To the mother:* Inhalation agents may cause nausea, respiratory depression, changes in blood pressure and heart rate, and elevated temperature and may increase the incidence of postpartum hemorrhage. The most serious, though rare, risk of general anesthesia is inhalation of vomited material, which can cause pneumonia and possibly death. Modern anesthesia technique minimizes these risks. There is a much lower possibility of side effects with self-administered analgesia due to lower drug concentration. ♦ *To the baby:* Inhalation agents may cause respiratory depression, drowsiness, poor muscle tone, and low Apgar scores.

General Analgesia and Anesthesia

General analgesia refers to a reduction of pain and awareness. *General anesthesia* refers to a total loss of both sensation and consciousness. For labor and birth, general analgesia and anesthesia are achieved by inhalation of a gas. General analgesics and anesthetics take effect almost immediately. In fact, they act more quickly than any other form of systemic medication.

The main difference between general analgesics and general anesthetics is in the concentration of the gas used (percent of drug and percent of air). A lower concentration reduces pain awareness but does not remove it completely. The mother sometimes holds the mask and uses it herself for analgesia, whereas an anesthetist always gives general anesthetic. General anesthetics are rarely used for vaginal births because the mother's participation in delivery is needed. They are used in the following situations:

♦ Emergency cesareans, when a rapid loss of sensation is required

♦ In small or rural hospitals that cannot offer regional anesthesia at all hours

♦ In the rare instance that an epidural or spinal block cannot be placed

♦ When the woman cannot tolerate a regional anesthetic

Under such circumstances, the benefits of general anesthesia outweigh its risks. Otherwise, regional anesthesia is preferred.

General anesthesia is achieved through a two-step process. First, an "induction agent" is given intravenously. This quickly makes the woman very relaxed and semiconscious. Then she inhales a gas that causes complete loss of consciousness. A tube is inserted into the woman's trachea (windpipe) to keep her airway open and to allow administration of the anesthetic. Because an unconscious person may vomit, the tube is there to help prevent her from inhaling the vomited material.

Regional and Local Analgesia and Anesthesia

A *regional* or *local* block causes a decrease or total loss of sensation (numbness) in a specific area or region of your body. An anesthetic is injected near particular nerves; this blocks the transmission of impulses over those nerves. The major functions of nerves are to conduct sensations (including pain) to your brain and to control activity of your muscles or organs. These functions are diminished by regional or local anesthetics. Lower doses of anesthetic take away pain and other sensations without taking away all muscle control. Higher doses remove both sensation and the ability to use your muscles. Higher doses are also likely to affect your baby more than lower doses. Other factors also influence your response and your baby's: the medication selected, the area injected, the technique of administration, your individual bodily response, and your baby's condition during labor. Regional and local anesthetics do not affect your mental state. You do not become groggy, sleepy, or confused, as you do with most systemic pain medications.

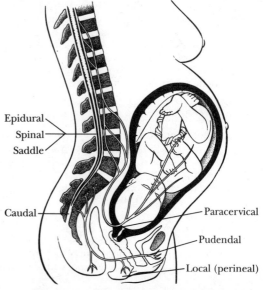

Placement of Regional and Local Blocks

Regional and Local Analgesia and Anesthesia

The placement of the anesthetic or analgesic determines the area where sensation is reduced and pain is relieved. The anesthetic is usually one of the "caine" drugs — bupivacaine (Marcaine), lidocaine (Xylocaine), chloroprocaine (Nesacaine), and mepivacaine (Carbocaine). The narcotics that may be used include morphine (Duramorph), fentanyl (Sublimaze), sufentanil (Sufenta), and others.

Epidural block

Placement of anesthetic
- In lumbar region of back, between vertebrae into the epidural space
- Given while you lie on your side

Area of pain relief
- In standard block: abdomen, back, buttocks, perineum, and legs
- In segmental block: abdomen and back only

Time given
Usually after cervix has dilated 4 to 5 cm's, sometimes as early as 2 cm's

Comments: Most commonly used regional block. Amount of pain relief and side effects depend on the timing of administration and concentration and total dose of the anesthetic. Possible side effects include the following: maternal fever;[a] a drop in maternal blood pressure; limited mobility of the mother; a slowing of labor, fetal rotation, and descent; diminished ability to push; and increased need for Pitocin, forceps, vacuum extraction, and cesarean birth.[b] Subtle, short-term neurobehavioral effects in the newborn may be present. Mother may have backache after birth.[c] Possible spinal headache if dura is punctured. Standard epidural often used for cesarean birth.

Epidural or spinal with a narcotic or combination narcotic/anesthetic

Placement of anesthetic
- In lumbar region of back, between vertebrae
- For epidural, into epidural space
- For spinal, through dura into subarachnoid space

Area of pain relief
Lower trunk and perineal area

Time given
- For labor, usually after cervix has dilated 4 to 5 cm's, sometimes as early as 2 cm's
- After cesarean birth

Comments: First used in the late 1980s, primarily for postcesarean pain relief. Now sometimes used during labor. Provides prolonged pain relief without loss of sensation or ability to move. Pain relief may last from several hours up to 24 hours or more. Close monitoring of the mother required for 24 hours as side effects may be delayed. Side effects of the narcotic epidural for the mother may include itching, difficulty in urination, nausea, vomiting, and rarely, respiratory depression. The effects on the mother and the fetus/newborn are less than with the epidural or spinal block using only a local anesthetic or with systemic use of narcotics because of the lower total drug dosage.

Caudal block

Placement of anesthetic
- At top of crack in buttocks, into the caudal canal at base of sacrum
- Given while you lie on your side or in knee-chest position

Area of pain relief
Abdomen, back, buttocks, perineum, and legs

Time given
After 5 cm's dilation

Comments: Most patients receive good anesthesia. May slow labor by reducing uterine contractility. May cause drop in maternal blood pressure, which leads to a drop in fetal heart rate. Diminishes urge to push and bearing-down reflex and impairs normal rotation and descent of baby, increasing need for forceps or vacuum extractor. Subtle short-term neonatal neurobehavioral alterations have been observed. Used less often today than the epidural block.

Spinal or saddle block

Placement of anesthetic
- Usually between third and fourth lumbar vertebrae through the dura into the subarachnoid space
- For spinal you lie on your side
- For saddle you sit up

Area of pain relief
- For spinal: trunk and legs from breasts to toes
- For saddle: low abdomen, inner thighs, perineum, and buttocks

Time given
- Late first stage
- Second stage

Comments: Spinals not usually given for vaginal birth, but often used for cesarean birth. Saddles occasionally given for vaginal birth or when forceps are needed. Nearly 100 percent of patients receive good anesthesia. Possible spinal headache afterward; possible drop in maternal blood pressure with resulting side effects. Mother may have difficulty with urination later. Frequently slows labor by reducing pelvic floor muscle tone and diminishing mother's bearing down effort. Similar fetal and neonatal effects as with caudal and epidural anesthesia.

Paracervical block

Placement of anesthetic
Two injections into the cervix

Area of pain relief
Cervix and lower segment of uterus

Time given
Between 4 and 10 cm's of dilation

Comments: May be repeated as needed. Rarely used today because of possible adverse effect on fetus/newborn. Anesthetic readily enters maternal circulation and crosses to the fetus, sometimes causing marked slowing of fetal heart rate, and in the newborn diminished muscle tone and delay in neurobehavioral responses. There may be a transient decrease in intensity and/or frequency of uterine contractions.

Pudendal block

Placement of anesthetic
Injections into both sides of vagina to block pudendal nerves

Area of pain relief
Vagina and perineum

Time given
- Second stage
- Third stage

Comments: Not 100 percent effective. Used for discomfort during delivery or when forceps or vacuum extraction are needed, or for episiotomy or its repair. May inhibit bearing-down reflex and impede fetal rotation and descent by relaxing muscle tone of perineum. Sometimes causes short-term neonatal neurobehavioral changes.

"Local" infiltration

Placement of anesthetic
Several injections around the vagina

Area of pain relief
Perineum

Time given
- Second stage
- Third stage

Comments: Given for episiotomy or after birth for repair of episiotomy or tears. May increase perineal tissue damage when given before birth.

[a] Fusi et al., "Maternal Pyrexia Associated with the Use of Epidural Analgesia in Labour," *Lancet* 8649 (3 June 1989): 1250.

[b] K. Dickersin, "Pharmacologic Control of Pain during Labour," in *Effective Care in Pregnancy and Childbirth,* edited by I. Chalmers, M. Enkin, and M. Kierse (Oxford: Oxford University Press, 1989): 913; J.A. Thorp et al., "The Effect of Continuous Epidural Analgesia on Cesarean Section for Dystocia in Nulliparous Women," *American Journal of Obstetrics and Gynecology* 161 (September 1989): 670.

[c] C. MacArthur et al., "Epidural Anaesthesia and Long Term Backache after Childbirth," *British Medical Journal* 301 (7 July 1990): 9.

The difference between local and regional anesthesia is in the location of the injection. Local anesthetics are injected in the skin, muscle, or cervix. They block sensation in a small, or local area near nerve endings. The paracervical block numbs the cervix; the pudendal block numbs the vagina; the perineal block numbs the perineum. Regional anesthetics are given in the lower back near nerve roots in the spinal cord and affect the region of the body where the nerves and their branches go (as small an area as the abdomen and lower back only, or as large an area as the entire body below the chest). Regional blocks provide pain relief in a much larger area than local blocks, while using smaller amounts of medication. Spinal, saddle (a low spinal), epidural, and caudal blocks are types of regional blocks.

The goal with anesthesia is to provide good pain relief without unfavorable side effects. In recent years, anesthesiologists have developed a technique called *regional analgesia* (a "light epidural," "band anesthesia," or "segmental block"), which reduces pain but does not remove all sensation. It also causes fewer side effects than standard regional anesthesia. To achieve analgesia rather than anesthesia, anesthesiologists use lower concentrations of the anesthetic. Another method, which has recently been introduced, is to combine the anesthetic with small doses of narcotics. Even with these advances in anesthesia technique, there remain potential side effects on you, your labor, or your baby. (See the chart on page 212.)

Procedure for Regional Blocks

The procedure for regional blocks is as follows:

1. The mother is given intravenous (IV) fluids to help reduce the chance of a drop in blood pressure and to enable administration of drugs, if necessary.

2. The mother lies on her side with her body curled, or she sits up, leaning forward. The anesthesiologist cleans the area (the antiseptic often feels cold), numbs the skin with a local anesthetic, and injects a small test dose of the anesthetic into the appropriate place in the lower back. (See the illustration on page 215 for the exact location of the injections.)

3. If there are no problems with the test dose, the full dose is injected. Within a few minutes the mother begins to notice the effects (tingling, numbness), and within fifteen to twenty minutes she will probably experience good pain relief.

4. If desired, a thin plastic catheter may be inserted and left in place at the injection site so that more anesthetic may be given, providing *continuous anesthesia*. Repeated injections or a continuous infusion pump adds anesthetic through the catheter for longer-lasting pain relief.

5. The mother's blood pressure and pulse are checked frequently, and labor contractions and the fetal heart rate are closely monitored. If the mother's blood pressure drops, the anesthesiologist may give her *vasopressors* to raise it. If her contractions slow down, the caregiver may use Pitocin to augment them.

Other Factors to Consider

♦ Midwives administer only the local or perineal block.

♦ Family physicians and obstetricians administer paracervical, pudendal, and local blocks.

♦ An anesthesiologist or nurse anesthetist administers epidural, caudal, spinal, and saddle anesthesia. There is an additional fee for the services of these specialists. Some small or rural hospitals do not have enough staff to provide twenty-four-hour obstetric anesthesia services. When anesthesia personnel are not available, they rely on simpler methods—systemic medications, local blocks, or general anesthesia.

♦ Both spinal and saddle anesthesia require puncture of the dura, the tough covering surrounding the spinal cord and cerebral spinal fluid. A spinal headache may result from this type of anesthesia. If the mother has a headache when her head is elevated but not when she lies flat, it is called a spinal headache. Whether mild or severe, the pain is caused by a leak of cerebrospinal fluid (the fluid surrounding the spinal cord and brain) through the puncture site in the dura. The headache usually disappears within a few days or weeks as the dura heals and closes the puncture site. If the headache lingers, a "blood patch" may be made by injecting a small amount of the mother's blood into the area next to the puncture site. A clot then forms and seals the puncture. This technique is usually effective for immediate and permanent relief of spinal headache.

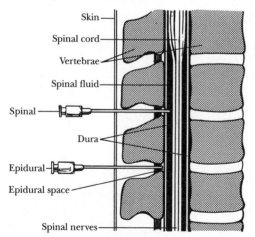

Placement of Spinal and Epidural Blocks

♦ With epidural and caudal anesthesia the anesthetic is injected outside the dura in the epidural or extradural space. A spinal headache rarely accompanies this type of injection, and only if the dura is penetrated unintentionally.

♦ Epidural and caudal blocks are more difficult to administer and are slower to take effect than spinal and saddle blocks.

♦ In most urban areas, the epidural block is the most widely used of all the regional blocks. The caudal block has been replaced by the epidural block almost everywhere.

♦ Vasoconstrictors (such as epinephrine) are sometimes added to the "caine" anesthetics (such as lidocaine and marcaine) in hopes of slowing systemic absorption of the drug and prolonging the duration of the anesthesia. Vasoconstrictors sometimes alter the mother's heart rate and blood pressure.

♦ Where available, regional anesthesia (epidural or spinal) is preferred for cesarean birth rather than general anesthesia because it has fewer side effects and allows the mother to be fully conscious.

Postpartum Medications

While you may need no medications at all after the baby is born, there are many available for a variety of purposes: oxytocics to keep the uterus contracted; sedatives to help you sleep; laxatives and stool softeners to help bowel function; lactation suppressants for those who choose not to breastfeed; pain medications for "afterpains" (see page 225) or postcesarean or perineal stitch pain; antibiotics for infection; and vitamins to improve your nutrition. In the past, a nurse would give prescribed medications at designated times or when the mother requested medication for pain relief or other discomforts. Today, caregivers recognize that most mothers are able to determine their own medication needs. They have developed self-administered medication (SAM) programs that give women more responsibility for their own use of medications and help prepare them to use medications safely at home.

Many hospitals offer patient-controlled analgesia (PCA) for mothers following a cesarean birth. With PCA, you have an intravenous (IV) drip in place. Whenever you need pain relief you can press a button to release a small dose of narcotic into the intravenous fluid. You have greater control over your comfort and more rapid pain relief. Maintaining consistent, safe blood levels of the drug helps decrease the sedative effect of the narcotic, which makes you less drowsy. The PCA unit is used for 24 to 48 hours following a cesarean birth. Mothers on PCA often use less total medication and are usually less groggy than those receiving injected or oral narcotics. PCA has the disadvantage of requiring an IV in place, which might be unnecessary otherwise. It makes movement in and out of bed and baby care more awkward and cumbersome.

The epidural or spinal narcotic offers another approach to pain relief after a cesarean or a difficult vaginal birth. If you have a regional block for labor or a cesarean birth, it may be possible for you to have a long-acting narcotic injected into the epidural catheter soon after the birth. It provides good pain relief for up to twenty-four hours without causing drowsiness, making it relatively easy for you to get out of bed and maintain normal activities. Itching all over is a frequent side effect of epidural narcotics. Another rare though potentially serious side effect is delayed respiratory depression in the mother. Epidural narcotics require that the nurse observe the mother frequently. This method of pain relief is not yet widely available.

Other Medications Used for Childbirth

During childbirth and the early postpartum period, medications may be used to prevent or treat conditions that pose a health risk to you and/or your baby. The following chart describes drugs frequently given to the mother, their purposes, potential benefits, and possible risks. Medications routinely given to the baby are described on page 242 in chapter 13.

Medications Used for Reasons Other than Pain Relief

Purpose	Name	Benefits/advantages	Risks/disadvantages
To stop preterm labor *(labor suppressants or tocolytic agents)*	♦ ritodrine (Yutopar) ♦ terbutaline (Bricanyl, Brethine)	These drugs, given intravenously, subcutaneously (beneath the skin), or orally, are used to inhibit uterine contractions in an attempt to prevent preterm birth. They are usually not used before 20 weeks or after 35 weeks gestation. Labor suppressants should be used with caution if the mother has high blood pressure, heart rhythm disturbances, preeclampsia, or diabetes. They are not used to stop preterm labor when it is judged that the baby would be better off being delivered (for example, in some cases of intrauterine growth retardation or infection following ruptured membranes). Tocolytic agents may be given to promote uterine relaxation before an external version, a procedure to turn a fetus from the breech position.	♦ *To the mother:* Labor suppressants are ineffective if active labor is established (the cervix is effaced or already dilating). Unwanted effects are usually controllable through dosage adjustment. They may include rapid heart rate, tremors, increased blood pressure, lowered blood potassium levels, elevated insulin and glucose levels, and pulmonary edema (fluid in the lungs). Prolonged and continuous high dose therapy with a labor suppressant may cause desensitization to the drug resulting in recurrence of preterm labor. Use of subcutaneous pump therapy with low doses of terbutaline minimizes this effect. ♦ *To the baby:* Labor suppressants may increase the fetal heart rate. Infrequently reported neonatal symptoms include hypoglycemia (low blood sugar), lowered blood pressure, and decreased calcium levels.
	♦ magnesium sulfate	This may be given intravenously for 24 to 48 hours to suppress and stabilize uterine activity before a woman is sent home with long-term terbutaline subcutaneous pump therapy or oral tocolytics.	Same as those listed below for magnesium sulfate use.
To stimulate fetal lung maturation	*Corticosteroids:* ♦ betamethasone ♦ dexamethasone	These drugs may be used in preterm labor at about 24 to 34 weeks gestation to hasten maturing of the fetal lungs. The drug is given to the mother by injection at the time of admission to the hospital and again 12 to 24 hours later. Corticosteroids may reduce the incidence and severity of Respiratory Distress Syndrome (RDS) in the premature baby and may reduce the possibility of other serious complications, such as intracranial hemorrhage.	There is a lowered resistance to infection in the fetus/newborn and the mother. It may increase the risk of maternal pulmonary edema when used with ritodrine or terbutaline.

continued

Purpose	Name	Benefits/advantages	Risks/disadvantages
To manage preeclampsia and treat elevated blood pressure	♦ magnesium sulfate	Magnesium sulfate is used to prevent or control seizures when the mother has severe preeclampsia. It is given by injection or intravenously.	♦ *To the mother:* Side effects of magnesium sulfate include flushing (warm face), sweating, hypotension, and diminished reflexes. Magnesium sulfate increases the effects of other drugs that depress the central nervous system such as barbiturates and narcotics. ♦ *To the baby:* Though the use of magnesium sulfate does not usually pose a risk for the fetus or newborn, babies are closely monitored for signs of toxicity during the first 24 to 48 hours. Adverse effects include muscle weakness, respiratory depression, and loss of reflexes.
	Antihypertensives: ♦ hydralazine (Apresoline) ♦ labetalol (Normodyne, Trandate)	These drugs, which dilate blood vessels, may be used to lower the mother's blood pressure when it is dangerously high. Hydralazine can be given intravenously (IV), intramuscularly (IM), or by mouth. Labetalol can be given by IV or by mouth.	♦ *To the mother:* Hydralazine may cause headache, rapid or irregular heart rate, nausea, vomiting, diarrhea, or difficulties with urination. Labetalol may cause slowing of the heart rate, shortness of breath, and drowsiness. ♦ *To the baby:* Use of hydralazine has not been associated with drug-induced fetal effects. The effects of labetalol on a laboring woman and fetus have not been well studied. These drugs should not be used unless the expected benefit clearly justifies the potential risk to the fetus.
To stimulate uterine contractions	*Oxytocics:* ♦ Oxytocin ♦ Pitocin ♦ Syntocinon	These drugs stimulate the rhythmic contractions of the uterus, increasing the frequency and intensity of the contractions. They are given intravenously to start labor contractions (induction), to strengthen contractions during labor (augmentation), or to control postpartum bleeding.	♦ *To the mother:* Sensitivity to the drug varies. Elevated blood pressure, heart rate irregularities, nausea, vomiting, and uterine hypertonicity (prolonged, strong contractions) are possible. Oxytocics may cause water intoxication, especially if combined with excessive fluid intake. Postpartum hemorrhage may ensue after Pitocin is stopped. ♦ *To the baby:* These drugs may slow the fetal heart rate, cause fetal heart rate irregularities, and deprive the fetus of oxygen if prolonged contractions occur. Some studies found an increased likelihood of jaundice in the newborn.

Purpose	Name	Benefits/advantages	Risks/disadvantages
To stimulate uterine contractions (continued)	♦ methyl-ergonovine maleate (Methergine)	Methergine is given by injection or orally; it helps control postpartum uterine bleeding due to uterine atony.	Side effects include nausea and vomiting, elevated blood pressure, headache, sweating, and ringing in the ears.
	♦ prostaglandins	There are many prostaglandins. Prostaglandin E_2 (PGE_2) is inserted as a gel within or near the cervix to hasten ripening (softening) of the cervix and increase uterine contractions. It is used either to start labor or as a prelude to induction with Pitocin. Another form of prostaglandin ($PGF_2 \alpha$) is sometimes used to control postpartum hemorrhage. It is given intramuscularly (IM), but can be injected directly into the uterine muscle.	Possible side effects of prostaglandins include overstimulation of the uterus, nausea, vomiting, diarrhea, and shivering. PGE_2 may lower the blood pressure, while $PGF_2 \alpha$ may raise it. Side effects are influenced by dosage and placement of the drug. Prostaglandins are not universally available in all U.S. hospitals.
To prevent milk production *(lactation suppressants)*	♦ bromocriptine (Parlodel)	Parlodel, acting on the pituitary gland, inhibits prolactin secretion and may control breast leakage and engorgement. It is given orally soon after delivery and continued for 2 to 3 weeks.	Once Parlodel is stopped, 18 to 40 percent of patients experience rebound breast secretion, congestion, and engorgement.[a] Side effects include low blood pressure, headache, dizziness, and nausea. Ovulation after birth may occur earlier than usual. It is very expensive and no more effective than ice applications or breast binding. The use of this drug as a lactation suppressant is being reviewed by medical professionals.

[a] *1990 Physician's Desk Reference*, 44th ed. (Oradell, NJ: Medical Economics Co., 1990), 1947.

Chapter 12

Postpartum Period

The postpartum period, the first six to eight weeks after childbirth, is a time of physical and emotional readjustment. The reproductive organs return to their prepregnant state. The family incorporates and accepts a new person into the home. Each parent changes his or her role within the family to cope with the demands of the new baby.

Every family's adjustment is unique. Some families find a comfortable new balance within weeks, while others take months or longer. Many variables affect the family's experience, including the temperament of the baby, medical complications for the mother or baby, the amount of available help, economic resources, experiences with infant feeding and care, parents' expectations of themselves and each other, single parenthood, blended families, and the flexibility of the parents. If you understand the common problems associated with the postpartum period, you can put the experience in perspective and plan to get the help you will need.

Prenatal Preparations for Post Partum

Before the baby is born, do some after-birth planning. Here is a checklist of suggestions.

♦ Choose a doctor, clinic, or nurse practitioner to provide health care for your baby. Interview people before the baby is born and choose one who is well-qualified, who is warm and caring, whose office is close to your home, and who meets the requirements of your insurance company, if applicable.

♦ Pack your bag for the hospital (include items for labor, post partum, and the baby's trip home), or gather supplies for a home birth.

♦ Acquire (beg, borrow, or buy) the necessary clothing, supplies, and equipment for the baby (see the next page).

♦ Buy diapers or sign up with a diaper service.

♦ Arrange a convenient baby care area and a sleeping area. For the dressing and diaper changing area, have a padded surface to lay the baby on and have clothing, diapers, waterproof pants, moistened wipes, pins, diaper rash ointment, and a diaper pail within arm's reach. For sleeping, have a basket, a baby carriage, a crib, or a cradle where the baby can be safely placed.

♦ Make sure all the baby's borrowed clothes are clean. New clothes are sometimes softer and more comfortable after they have been washed.

Your Baby's Layette

Use the following as a guide in getting what you need for your newborn baby.

Bed	♦ 2 bassinet sheets (if you are using a bassinet) ♦ 2–4 crib sheets ♦ 3–6 receiving blankets ♦ 1–2 crib quilts ♦ lambskin (optional) ♦ 2–4 waterproof pads for crib and lap
Diapers	♦ diaper service (arrange for this before the baby comes), or ♦ 4 dozen cloth diapers, or ♦ 4 dozen disposable diapers (newborn size) ♦ 3–6 waterproof pants for use with cloth diapers ♦ 4–6 diaper pins (if necessary) or diaper clips ♦ 3–6 washcloths to clean baby when diapering ♦ cotton balls for diaper area cleaning ♦ diaper wipes ♦ diaper pail (if using own cloth diapers) ♦ diaper ointment such as Bag Balm or Desitin (ask caregiver) ♦ hair dryer to dry baby's bottom
Bath	♦ 2–4 hooded towels or soft towels ♦ 2–4 baby washcloths ♦ baby soap and shampoo (Ivory bar soap is fine) ♦ baby bath tub (optional) ♦ large foam pad (to place beneath baby in the tub or sink) (optional) ♦ cotton-tipped swabs
Baby clothing (some large babies are born too big for newborn-sized clothing)	♦ 4–8 undershirts (snap type are easiest to use) ♦ 3–6 gowns with drawstring closure ♦ 2–4 stretch suits with feet ♦ 2 blanket sleepers (depends on season) ♦ 1–2 sweaters (depends on season) ♦ 1–3 pairs of booties or socks ♦ 2–4 small bibs ♦ 1 hat for newborn ♦ 1 hat (appropriate for season) ♦ snowsuit (during cold weather)
Baby equipment	♦ bassinet (optional) ♦ crib ♦ bumper pads for crib ♦ changing table ♦ car seat (mandatory in most states and provinces) ♦ dresser ♦ soft front pack baby carrier ♦ carriage or stroller ♦ baby swing (optional) ♦ liquid acetaminophen ♦ thermometer (rectal or one designed for babies) ♦ blunt-tipped nail scissors or baby nail clippers ♦ massage oil (optional)

♦ Buy or borrow a book on infant care and one on breastfeeding.

♦ If you intend to breastfeed, get two or more nursing bras and breast pads. Find out where you can obtain other supplies if needed. Get the names and phone numbers of local breastfeeding experts who can advise you.

♦ Clean your house. It may be the last chance you have for quite a while. If you have been accumulating piles of papers, magazines, and clothing, get rid of what you don't need. The baby and accompanying items take up a lot of space.

♦ Plan two weeks worth of meals and make up two related grocery lists: (1) nonperishable items needed for those meals and (2) perishable items needed for each meal. Shop for list number 1 before the baby is born and have list number 2 ready to consult when the time comes. Make sure the meals you plan are very easy to prepare.

♦ Prepare some dishes in advance and freeze them.

♦ Line up postpartum help: your mother, mother-in-law, relatives, friends, or hired help. If planning to hire someone, look into businesses and individuals that specialize in postpartum help. Find out their rates, their training, the usual duties performed, and whether they are bonded. If friends or loved ones will come to help, recognize that this is a working visit for them and you are not supposed to be the perfect hostess. The main purpose of having help is to enable you to accomplish your priorities: establishing successful feeding and care of your baby; getting adequate rest and nutrition; having your partner get to know the baby and catch up on rest; having time together as a family; and having time to visit with the kind loved ones who are helping you.

♦ If you have a short maternity leave (less than three months) begin investigating options for day care: family members; informal arrangements with friends or individuals who provide one-on-one care; institutional day cares; and nannies or *aux pairs*. Find out about costs, safety arrangements, ratio of adults to children, and availability of day care when you need it.

♦ Make a list of important phone numbers and post it near the phone. You may include the following:

> The baby's doctor
> Your doctor/midwife
> Hospital/birth center
> Hospital emergency
> Emergency aid service
> Your childbirth educator
> Diaper service
> Breastfeeding counselor

Postpartum Physical Adjustments

Your body makes numerous physical adjustments in the first days and weeks after childbirth. You may feel uplifted and energetic immediately after the birth and for the next few days or weeks. Or you may feel exhausted and let down. Most women experience sudden changes in their moods, and all new mothers get tired and need rest. After birth, your body undergoes rapid physical and hormonal changes. These changes are normal but can be complicated by fatigue, which undermines your sense of well-being and confidence in your ability to cope with a new infant and a changing lifestyle. Fathers and partners often experience similar problems of adjustment; their moods fluctuate and they feel tired. In addition, your needs for help, the baby's almost constant and sometimes puzzling needs, and the unpredictability of the baby's schedule all contribute to fatigue. You all may benefit from help from family and friends. Plan ahead for this possibility.

Early Recovery Period

Immediately after the birth, your caregivers closely observe your physical condition to assess your recovery. They frequently check your temperature, pulse, respiratory rate, and blood pressure. They also monitor the amount and character of your lochia, the size, firmness, and position of your fundus, and the functioning of your bladder and bowel.

Uterus

Through the process called *involution*, the uterus returns to its prepregnant size five or six weeks after birth. Immediately after the

Warning Signs during Post Partum

Report to your caregiver any of the following signs, which may indicate a problem requiring treatment.

Warning signs	Possible problems
Fever	♦ Uterine infection ♦ Bladder or kidney infection ♦ Breast infection—mastitis ♦ Other illness
Burning with urination, or blood in the urine	♦ Bladder infection
Inability to urinate	♦ Swelling or trauma of urethral sphincter
Swollen, red, painful area on leg (especially the calf) that is hot to the touch	♦ Thrombophlebitis—development of blood clot in blood vessel (do not massage)
Sore, reddened, hot, painful area on breast(s) in addition to fever and flu-like symptoms	♦ Breast infection—mastitis
Passage of large red clots, pieces of tissue, or return of bright red vaginal bleeding after flow (lochia) has decreased and changed to brownish, pink, or yellow	♦ Retained fragment of placenta ♦ Uterine infection ♦ Overexertion
Foul odor to vaginal discharge; vaginal soreness or itching	♦ Uterine infection ♦ Vaginal infection
Increase in pain in episiotomy site; may be accompanied by bleeding or foul smelling discharge	♦ Infection of episiotomy ♦ Reopening of incision or tear ♦ Stitches give way
Slight opening of cesarean incision; may be accompanied by foul discharge and blood	♦ Infection of cesarean incision
Feeling depressed, uncontrollable crying, inability to sleep or eat, extreme anxiety or agitation	♦ Postpartum depression

birth of the placenta, the uterus weighs between two and three pounds and the fundus can be felt midway between the navel and the pubic bone. During the next two days, it remains approximately the same size and feels like a tight muscle the size of a grapefruit. To help maintain the firmness of the uterus and prevent heavy blood loss from the placental site, you or your nurse massages the uterus, stimulating it to contract (see page 160 for instructions). Nursing your baby also helps contract your uterus.

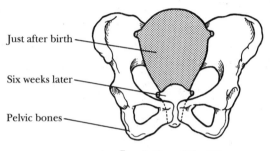

Just after birth

Six weeks later

Pelvic bones

Involution of the Uterus

A week after the baby's birth, your uterus weighs from one to one and one-half pounds. After two weeks, the uterus lies within the pelvis and weighs about a half-pound. By the end of five or six weeks, it weighs two to three and one-half ounces, and it has nearly returned to its previous size.

During involution, *lochia* (bloody discharge) flows from the uterus. For the first few days after birth, the red lochia is heavy. The amount of flow may change with your activity or body position. Lochia is generally heavier when you change positions (standing or sitting up after lying down), and during breastfeeding, and it often has a "fleshy" odor. Within ten days, the lochia diminishes and becomes pale pink in color. During the next several weeks, it becomes yellowish white, white, or brown. It may continue for as long as six to eight weeks. (See the chart on the previous page for warning signs regarding the lochia.)

Afterpains

Afterpains, the uncomfortable and sometimes painful contractions of the uterus after birth, often occur while you are nursing and are more common if you have had a child before. To ease the pain, relax and use slow breathing patterns. Afterpains usually disappear after the first week.

Cervix and Vagina

With the completion of involution, the cervix has returned almost to its prepregnant size, but the outer opening of the cervix remains somewhat wider.

The vagina gradually regains its tone, but the labia remain somewhat looser, larger, and darker than they were before pregnancy.

Breasts

Breastfeeding mothers. For the first twenty-four to seventy-two hours after birth, your breasts secrete *colostrum,* a yellow fluid that is your baby's first milk. Mature breast milk appears between the second and fifth day. At this time your breasts may feel full, hard, hot, and painful. This is *engorgement.* With frequent nursing for at least ten minutes on each breast, this initial engorgement may not occur or will soon subside. (See chapter 14 for more information on breastfeeding.)

Nonbreastfeeding mothers. The same initial changes will probably occur for you as for breastfeeding mothers, but you may be given medication immediately after delivery and during the next few days to suppress lactation. (See page 219.) Even so, you may still produce milk. Binding your breasts, ice packs, and the avoidance of breast stimulation are at least as effective as the lactation suppressants in diminishing milk production and decreasing your discomfort. Do not express milk from your breasts since this will stimulate your breast to produce more milk.

To Bind and Ice Your Breasts

Use an extra wide elastic (Ace) bandage or a tightly woven band of cloth about 12 inches by 6 feet. Wrap it tightly around your chest 2 or 3 times, being sure to flatten your breasts. Pin in place. Rewrap every few hours. This will compress your breasts and reduce milk formation. Wear binding 24 to 48 hours.

Every 4 hours or so during the daytime, ice your breasts for at least 20 minutes. This will provide temporary relief of pain (analgesia) and help reduce the tissue inflammation and swelling that accompanies engorgement. Use a sports ice bag or several bags of frozen peas or corn over your breasts and hold them in place with the binding. These may be refrozen for repeated use.

Your caregiver may suggest the use of ibuprofen or acetaminophen for pain relief.

Circulatory Changes

Some blood loss is a natural result of birth. Average blood loss during an uncomplicated vaginal birth amounts to about seven ounces (or almost one cup). If you have had an episiotomy or a sizable tear, you may have lost ten ounces of blood or more. You will continue to lose blood in your lochia for a few weeks, but do not be alarmed. In pregnancy, you accumulated extra blood and fluid so that such a loss during and after birth is not harmful.

In the early postpartum period, you will lose the extra fluid accumulated during pregnancy by urinating large quantities and perspiring heavily. As a result, you will lose as much as five pounds during the first five days after birth.

Abdominal and Skin Changes

After birth, your abdominal muscles are lax and it takes six weeks or more for them to regain their tone. Your stretch marks will fade but not completely disappear. If you have had an increase in skin pigmentation, it will fade. There will also be a gradual reversal of any increase in hair growth.

Hormonal Changes

After delivery, your body undergoes sudden and dramatic changes in hormone production. When the placenta is delivered, estrogen and progesterone levels drop abruptly and remain low until your ovaries begin producing these hormones again. If you breastfeed, your production of other hormones (for example prolactin and oxytocin) increases and remains high until you wean your baby.

Return of Menstruation

If you are not breastfeeding, you will probably begin menstruating again four to eight weeks after delivery. If you are breastfeeding, you may not menstruate for several months, though ovulation can occur during this time. Your first few menstrual periods following delivery may be heavier than usual, but will soon return to normal.

Self-Care after Birth

Rest and Activity

♦ Adequate rest is essential to recovery. Try to rest or sleep when the baby sleeps. Even if you are feeling well rested, you should take a daily nap. Go to bed early whenever possible, especially while you are waking up for night feedings. Your goal should be to get as much total sleep in a twenty-four-hour period as you normally need to function well. If, before you became pregnant, you needed seven to eight hours of sleep a night, then you should get that much sleep now, even if it has to be broken up into shorter periods.

♦ If your labor and birth were normal, it is safe to begin postpartum exercises within a day or two. (See pages 230–34.) Do not, however, feel guilty if you cannot find the time or the motivation for a few weeks.

♦ Gauge your activity by how you feel. It is wise to establish priorities about working inside and outside the home, to follow your caregiver's guidelines about activity, and to take advantage of all offers of help.

Perineal Care

Special care of the perineum is suggested, especially if you have had stitches for an episiotomy or tear. The basic goals of perineal care are to prevent infection, to relieve pain, and to promote healing. Your stitches dissolve and the tissue is usually healed within four weeks, though you may feel discomfort for some time. Discomfort during intercourse may persist for several months. See your caregiver if the discomfort persists. It may be treatable.

♦ Apply an *ice pack* to the perineum as soon after birth as possible to reduce pain and swelling. You can use it intermittently for up to twenty-four hours; then application of heat is used to promote healing.

♦ Frequent *pelvic floor contraction exercises* (Kegels) encourage the healing of your episiotomy or any tears, reduce the swelling in the area by increasing circulation, and help restore the muscle tone in the pelvic floor. You may begin to do Kegels immediately after birth.

♦ After you urinate, clean yourself by pouring warm water over your perineum from the front toward your rectum. *Peri bottles* are often provided for this in the hospital. Remember to take yours home with you.

♦ Always wipe yourself from front to back to prevent infection of the perineum from organisms in the rectal area.

♦ A *sitz bath* can relieve perineal soreness. Sit in a clean tub of warm water for twenty minutes. You may receive a portable sitz-bath basin from the hospital that can be placed on the toilet. (Do not use this water for washing. A shower is preferable for washing until your stitches have healed.) Then lie down for fifteen minutes or more to decrease perineal swelling caused by the warm water. If you desire, use cold water in your sitz bath. It is soothing and does not increase swelling.

♦ *Cold or hot packs* placed on your perineum for twenty to thirty minutes may be soothing. Place a layer of cloth or towel between the pack and your skin to protect your skin from excessive heat or cold. The pack should feel comfortable. If it is too hot or too cold, remove it.

♦ A *heat lamp* brings soothing, dry warmth to your sore perineum. In years past, when hospital stays lasted several days, the heat lamp was used routinely twice a day. You can set up your own heat lamp at home. Use a high intensity lamp or a goose-neck desk lamp (with a forty-watt bulb). Do not use a sun lamp or ultraviolet bulb, which would burn you. Sit on your bed with your legs spread. Situate the lamp about eighteen to thirty inches from your perineum, shining directly on it. Making sure it will not tip over, pull a sheet over your lower body and the lamp. Lie back and relax for about twenty minutes. Repeat two or three times a day.

♦ *Witch hazel,* available in drug stores, relieves soreness. Soak a cotton ball in witch hazel and pat it on your stitches, or buy commercial pads containing witch hazel such as Tucks and put them on your sanitary pad, which will hold them against your perineum. You may use witch hazel as often as you wish. Witch hazel also soothes pain from hemorrhoids.

♦ Lie down and rest as often as you can.

♦ Do not use tampons before your postpartum checkup.

♦ Do not douche.

Elimination

♦ At first, urination may be difficult because of slack abdominal tone, soreness and swelling around your urethra, or other factors. If you have trouble, relax, drink lots of liquids, pour warm water over your perineum to start your flow, or try to urinate in the shower or bathtub. If you are unable to urinate, you will need to be catheterized to empty your bladder.

♦ You may become constipated after delivery because of lax abdominal muscles or the soreness of the perineum, episiotomy, or hemorrhoids. Iron supplements may also contribute to constipation. You can avoid constipation by eating fresh fruits, vegetables, and whole-grain cereals and drinking plenty of water. Walking, exercising your abdominal muscles, and responding when you have the urge to move your bowels rather than postponing it, will help restore normal bowel function.

♦ Supporting your perineum by gently pressing toilet tissue at the episiotomy site can help relieve soreness when you are bearing down for a bowel movement; this will help if you are afraid of hurting yourself while straining.

If these suggestions do not help you, your physician or midwife may prescribe stool softeners, suppositories, or an enema.

Hemorrhoids
There are several ways to reduce the discomfort of hemorrhoids and promote healing:

♦ Avoid constipation.

♦ Try the pelvic floor contraction, or Kegel, exercise (see page 97), with emphasis on the muscles around the anus.

♦ Modify for home use any hospital procedure that helped, such as witch hazel and sitz baths (see the previous page).

♦ Your physician or midwife may prescribe medication. Surgical treatment of hemorrhoids is sometimes necessary in extreme cases.

Bathing
You will find that attitudes and advice about tub baths and showers vary depending on your condition and your caregiver's opinions. Showers are used in most hospitals and can be continued at home. Sitz baths are not used for washing, only for soaking the perineum. Ask your physician or midwife about baths at home.

Nutrition
♦ Continue healthful eating as you did during pregnancy (see chapter 4 for more information).

♦ To lose any extra pounds remaining after birth, do not go on an extreme slimming diet. Most new mothers lose weight gradually over a period of several months with no special effort. If you choose to reduce, a weight loss of one to two pounds a week is suggested for most mothers.

♦ If you are breastfeeding, drink to thirst, and include a quart of milk or its equivalent. (See pages 269–71 for specific advice.)

♦ Make sure your diet contains plenty of roughage so you will not become constipated.

♦ Your physician or midwife may recommend that you continue your prenatal vitamins and iron supplement.

Early Discharge
If you and your baby are doing well, you may have the option of leaving the hospital within twenty-four hours after the birth. You might prefer a "short stay" or early discharge to save money or to get back to your other children and to the comforts of your home—your own food, your own bed, and your familiar surroundings. Some insurance companies cover only twenty-four hours in the hospital after a vaginal birth.

If you choose an early discharge you will have less time to learn about baby care and breastfeeding from the nurses. If at all possible, you should have help at home at least during the first few days. You will need to learn what observations to make of yourself and your newborn for problems that need medical care. You will need resources you can call upon if you have any concerns. Many hospitals offer a class and educational materials. Some provide a home visit by one of their nurses to check on you and your baby, answer questions, and offer practical advice. You should plan to contact your caregiver or a public health nurse within a few days after you come home for a checkup and a chance to ask questions. A helpful pamphlet on early discharge is *The First Days after Birth: Care of Mother and Baby* (see Recommended Resources).

Practical Help

Since getting enough rest is essential but also very difficult, think of ways to minimize your work. Accept all offers of help and direct it to meet your needs: ask someone to cook a meal or two, do the laundry, do the grocery shopping, vacuum and dust, or keep an eye on the baby while you get some uninterrupted sleep. If friends are wearing you out, tell them you are exhausted, excuse yourself with your baby if you prefer, and retire to the bedroom. This is no time to take on the role of perfect hostess. Many families hire part-time household help for a few weeks after the birth. Agencies specializing in postpartum home care exist in many communities.

Postpartum Examination

It is important that you have a postpartum checkup within three to eight weeks after delivery. A general physical examination, which includes a pelvic exam, assesses your recovery and gives you a chance to discuss with your midwife or doctor any physical problems, your out-of-the-home work schedule, and your preferences for family planning. If you notice any of the warning signs in the chart on page 224, you should call your caregiver rather than wait for your scheduled postpartum visit.

Your physician or midwife will recommend Pap tests on a regular schedule. This test is painless and effectively detects the early symptoms of cervical cancer.

Breast Self-Examination

Your caregiver will also recommend a monthly breast self-examination. The best time to check your breasts is right after your menstrual period. While only a small percentage of breast changes indicate cancer, you should report any thickening, lumps, or nonmilk discharge to your physician. Here is how to conduct a breast self-examination:

♦ You can examine your breasts while bathing or showering. Wet skin allows your fingers to slip easily over your skin. Flatten your fingers and move them gently over every part of each breast, feeling for any lump or thickening.

♦ Standing in front of a mirror, look at your breasts with your arms at your sides, then with your arms raised over your head. Look for changes in contour, swelling, dimpling of the skin, or changes in the nipple.

♦ You should also examine your breasts while lying down. To check your right breast, put a pillow under your right shoulder and place your right hand under your head. With your left hand (fingers flat), press gently around your breast in a circular motion. Making smaller circles, gradually move in toward the nipple, until you have examined your entire breast (including the nipple). Repeat this procedure on your left breast after switching the pillow and placing your left hand behind your head.

Breast self-examination is less reliable during breastfeeding because changes in size and shape occur every day. If you are breastfeeding, it is best to check your breasts right after a feeding. Until your periods resume, mark a calendar as a monthly reminder to check your breasts. While you are weaning and your milk supply is diminishing, you may find lumps in your breasts. This is common, but if you feel unsure about the condition, call your physician or midwife.

Sexual Adjustments

Some women and men want to resume intercourse as soon as possible after the birth. Others may prefer to wait or may even feel afraid. Obviously, a sore perineum, a demanding baby, lack of help, and extreme fatigue will affect your ability to relax and enjoy making love. You still need to feel loved, however. If you are not ready to resume intercourse, cuddling and "pleasuring" (touching and enjoying each other's bodies sensually with or without orgasm and without pressure to have intercourse) can help you both to relax and show your love. Keep your sense of humor and be honest with each other about your feelings.

Doctors sometimes routinely recommend that new mothers refrain from intercourse for six weeks, but this is a somewhat arbitrary and outdated suggestion. It is probably safe to have intercourse when your stitches heal, your vaginal discharge declines, and you feel like it. But be gentle. You will probably be sore at first. After birth, you will have a decrease in vaginal lubrication because of hormonal changes; if you are breastfeeding, this will continue. Any sterile, water-soluble lubricant, such as K-Y Jelly or a contraceptive cream, can help. Keep in mind that conception can occur whether or not menstruation has resumed. A condom in combination with spermicidal foam, cream, or jelly is safe and effective soon after birth. Your physician or midwife can help you choose a satisfactory family planning method.

Postpartum Exercise

The exercises described here (including some that you practiced during pregnancy) will help you recover your former contours and strength during the postpartum period. With your doctor's or midwife's approval, you can start the first two exercises described below as early as one hour after delivery. If you have had a cesarean birth, however, you should check with your doctor before starting to exercise.

In addition to gentle conditioning, many new mothers want to resume more vigorous exercises. Check first with your caregiver. You can begin by taking brisk walks. Besides being an excellent conditioning exercise, it is easy to take the baby along. Getting out of the house and walking can lift your spirits and often calms a fussy baby. If you find exercising on your own difficult, consider joining a postpartum exercise class (check the Yellow Pages or call your local recreation or fitness center) or use one of the excellent videotapes on postpartum exercise now available.

After birth, two areas of your body need special attention—your abdominal muscles and your pelvic floor. You can see that your abdomen is not as flat as it was. After months of stretching, it needs toning and conditioning. At the same time, the pelvic floor muscles need exercise to increase circulation, to reduce swelling and promote healing in the perineum, and to restore vaginal muscle tone. The pelvic floor muscles need support while you exercise your abdominal muscles, so when you are doing abdominal exercises, first contract the pelvic floor muscles.

Exercises

After the birth of your baby, you may think you do not have time to exercise. Luckily, these exercises can be done while you go about your daily tasks. For instance, each time you change a diaper you can contract

Checking for Separation of the Rectus Muscles

Before you begin any abdominal muscle exercises (other than the pelvic tilt), check for separation (or diastasis) of the rectus muscles, the muscles that run up and down, from your chest to your pubic bone. Like a zipper opening under stress, the connective tissue between these muscles may have responded to the stretching during pregnancy by separating painlessly and without bleeding. This separation protects the muscles from stretching excessively. It is normal, but requires some special attention for a while to help close the separation.

To test for separation of the rectus muscles, lie on your back with your knees bent. Press the fingers of one hand into the area just above your navel (fingers should be together and horizontal). Slowly raise your head and shoulders off the bed or floor. The rectus muscles will tense, allowing you to detect any gap. A slight gap (the width of one or two fingers, placed side by side) indicates normal muscle weakness after pregnancy. An extreme gap between the muscles (three or four fingers wide) indicates that you need some preliminary work before you begin strenuous abdominal exercises. Strenuous exercise in the presence of a wide separation only increases the separation and defeats the purpose of the exercise.

To help close the separation, begin with the following exercise. After the gap has narrowed to the width of one or two fingers, proceed to the leg sliding, sit-back, and diagonal/central lift exercises.

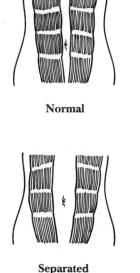

Normal

Separated

Head lift exercise
Lie on your back with your knees bent; cross your hands over your abdomen, placing them on either side of your waist. Breathe in. As you exhale, raise your head off the floor or bed; at the same time, pull the rectus muscles toward the midline with your hands. Hold for a slow count of five. Slowly lower your head back down. Repeat 5 times in 3 or 4 sessions per day.

---

the pelvic floor muscles or do several pelvic tilts. Before a feeding you can do wide arm circles. Once every day or two, sit on the floor and perform the exercises that are done in this position. You can also combine baby play with the last four exercises in this chapter. Do not overdo it. If you experience any pain, discontinue that exercise for a while. You practiced many of the following exercises when you were pregnant. Refer to the pages indicated to review the complete descriptions.

Pelvic Floor Contraction (page 97)
Starting right after birth, gently tighten and then relax the muscles of your perineum. You can perform this exercise when you are lying down, sitting, or standing. You may not feel the contractions of these muscles at first, but if you did this exercise before delivery, you will know how to do it now. Start by doing two to three contractions each hour for the first few hours, then progress to five contractions several times a day. At first you may only be able to hold the contraction for

two to three seconds. After a few days, hold the pelvic floor contraction for three to five seconds. Gradually work up to ten, then twenty seconds.

To test your progress, occasionally try this exercise while you are urinating by partially emptying your bladder, then stopping the flow. Do not be discouraged if you cannot do this at first. Test the strength of your pelvic floor muscles by noting how successfully you can stop the flow of urine during midstream.

Pelvic Tilt (pages 98–99)

This exercise will help tone and strengthen your abdominal muscles, relieve backaches, and help you maintain good posture. Soon after the birth, lie flat in bed or on the floor with your knees bent. Tighten your abdominal muscles to tilt your pelvis, and press your lower back into the bed for a count of two or three. Increase gradually to a count of five. After a few days, do pelvic tilts while standing, sitting, or on hands and knees.

Leg Sliding

This exercise helps strengthen the lower abdominal muscles.

Lie on your back with your knees bent and your feet flat on the floor. Your feet will slide better if you wear socks or stockings.

Place one or both hands beneath the small of your back.

Press your lower back to the floor and maintain a pelvic tilt. Slowly slide your feet along the floor, away from your body, extending both legs until you feel your lower back begin to come up off your hands and the floor. At this point, stop sliding your legs and bring your legs back to the starting position, one at a time.

Repeat the exercise five times per day. Remember to extend your legs only as far as you can without your lower back rising off your hands. As your abdominal muscles become stronger you will be able to extend your legs completely and still keep your lower back flat.

Sit-Back

A week or two after the birth, begin this exercise, which strengthens the abdominal muscles. This and the central/diagonal lift (described below) are safer and more effective than sit-ups, which require jerking movements and can unduly strain the abdomen and lower back. The sit-back is smooth and safe because it is tailored to your strength and because you do not have to overcome the force of gravity at the beginning of the exercise.

Sit with your knees bent, feet flat on the floor, and your arms stretched out in front of you. Lean back, but only as far as you can without feeling weak or losing control of the position. In other words, when you begin to feel unsteady or weak you have found your limit. Sit back up. Gradually increase the distance you lean back as you build strength. Soon you will be able to lean all the way down to the floor. Folding your arms across your chest makes the exercise more difficult. Later try it with your hands clasped behind your head.

Central/Diagonal Lift

These exercises strengthen your abdominal muscles.

The central lift. Lie on your back with your knees bent, and your feet flat on the floor. Breathe in, tilt your pelvis, and keep your lower back pressed toward the floor. While breathing out, raise your head and shoulders from the floor, reaching your outstretched arms toward your knees. Move smoothly and keep your waist on the floor. When your shoulders are raised about eight inches, hold the lift for a slow count of five. Relax and gently lie back. Do not use sudden jerky movements. At first, repeat about five times daily.

The diagonal lift. By rotating your upper body to the left or right as you raise your head and shoulders, you can strengthen different abdominal muscles (the oblique muscles). Remember to begin, as with the central lift, by breathing in and tilting your pelvis. While breathing out, raise your upper body diagonally by rotating to the left, and reach toward the outside of your left knee. Hold for a slow count of five. Repeat, rotating toward your right side. Do the exercise five times daily on each side. Your movements in the central and diagonal lifts should always be smooth, not jerky.

As you strengthen your abdominal muscles, you can increase the benefits of the central and diagonal lifts by folding your arms across your chest and later clasping them behind your head. Gradually increase the number of repetitions from five to ten per day.

Wide Arm Circles

This exercise helps increase circulation in the breasts and may help prevent or relieve clogged milk ducts (page 282).

Stand, kneel, or sit with arms straight and extended to the side. Move both arms in large, wide circles, first in one direction, then in the other. Try this exercise without a bra on. Do five to ten rotations in each direction, once to several times a day or once before each feeding.

Relaxation and Slow Breathing

Because the postpartum period is stressful, it is wise to use the same relaxation techniques you found helpful during pregnancy and childbirth. Try five minutes of slow breathing and passive relaxation during a hectic day and see how it relaxes and refreshes you. These techniques are also useful for afterpains, which occur during breastfeeding and at other times, especially in women who have had more than one child.

Exercising with Your Baby

Shaping up can be fun for both you and your baby. These exercises, which combine conditioning for you with play for your baby, are designed as all-around toners for the abdomen, arms, legs, and buttocks.

Up, Up, and Away (Arm Toning)

Starting Position: Lie on your back with your knees bent and feet flat. Place your baby face down on your chest, holding him under his arms.

Exercise: Slowly and gently raise the baby off your chest. Gently lower the baby back onto your chest.

Repetition: Repeat five times.

The Twist (Hip Walking)

Starting Position: Sit on the floor with legs extended. Hold your baby on your thighs, with his head and shoulders cradled in your hands.

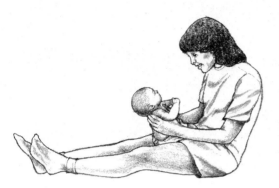

Exercise: "Walk" forward on your buttocks, twisting as you go. Then "walk" backward.

Repetition: Repeat four or five times.

Rocking (Central Lift)

Starting Position: Lie on your back with hips and knees bent and lower legs parallel to the floor. Place your baby face down on your shins, with his eyes peeking over your knees. Hold him under the arms.

Exercise: Tuck your chin, slowly raise your head and shoulders, and rock forward. (This is like a gentle central lift.) Then gently rock back, lowering your head to the floor. Avoid holding your breath.

Repetition: Repeat five times.

Rolling (Sit Back)

Starting Position: Sitting on the floor with knees bent, feet flat on the floor, hold your baby against your chest or rest the baby on your thighs.

Exercise: Gently lean back as you would in the sit-back exercise (page 232). Roll back about halfway, then return to an upright position.

Repetition: Work gradually up to five repetitions.

Adjusting to Parenthood

The first weeks after birth present a sudden leap into parenthood. A good start sets the stage for strong family bonds and commitment to the requirements of parenting. If you and your partner are nurtured and helped at the beginning, you will have more to give to your baby. The early weeks are not always easy. Following is some advice on the difficult aspects of adjusting to parenthood.

Postpartum Emotional Difficulties

After childbirth, you will experience in various degrees the emotional ups and downs associated with post partum. These emotional fluctuations may be partly due to the drastic change in hormone levels, to fatigue, to inexperience or lack of confidence with newborn babies, to loneliness or isolation from supportive adults, and to the constant fulltime demands made by the baby. For some women, these emotional fluctuations are minor, or they decrease within a few weeks. For others, they are overwhelming and long-lasting, creating feelings of anxiety, depression, or an inability to cope.

If you have such feelings, even with adequate rest, you might benefit from counseling by a professional who has expertise in postpartum emotions. In many communities, postpartum depression support groups exist to help new mothers who feel depressed or overwhelmed. Your childbirth educator may be able to help you find such a group or refer you to a counselor.

Following is a list of the more serious signs, which may indicate postpartum depression. If you have these, do not just wait for them to go away. Tell a loved one, a support group, or a counselor.

Depression. The "baby blues" commonly occur in the early postpartum weeks and are shortlived and temporary. However, if the blues continue and you feel very sad, hopeless, and depressed, tell your partner and seek help from your caregiver, a support group, or a specially trained counselor.

Excessive talking, worrying, or crying. If you find yourself talking compulsively, crying frequently without being able to stop, or if you are preoccupied with worries, seek help.

Extreme changes in appetite. A common sign of depression is a loss of appetite. If you find you are never hungry and have to force yourself to eat, and this loss of appetite lasts more than a couple of days, seek help.

Inability to sleep. If you cannot rest or sleep, if you feel constantly agitated and unable to relax, these too can be signs of depression. If a warm bath, a walk without the baby, a massage, a cup of herbal tea or warm milk, and the relaxation skills you

learned during pregnancy do not help, seek counseling.

Inability to care for your baby. If you are excessively worried about your baby, or cannot care for her (soothing, feeding, and changing), seek help.

By getting professional help when you need it, you will probably feel an almost immediate sense of relief. The opportunity to explore your feelings and come up with some solutions gives you hope and a sense of control that you may have lost temporarily.

A Note to Partners

Once your baby is several days old and the newness and luster of a brand new baby has worn off, the constant demands and frequent crying of a newborn begin to tax everyone's endurance and patience. It may seem to you that the baby's mother is better able than you to soothe your baby and meet her needs, especially if she is breastfeeding. But if this is her first baby, she is as new at parenthood as you are. She may feel the burden of a new baby is too great if she does not have your daily support and help with baby care.

This time with a new baby should not be missed. Despite the baby's crying and your frustration at not always knowing what your baby needs, spending time caring for your baby during these early months will provide you with lifelong memories as you watch her personality emerge and unfold. Acknowledging that both of you are under a lot of stress and then sharing the work and joy of parenting will strengthen your relationship and your family.

Parenting

Each parent needs to develop his or her own comfortable relationship with the new baby. Try not to interfere with each other or protect each other from the realities of baby

—photograph by Lise Alexander/Beginnings

She will be a baby for only a short time. Enjoy it!

care (like diapers and crying). Support each other. You do not have to do things the same way to appreciate each other as parents. Distinguish between small problems and large ones. Let the small problems (diapers on backward, pajamas inside out) go so you can work out the large ones together. If you have different approaches to the baby's crying, try to talk about your views and arrive at a comfortable compromise. The price paid for one parent always getting his or her way ("Well, I figured she was the mother," as one father put it) is that the other parent begins to feel discouraged, incompetent, and less involved. Parents need to become aware of their goals and feelings about parenthood, and it does not happen overnight. It is an ongoing process.

Unfortunately, parenting is not an instinctive skill. No one is born with the ability to parent. But you can learn. The ability to parent depends on how your parents treated you; experiences you have had with young children (younger sisters, brothers, or other children you have cared for or taught); your knowledge of the physical, emotional, and intellectual needs of infants and children; the examples of parenting you see around you; and the temperament and special needs of your baby. Even if you have not had experience as a big sister or brother or as a babysitter with children, you can still learn about your infant's needs and development by reading, attending parenting classes, or observing your baby's behavior and her responses to your care. You can also observe other parents with their children. You will like some of the parenting styles you see; you will not like others. Try to figure out the differences and why you like some and not others so you can develop your own parenting style.

A Baby Changes Your Life

How will this new family member affect your partner's and your relationship as a couple? How will the new baby affect your roles at home and away from home? How will you share the housework and baby care? How will you find time to relax, to be close, and to make love? How will you arrange to get away from home? Ask yourself these questions periodically. The answers may change as time goes on. At some point you may have to figure out which of your commitments are important and which can be dropped. You do not need a lot of external pressures when you begin your family life. Support from relatives, friends, and babysitters can help you work out your priorities.

In addition to the overnight changes that occur to you as an individual when you become a parent, there are also changes occurring in our society—transitions in family roles, both inside and outside the home. This may mean that you and your partner anticipate different roles for yourselves as mother and father than the roles your parents played. Your actual feelings about being a mother or father, based on your memories of your own parents, may not mesh very comfortably with your new expectations. This may be particularly true if you are exploring new arrangements in your family and do not have any role models for guidance and reassurance.

The challenges of parenting increase for the single parent. The time, energy, and emotional demands are much greater. Parent support groups and parent-infant classes can be very helpful. Other single parents and friends may also be a source of support and help.

Parenting a small infant is a time of disequilibrium. To keep this period in your life in perspective, take a look at the "pie of life" chart on the next page. While you will be a parent for the rest of your life, this time with your infant is short and represents only a small portion of your life. Enjoy it!

The "pie of life" graphs the predictable phases in your life. Roughly one third of your life is spent before you have a child.

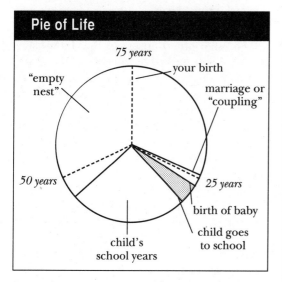

Pie of Life

75 years

your birth

"empty nest"

marriage or "coupling"

50 years

25 years

birth of baby

child goes to school

child's school years

During this period, you develop as an individual and form a relationship (marriage or other) that leads to the decision to bear a child. Another third is spent bearing and rearing a child or children. The last third is spent with an "empty nest"; the children have left, and you and your partner, if you are still together, once again find yourselves as a couple. It is possible that a woman will spend the last years of her life a widow, since women usually live longer than men.

Notice how small a slice is the time you spend bearing children and caring for them before they enter school. This time in your life is very short, although it is probably the most demanding and stressful for both individuals and couples. It is during this period that many couples, so caught up in caring for the children and possibly pursuing one or two careers, neglect the little things that keep them close to each other. Make time for conversation, fun, and shared activities.

In addition, it is important not to neglect your individual interests, even though they must take a lower priority when the baby and young child need so much of your attention. Pursuing individual interests keeps you growing as a person, not only as a parent or a worker. Later in your life you will find that what you did during this brief childbearing period played an important part in your individual growth and the development of your family.

Chapter 13

Caring for Your Baby

New parents are often surprised at the physical appearance of their newborn. The size and shape of the head, the baby's initial dusky blue color, the presence of vernix and streaks of blood, the beautiful hands, the enlarged reddened genitals, and the baby's size make a strong first impression. You will probably find that you cannot take your eyes off your new baby.

Your Newborn's Appearance

Body

The average full-term baby weighs seven to seven and one-half pounds and measures about twenty inches. A newborn baby's shoulders are narrow, his abdomen protrudes, his hips are small, and his arms and legs are relatively short and flexed.

Head

Your baby's head is large in proportion to the rest of his body.

Your baby's head may be elongated or molded from pressures within the pelvis during labor and birth. This is called *molding*. It returns to a normal round shape within a few days. Occasionally the scalp is bruised and swollen, but this will disappear in time.

Babies are born with two *soft spots* or *fontanels*—areas where the bones of the skull have not completely fused. There is a large, diamond-shaped soft spot on the top front portion of the head, while a smaller, triangle-shaped spot lies at the back. The larger one usually closes by eighteen months, the smaller one by two to six months. The membrane covering the fontanels is thick and tough, so brushing or washing the scalp will not hurt your baby.

Hair

Some babies are born with full heads of hair, while others are virtually bald. Fine, downy body hair, called *lanugo*, may be noticeable on your baby's back, shoulders, forehead, ears, and face. It is most pronounced in premature babies. Lanugo disappears during the first few weeks.

Eyes

Fair-skinned babies usually have gray-blue eyes; dark-skinned babies have brown or dark gray eyes. If his eye color is going to change, it usually does so by six months. The tear glands of many newborns do not produce many tears until about three weeks of age.

Blister on the Lip

Intense sucking often causes a painless blister on the center of your baby's upper lip. Sometimes the sucking blister peels. It disappears gradually as the lip toughens.

Skin

At birth, your baby's skin is grayish-blue, wet, and streaked with blood and varying amounts of vernix, a white creamy substance. Within a minute or two, when your baby begins breathing, the skin color changes to normal tones, beginning with his face and trunk and soon reaching his fingers and toes.

Obstructed sweat and oil glands cause small white spots called *milia* on your baby's nose, cheeks, and chin. When the glands begin to function, which may take several weeks, the milia disappear. You do not need to treat the condition or try to remove the whiteheads; simply wash his face with water.

Fair-skinned newborn babies often look blotchy, with areas of redness and paleness. After a few weeks the baby's skin has a more even color, but becomes more mottled-looking when he is cold.

Many babies have peeling skin, particularly at the wrists, hands, ankles, and feet. Overdue babies peel more than term babies. This is normal and no treatment is necessary.

Vernix caseosa, a white, creamy substance that protected your baby's skin before birth, often remains in skin creases even after bathing. There is no need to remove the vernix. Gently rub it into your baby's skin.

Stork bites and *angel kisses,* red areas on the skin formed by the collection of tiny superficial blood vessels, often appear on the back of the baby's neck, eyelids, nose, or forehead. They redden when the baby cries. They are not permanent birthmarks and are not caused by injury during birth. Although they usually fade or disappear within nine months, some, especially those on the neck, may remain longer.

Mongolian spots, areas of dark pigment, commonly appear on the lower back and buttocks of some dark-skinned babies. The

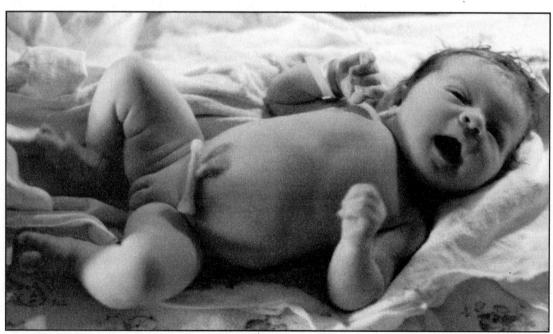

—photograph by Lise Alexander/Beginnings

A newborn's shoulders are narrow, her abdomen protrudes, her hips are small, and her arms and legs are short and flexed.

spots look like "black and blue" marks or bruises, but they are not bruises. They gradually fade and usually disappear by age four.

Breasts

Due to maternal hormones, both male and female babies may have swollen breasts. Some babies even leak milk from their nipples. This is normal and needs no treatment. Do not try to express milk from your baby's nipples as this may cause infection; the condition will disappear within days.

Umbilical Cord

A newborn baby's umbilical cord is bluish-white in color and one or two inches long immediately after it is cut. Some hospitals apply triple dye to dry the cord area and prevent infection. The triple dye will color the cord and skin purple. The umbilical cord dries, shrivels and darkens, and falls off spontaneously between the first and third weeks. It is important to keep the cord clean and dry, so do not cover it with diapers or plastic pants. Wipe around the base of the cord daily with a cotton swab dipped in water. Formerly, advice for cord care included keeping the cord dry by using alcohol swabs and giving sponge baths until the cord had fallen off. Alcohol, however, is potentially irritating and may be no more effective than water. Sponge baths are more chilling than tub baths and are of questionable benefit.[1] Many physicians now recommend swabbing with water and giving tub baths from the beginning. The important point is to keep the cord dry and clean. After bathing or cleaning the cord, dry the area with a dry cotton swab. If there is a foul odor, redness, or discharge with pus, report it to your baby's health care provider.

Genitals

Maternal hormones may cause swollen genitals in both male and female newborns. Female infants may discharge a milky or bloody substance from the vagina. Male infants may have an unusually large, red scrotum. These conditions are normal, temporary, and do not require treatment.

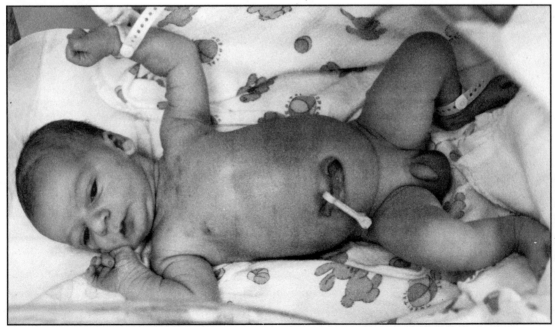

—photograph by Lise Alexander/Beginnings

A newborn's umbilical cord is one or two inches long after it is cut, and the genitals are often red and swollen.

Newborn Tests and Procedures

Routine care of the newborn includes many tests and procedures. These vary somewhat among health care providers and institutions. The following table describes many newborn routines and tests. Try to find out which ones are used by your health care provider and what choices you have.

Test or procedure	Where required	What it is	Comments
Vitamin K	Variable; required in most states and all provinces	Vitamin K is administered by injection into the thigh or given by mouth soon after birth to help in the process of blood clotting and to prevent a bleeding disorder of the newborn, called hemorrhagic disease.[a]	The American Academy of Pediatrics has approved both oral and injectable forms, but some states (and caregivers) allow only the injectable form because they believe it is better absorbed. Once feeding is established, the baby makes her own vitamin K, but this takes about one week. Breastfed babies are slower to produce adequate amounts of vitamin K than those fed formula.
Newborn eye care or prophylaxis	Almost all states and provinces; parents, in some instances, can sign a waiver to avoid procedure	Silver nitrate drops or erythromycin or tetracycline ointments are placed in the eyes within an hour or so after birth to prevent infection (ophthalmia neonatorum) and possible blindness if the newborn is exposed to the bacteria causing gonorrhea in the birth canal. Erythromycin also decreases the risk of an eye infection caused by chlamydia.	Silver nitrate causes redness, swelling, and discharge from the eyes. The antibiotics erythromycin and tetracycline usually do not. All cause temporary blurring of vision. Delaying the procedure up to the allowed one hour gives you some time with the baby when she is alert and can see clearly. Eye prophylaxis cannot prevent all possible eye infections, such as those caused by Herpes simplex virus, Group B streptococcus, or Hemophilus influenzae biotype IV. Some researchers now suggest that eye prophylaxis is overused. Rather than treating all babies, they believe women should be tested for chlamydia and gonorrhea and treated if necessary. Only those babies whose mothers have the infection would receive the treatment.[b] These recommendations are unlikely to change state or provincial requirements for a long time.
Test for jaundice	If medically indicated	Blood taken by pricking the baby's heel is sent to a laboratory where the bilirubin level is determined. If the bilirubin level is high, the baby has jaundice.	The test is performed if the baby's skin and whites of her eyes are yellowish, which may indicate an elevated bilirubin level. Jaundice may result from prematurity, bruising of the baby during labor or birth, blood incompatibilities (Rh and ABO), sepsis (infection), exposure to certain drugs given to the mother in labor (for example, Pitocin, Valium), or liver or intestinal problems. Most jaundice is not harmful. (See page 249 for a more detailed discussion of jaundice and its treatment.)

Test or procedure	Where required	What it is	Comments
Test for hypoglycemia	If medically indicated	Blood obtained by a heel stick is tested for hypoglycemia (low blood sugar).	The test is performed if the baby is larger than average or is thought to have low blood sugar, which may occur when the mother is diabetic, when the baby becomes chilled, when the baby is preterm or postmature, or when the mother has received large amounts of intravenous dextrose and water (a sugar solution) in labor. Hypoglycemia can lead to difficulty with breathing and, in the most severe cases, death. Treatment includes frequent breast-feeding or formula feeding and/or feedings of sugar water (5 or 10 per-cent dextrose solution). In more seri-ous cases the baby may be given intravenous dextrose.
Test for PKU (phenylketonuria)	In all states and provinces	Blood is obtained by a heel stick after 24 hours of age and tested for elevated phenylalanine levels. For greater accuracy, this procedure may be repeated at 7 to 14 days. The test is 95 percent accurate.	PKU is an inherited metabolic disease occurring in 1 infant in every 10,000 to 25,000 in the United States. With this disease, the infant is unable to digest phenylalanine (an amino acid), which builds up in the blood. If untreated, PKU causes mental retardation. Treat-ment with a low phenylalanine formula in infancy and diet through adoles-cence is very effective in preventing retardation.[c]
Test for hypothyroidism	In all states and provinces	Blood is obtained by a heel stick after 12 hours of age and tested for T_4 (thyroid hormone) level. If low, another blood test for thyroid stimu-lating hormone (TSH) is performed at the same time on the same blood sam-ple as the PKU test.	Hypothyroidism (low production of thyroid hormone) occurs in 1 in every 3,600 to 5,000 newborns in the United States. There is a higher incidence among females, offspring of mothers with thyroid disorders, and those who have had other children with thyroid disorders. The condition can be tran-sient or long-term. Treatment with replacement hormone avoids serious long-term effects, including mental retardation, growth failure, deafness, and neurological abnormalities.[d]
Test for galactosemia	Variable; cur-rently required in most states and 2 provinces; in others per-formed if medi-cally indicated	Blood is obtained after breast or for-mula feeding and is tested for elevated galactose content, which indicates an inability to digest and utilize galactose (milk sugar).	Galactosemia, an inherited disease, occurs in 1 in 60,000 to 80,000 infants. Without treatment, galactosemia is fatal. Treatment is a diet that is galactose free.[e]

continued

Test or procedure	Where required	What it is	Comments
Test for sickle cell anemia	Variable; performed if medically indicated	Blood is obtained by heel stick any time after birth and tested for the presence of sickle-shaped red blood cells.	Sickle cell anemia is an inherited disorder resulting in the production of abnormal red blood cells that are sickle-shaped. In the United States, it occurs in 1 in 400 people of African descent. Less severe forms occur in people of Arabic, East Indian, Middle Eastern, and Southern European descent. Screening is 97 percent accurate. This disease causes anemia, severe joint pain, bone deterioration, serious infections, and death. Treatment includes antibiotics and immunizations to prevent or treat infection, and avoidance of high altitudes, dehydration, exposure to cold, and excessive exertion.[f]

[a] American Academy of Pediatrics and American College of Obstetricians and Gynecologists, *Guidelines for Perinatal Care*, 2d ed. (Elk Grove, IL: American Academy of Pediatrics and American College of Obstetricians and Gynecologists, 1988): 88; S.S. Caravella et al., "Health Codes for Newborn Care," *Pediatrics* 80 (July 1987): 1.
[b] "Newborn Eye Care," Washington State Perinatal Newsletter 1 (April 1987): 1; S.S. Caravella et al., op. cit.: 1.
[c] American Academy of Pediatrics, "Newborn Screening Fact Sheets," *Pediatrics* 83 (March 1989): 449; C. Holtzman et al., "Descriptive Epidemiology of Missed Cases of Phenylketonuria and Congenital Hypothyroidism," *Pediatrics* 78 (October 1986): 553.
[d] Ibid.; American Academy of Pediatrics, "Newborn Screening for Congenital Hypothyroidism: Recommended Guidelines," *Pediatrics* 90 (November 1987): 745.
[e] American Academy of Pediatrics, "Newborn Screening Fact Sheets," *Pediatrics* 83 (March 1989): 449.
[f] Ibid.

Your Newborn's Senses

Until recently, we believed that new babies were extremely limited in their range of responses. We thought that a wet diaper, hunger, or colic were the only things that brought out a response in a new baby. We believed that babies could not see at birth, and when they finally did see, they could not discern color. We also believed that babies could not hear because their ears were full of mucus and fluid. And we thought that babies could be spoiled if they were picked up every time they cried. How we underestimated babies!

After years of study, we now recognize some of the newborn's amazing capabilities. Consider the following.

Seeing

When he is quiet and alert, your baby can focus on objects seven to eighteen inches away. He prefers to look at human faces, complex patterns, and slowly moving objects—particularly shiny objects with sharply contrasting colors. Your newborn can follow a slowly moving object in a 180 degree arc above his head (if the object catches his attention).

Hearing

Infants hear from birth and react to sound. They respond to voices (especially female, which is why people often unconsciously raise the pitch of their voices when talking to babies). Your baby heard your heartbeat, your voice, your partner's voice, and other internal and external noises while inside you. He may become calm or alert when he hears these familiar sounds (when you hold him close or talk to him) or when he hears similar sounds (such as a dishwasher, a washing machine, or certain music). He will also startle at sudden, loud noises.

Smell

Your baby has a refined sense of smell. Within the first week, he recognizes differences in smells and can even tell the difference in smell between his own mother's milk and another mother's milk.

Taste

Babies may react to sweet, sour, salty, and bitter tastes, preferring sweet substances.

Touch

Your baby enjoys being stroked, rocked, caressed, gently jiggled, and allowed to nestle and mold to your body while being held. He also likes comfort and warmth—not too hot or cold. He enjoys swaddling when he is young and freedom of movement as he grows older.

Infant Cues

From birth, your baby has the ability to let you know a lot about what she wants, likes, and does not like. The efforts she makes to communicate with you are called *infant cues*. As you get to know your baby better, you will be able to interpret her cues more easily.

Communication Cues

Although a newborn baby cannot smile or talk, she has other ways to communicate with you. Of course, fussing and crying are ways to tell you she is hungry, lonely, or uncomfortable. Rooting or sucking her hand tells you that she is hungry. Heavy eyelids tell you she is sleepy. But when your baby is in a calm, quiet, alert state, she uses all kinds of subtle ways to get your attention and keep it. As you begin to recognize these, you will be impressed by how much your baby can tell you.

Your baby uses her eyes to capture your attention and get you to look at her and talk to her. Her eyes brighten and open wide, and she stares at you intently. She explores your face, which she finds especially appealing. If you ignore this cue or look away, she may vocalize or move her arms to catch your attention. And as you return her gaze, a quiet dialogue begins. She may interrupt the dialogue by turning or looking away when she needs a rest and time to process what she has seen. After a brief rest, she may return her gaze to you. Returning her gaze when she wants to explore your face, and then giving her a chance to turn away and rest without you coaxing her to look back at you shows your sensitivity to her needs.

Feeding Cues

Newborn babies' hunger cues are not always clear. In fact, they often feed best when they are not showing obvious signs of hunger. You should offer a feeding whenever your baby wakes up, even if she doesn't seem hungry. If you wait too long, your baby may cry too hard to be able to feed.

Your baby may show her hunger by stroking her jaw with her fists, sucking on her lip, fingers, or fist, or rooting toward anything that touches her cheek. Pay attention to these early cues and feed her right away to help ensure a calm feeding.

When full, your baby lets go of the nipple, slows her sucking, yawns, dozes off, or makes a pucker face.

Soothing Cues

Your infant is the best person to teach you what calms her and what stimulates or agitates her. When your soothing efforts are effective, her fussiness lessens, she becomes more calm, and she relaxes and molds to your body as you hold her. If your jiggling, attempts to feed, or efforts to burp agitate her, she becomes more active and fussy and she stiffens. Coping with crying is one of the greatest challenges of parenthood, but in time you will figure out what soothes your baby (see page 253 for more on crying).

Parent-infant classes can help you learn more about your baby's cues, as can your baby's doctor, nurse, your childbirth educator, or other experienced parents. The book *The Amazing Newborn,* listed in Recommended Resources, is an excellent source on newborns. Take advantage of these resources—they can help you enjoy and understand your baby better.

Development and Growth

Each baby is an individual with a unique temperament and personality. Your new-born differs from others in his appearance; activity level; response to pain, hunger, or boredom; and sleeping and eating patterns. Your child is like a puzzle; it will take time for you to figure him out. If you remember that your child is an individual, not a reflection of you, it will make the job of parenting easier. Some babies are more difficult to live with than others. An infant who has a combination of intense reactions, irregularity, slow adaptability, and a high activity level is difficult to care for; you will need to be more patient and flexible parents. As you get to know your baby, you will learn about his temperament and learn to care for him in a more effective or satisfying way.

Developmental Milestones

Here is a list of developmental characteristics and behaviors and the ages at which your baby is most likely to begin to show them. If your baby is premature, these milestones may occur somewhat later.

Developmental characteristic	Approximate age
Looks or stares at your face	Birth to 4 weeks
Follows an object with her eyes for a short distance	Birth to 6 weeks
Holds her head off the bed for a few moments while lying on her stomach	Birth to 4 weeks
Pays attention to sound by becoming alert, or turning toward it	Birth to 6 weeks
Smiles or coos when you smile, talk, or play with her	3 weeks to 2 months
Holds her head upright while lying on her stomach	5 weeks to 3 months
Holds her head steady when upright	6 weeks to 4 months
Brings her hands together in front of herself	6 weeks to 3½ months
Laughs and squeals	6 weeks to 4½ months
Rolls over from front to back or back to front	2 months to 5 months
Grasps a rattle placed in her hand	2½ months to 4½ months

While your baby's temperament tends to change little over time, his abilities and size will change rapidly. Remember that normal development patterns vary widely from one baby to the next. Do not feel anxious if your baby takes a developmental step later or earlier than someone else's infant. His developmental pattern is uniquely his own. If, however, you notice that your baby misses some of the developmental steps listed on the previous page or is consistently behind in the age when he begins to do them, bring it to the attention of the baby's doctor or nurse practitioner. Early detection and treatment may improve long-term development.

Your Newborn's Reflexes

Your baby is born with many normal reflexes. As he matures, many of these early reflexes or reactions will disappear. In the newborn exam, a nurse or doctor checks these reflexes, which are a sign of his good neurological health. There is no relationship between these reflexes and your baby's future intelligence.

Awake or asleep, your baby yawns, quivers, hiccups, stretches, and cries out without apparent reason. Many of these behaviors are reflexive in nature; he cannot control most of his movements.

Other reflexes are protective. Coughing helps move mucus or fluid from his airway and relieves irritation. A new baby sneezes when his nose is irritated or a bright light shines in his eyes. He blinks if his eyelashes are touched, and he pulls away from a painful stimulus, such as a pinprick in his heel. If he is lying on his stomach, he lifts his head and turns it to the side to avoid smothering. If you place an object over his nose and mouth, he twists away from it, mouths it vigorously, or attempts to knock it off with his arms. A newborn is not helpless.

Some reflexes have specific names. The *Moro* or "startle" reflex occurs when your baby is alarmed or surprised. He suddenly flings his arms and legs out and straightens his body. The *grasp* reflex occurs when you place your finger in his palm; he responds by firmly grasping your finger. The *automatic walking* or *dance* reflex occurs when the baby feels pressure on the bottoms of his feet. If you support him upright with his feet bearing some weight, he will alternately move his feet as if walking. Your baby is born with well developed *sucking* and *swallowing* reflexes; these survival reflexes enable him to eat and thrive. He eagerly sucks on a breast or bottle nipple and swallows the milk, and when in need of soothing himself, he sucks on his fingers or yours. The *rooting* reflex is especially pronounced when he is hungry. Stroke his cheek with your finger and he turns toward the touch with his mouth open and searching. Tickle his lips and he will open his mouth wide. These reflexes are but a few your baby has to help him adapt and live outside your uterus.

Sleeping and Waking

After an initial period of wakefulness after birth, many babies sleep deeply until they are twenty-four hours old. They rouse only briefly and may not be very interested in feeding; others are just the opposite, waking, fussing, and feeding frequently. Both are normal. Your baby's sleep cycle is closely related to how often she eats. After adjusting to her new environment, a baby will sleep twelve to twenty hours in a twenty-four-hour period. Early on, her sleeping periods may be short but frequent.

When your baby is older, she may awaken at night and then settle back to sleep. However, a newborn may need to be fed, walked, rocked, changed, sung to, massaged, or otherwise soothed before going back to sleep. Many new parents wonder when to get up and feed the baby. When your infant is awake and hungry, she will cry, root and suck at anything close by, and wave her arms and legs vigorously.

Where your baby will sleep depends on your personal preference. A newborn should sleep on a firm surface and in a safety-approved crib, bassinet, or similar piece of furniture. Many babies sleep some of the time in their parents' bed.

Sleep-Activity States

Six states of sleep and wakefulness have been identified in the infant: deep sleep, light sleep, drowsy state, quiet-alert state, active-alert state, and crying. While each state has specific characteristics, the way babies change from state to state varies. Some move gradually from one state to another, while others make abrupt transitions. Some spend more time asleep, or quiet alert, or crying than others. You cannot completely control your infant's states; they are somewhat determined by personality.

Being able to identify the state your baby is in helps you give appropriate care. The following descriptions of each state explain their implications for parenting.[2]

Sleep States

Deep sleep. In this state your baby is very still and relaxed; her breathing is rhythmic. She occasionally jerks or makes sucking movements with her lips, but rarely awakens. You cannot feed or play with your baby in this state. If you manage to rouse her at all, she will stay awake only for a moment, then resume a state of deep sleep. Take this opportunity to rest or sleep, make a phone call, take a bath, or spend some time with your partner.

Light sleep. This state of sleep is the most common in newborns. Your baby's eyes are closed, but they may move behind her lids. In light sleep she moves, makes momentary crying sounds, sucks, grimaces, or smiles. She breathes irregularly. She responds to noises and efforts to arouse or stimulate her. Sometimes she awakens to a drowsy state or remains in this state and falls into a deep sleep.

Many parents rush to care for a baby who moves and makes mewing or crying sounds. Often, however, the baby is not ready to wake up. Wait a few moments to see if the baby is entering the drowsy state and needs care or is falling back to sleep.

Awake States

Drowsy. In this state your baby appears sleepy, her activity level varies, and she may startle occasionally. Her heavy-lidded eyes, opening and closing for brief periods, lose focus or appear cross-eyed. She breathes irregularly and reacts to sensory stimuli in a drowsy way. She either returns to sleep or becomes more alert. If you want your baby to return to sleep, avoid stimulating her. If you want her to wake up, talk to her, pick her up, massage her, or give her something to suck or look at.

Quiet alert. This state, which usually precedes a long sleeping period, is pleasing and rewarding for parents. Your baby lies still and looks at you calmly with bright, wide eyes. She breathes with regularity and focuses attentively on what she sees and hears. By providing something for her to look at, listen to, or suck on, you will encourage her to stay in this state. You can sing and talk to your baby, or try some of the infant exercises described on pages 256–57. Take time to enjoy these moments of eye contact, alertness, and calm.

Active alert. In this state your baby is readily affected by hunger, fatigue, noises, and too much handling. She cannot lie still; she may be fussy. Her eyes are open but do not appear as bright and attentive as in the quiet-alert state. She breathes irregularly and makes faces.

When your baby reaches the active-alert state, it is time to either feed or comfort her. If she is not hungry, she probably needs less stimulation. If you act immediately, you may bring her to a lower, calmer state before she enters the crying state.

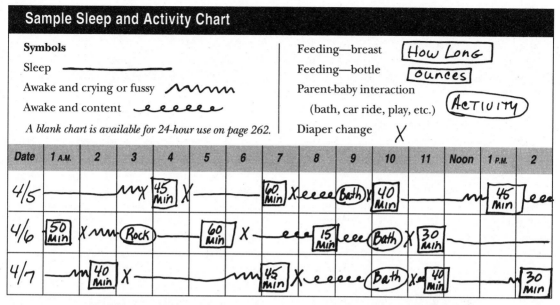

Sample Sleep and Activity Chart

Symbols

Sleep ————————

Awake and crying or fussy ∿∿∿

Awake and content ᘒᘒᘒᘒᘒ

A blank chart is available for 24-hour use on page 262.

Feeding—breast [How Long]

Feeding—bottle [ounces]

Parent-baby interaction
(bath, car ride, play, etc.) (Activity)

Diaper change X

Crying. A crying baby is difficult for every parent. Keep in mind that your baby has only one way of telling you she cannot cope anymore. If she is overstimulated, tired, sick, hungry, frustrated, wet, cold, too warm, or lonely, she says so by crying. She also moves her body actively, opens or closes her eyes, makes unhappy faces, and breathes irregularly. Sometimes crying is a release, a self-comforting mechanism that enables her to enter another state. At other times, she needs you to feed or comfort her. See page 253 for more on crying.

Recording Your Baby's Sleep and Activity

Sometimes parents are puzzled by their baby's apparent unpredictability and are unaware of any consistency in the daily pattern. If that is true for you, make a chart like the one above to record your baby's activities and sleep periods for a week. This chart, which was adapted from the Sleep-Activity Record of the University of Washington School of Nursing, will show you how long and when your baby sleeps, is awake and content, or awake and crying. You will also see the large amount of time

you spend diapering, feeding, and caring for your baby. After using the chart for a week, you can often see that your baby does follow a fairly consistent pattern. As your baby matures, the sleep and activity patterns will undergo further changes.

Common Concerns about Newborns

Newborn Jaundice

A yellow tint to the baby's skin and in the whites of the eyes, called *jaundice*, is caused by large amounts of bilirubin in the blood. (Bilirubin forms normally as red blood cells break down.) Because a newborn's liver is immature, he is less able to handle the bilirubin in a normal way until he is a week or two old. Mild jaundice (sometimes called "physiological jaundice") is considered harmless and occurs in about 50 percent of full-term and 80 percent of premature babies. It is the most common type of jaundice in newborns. It usually appears on the second or third day after birth, peaks, and then goes away, disappearing before the end of the second week.

249

Jaundice can also be the result of certain blood incompatibilities, such as when the mother is Rh negative and her baby is Rh positive, or when certain differences in the mother's and baby's blood types exist, (referred to as an ABO incompatibility). Jaundice is sometimes associated with infection, significant bruising of the baby during birth, or certain drugs taken by the mother during labor (for example Pitocin, some sulfa drugs, and Valium).

Very rarely, jaundice occurs with breast-feeding. With "breast milk" jaundice, the bilirubin levels begin to rise after the third day of age and usually peak between the seventh to tenth day. Diagnosis is made by ruling out all other possible causes. (See pages 281–82 for more on breast milk jaundice.) You may be the first to notice jaundice in your baby. If so, notify your baby's doctor or nurse.

If significant jaundice occurs, your doctor will order a test of the baby's blood, obtained by a heel stick, to measure the blood's bilirubin level and look for other causes such as infection. If the bilirubin level is high, the baby may be treated with phototherapy (light therapy) or in severe cases, with an exchange transfusion, in which all the baby's blood is removed and replaced with intact red blood cells. If jaundice is associated with infection, the baby will receive antibiotics. With phototherapy, the naked baby wears eye patches to protect his eyes and is placed under special lights (bililights) that help to break down the bilirubin in the skin. A newer form of phototherapy utilizes a plastic body wrap and fiberoptic lights. The baby does not wear eye patches and the parents can feed and hold the baby without interrupting treatment.

Among physicians, there is a lack of consensus as to the effectiveness of phototherapy, the circumstances under which treatment is desirable, and just how serious jaundice may be. Newborn jaundice is a field of great research activity (see Recommended Resources and pages 281–82 for more on jaundice).

Circumcision

Circumcision, the removal of the foreskin covering the head (glans) of the penis, is probably the oldest surgical operation known, dating back some six thousand years. It is a ritual of the Jewish religion and one of the puberty ceremonies of some Islamic, African, and New Guinean cultures. It is also commonly performed in North America, more in the United States than Canada, for nonreligious reasons as a matter of parental choice. Performed by physicians (usually the obstetrician or family physician), circumcision is a surgical procedure that requires written permission from the parents. Since the decision about circumcision is up to you and your partner, discuss the subject during pregnancy when you have more time to gather information.

While you are making this decision, you might consider whether other males in the family, schools, and community have been circumcised. You may feel that your son should look the same. In reality, however, the rate of circumcision today is about 60 percent in the United States (much lower in Canada), so the social pressure to circumcise may be lower than ten or twenty years ago when circumcision rates in the United States were much higher. In Canada, circumcision has never been routinely performed for nonreligious reasons. The circumcision status of a child may have no greater implications than the other physical differences that exist between individuals.

Facts to Consider

♦ There are no legal and few medical reasons for circumcising the male newborn.

♦ The American Academy of Pediatrics has no recommendations regarding routine circumcision, only that parents be well-informed before making the decision.[3]

♦ Circumcision should not be done for sick

infants, infants with bleeding disorders, and infants with hypospadius, an anomaly where the urethral opening is on the underside of the head of the penis.

♦ The procedure usually takes less than a half hour. Healing takes seven to ten days.

♦ The newborn will feel pain.

♦ Local anesthesia is sometimes used. This reduces but does not eliminate all pain associated with circumcision. Complications from the anesthesia are rare and consist of local tissue damage, bruising, and subtle alterations in some reflexes.

♦ Complications from the circumcision procedure itself occur 0.5 to 2 percent of the time. These range from the minor to the serious and include infection, bleeding, irritation of the head of the penis from the friction of wet diapers, pain on urination, and scarring of the urinary outlet.

♦ There is a fee, which may be covered by health insurance.

♦ Some studies note an increased incidence of cancer of the penis in uncircumcised males. This may be due to the combination of being uncircumcised and having poor hygienic care of the penis. The American Academy of Pediatrics recommends that parents and then the child as he grows older make a lifetime commitment to careful hygienic care of the uncircumcised penis to reduce the potential risk of penile cancer.[4]

♦ Some studies, though not conclusive, have found an association between not being circumcised and urinary tract infection. Again, good hygienic practices may negate this possibility.[5]

♦ Contrary to previous reports, there is no evidence that circumcision prevents cancer of the prostate gland, nor does it prevent sexually transmitted diseases.

♦ There is no evidence that circumcision or noncircumcision affects sexual performance.

Care of the Circumcised Penis

If you choose to have your son circumcised, ask the medical staff about care of the penis. They often suggest frequent diaper changes, gentle washing with soap and water, and application of Vaseline or petroleum jelly to aid healing and prevent irritation. You can expect very slight bleeding, but report any excessive bleeding or swelling to your doctor. Some babies sleep more comfortably on their sides until the area has healed.

Care of the Uncircumcised Penis

The foreskin of an uncircumcised newborn does not usually retract (pull back). It is normally joined to the glans, so avoid forcing it back over the end of the penis. It will gradually become looser, and between three and five years of age most boys' foreskins are fully retractable. Normal bathing provides adequate cleansing during infancy.

Spitting Up

Many babies spit up milk during or after a feeding. Some babies spit up more than others. Your baby is more likely to spit up if he cries hard before a feeding, eats too much too quickly, or swallows air during the feeding. Some babies have an immature sphincter muscle at the top of their stomachs, which allows milk to come up with air bubbles. Spitting up is usually not harmful, but you can reduce it by burping your baby during and after feedings (burp newborns after each breast or after each two ounces of formula), not overfeeding him, handling him gently, and positioning him in the following ways after feeding: on his side, sitting in an infant or car seat with his head elevated twenty to thirty degrees, or laying him on his tummy. Babies outgrow the tendency to spit up by five to nine months of age.

If spitting up seems to be associated with pain, call your baby's doctor. Continuous or frequent forceful (projectile) vomiting is more serious and can lead to dehydration. If your infant vomits after two or three consecutive feedings, consult your baby's doctor.

Bowel Movements

A newborn's stool pattern is different from an adult's. Your baby's first bowel movements will consist of *meconium*, a sticky, green-black substance present in the intestine before birth. For two to six days following birth, his stools will be a mixture of meconium and milk by-products, spinach-green or yellow in color. Later, your baby will have yellow, green, or brown stools with or without curds. The frequency and consistency of stools depend on the individual baby and on the food he is fed. Breastfed babies should have a stool after each feeding or at least three or four large runny stools a day once your milk is in. Formula fed babies may have fewer stools.

Constipation, hard, dry stools that are difficult to pass, is rarely found in breastfed babies. Some older breastfed babies have only one bowel movement per week. These babies are not constipated; their more mature digestive systems are efficiently using more of their mothers' milk. Call your doctor, however, if your baby seems constipated.

Your baby probably has *diarrhea* if his stools are mucousy, foul smelling, more frequent than usual, blood-tinged, or watery (the diaper shows a water ring around the stool). When in doubt, note the color, consistency, and frequency of your baby's stool; then call your doctor.

Diaper Rash

Many substances can irritate your baby's skin, including urine and stool, some laundry products, inadequate diaper washing, or chemicals used in some disposable diapers. To prevent or treat diaper rash caused by urine, change diapers frequently, rinse the diaper area with water at each change, and avoid plastic pants, which retain moisture.

You can reduce irritation from laundry detergents by running the diapers through an extra rinse cycle or by changing to a milder product, such as Dreft. To reduce the amount of ammonia retained in the diapers, add half a cup of vinegar to the diaper pail or the rinse water.

Other treatments for diaper rash include exposing the rash to fresh air for a few hours each day, blow-drying your baby's clean bottom with a hair dryer set at medium heat, or applying a commercial ointment to the clean, dry, irritated skin. (You can remove the heavy white ointment with a cotton ball moistened with baby oil.) If diaper rash persists, consult your physician.

Facial Rashes

Mild rashes on the face commonly occur in the first months of life. The rashes—smooth pimples, small red spots, or rough red spots—come and go and rarely require treatment.

Prickly Heat

This common, warm-weather rash appears on overdressed or overwrapped babies. Found most often in the shoulder and neck regions, prickly heat looks like clusters of tiny pink pimples surrounded by pink skin. As it dries, the rash becomes slightly tan. Prickly heat may look worse than it apparently feels to your baby. To avoid this rash, keep him from becoming overheated.

Cradle Cap

Cradle cap is a yellowish, scaly, patchy condition found on the scalp or sometimes behind the ears. Daily washing or brushing of the scalp may prevent cradle cap and will help treat it if it does appear. Comb or brush out the scales, using a baby comb, fingernail brush, or soft toothbrush; wash with mild soap. Continue this procedure until the scales are gone. Neither baby oil nor vegetable oil helps.

Newborn Breathing Pattern

Periods of irregular breathing are normal in newborns but may be frightening to new parents. When your baby is sleeping, he will snort, gasp, groan, and even occasionally pause in his breathing. These irregularities disappear in a month or two.

Crying

A newborn who is not eating or sleeping may spend a lot of time crying, and most parents feel frustrated when they cannot understand why their baby cries. This is a natural reaction. Remember to stay as calm as possible. Your tension is contagious; move slowly and calmly around a crying infant.

After you have ruled out hunger, consider whether the baby needs cuddling, rocking, walking, or your attention. Is he overdressed, underdressed, sick, or bored? Does he need to burp? Does he have diaper rash or colic? Is he just plain tired? Exhaustion commonly causes crying. If nothing seems to calm him, he may simply need to be put to bed and allowed to cry a while to settle himself. (Set the timer between five and fifteen minutes or it may seem like an eternity.) Patting or stroking his bottom or back or gentle rocking may also help him relax.

Many infants have a regular fussy time every day. Unfortunately this period often occurs in the late afternoon or evening, when everyone else in the house is tired and wants peace. You might find that attention and cuddling quiet him down. If not, consider these suggestions:

♦ Babies love motion, so try a swing, rocker, front pack, or sling, or a walk in a stroller. You can even go for a ride in the car.

♦ Wrap your infant snugly in a receiving blanket. Many newborns love the security this provides.

♦ Let the baby suckle and comfort himself at your breast. Or, let him suck on your clean finger with your fingernail placed against his tongue. Once your milk supply is well established, try giving your baby a pacifier. Wet the pacifier first in water.

♦ Play music, turn on the radio or television, or sing. The dishwasher, washing machine, clothes dryer, or vacuum cleaner may provide soothing noises.

♦ Your baby may be bored; put him in the center of family activity. Keep in mind, however, that some babies get overstimulated and need quieter surroundings.

♦ Try letting your baby rest on a lambskin—this is soothing to some babies.

♦ If the baby's fussy time occurs at dinner, try preparing dinner early.

Some parents fear that if they give their babies too much attention, they will spoil them. A newborn, however, cannot be spoiled. He needs feeding, attention, cuddling, and handling to develop a trust in your ability to meet his needs. Enjoying and responding to your baby is not spoiling him. When your infant cries, he needs more care, not less. Your newborn infant is not manipulating you when he cries for attention; he simply has no other way to tell you he needs something. You might have trouble figuring out exactly what he wants, but pick him up, cuddle him, and trust your instincts and feelings.

Colic

Colic is another reason that babies cry. No one knows the exact cause of colic, so it is sometimes difficult to confirm. You may suspect colic, however, if your baby cries inconsolably at about the same time every day — often between 6 and 10 P.M. or after most feedings. The infant draws his knees up in pain and screams loudly for two to twenty minutes; then the crying stops, only to resume later. He may pass gas from the rectum. Despite the apparent discomfort, colicky babies seem to thrive.

Try comforting your baby by doing the following:

♦ Using a comfort hold that provides pressure against his abdomen: lying on his abdomen across your lap or on a hot water bottle wrapped in a towel, sitting on your hip facing away from you, or lying on your arm looking away from you.

Comfort Holds

♦ Letting him suck on your breast, pacifier, or finger.

♦ Walking or rocking him.

♦ Maintaining a tension-free atmosphere as much as possible. This may mean getting away from a colicky baby for a while.

♦ Swaddling him, holding him close, or putting him in a front pack.

♦ Talk to your caregiver to determine whether food sensitivities might be contributing to the problem.

The colicky period is very stressful for parents. It may seem impossible to maintain a calm atmosphere. Try to keep in mind that colic does not produce any lasting harmful effects and that it usually disappears by the third or fourth month. Consult your doctor if constant crying is associated with vomiting, a cold, a fever, or hard stools.

Special Babies

Premature Infants

An infant born before thirty-seven weeks and weighing less than five and one-half pounds is considered *premature*. Her appearance and physical abilities depend to some extent on just how early she was born. A premature infant looks different from a full-term infant—she is small, limp, and frail; her skin is reddish and appears tissue-paper thin; and she has little or no fat or muscle. Her head appears disproportionately large. Vernix and lanugo are abundant, fingernails and toenails have not grown out, and her tiny ears are soft and hug her head. Her cry is more feeble, and she is more difficult to soothe than a full-term infant.

A premature infant is physically vulnerable until she grows older. She sucks weakly, and her swallow and gag reflexes are unreliable. Tube feeding is sometimes necessary. Because her body temperature is unstable, often below normal, she is usually kept in a temperature-controlled isolette. Breathing may be more difficult—her respirations are irregular, rapid, and often shallow because her lungs are immature. She may need oxygen and help with breathing. Her ability to absorb food is less efficient than that of a full-term infant, although her need for nutrients, especially calories, protein, iron, calcium, zinc, and vitamin E, may be greater.

Giving birth to a premature infant may be upsetting and frightening. Your premature baby needs special medical attention that may separate her from you, but she also needs to be touched, stroked, and talked to, even while inside the isolette. Today, most modern hospitals encourage you to visit and care for your premature infant. If she cannot suckle at your breast, you can express milk, which can be fed to her through a tube from her mouth to her stomach or from a bottle with a soft "premie" nipple. Your milk is different from the milk of a mother of a full-term baby, and is better suited to the nutritional needs of your premature infant. By feeding and touching her, you help your baby through this difficult time.

Parents often feel guilty or responsible for the premature birth of their baby, even though in over 50 percent of premature births no specific cause of prematurity can be found. In the majority of the remaining cases, where the cause is known, the parents could have done nothing to prevent an early birth. For more on preterm labor, see pages 179–80.

Parent support groups provide information, assistance, and emotional support to the parents of a premature infant. In addition to listening with understanding and giving practical suggestions, members of a support group may even supply you with clothing or patterns for clothing small enough for your baby. If you would like more information about premature babies, check with your local childbirth education group, caregiver, or hospital, or write to Parents of Prematures, P.O. Box 3046, Kirkland, Washington 98083. You can call them at (206) 283-7466.

Small for Gestational Age Infants

In the past, some full-term babies who weighed less than five and one-half pounds were wrongly called premature. Babies who are small in size and weight for the length of pregnancy are more appropriately called *small for gestational age—SGA*. This condition may have any of several possible causes: an inadequate transfer of nutrients across the placenta to the baby; the effects of some drugs taken during pregnancy such as alcohol or cocaine; some congenital and genetic malformations; and certain infections of the fetus, such as rubella and toxoplasmosis.

The SGA baby presents some special challenges to the parents. These babies, like other high-need infants, do not move easily from state to state (for example from active to quiet alert or from drowsy to deep sleep). They are often fussy and more difficult to soothe than other infants. Parents of SGA babies have to spend a great deal of time calming and quieting their babies. Techniques that seem to work include frequent feeding, gentle rocking, talking quietly, and maintaining a calm environment. These parents soon learn that their babies can handle only one source of stimulation at a time. Too much stimulation, such as talking to the baby while feeding, making eye contact, or jiggling her while talking overwhelms this intense baby and causes her to cry or become agitated.

Over time, the SGA baby matures and becomes less intense and fussy. Your sensitivity to her special needs helps her while she matures.

Postmature Infants

A baby is considered *postmature* if she is born well after the anticipated due date and exhibits the following characteristics: the absence of lanugo; little vernix; long fingernails and toenails; loose skin; pale, dry, peeling or cracked skin; and unusual alertness. In postmaturity, the amniotic fluid may be scant or stained with meconium. True postmaturity is rare even in babies born two or more weeks after their due date, but if your pregnancy lasts beyond forty-one or forty-two weeks, your caregiver will test for fetal well-being (see chapter 3). If the test results indicate that your baby is not thriving, your caregiver may want to deliver the baby before spontaneous labor begins. Most post-mature babies are treated the same as any full-term infant. If the postmaturity has caused special problems, they will be treated as needed.

Playing with Your Baby

Play is more important to babies than it is to adults. For an adult, play is usually a form of recreation; for a baby, it is a means of learning about himself and the world around him. When he grabs and shakes a rattle, gums and chews a teething ring, squashes and squeaks a rubber duck, he is learning that he can make things happen. He learns about himself, as well as about the objects he is playing with.

When you talk, coo, laugh, hug, and kiss your baby, he learns that certain things he does make an impact on you. Learning activities (play) for a baby during an average day might include singing and talking; caressing, touching, and cuddling when changing or feeding him; a massage after a bath; baby exercises; moving to different rooms; games, such as peek-a-boo; and playing with appropriate toys.

Baby Exercise

Much has been written about baby exercise, and some community centers feature classes in infant stimulation and parent-baby exercises. The purpose is twofold: to educate parents about their infants' physical growth and development, and to teach parents some appropriate and fun ways to play with their babies. By using these simple exercises, you not only play with your baby, but you learn more about his capabilities and limitations.

These exercises will probably not speed up your baby's development, since growth and development normally occur in an orderly and predictable fashion with or without infant exercise. But you can enhance your baby's development by giving him the chance to use the muscles he is already learning to control.

The baby exercises discussed in this section are designed for babies one week to three months old. (Exercises for mother *and* baby are described on pages 233–34.) A young baby (one to six weeks) may have tightly flexed legs and arms. If you gently jiggle or pat his hands, arms, or legs, you may help relax his muscles and they will move more easily. Keep your movements slow, gentle, and rhythmic. Try singing songs to him as you move his limbs. After a few sessions, he will relax and seem to anticipate the movements.

Exercise or play with your baby when he is in the quiet-alert state—wide awake, calm, and attentive. If he is fussy, hungry, upset, or sleepy, chances are you will not enjoy yourselves. Unless otherwise noted, do the following exercises on the floor or on a firm surface. As your baby grows older, you may want to do other exercises.

Arm Cross
Aim: To relax chest and upper back muscles.

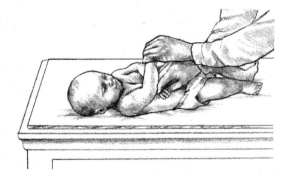

Exercise: With your baby on his back, place your thumbs in your baby's palms. When he grasps them, open his arms wide to the side. Bring them together and cross his arms over his chest. Repeat slowly and gently, using rhythmic movements.

Arm Raising

Aim: To facilitate flexibility of the shoulders.

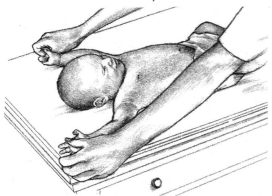

Exercise: With your baby on his back, grasp your baby's forearms or hands. Raise them over his head, then lower them to his sides. Repeat slowly and gently, using rhythmic movements. Alternate arms—while one goes up, the other goes down.

Leg Bending

Aim: To facilitate flexibility of hips; may help baby pass gas.

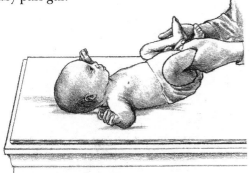

Exercise: With your baby on his back, grasp lower legs and gently bend his knees up toward his abdomen and chest. Gently lower his legs until they are straight. Repeat several times. Alternate, bending one leg while straightening the other.

Inchworm

Aim: To bring about extension of legs and back.

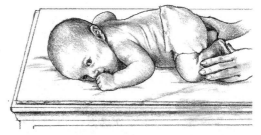

Exercise: With your baby on his tummy, bend his knees under him, holding his feet with your thumbs against the soles. Thumb pressure on his soles will cause him to straighten his legs and move forward like an inchworm.

Baby Bounce

Aim: To comfort baby or ready the baby for play.

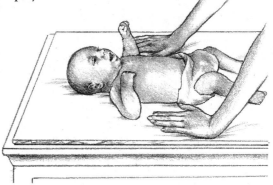

Exercise: Place your baby on his back or tummy on a foam rubber pad, bed, your lap, or any soft, bouncy surface. Slowly and gently press the bouncy area around the baby (or bounce baby on your lap) so the baby rocks up and down. Use a gentle, rhythmic up-and-down motion, and he will relax. You may also try patting your baby rhythmically on his chest, back, arms, and legs.

Baby Massage

Massage is the language of touch. With a massage, you can calm and soothe your baby and communicate your love and care. During massage, keep the following points in mind. A nice way to start is with a bath. Then, after making sure the room is warm, remove the towel or receiving blanket, and put your baby on the floor. (You can also sit with the baby on your lap or kneel in front of him.) Baby lotion and baby oil soak into the skin too fast, so use vegetable oil, massage oil, or cornstarch. Put the oil or cornstarch on your hands first, then rub your hands together to warm them. Tell your baby what you are doing or sing a song. Rub gently during the first month; as the baby gets older, you can exert more pressure. Once you have touched the baby, keep at least one hand in contact with him until the massage is over. Don't massage your baby's trunk if his stomach is full. Be sensitive and responsive to his reactions; stop if he is not enjoying himself.

If he is enjoying himself, and he probably is, here are some motions you can try:

♦ Stroking with your open palms

♦ Stroking with the thumbs or fingers

♦ "Raking" with the tips of the fingers

♦ Tapping lightly with the tips of the fingers

♦ Massaging arms or legs with a wringing motion

♦ Doing whatever feels good to you and makes the baby happy

Babysitters

Childrearing is physically and emotionally demanding. You may need some time to maintain your sense of self and your relationship as a couple. When you go out, you will need a babysitter—a grandparent, friend, relative, member of a babysitting cooperative, or hired babysitter. Unless you have confidence in the sitter, however, you will not enjoy your time away from your baby.

What are the characteristics of a good sitter? If he or she is an older person, make sure the sitter's strength, hearing, and alertness are adequate to care for your baby and handle an emergency. If the sitter is a teenager consider his or her past experience, training, age, rapport and confidence with babies, and familiarity with emergency measures. Ask for references.

Car Safety

Be sure that your baby is restrained in a dynamically tested and appropriately attached car seat whenever riding in a car. In many states and provinces, this is required by law. Your baby is safest when her car seat is attached to the center of the rear seat. A child accustomed to a safety device from an early age gets used to it and only occasionally protests. Never leave your baby alone in a car. Remember that everyone in the car should "buckle up," since other passengers are endangered if even one person is not restrained.

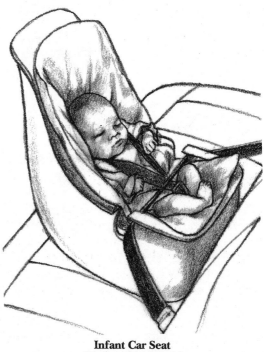

Infant Car Seat
(birth to 20 pounds)

Medical Care

Immunizations

Immunizations protect your child from certain potentially serious diseases. Since many of these illnesses occur in the first years, it is important to immunize your child early and keep to a regular schedule. Immunizations are given at your doctor's office or, for a minimal fee, at public health clinics.

The first vaccinations immunize against diphtheria, whooping cough (pertussis), tetanus (DPT), *Haemophilus influenzae* type B (Hib), and polio. The DPT and Hib vaccines are given by injection; the polio vaccine by mouth. Later, measles, mumps, and rubella vaccines (MMR) may be given by injection, either alone or in combination. In addition, boosters of DPT, Hib, and polio vaccines are given. Some caregivers are now immunizing against hepatitis B virus (HVB).

Keep a record of your child's immunizations. These records will be required by day cares, schools, and camps throughout his life. If the immunization schedule is interrupted, resume it where you left off in the series, rather than beginning again.

Possible Reactions

Many parents are concerned about the risks from immunizations and possible adverse reactions in their infants. It is true that each vaccine carries possible risks as well as benefits. Health care providers believe that in almost all cases, the risks of potentially serious childhood diseases greatly outweigh the risks of immunizations.

Following a DPT injection your baby may have local pain and tenderness at the injection site, a slight fever, and mild irritability for one or two days. Your doctor may suggest that you give acetaminophen to your baby to relieve these symptoms.

On rare occasions, severe adverse reactions occur. If your baby cries inconsolably, develops a high fever, has convulsions (shaking or unresponsiveness), or becomes limp

Immunization Schedule	
Birth–2 months	DPT (Diptheria, Pertussis, Tetanus) Polio Hib (*Haemophilus influenzae* type b)
3–4 months	DPT Hib Polio (optional)
4–6 months	DPT Hib Polio
12 months	Tuberculosis test
15 months	MMR (Measles, Mumps, Rubella) Hib
16–24 months	DPT Polio
4–6 years	DPT Polio
12 years	MMR
12–16 years	Td (Tetanus-Diptheria)
Every 10 years thereafter	Td

or pale, notify your doctor immediately.

DPT injections are usually not given to an infant who had a serious reaction to a previous injection, to an infant who is ill, or to an infant who has had previous convulsions or other nervous system problems.

Reactions to the Hib vaccine include redness and swelling at the injection site and a mild fever. About 1 percent of those vaccinated have a higher fever (above 101.4 degrees Fahrenheit [38.5 degrees Celsius]). Fever and tenderness at the injection site last about a day or two. Rare allergic reactions have also been reported.

Reactions to the polio vaccine are uncommon. In rare instances (one in five to ten million doses), symptoms of polio (such as high fever, muscle weakness, or paralysis) appear in the person who is vaccinated or someone who comes in contact with that person. For example, the person who changes the diapers of the infant may be exposed to polio because the virus is shed in the baby's stools up to two months after the vaccination. Individuals whose immune systems are depressed due to drugs or illness should not provide care for a recently immunized infant. Others should wash their hands well after every diaper change.

Following an MMR injection, a child may develop a mild fever. Seven to twelve days later, he may develop a rash and fever that lasts a day or two. Some children develop mild, brief joint pain two weeks or so following the vaccination, which may show up as a limp. If any other symptoms such as high fever or convulsions occur (a very rare event), these should be reported to your doctor immediately.

When to Call the Doctor

If you are worried about an illness in your baby, call your doctor. Before you call, however, give careful thought to, and then note on paper, your baby's temperature and all the symptoms that worry you. Here are some things your doctor may wish to know:

Physical symptoms. Abnormal temperature, breathing difficulties, coughing, vomiting, diarrhea, constipation, fewer wet diapers, rash.

Behavioral symptoms. Loss of appetite, listlessness, unusual fussiness or irritability, change in typical behavior and activity level (for example, if your baby loses interest in his surroundings or is unable to muster a quiet smile).

Home treatment. What have you done to treat the illness, and how has your child responded? Have you given your child any medications? What and when?

General considerations. Has there been recent exposure to illness? Is anyone at home or day care sick?

Have a paper and pencil handy to write down your doctor's suggestions. Also, know your pharmacist's phone number, as the doctor may want to call in a prescription.

Colds

It is normal for babies to have a slight, stuffy, rattly noise in their noses. Your infant probably has a cold, however, if he has a very runny nose, is fussier than usual, has trouble eating and sleeping, and perhaps has a slight fever.

To lessen the chance of a cold, minimize the number of visitors (adults and children) when the baby is very young. People with colds should stay away. You will probably want to consult your physician for your baby's first cold. He or she may suggest a cool-mist vaporizer, sleeping in a semireclined position (place a folded blanket or pillow under the head end of the mattress), clearing the nostrils gently with a bulb syringe, using nose drops, or giving medication.

Medications

Use the following guidelines when giving medications or vitamins to your baby:

♦ Give only the medication your baby's doctor specifies. Aspirin, even baby aspirin, is no longer recommended for infants and children because of its association with Reye's Syndrome, a very serious disease.

♦ Use a medicine dropper placed between the baby's cheek and gum. Let the infant suck the medication, or gently squirt it in. You might try placing the dropper next to a pacifier or your finger.

♦ Pour medication into an empty bottle nipple and have the baby take it all; fill the emptied nipple with water and have the baby take all that too, to ensure that the baby has received a full dose.

◆ Do not put medication in formula, juice, or water. You will be unsure how much your baby has received if he refuses to finish it.

A Word about SIDS (Sudden Infant Death Syndrome)

Almost every parent worries about SIDS at some time. You may know someone whose baby died of SIDS, or you may have read about it. There is no way to minimize the loss and grief caused by SIDS, but the following facts might help you put your fears and worries into perspective:[7]

◆ SIDS is not caused by a baby's parents; it cannot be predicted and it cannot be prevented. SIDS even occurs in the hospital.

◆ About two to three deaths per thousand live births in the United States are caused by SIDS.

◆ Ninety percent of SIDS deaths occur between two and six months of age.

◆ Death occurs quickly and painlessly and is not the result of suffocation, asphyxiation, or regurgitation.

◆ SIDS is not caused by immunizations; in fact, statistically SIDS deaths occur more commonly in infants who have not been immunized.

◆ Families who have lost a previous baby to SIDS are no more likely to lose subsequent babies to SIDS than any other family.

◆ SIDS is not contagious.

◆ No one is to blame for SIDS.

It is helpful to remember that SIDS occurs rarely. However, if you have lost a baby to SIDS, be assured there was nothing you could have done to cause, predict, or prevent it. SIDS support groups are available to help parents cope with their loss. Your doctor, public health nurse, or childbirth educator can help you locate a group. Or contact the SIDS Alliance, 10500 Little Patuxent Parkway, Suite 420, Columbia, Maryland 21044, (800) 221-7437.

Conclusion

Getting to know and falling in love with your new baby begins before birth and continues over time. If you know what to expect, what is normal, and how to interpret her cues, and if you can appreciate that she has her own unique personality, your role as a parent will be easier and more satisfying. Remember, no one loves your baby or cares more about her well-being than you. She senses this and thrives on your love.

Sleep and Activity Chart

Symbols

Sleep ⎯⎯⎯

Awake and crying or fussy ∿∿∿

Awake and content ‿‿‿

Feeding—breast (HOW LONG)

Feeding—bottle (OUNCES)

Parent-baby interaction (bath, car ride, play, etc.) (ACTIVITY)

Diaper change X

Date 1 A.M.	2	3	4	5	6	7	8	9	10	11	Noon 1 P.M.	2	3	4	5	6	7	8	9	10	11	12 P.M.

Chapter 14
Feeding Your Baby

During pregnancy, a baby grows rapidly from a fertilized egg to a mature baby weighing around seven pounds. All the baby's nutritional needs are met by his mother's body. For the newborn, growth also continues at a rapid rate, but now he is dependent on milk to supply the nutrients necessary for the extraordinary growth occurring in the first months of life. The full-term infant will generally double his birth weight by five months and triple it by one year, and he will grow ten to twelve inches longer than he was at birth.

Two important organ systems are not fully developed at birth—the skeletal system and the central nervous system, which includes the brain. Because the most rapid growth of the skeleton occurs in fetal life and during the first year of life, malnutrition at these times can cause a delay or abnormalities in growth and maturation. There are two rapid periods of brain growth—between fifteen and twenty weeks of fetal life and from thirty weeks of fetal life until one year of age. In fact, by one year, the brain has grown to 82 percent of its adult size. It is not surprising, then, that malnutrition, especially before six months of age, can permanently impair brain development and function.[1]

Parents have the very important responsibilities of providing their baby with foods to promote healthy growth and feeding their baby in a caring and loving way to foster emotional development. The way parents meet their baby's nutritional needs greatly influences both the physical and emotional well-being of the baby.[2]

Feeding Guidelines

Knowing how infants were fed in the past will help you better understand infant nutrition today. You may wonder why you were fed cereal so soon in your babyhood and why your baby's doctor now encourages you to delay solid foods for your baby for several months.

In the early 1900s, most babies were breastfed or fed modified cow's milk for the first year of life. Other foods were seldom offered, except cod liver oil to prevent rickets and orange juice to prevent scurvy. From about 1920 through the next half-century, solid foods were offered earlier and earlier (even in the first week of life) to supply the baby with iron, vitamins, and a more varied diet. Parents and their doctors believed that introducing solid foods early would not only improve babies' nutrition but would also help them sleep through the night sooner (a myth). And they hoped their babies would grow chubby and round. Also at this time, the practice of breastfeeding declined because it was thought to be old-fashioned, and bottle feeding, seemingly more scientific, became highly popular. By 1940, fewer than half of all babies in the United States were breastfed; and by the late 1960s, fewer than a quarter of all babies in the United States were breastfed.

By 1975 a change had taken place. Breastfeeding was becoming increasingly popular, partly because it reflected the "back to nature" movement of the time and partly because it was discovered to have previously unrecognized emotional and health benefits to baby and mother. The return to breastfeeding was led by La Leche League International. By 1979, over 50 percent of American mothers breastfed their babies. Today, over 60 percent of mothers choose to breastfeed their newborns. In addition, in the 1970s, nutritionists began advising mothers to delay introducing solid foods until their infants were at least four to six months old, because they recognized that infants are not physically or developmentally ready to handle solids before this age. They found that early introduction of solid foods contributed to food intolerances, allergies, or inappropriate caloric intake. If high calorie foods are given, the baby may be overfed; if low calorie foods are given, the baby's growth may falter.

In 1980 the American Academy of Pediatrics Committee on Nutrition published guidelines for infant feeding for the first year of life.[3] Three overlapping feeding periods were defined: the nursing period, during which breast milk or an acceptable formula is the only food in the infant's diet; the transitional period, during which solid foods are offered in addition to breast milk or formula; and the modified adult period, during which most of the infant's food comes from the family table, along with breast milk or formula. This chapter will focus on the first feeding period—the nursing period—and will discuss the parents' and infant's role in feeding when milk is the only food in the baby's diet.

Breast Milk or Formula?

The decision whether to breastfeed or formula feed is a personal one. Before making up your mind, try to become informed about each method of feeding. What are the advantages and disadvantages? Under what circumstances is breastfeeding superior to formula and vice versa? Do you have support and commitment from loved ones, friends, and your baby's doctor for your decision? After gathering the facts, it might be helpful for both you and your partner to list all the reasons for, and drawbacks against, each feeding method.

Why Breast Milk Is Recommended

Breastfeeding is recommended for many reasons:

♦ The nutritional composition of breast milk is ideal for human babies.

♦ Breast milk is easily digested.

♦ Breast milk contains antibodies that help protect the baby from infections.

♦ Breastfeeding reduces the possibility of allergies.

♦ Breastfeeding aids involution (the return of the uterus to its normal size).

♦ Breastfeeding, because it requires close physical contact, allows the mother and baby to have an intimate relationship for feeding.

♦ Breastfeeding is both convenient and economical.

Success in breastfeeding is more likely if it appeals to both you and your partner and if you have the support of your friends, loved ones, and your baby's health care provider. If you are committed to the value of breastfeeding, you will be more likely to persist when common temporary problems arise, such as sore nipples or fatigue, or if you are confronted with such challenges as returning to work, mastitis, and infant illnesses.

When Breast Milk Is Not Recommended

There are certain rare instances, however, when breastfeeding may not be recommended or possible:

♦ If the mother has had extensive breast-reduction surgery in which the areola was moved (thereby severing the nerves to the areola), if circulation to the breast was impaired, or if the duct system within the breast was altered

♦ If the mother has untreated tuberculosis

♦ If the mother is HIV infected

♦ If the mother has herpes sores on her areolae

♦ If the mother receives significant amounts of certain drugs, such as chemotherapeutic drugs for cancer

♦ If the mother uses cocaine

♦ If the baby has galactosemia (a rare condition where the baby is unable to digest the sugar in the milk)

♦ If the mother would be uncomfortable, resentful, or unhappy breastfeeding

Prenatal Preparation for Breastfeeding

If you have chosen to breastfeed, the first step is to become familiar with your breasts. Look at yourself in the mirror, keeping in mind that while the size and shape of breasts and nipples vary from woman to woman, these factors have virtually no effect on your ability to produce enough milk for your baby. You may notice that your breasts are larger now and possibly more tender than they were before you became pregnant. The veins are more visible. The Montgomery glands (the small bumps on your areolae) are also larger. Colostrum, which has been present in your breasts since the middle of pregnancy, may leak from your breasts or appear as a dried crust on your nipples. If leaking does not occur, do not worry; you will continue to produce colostrum. All these changes are positive signs that your breasts are preparing to produce milk for your baby.

Women are sometimes advised to express colostrum from their breasts as another way to prepare for breastfeeding. The benefits of this practice probably do not outweigh the possible risk of causing preterm labor by stimulating the breasts. Use other methods instead.

Conditioning or toughening your nipples to prevent soreness has not been shown by any large, scientific study to be effective. In fact, sore nipples are usually due to poor positioning of the baby's mouth on the areola (a poor latch). Most women experience a little nipple soreness in the first few weeks of breastfeeding, usually when the baby first latches on. This soreness should fade within a few minutes. You should avoid using soap, tincture of benzoin, or alcohol on your areolae and nipples, as these products dry the skin. You might also try exposing your nipples to sunshine or to the air for several minutes daily. In regions of the world where women's breasts are not covered with clothing, problems with sore nipples are rare.[4]

An important part of preparing for breastfeeding is to take a breastfeeding class or get a comprehensive book on breastfeeding (see Recommended Resources). You will learn what to expect and how to feed your baby.

Flat or Inverted Nipples

Because flat or inverted nipples can cause problems with initial breastfeeding, you need to know whether you have them so you can begin treatment in late pregnancy. Check yourself for flat or inverted nipples by placing your thumb above and forefinger below your breast on the edge of your areola and gently compressing your areola. This simulates the action of your baby's mouth on your areola during feeding. The nipple should protrude or stick out. If it flattens or indents, you have a flat or inverted nipple. This problem may make feeding difficult because the baby cannot grasp enough of your areola in his mouth to suckle well.

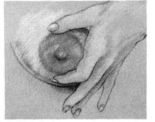

Finger Placement for Checking Nipples

Regular   **Flat (retracted)**

For Flat or Inverted Nipples

Flat or inverted nipples can sometimes be helped to protrude by using the following techniques to stretch the underlying tissue and help the baby attach.

Caution: Stimulation of the nipples sometimes causes uterine contractions and could theoretically cause premature labor in a woman at risk. Discontinue nipple stimulation if it causes contractions.

Breast cups or shells. These two-piece plastic dome-shaped cups or shells are placed over the areola to draw out the nipple. The cups work by exerting a continuous, gentle pressure on the areola, causing the nipple to protrude through an opening in the inner plastic ring.

Breast Cup or Shell

Wear these cups in the last trimester of your pregnancy, starting with an hour each day and gradually working up to several hours. Because the skin may become moist under the plastic, be sure to dry your nipples each time after you wear the shells, or choose a shell that has air holes for constant ventilation. You may continue to wear these cups after the baby is born if your nipple problem persists. For a short time after removing the cups, your nipple will protrude more than usual—perhaps enough to help your baby latch on more successfully.

Nipple stretching. Stretching the nipple tissue several times a day during the last weeks of pregnancy may help correct flat or inverted nipples. Try the following stretching exercises:

◆ Grasp your areola just behind the nipple with your thumb and fingers. Draw your nipple out to the point of discomfort, hold several seconds, and release. You may also roll your nipple between your thumb and fingers while the tissue is stretched.

♦ Place your thumbs at three and nine o'clock positions at the edge of your areola. Gradually stretch the skin and nipple by pressing and moving your thumbs away from each other. Repeat at twelve and six o'clock positions. This is called *Hoffman's Technique.*

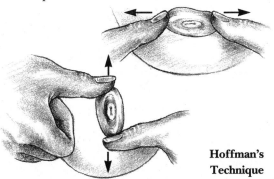

Hoffman's Technique

♦ Your partner's sucking on your nipples during lovemaking stretches the nipples and can be helpful.

Prenatal preparation provides important emotional benefits, too. Until pregnancy, the breasts are perceived by most people primarily as sexual objects; a change in attitude toward them is helpful for successful breastfeeding. Handling your breasts, checking your nipples, and taking a breastfeeding class help you and your partner make this important transition to thinking of the breasts in terms of their function—nourishing a baby.

Breastfeeding

Anatomy of the Breast

The breasts are well designed to make milk. The internal structures change during pregnancy so that your breasts can make colostrum (the first milk) when the baby is born. As soon as you become pregnant, the duct system inside your breasts begins to develop and enlarge in response to estrogen. The milk-producing glands begin to increase in size in response to pro-gesterone. Blood supply to the breasts also increases to support this growth and later to supply the nutrients in breast milk.

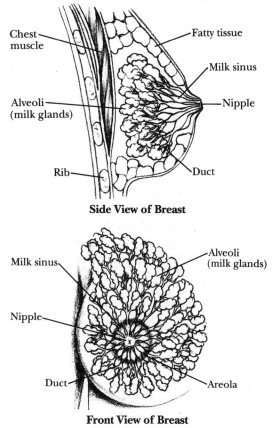

Side View of Breast

Front View of Breast

The illustration shows a cross section of the breast. Each breast contains fifteen to twenty *lobes,* or milk-producing units. Each lobe has approximately twenty to forty *lobules;* within each lobule are numerous *alveoli* that contain the milk-producing cells. Milk flows from the alveoli through the *ductules* into longer *lactiferous ducts.* It then enters the *milk sinuses* located under the areola and leaves the breast through many *nipple* openings. As the infant compresses the sinuses with her lips and gums and massages the extended areola with her tongue, she draws milk into her mouth. The *Montgomery glands,* small glands on the areola, secrete a lubricating substance that keeps the nipple supple and helps prevent infection.

Milk Production

Two hormones, prolactin and oxytocin, play a significant role in milk production and milk ejection (flow). The infant suckling at your breast stimulates the release of prolactin by the anterior pituitary gland, located in your brain. The prolactin in your bloodstream causes the cells in the alveoli to draw water and nutrients from your blood to make milk. In the same manner, oxytocin is released into your bloodstream by the posterior pituitary gland in response to the infant's suckling (or sometimes just by thinking about the baby or hearing a cry). Oxytocin causes the small muscles around the milk-producing cells to contract, releasing milk. It also widens and shortens the ducts, facilitating milk flow. This process is called the *let-down reflex.* You probably will not be aware of a let-down until your mature milk is in. You may feel the let-down as a tingling, itching, or burning sensation in your breasts, or you may experience no sensation even though your baby is getting your milk. The sensations of let-down vary widely. While the first let-down is most noticeable, you will have many let-downs during a feeding.

The amount of milk you produce is generally controlled by the "supply and demand response." The more your baby suckles at your breast, the more milk you produce. Delaying feedings by using a pacifier, offering supplements of water or milk, or attempting to place your baby on a three- to four-hour feeding schedule will decrease your milk production. Breast surgeries and some maternal illnesses can also affect milk production. Feeding frequently, in response to your baby's hunger cues, and for at least ten to twenty minutes at each breast, will increase your milk production in most instances.

Composition of Breast Milk

The first milk produced by the breasts, *colostrum,* is a yellowish fluid that is higher in protein and lower in fat than mature milk. It is ideally suited to the newborn's needs: it provides a laxative effect that helps to speed the passage of meconium; it helps establish the proper balance of bacteria in the infant's digestive tract; and because colostrum is rich in antibodies, it protects the infant from infection. *Transitional milk* is produced next. It is higher in fat and calories and lower in protein and antibodies than colostrum. Soon, the *mature milk* comes in, containing more calories than both the transitional milk and colostrum. Its components include the following:

Water. Water is the largest constituent of breast milk.

Fats. Fats account for most of the calories in human milk. Cholesterol, a fat in human milk, is necessary for proper growth. In addition, it is thought to trigger the enzyme systems that later help the adult to safely utilize cholesterol. Other fats in human milk aid digestion by helping to form a soft curd in the infant's stomach.

Carbohydrates. Lactose (milk sugar), the primary form of carbohydrate in human milk, is present in greater quantities than in cow's milk. It helps the infant absorb calcium and is easily metabolized into two simple sugars that are necessary for the rapid brain growth occurring in infancy.

Proteins. Whey and casein constitute the proteins in milk. Whey is the primary protein in human milk. It is easily digested and becomes a soft curd from which nutrients are easily absorbed. By contrast, casein is the primary protein in cow's milk. When cow's milk is fed to a human baby, the casein forms a rubbery curd, which is less easily digested. Other components of the milk proteins have an important role in protecting the infant from disease and infection. This helps to explain why breastfed infants have a significantly lower incidence of respiratory infections and diarrhea than for-mula-fed infants.[5]

Vitamins and minerals. Some of the vita-mins and minerals present in breast milk deserve special attention. Although iron is present in human milk only in small quanti-ties, it comes in a highly absorbable form. A full-term, healthy, breastfed baby rarely needs iron supplementation before six months of age.[6]

Though rare, rickets has been seen in breastfed infants. As a result, the American Academy of Pediatrics recommends that when breastfed babies and their mothers have little exposure to sunlight due to cli-mate or clothing, the baby should be sup-plemented with vitamin D.[7]

Fluoride in drinking water has a minimal effect on the fluoride levels in breast milk. Some experts believe that breastfed infants should be supplemented with fluoride. Oth-ers question the necessity of supplementing during the early months of infancy. Discuss fluoride supplementation with your baby's doctor or your dentist. Some people are concerned about the safety of fluoride sup-plementation, but there are no reports of harmful effects when used as prescribed.

Changing Composition of Breast Milk

Milk varies in composition during a single feeding. The first milk early in the feeding, called the *foremilk*, is continuously secreted into the lactiferous ducts between nursings. It represents a small amount of the milk vol-ume in each feeding. The *hindmilk* consti-tutes the remaining portion of the feeding. It is released with the let-down reflex. Hind-milk contains more fat and protein than foremilk, and provides more of the calories your infant needs to thrive. As your infant grows, her requirements for nutrients change and the composition of your breast milk changes according to her needs.

Diet for Breastfeeding

By the time your baby is one month old, you will be producing about twenty ounces (two-and-one-half cups) of milk each day. By three months, you will produce about twenty-three to twenty-five ounces a day, and by six months, you will produce about twenty-five to twenty-seven ounces a day. When you introduce solid foods, the amount of milk you produce may decline.

How will you manage to produce so much milk? Your diet plays an important part. A good prenatal and postpartum diet in addition to sufficient liquids, adequate rest, and frequent stimulation of your breasts by your baby's suckling help you to produce all the milk your baby needs. In addition, a good diet prevents your body from being depleted of the nutrients you need to feel well and remain healthy.

During pregnancy, your body prepared for lactation by storing energy in the form of five to seven pounds, which provides some of the extra calories necessary for milk production in the early months. In addi-tion, during lactation your body has the added advantage of being more efficient in absorbing nutrients from the foods you eat. Still, you may also need extra calories beyond your normal recommended daily requirement.

If, after the initial large weight loss in the first month or so following birth, you are still heavier than your recommended weight (allowing for two to four pounds for the weight of your lactating breasts), you may want to go on a reducing diet. It is best to lose only one or two pounds per week and avoid fad or crash diets. Losing weight at this rate and not more rapidly, you will meet your nutritional needs and maintain a suffi-cient quantity of milk. The amount of food and the number of calories you need each day depends on a variety of factors. If you are quite active, have a large baby, or are nursing more than one baby, you may need to consume more calories each day to maintain your weight. On the other hand, if you are less active or are supplementing with formula, you may not need extra calories. The best advice is to continue to eat good foods just as you did in pregnancy and to let your weight guide your calorie intake. Regular exercise helps control weight, too.

Foods to Eat

Your diet while nursing should include some extra protein, more calcium-containing foods, more vitamins, and more fluids than your normal diet. (See chapter 4 for lactation requirements.) But you can easily get the foods you need by eating a balanced diet similar to your pregnancy diet. In addition, you might drink more milk, continue to take your prenatal vitamins, and pay attention to your fluid intake. Two to three quarts of fluids a day are helpful for milk production. If you feel you are not getting enough liquids, pay attention to how concentrated (yellow) your urine is. If it is deep yellow, you probably need more liquid. On the other hand, too much liquid can interfere with let-down.

With the lack of sleep and the sometimes overwhelming responsibility of caring for a newborn, you may feel too tired to even think about eating or drinking. Loss of appetite and tiredness are your body's ways of telling you that you need to put a priority on rest and on caring for yourself. If you severely limit your calories, your milk production will decline, and over time, your body's stores of important elements such as calcium will be depleted.

Food Sensitivity

Your breastfed baby will probably tolerate your milk well, no matter what you eat. But there is a slim chance that he will react adversely to a particular food or group of foods.

A baby who has a strong family history of food allergies may have allergic reactions to some foods that his mother eats. The most common foods with the potential to cause these reactions include cow's milk, eggs, fish, shellfish, and nuts.

If you notice that your infant has a chronic runny nose, diarrhea, or a rash, discuss the possibility of a food allergy with your baby's doctor or a lactation counselor. They may be able to help you identify the problem and provide you with nutritional guidelines.

Drugs in Breast Milk

Many nursing mothers wonder whether drugs appear in breast milk and have an effect on their babies. With a few exceptions, any drug you take will be present to some degree in your breast milk. Some drugs do not present a problem for your baby, while others do. Here is information on some of the commonly used drugs and some dangerous drugs that may cause problems for your baby:

♦ *Vitamin B_6*, when taken in large doses (more than the amount in most prenatal vitamins), may inhibit lactation in sensitive women. Check the amount in your prenatal tablet. The RDA (Recommended Daily Allowance) for B_6 is 2.1 milligrams during lactation. Some tablets contain as much as 10 milligrams. If your milk output is low, consider B_6 as a possible cause.

♦ Some mothers have found that if they consume large quantities of *caffeine,* found in beverages such as coffee and cola, their babies become fussy. Very little of the caffeine you consume is present in your breast milk, but if you suspect your baby's fussiness is aggravated by caffeine, try reducing or eliminating caffeine from your diet. Large amounts of chocolate may have a similar effect on your baby. Chocolate contains theobromine, which is similar to caffeine.

♦ The *alcohol* content in breast milk is approximately equal to the concentration in your blood. Therefore, the effects on the baby correspond to the amount you have consumed. Too much alcohol can inhibit the let-down reflex and reduce the amount of hindmilk available to the baby. Though an occasional drink has not been proven harmful, it is probably wise to limit or eliminate alcohol consumption during lactation. The more recent findings on alcohol raise questions about the advice given in some older books on breastfeeding that recommended beer or other forms of alcohol to stimulate the let-down reflex. They did not take into account potential effects on the baby and the inhibiting effects of excessive alcohol on milk ejection.

♦ Heavy *smoking* has been shown to reduce milk production,[8] reduce the vitamin C content of milk, and increase the incidence of nausea, colic, and diarrhea in infants.[9] Smoking near the baby increases the incidence of pneumonia and bronchitis in the baby.[10] As in pregnancy, it is wise to abstain or to limit smoking during lactation and to avoid smoking in the presence of the baby. Marijuana use is inadvisable, too, for all the same reasons as smoking tobacco, in addition to the effect of the active drug in marijuana on your developing baby. A drugged baby has less opportunity to develop socially, physically, and emotionally in an optimal way.

♦ *Cocaine* use during lactation should be avoided. Cocaine will be present in breast milk and can affect the baby at least as profoundly as an adult. It can cause serious changes in heart function and is associated with an increased incidence of Sudden Infant Death Syndrome (SIDS).

♦ Check with your doctor, midwife, baby's doctor, or pharmacist before taking any *prescribed* or *over-the-counter drugs.* If you need medication, remind your doctor that you are breastfeeding so he or she will choose the medication best suited for you and your baby.

Breastfeeding Basics

First Feedings

You can help establish your milk supply and avoid some early breastfeeding problems by nursing your baby as soon after birth as possible and by allowing your baby to suckle frequently. When mothers breastfeed within an hour after birth and feed their babies frequently, their milk comes in sooner (within twenty-four to forty-eight hours after birth) and engorgement is less of a problem than when they wait to begin breastfeeding.[11]

The first feeding is special. You and your baby get to know each other better and begin the beautiful, synchronous interaction that characterizes breastfeeding. If you have never breastfed before, the technique of feeding may seem awkward and cumbersome at first. But you can be reassured that the skill of breastfeeding improves with experience. Here are some suggestions:

♦ Breastfeed your baby as soon as possible after birth. Babies are often more alert and interested in feeding in the first hour after birth than during the next twenty-four hours.

♦ Use the help of experienced staff or request privacy if you feel confident about initiating feeding without help.

♦ Get into a comfortable position. If you nurse right after delivery, sit comfortably supported or lie on your side. If you have had a cesarean, try sitting in bed with the baby across your lap on a pillow or positioned beside you in a "clutch" or "football hold" for the greatest comfort. (See page 280.)

Lying on Your Side

♦ Nurse your newborn in an atmosphere of calm and tranquility, if possible; this will help you relax and allow you and your baby to concentrate on feeding. You might need to ask visitors other than your partner to leave for the first feeding.

What to Do

1. Make yourself comfortable with your baby's body tipped toward you. Cradle your baby's head comfortably in the crook of your arm. Let her back rest on your forearm and cup her buttocks in the palm of your hand (this is called the cradle hold).

2. Grasp your breast with your free hand behind (not touching) your areola with thumb on the top and four fingers below. Compress the breast with your thumb and forefinger, centering your nipple with the baby's mouth.

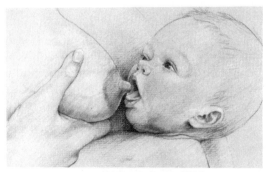

Wait until Mouth Opens Wide

3. Stroke or tickle your baby's lips with your nipple to stimulate her rooting reflex and to get her to open her mouth. Once her mouth opens wide (as wide as a yawn), pull or roll her rapidly toward you and hold her close, so that she is pressed tummy to tummy against your body. Be patient, because it sometimes takes a long time before your baby opens her mouth wide enough. Just keep stroking her lips. Bring your baby to your breast rather than bringing your breast to your baby.

4. Make sure to get as much of your areola as possible in your baby's mouth to ensure a good latch. (Her nose will be touching your breast.) Unless your breasts are quite large, she can still breathe. She will not allow herself to smother. If you feel you need to help her to breathe more easily, lift your whole breast a little and bring her buttocks in closer to rearrange her position and give her more breathing space.

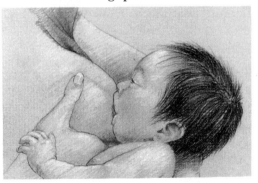

Good Latch

5. Let your baby suckle at the first breast for as long as she wishes (at least ten to fifteen minutes), and then offer the second breast. This advice is much more appropriate than the instructions that you might get to limit feedings at each breast to five minutes or fewer in hopes of preventing sore nipples. Five minutes is hardly enough time to get started. During the first feedings after birth, the let-down reflex may not take place for three minutes or more after you begin the feeding. Once breastfeeding is established, the let-down occurs within seconds after the baby begins to suckle.[12] Research has shown that limiting the amount of time your infant spends at the breast merely delays rather than prevents the onset of sore nipples. The most critical factor in nipple soreness is the baby's latch (described above). When the baby's mouth is properly positioned on the nipple, soreness is rarely a serious problem.

6. When your baby is finished nursing at one breast, she will stop sucking and release the breast. If you need to take the baby off the breast, do so by placing a finger in the corner of her mouth until you break the suction. Then move her away from your breast.

7. Burp the baby, but do not be concerned if the baby does not burp until your milk comes in.

8. Allow your baby to nurse from the other breast.

Initial Nursing Difficulties

Some babies seem to know how to feed right from the beginning, while others seem uninterested, sleepy, or have difficulty latching on to the nipple. If you have difficulty getting started, the following suggestions may help:

♦ If your baby is sleepy, make sure she is not swaddled too snugly. Talk to her, stroke her arms and legs, and wiggle her toes. Make her a little uncomfortable. Do not pry your baby's mouth open. Be patient and in time she will be ready.

♦ Arouse your baby's sense of taste and smell by expressing a few drops of colostrum and rubbing your nipple on her lips.

♦ Hold your baby close enough to you so that she can get as much of the areola in her mouth as possible and can compress the milk sinuses with her lips and gums.

♦ Ask for help from a breastfeeding counselor, experienced nurse, your childbirth educator, your baby's doctor, or your caregiver.

The initial nursing may be different than you expected. Your baby may tentatively lick and mouth your breast; she may struggle to get your areola in her mouth. Or she might immediately latch on to your areola, tug, and suck vigorously. Energetic nursers sometimes grasp and pull on the nipple so firmly they surprise you and cause some pain. You may experience painful uterine contractions (afterpains) with the let-down reflex, especially if this is not your first baby. Relaxation and slow breathing may help in either case.

Do not despair if your baby does not nurse on the first try. Whether she suckles or not, the stimulation of her nuzzling, licking, and being close to your body encourages milk production. Sometimes babies are tired from a long labor or drowsy from the effects of some medications. Perhaps you also are tired following a long, difficult labor. Rest and nourishment will relieve your fatigue, just as rest and time will help your baby. With your patience and perseverance, she will almost certainly learn to nurse quite efficiently.

Burping Your Baby

Babies sometimes swallow air along with milk while breast or bottle feeding. You should burp your baby during and after feeding to help her get rid of the air. Try these burping methods to find the one that is most effective for your baby. With each method, use a burp cloth to protect your clothes. If there is no burp after several minutes, just lay her on her tummy or side or continue feeding.

Over-the-shoulder. Place your baby high on your chest with her head peeking over your shoulder. Support her well across her back and buttocks. Gently pat or rub her back until you hear a burp.

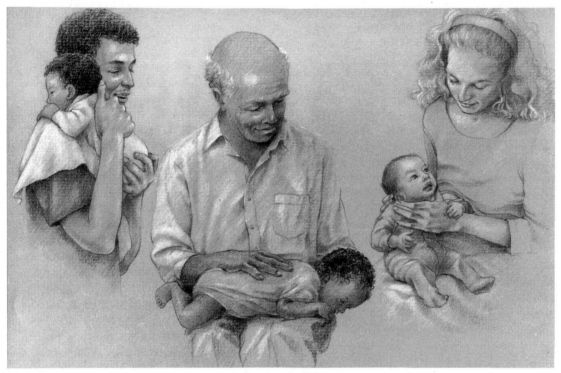

Burping Positions

Over-the-lap. Place your baby on her tummy across your lap. Gently rub or pat her back until you hear a burp.

Sitting and rocking. Sit your baby sideways on your lap. Place your thumb and first finger under her chin with your palm supporting her chest and your other hand supporting her back. Gently rock her back and forth. You might lightly rub or pat her back until you hear a burp.

Frequency of Feeding

Breastfeeding on demand means feeding the baby when she is hungry rather than on a schedule. It probably means feeding every one to three hours. Breastfeeding eight to eighteen times in twenty-four hours is the best way to establish an adequate milk supply. Begin each successive feeding with the breast your baby last nursed from, since babies usually nurse most vigorously at the first breast. This will make sure that both breasts get an equal amount of stimulation. You might use a safety pin in your bra strap to remind you which side to begin with, or palpate your breasts and begin feeding on the side that feels more full. Feed from the first breast for as long as the baby is interested (ten to twenty minutes on average) and then offer the second.

If your baby remains with you in your hospital room, you will know when she needs to be fed. But if she spends some or most of her time in the nursery, you will want to ask the nursing staff to bring your baby to you when she is hungry, day or night. Also keep in mind that full-term, healthy babies do not need supplementary bottles of formula, sugar water, or water if they are breastfed frequently and on demand from both breasts. Their requirements for nourishment and fluids will be met as long as breastfeeding is not limited. Policies restricting feeding time are often based on requirements for formula-fed babies and cannot be applied to breastfed babies.

Supplementary bottles of formula and water have several disadvantages. Formula and sugar water contain calories that diminish your baby's hunger and interfere with her desire to nurse. Furthermore, sucking on a bottle nipple is entirely different from suckling on your breast, and it can result in "nipple confusion," the inability to nurse well at both breast and bottle and the development of faulty sucking patterns, conditions that are difficult to treat. If nipple confusion does occur, it may help to avoid the use of bottle nipples and pacifiers until nursing is well established. If for some reason your baby must receive supplements of water and formula in the first several weeks, it may be helpful to offer them by a Supplemental Nutrition System (SNS), a medicine dropper, a cup, or a syringe feeder to avoid nipple confusion. The Supplemental Nutrition System and syringe feeder include a container of milk attached to a tube that is placed alongside the mother's nipple. As the baby suckles, milk from the container flows through the tube and the baby gets extra milk, along with breast milk. The baby does not use a rubber nipple.

How to Know When Your Milk Comes In

You will know your milk has come in when your baby begins to gulp and swallow rapidly while nursing. You may see some milk in the corners of her mouth; your breasts may be heavy, hard, and tender; you may feel the tingling sensation of your milk letting down; and milk may drip from your other breast while your baby is nursing.

First Weeks

In the early weeks after birth, your baby will nurse every one to three hours. Over time, your baby will consume more at each feeding, and reduce the total number of feedings each day.

Babies do not always nurse on a regular schedule. Sometimes they nurse four or five times in five or six hours and then sleep for a stretch of several hours. If your baby sleeps five to six hours at a stretch at night, be sure to feed her frequently during the day so she will get all the nourishment she needs. If your baby sleeps a great deal during the day and awakens frequently at night to feed, you may try awakening and feeding her every two to four hours during the day in order to change the night-feeding pattern. This is worth trying, but not always successful.

Generally, avoid pacifiers in the early weeks. Besides causing nipple confusion, they may satisfy your baby's sucking needs while interfering with nursing and adequate nutrition. Some babies are happy to suck pacifiers and not eat. These babies will not gain weight well. Other babies seem to nurse constantly without ever giving their mothers a rest. Offering a pacifier to a baby who is nursing well will have less impact on breastfeeding than offering one to a baby who feeds less vigorously and frequently.

Growth Spurts

At about three weeks, six weeks, three months, and six months, your baby may suddenly change her feeding pattern and return to more frequent nursing. She may be fretful, irritable, and more sensitive to stimuli during this time, and she may seem to need to nurse constantly. She is probably experiencing a growth and developmental spurt, and nursing frequently is her way of stimulating you to make more milk to meet her needs and to comfort herself. Do not be troubled by her increased demands. Usually, within about a week, your baby's needs will level off once again.

Enhancing Milk Flow

Breast massage before a feeding or breast pressure during a feeding enhances the flow of milk from your milk-producing glands. If done before feeding or pumping, breast massage speeds your let-down reflex. An impatient, fussy baby will latch to the breast more easily if she does not have to wait long for the milk to flow abundantly. Pumping is often more productive if you "prime" your breast first with breast massage.

Before a Feeding

There are several techniques for massaging your breasts before feeding:

♦ Cup your hands around your breasts and stroke gently but firmly from the chest wall toward the areola. This is best accomplished if you are not wearing a bra.

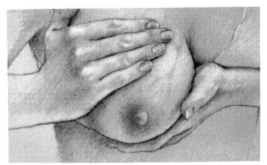

Massage before a Feeding

♦ Massage sections of your breast with circular motions using your fingertips. Massage from the chest wall toward the areola.

♦ Gently jiggle or shake your breasts.

♦ Stroke your breast lightly with a comb or your fingertips from the chest wall toward the areola.

♦ In addition, try visualizing the milk flowing while massaging your breasts. This may help the let-down.

During a Feeding

Breast pressure during feeding enhances milk flow, helps to empty clogged ducts and makes more high calorie hindmilk available to the baby.[13] This technique is especially useful for sleepy babies, babies with a less vigorous suck, and babies who are gaining weight slowly.

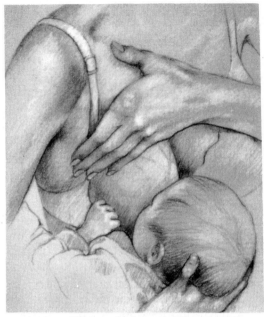

Massage during a Feeding

Once the baby has latched well, pay attention to her pauses in suckling. When she pauses, gently press your fingertips against the milk-producing glands located in the upper outer quadrant of your breast, near your underarm. You will notice a burst of suckling as milk is pressed toward the milk sinuses and into your baby's mouth. If the baby pauses again, rotate the position of your fingertips and press another quadrant of your breast. Be careful not to press too close to your areola as this can interfere with your baby's latch.

Involving the Family

Although you are the one who produces milk and feeds your baby, your partner's and family's support and encouragement are often the key factors in keeping you going in the face of difficulty. Your family can help you eat and drink well, allow you to rest by caring for the baby, and shield you from unnecessary stress. If they can relieve you of some or all of your day-to-day chores, you will be free to devote yourself to caring for yourself and establishing breastfeeding.

Some Early Breastfeeding Problems

Almost every woman has some problems or questions with breastfeeding in the first weeks after birth. Some of these are common and predictable and can be handled quite easily. Others are more serious and require more information and assistance. Following are some of the more common breastfeeding problems and suggestions for solutions.

Is the Baby Getting Enough Milk?

A number of signs can tell you if your baby is getting enough milk. A baby who feeds well every two hours or so for twenty to forty minutes with occasional shorter or longer periods between feedings will have six to eight wet diapers each day. After passing his meconium stool, a breastfed baby may have a loose stool with each feeding, or at least three or more stools a day for the first month. It is common to have a stool after every feeding. Later, as he matures, he may have a bowel movement every other day or even once a week. Your baby's elimination patterns along with his contentment after being fed are good indications that he has received enough milk. Most importantly, your baby's doctor will watch his weight gain and growth to determine if he is getting enough milk. Most babies lose weight shortly after birth—as much as 5 to 10 percent of their birth weight. They usually regain it within two or three weeks. If your baby's weight gain seems to be slow, it could be due to any of the following factors.

Limited sucking time. The let-down may not occur if suckling is limited to a few minutes on a side. This means that the baby will not get the high-calorie hindmilk and will not gain as expected. Your baby needs at least ten to twenty minutes of vigorous suckling at each breast to get the hindmilk.

Gas bubbles. Swallowed air can make the baby feel full. Be sure to burp your baby before changing to the other breast and after the feeding.

Scheduled feedings. A newborn breastfed baby, especially a slow-gaining baby, needs to be fed more frequently than every three or four hours. Allow your infant to nurse on demand or whenever he seems interested (at least eight to eighteen times in twenty-four hours).

Sleepy baby. If your baby is very drowsy during the feeding, pauses for long intervals, or even falls asleep, he may spend a long time at the breast without getting much milk. To wake up your baby, try stroking the soles of his feet with your fingernail or rubbing his thighs or tummy. Avoid wiggling your breast or rubbing his cheeks which may dislodge a good latch and interrupt the feeding. If these techniques are not enough, make sure he is not overbundled. Then try burping him and switching to the other breast, which can be done several times during one feeding to keep him awake. You may also use breast massage (see page 276) to press milk down toward the nipple and interest him with the flow of milk.

If your baby goes for long stretches without feeding, try waking him every two to three hours during the day and every four hours at night. If the baby was preterm or has had other problems, your doctor may suggest feeding more frequently.

If your baby is sleeping so soundly that you simply cannot rouse him, it is better to wait a half hour and try again than to continue the frustrating and futile effort of waking up a baby who is deeply asleep. If this happens often, record the baby's feeding and sleeping on the Sleep and Activity Chart (page 262) for two or three days and call your baby's doctor with this information.

Limiting feedings to one breast. Offering only one breast at each feeding may result in inadequate milk production. Switch to the other breast after your baby finishes feeding at the first breast. The baby might nurse very little on the second breast at first, but he will nurse more as he grows.

Nonnutritive sucking. Some infants satisfy their sucking needs without nursing by sucking on their own fists, fingers, tongues, lips, or pacifiers, or by chewing and sucking on the tips of their mother's nipples. Once their sucking needs are satisfied in this way, they may not appear hungry, leading their mothers to think they do not want to nurse. These babies may have problems gaining weight.

Difficulty with the let-down reflex. Anxiety, fatigue, inadequate nipple stimulation, and excessive amounts of alcohol, caffeine, and smoking all may inhibit the let-down reflex.

Fatigue, insufficient intake of fluids and calories, or poor diet. These may reduce your milk supply but are less common reasons for inadequate milk supply. Spend a day in bed with the baby to replenish a declining milk supply. Pick a day when you have help with meals, household chores, telephone calls, and your other children. Spend the day nursing your baby as often as possible, eating and drinking well, sleeping, nurturing yourself, and letting others nurture you. Besides helping to restore your milk supply and helping you catch up on needed rest, this is a wonderful way to learn more about your baby. Then, over the long term, pay attention to your need for rest, to your food and fluid intake, and to the quality of your diet.

Poor latch. If the baby has not positioned his mouth properly on the nipple, he will not be able to compress the milk sinuses well and will not stimulate a let-down reflex. If the baby's mouth makes a "clicking" sound during sucking, it may indicate that the suction is breaking with each sucking

effort. For the whole feeding, hold the newborn baby tight against your body, close enough that his nose touches your breast. It is possible to start with a good latch and later have the baby's mouth slip down to the nipple tip as your arm tires. A pillow beneath your arm may prevent this. See page 272 for a description of a good latch.

Alternate Cradle Hold

Treatment

If you wonder if the baby is getting enough milk, try the following:

♦ Feed frequently and for at least ten minutes from each breast.

♦ Avoid pacifiers, at least in the beginning.

♦ Feed the baby whenever he indicates an interest in feeding (awake, alert, sucking fingers or fists), and try not to postpone feedings.

♦ Massage your breasts during feedings to increase the milk flow. (See page 276 for information about breast massage.)

♦ Nurture yourself. Rest or sleep when the baby sleeps. Get adequate fluids and eat well.

♦ Get help from a lactation specialist, your childbirth educator, a La Leche League leader (they are listed in the phone book), your doctor, or an experienced breastfeeding mother. A poor newborn weight gain (an indicator of insufficient milk) can be improved if an experienced person can help you figure out the cause of the problem and develop a plan for treating the weight gain problem.

Engorgement

Engorgement is an inflammation of the breast with swelling in the tissue surrounding the milk-producing glands. It is accompanied by an accumulation of milk in the ducts. It occurs when the "milk comes in," usually the second or third postpartum day. Your breasts swell, become firm and warm to the touch, and painful. Keep in mind that engorgement may be prevented or at least reduced by allowing the baby to nurse early and frequently for an adequate time and with a proper latch. Engorgement usually subsides after a few days. Pumping to remove the milk your baby does not take will relieve, not aggravate, engorgement.

Treatment

♦ Let the baby nurse frequently for as long as he wishes. You can feed him whenever he is awake and interested in feeding.

♦ Use warm packs or a warm shower before a feeding to help the milk flow.

♦ Express milk right before feeding to soften a hard, swollen areola and to make it easier for the baby to grasp. (Expression of milk is described on pages 283–84.)

♦ While feeding or pumping, massage your breasts (page 276) to enhance milk flow.

♦ Use an electric or mechanical breast pump after the feeding if nursing does not reduce the fullness.

♦ After feeding or pumping, apply cold packs to reduce blood flow to your breasts and to provide comfort.

Sore Nipples

Sore nipples may occur at any time but are most common during the first weeks of breastfeeding. Soreness may range from discomfort only when the infant first grasps the nipple to continuing pain throughout and between feedings. Sore nipples can almost always be treated successfully. In severe cases, the nipples may crack and bleed, but even these cases can be successfully treated without stopping breastfeeding.

Sore nipples are usually caused by improper positioning of the baby's mouth on the areola (improper latch). Flat or inverted nipples are more prone to soreness. Less commonly, sore nipples are due to overvigorous pumping or hand expression, a very vigorous baby whose gums clamp hard on the areola and whose suckling may scrape the tissue of the areola, or an infection of the areola. They are not prevented by prenatal nipple "toughening" exercises (rubbing or pulling the nipples), as was once believed. The common belief that limited suckling reduces or prevents nipple soreness has also been shown to be a myth.[14] Frequent unlimited suckling with a good latch is not associated with an increased incidence of sore nipples.

Treatment of Sore Nipples Due to Problems with Latch

♦ Check for proper latch and make adjustments if necessary. (See page 272.)

♦ Check your grasp of your breast. Your fingers should be below your breast and behind your areola. Your thumb is above and behind your areola. Using a "scissor-hold" (holding your nipple between two fingers) sometimes interferes with your baby's ability to latch if your fingers slip down over the nipple area.

Football or Clutch Hold

♦ Vary the feeding position. Feed your baby in a cradle hold, football hold, or lying down. The different positions change the placement of your baby's mouth on your nipple so that the pressure from your baby's suckling will not be in the same place all the time.

♦ Feed your baby frequently, and begin on the less sore side. Try to nurse for at least ten minutes on each breast, but avoid frequent "marathon" nursing sessions lasting longer than an hour.

♦ Soak a tea bag (black tea) in a small amount of hot water, making a very dark solution. Apply the tea solution to your areolae and dry with a hair dryer at low or medium heat held at arm's length. The tannic acid in the tea is thought to help the skin be more resistant to soreness. Sometimes applying warm, moist, tea bags to the sore area for ten to fifteen minutes after several daytime feedings is helpful. To protect your clothing, cover the tea bags with plastic wrap and pull up your bra flaps. Dry the breasts well after removing the bags.

♦ Dry both areolae well after each feeding by leaving bra flaps down and using a hair dryer or exposing them to sunshine briefly until dry. To keep the nipples dry, change nursing pads frequently if you are leaking milk during or between feedings.

♦ Express a small amount of breast milk and rub it over the sore area. The anti-infective properties of breast milk and other substances in the milk help the tissue to heal. Breast creams and ointments are sometimes recommended. While they may help in some instances, they may also cause irritation of the breast (for example if you are allergic to wool, lanolin may create a rash), or they may clog the Montgomery glands. If you use creams, apply the cream sparingly just over the sore area. Vitamin E oil should be used sparingly if at all as it can raise the baby's blood level of vitamin E to toxic levels. And it has been found that creams containing lanolin may also contain insecticides used to treat sheep from which the lanolin comes.

♦ Use perforated breast shells or cups between feedings to keep anything from touching your sore nipples and to keep them dry. (Such shells are manufactured by Medela and Egnell.) Sometimes these breast shells increase leaking.

♦ Apply a small ice pack (a zip-lock bag with frozen peas or corn works well) to the sore area for five minutes before feeding to provide some relief of pain as the baby latches on. Apply an ice pack again for twenty minutes following feedings. This relieves pain and aids healing by taking advantage of an increase in circulation that occurs after application of ice.

♦ Avoid using nipple shields. They are never a solution for a poor latch. They may be used in rare instances when sore nipples have been a long-standing problem. They offer only temporary relief and, because they prevent stimulation of the areola, they cause a decline in milk production.

Treatment of Sore Nipples Due to Overvigorous Pumping or Milk Expression

♦ Be sure to center your nipple in the breast pump cup (see page 284). When the nipple is not centered, friction to the areola is unevenly applied and your nipples become sore.

♦ Use only enough suction to cause milk to flow well. Too much suction stretches the areola too deep into the pump cup and may injure the tissue.

♦ When expressing by hand, use breast massage first. Express milk gently. Except when expressing from an engorged breast, hand expression should not hurt. Carefully and patiently express milk from your milk sinuses and avoid bruising the tissue.

♦ Use the measures previously suggested if your areola or nipple is sore, cracked, or bleeding.

Thrush (Yeast) Infection

If your nipple pain continues even between feedings; is sharp, deep, or searing; and persists even when you have a good latch, you might have a thrush infection. The areolae or nipples may appear slightly pink but are usually unremarkable in appearance.

If you or your baby have taken antibiotics, if you have had a vaginal yeast infection, or if your baby has or has had thrush, an areolar thrush infection is possible.

Treatment of Sore Nipples Due to Thrush

Consult your doctor or midwife. Thrush infections are most effectively treated by applying a prescription medication to your areola and to the baby's mouth and by treating any vaginal yeast infection.

Breast Pain on Let-down

Some women experience a sharp, deep pain behind the areola at the beginning of each feeding. The pain, which subsides when the milk is flowing, does not indicate a problem and will usually go away in time without treatment. It is probably caused by oxytocin, which shortens and widens the ductules and ducts and facilitates the flow of milk through them.

Physiologic Jaundice in the Newborn

Physiologic jaundice usually begins on the second or third day after birth. It is not a reason to discontinue breastfeeding or to give water or formula. (See pages 249–50 for a discussion of newborn jaundice.) Physiologic jaundice in breastfed babies is often the result of insufficient breastfeeding. In fact, it has been called "lack of breast milk" jaundice. The most effective way to prevent jaundice in the breastfed infant is to feed frequently and to not limit feedings. This will help the baby to have bowel movements, which is his way of excreting bilirubin. Since very little bilirubin is excreted in urine, water bottles are not helpful in preventing or treating jaundice.

Breast Milk Jaundice

Breast milk jaundice, a rare condition, does not occur until the baby is five to seven days old and is thought to be caused by a substance sometimes found in breast milk that interferes with the normal metabolism of bilirubin. The bilirubin accumulates, causing the jaundice. To slow the rise in bilirubin or reverse a high bilirubin level, you may be asked to stop breastfeeding and feed with formula for twelve to twenty-four hours. This is usually enough to lower bilirubin levels and is diagnostic for breast milk jaundice. If there is another rise, interrupting feedings once again may be suggested. Eventually the bilirubin levels fall or stay down and no other treatment is necessary. You should pump your breasts during the periods you are not nursing to maintain your milk supply.[15]

Interrupting breastfeeding in this way is very stressful when you are trying to establish your milk supply. You should be reassured that your milk is not "bad"; your baby is simply not able to handle it yet. Your baby is not likely to be harmed by this rise in bilirubin level.

Treatment

♦ Continue nursing your baby unless your baby's bilirubin levels are too high and continue to rise. Your doctor can help you decide if they are too high.

♦ If you are asked to interrupt breastfeeding, feed with formula and pump your breasts to maintain your milk supply. (You can save the milk to be used later.)

Leaking

Milk often leaks from the breasts in the first few weeks or months of nursing. This subsides as your breasts become more finely tuned and they "learn" how much milk to make and when to let it down. Leaking usually occurs when your breasts are very full, when you are feeding from the other breast, when you hear a baby cry, or when you are sexually aroused.

Treatment

♦ When you feel the milk starting to let down, press your hands or forearms firmly against your nipples to slow the flow of milk.

♦ Compress your nipple between your thumb and forefinger to stop the flow of milk.

♦ To prevent soaking your clothes, wear cotton or disposable breast pads and discard them when they become damp. Avoid breast pads with plastic liners.

♦ Wear plastic breast cups or shells, such as the ones used to make flat nipples protrude, for short periods of time when you want to keep your clothing dry. Because these cups

actually stimulate milk production, avoid using them for long periods. Discard any milk collecting in the cups and allow the nipples to dry well between wearings.

Clogged Ducts

Redness, pain, swelling, or a lump in the breast can mean either a clogged duct or mastitis (an infection). If these symptoms occur in an area in one breast and you do not have a fever or other flu-like symptoms, you may have a caked, clogged, or plugged duct. If untreated, this could lead to mastitis. Any lump that does not respond readily and go away with the following treatment should be evaluated by your doctor or midwife.

Treatment

♦ Apply a warm, moist pack to the sore area and leave it on for ten minutes. Repeat three to four times a day.

♦ Massage the area toward the nipple during feedings. (See page 276 for instructions in breast massage.)

♦ Avoid tucking clothing up under your arm during feedings; it may hinder milk flow.

♦ Avoid poorly fitting bras; they may obstruct milk ducts.

♦ Nurse frequently.

♦ Express milk after the baby has nursed if fullness remains. You may massage the full area to promote milk flow.

Mastitis

Mastitis is an infection of the breast, which can occur at any time while you are nursing. Presence of bacteria and lowered maternal defenses associated with such conditions as cracked nipples, fatigue, or stress may cause mastitis.

The breast may have a tender, reddened area or the whole breast may be involved. Symptoms include fever, chills, fatigue, headache, and sometimes nausea and vomiting. Many women feel as though they have a severe flu. If you have these symptoms, suspect mastitis and call your caregiver.

Treatment

♦ Continue to nurse from both breasts. The milk is not harmful.

♦ Rest and stay in bed until you feel better.

♦ Take antibiotics, if prescribed, for the full course of the prescription.

♦ Apply a warm, wet towel over the painful area to help increase circulation to the breast.

♦ Apply cold compresses after feeding to reduce congestion and pain in your breast.

♦ Drink ample water, juice, and other fluids.

♦ Avoid constricting bras and clothing so milk may flow easily. During feedings, breast massage may help.

♦ If mastitis occurs frequently during the course of breastfeeding, more prolonged low dose antibiotics may be helpful.[16]

Expressing and Storing Breast Milk

Expressing and storing your breast milk allows you to leave your baby for a while without altering her usual diet. Although awkward and slow at first, expression becomes easier with practice.

You will need clean hands, clean equipment, and bottles or disposable baby bottle liners (any container meant for food storage is fine). Pumping and expressing milk is most effective if you can do it while you are having a let-down reflex.

Getting Ready to Pump

♦ Nurse your baby and take advantage of the let-down reflex that comes during a regular feeding time. As your baby suckles, collect any milk that drips from the other breast, or pump that breast at the same time. It may take another person or a one-handed breast pump to express at the same time you feed your baby. Other good times to pump are following a feeding; when your baby feeds from only one breast (pump the unnursed breast); or when your baby skips a feeding or you feel particularly full of milk.

♦ Find a private, uninterrupted, warm environment for pumping or milk expression.

♦ Massage your breasts with your fingertips. Imagine the round shape as the face of a clock. Massaging at twelve o'clock, one o'clock, and so on, use your cupped hand and massage your whole breast. Start way back under your arms and at the outer boundaries of your breasts and massage toward your areolae, or use any of the massage techniques listed on page 276.

♦ Apply warm, wet towels to your breast.

♦ Relax and imagine your baby nursing and the milk flowing.

♦ Some mothers occasionally use a prescribed nasal Pitocin spray. This drug is expensive and has side effects such as headaches, and it may only work for a short time. If the other methods do not work, you might discuss this option with your doctor.

Expressing Breast Milk

There are many ways to express or pump milk.

♦ Expressing by hand is effective for many, and also inexpensive and convenient. Once milk is flowing, grasp your breast behind the areola with thumb above and one or two fingertips below. Lift your breast, press toward your chest and compress the milk sinuses between the pads of your fingers. Your milk may drip or spurt into a collecting container. At first you may obtain only several drops to a half-ounce. With practice, you will be able to collect more.

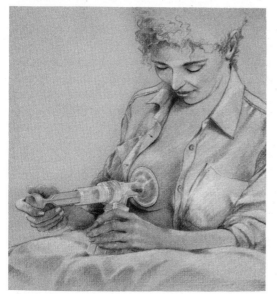

Manual Breast Pump

♦ You can buy or rent effective equipment designed for pumping your breasts. Your breastfeeding counselor, childbirth educator, La Leche League leader, midwife, or physician may help you select a pump. If only an occasional bottle is needed, hand expression or a small battery-operated pump is sufficient. If you need to pump large quantities (several bottles) a day, or if you are pumping milk to maintain your milk supply during a period when your baby is unable to nurse, you will probably need one of the large and powerful but gentle electric pumps. It may be helpful to know that you can never pump all the milk out of your breasts. There is always some there.

Using Expressed Breast Milk

Fresh. Feed the milk to your baby right after pumping.

Refrigerated. Use within forty-eight hours if kept at 40 degrees Fahrenheit (4° Celsius).

Frozen. Use within two months if your freezer is very cold (cold enough to keep ice cream very hard) or within two weeks if not very cold. It can be stored in a deep freeze for two to three months. Place the milk at the back of the freezer away from the door. One disadvantage of freezing milk over using it fresh or refrigerated is that freezing destroys some of the anti-infective properties.

To thaw frozen breast milk, hold the container under warm water until it is liquified, or let it thaw and warm slowly, six to eight hours, in the refrigerator. Do not overheat the milk since this destroys more of the anti-infective properties. There is no clear data about changes in breast milk defrosted by microwave, but the American Academy of Pediatrics advises against thawing or warming in a microwave as this has been associated with scald burns to the baby's mouth and throat due to "hot spots" in the milk.

Introducing a Bottle to a Breastfed Baby

You may want your baby to use a bottle when you are gone for a feeding or while you are at work. Some babies take a bottle with no problem, while others do not take it so easily. If you have a problem introducing a bottle to your baby, try the following suggestions:

♦ Wait until breastfeeding is well established before introducing the bottle. A baby who is still learning to breastfeed or who needs coaxing to latch on and remain latched is at risk of becoming "nipple confused." Usually, waiting until your baby is three or more weeks old is a good idea.

♦ If possible, put expressed breast milk into the bottle rather than formula. Providing a familiar milk may be helpful as your baby adjusts to sucking from a bottle.

♦ Sucking from a bottle is a new experience for the breastfed baby. Babies are able to learn something new most easily when they are calm and rested. Offer a half ounce or so of breast milk in a bottle following a feeding and during a time when you feel calm. The goal at first is to acquaint your baby with a bottle, not to replace an entire feeding.

♦ Sometimes babies take a bottle best from someone other than their mother. Other babies are happy to accept bottles from their mothers. You will discover what your baby prefers.

♦ You will probably feel better about leaving your baby once you are sure he will take milk from a bottle. Help your baby learn about bottle feeding well in advance of your returning to work, if possible.

♦ Occasionally, a baby absolutely refuses to take a bottle. (Usually this is a temporary situation for a baby in day care.) Fortunately, babies can take milk in other ways—from a small cup, a dropper, or a spoon. A small cup such as a shot glass or medicine cup works well. Sit the baby upright and tip a little milk into his mouth for him to swallow. A medicine dropper allows you to squirt small amounts between his cheek and gum, which he will swallow. Babies three months old or older can learn to use a small stiff straw.

Special Situations

Under certain circumstances, breastfeeding mothers and their babies need more support and persistence than usual to establish lactation. Many hospitals and community agencies have trained lactation specialists to help in these challenging situations. Your childbirth educator or baby's doctor can make a referral.

Premature Infants

Mothers who give birth to premature infants produce a milk that is different from the milk produced by the mother of a full-term infant. It is especially well suited to the unique nutritional needs of the premature baby—it is higher in protein, nitrogen, sodium, calcium, fat, and calories. The American Academy of Pediatrics Committee on Nutrition states: "At this time the Committee considers it optimal for mothers of low birth weight newborn infants to collect milk for feeding their own infants fresh milk."[18]

It is both possible and desirable to breastfeed when your baby is born prematurely. At a time when you may feel sad and worried about her well-being, it helps to know that you can do something important for your baby that no one else can do. If your baby is not yet able to suckle well, express your colostrum by using hand expression or a pump. Many hospitals have efficient electric breast pumps for this purpose. This expressed colostrum and milk can be fed to your baby by tube until she is able to suckle at your breast. Contact your hospital's nursing staff, a Parents of Prematures support group, a lactation specialist, or La Leche League for help in establishing lactation and in overcoming some of the obstacles you may encounter in the process.

Working Outside the Home

It is possible to breastfeed exclusively and work outside the home, if you wish, by expressing and storing milk to be fed to your baby while you are away. The more flexible your job, and the longer your maternity leave, the easier it will be for you to combine breastfeeding and work. You might consider finding part-time work, establishing a work schedule of longer days with an opportunity to take a long feeding break midday, or choosing a day-care setting near your work so you can nurse your infant during your breaks and at lunch time. But if feeding your baby during the work day is not an option, make arrangements for time and privacy to express or pump milk at work. The milk must be stored in a refrigerator or an ice chest and, unless it is frozen, fed to the baby the next day.

The age of your baby is a factor. If you are able to delay returning to work until your baby feeds less frequently, is taking solid foods, and is on a more predictable schedule, breastfeeding will be easier.

Some working mothers decide to breastfeed while at home and supplement with formula while they are away. The breasts are amazingly cooperative in producing enough milk as long as you nurse on a regular schedule for an adequate period of time. If your milk supply begins to dwindle, nurse frequently during the evening and days off

Breastfeed Whenever Possible

to stimulate your milk production. Mothers who are not able to pump at work can still breastfeed. This requires feeding frequently

when at home. Many babies go on a "reverse feeding schedule," feeding in the evenings and at night and taking few if any supplements at day care.

Relactation

It may be possible to reestablish lactation after you have stopped nursing or after you have been separated from your baby. However, it requires persistence and a commitment to succeed on your part as well as an interested baby. Frequent, round-the-clock nipple stimulation by massaging and suckling is most effective. You may use a Supplemental Nutrition System (SNS) or a Lact-Aid Nursing Trainer during your early nursing efforts. These devices encourage the baby to suckle at an empty or near-empty breast while receiving supplemental formula through a plastic tube that you place by your nipple. The baby sucks on the tube and your nipple. The suckling helps you produce milk while the device provides your baby with enough milk for growth. Your milk supply may be increased by using an electric pump following feedings. You can use the milk you pump in the tube feeding unit. Lactation specialists and La Leche League leaders who are knowledgeable about relactation can support and advise you if you decide to reestablish breastfeeding.

These same methods can be used by mothers who wish to breastfeed their adopted babies.

Breastfeeding and Fertility

Breastfeeding usually suppresses or delays ovulation and menstruation, especially if breast milk is the only food your baby receives and you nurse frequently around the clock. You cannot count on breastfeeding for birth control, however, because some breastfeeding women ovulate as early as several weeks post partum, while others do not ovulate for twelve to eighteen months. Because you can ovulate before menstruating, you cannot assume that breastfeeding will prevent you from becoming pregnant.

Your midwife or physician can advise you about the most appropriate methods of contraception while you are breastfeeding. Oral contraceptives, either estrogen-progestin or progestin only are not recommended for nursing mothers. The use of oral contraceptives has been associated with reduced milk production and potential harmful effects for the infant who receives them through the breast milk. These possible harmful effects must be weighed against the risk and personal cost of future pregnancies.

Formula Feeding

If you are formula feeding your baby before one year of age, the American Academy of Pediatrics recommends a commercially prepared formula. Evaporated milk formulas are not as well suited to your baby's nutritional needs. Whole, 2 percent, 1 percent, skim, and goat's milk are not considered good choices for infants under one year of age: they are difficult for infants to digest and lack some necessary nutrients. Your baby's doctor can recommend a formula for your baby and give you guidelines on how much to feed him. Because these commercial formulas are fortified with vitamins and minerals, your baby will not require a vitamin supplement. So if you change from breastfeeding to bottle feeding, discontinue any vitamins you gave him while nursing. An exception might be a fluoride supplement if your water supply does not contain fluoride.

Infant Formulas

Most infant formulas are made from cow's milk or from soy beans. They are available in ready-to-feed preparations, canned liquid concentrates, and a powdered form. The powdered formula is the least expensive; ready-to-feed is the most expensive, but it might be especially useful for trips where the water supply is questionable. If your tap water is fluoridated and you mix it with the concentrate or powdered formula, your baby will receive daily fluoride.

When preparing formula, carefully follow the directions on the can or package. If you use too little water, you can cause diarrhea, dehydration, and other problems for your baby. If you use too much water, your baby will not receive enough calories and nutrients.

Equipment

Your baby's doctor or your friends might offer suggestions about purchasing bottles and nipples. Your baby's doctor can advise you about whether to sterilize or simply to wash your baby's bottles with the family dishes. You need to handwash nipples. Be sure to squirt water through the holes to clean them.

Check the equipment before feeding your baby. The holes in the nipples are the right size if the formula drips out when you hold the bottle upside-down. If the milk comes out in a stream, the nipple hole is too big and your baby will feed too fast and his sucking needs will not be satisfied. If the milk drips too slowly or not at all, your baby will swallow too much air, tire, and perhaps not get enough during a feeding. If the nipple hole is too large, discard the nipple. If it is too small, pierce the hole with the tip of a clean, red hot needle and check it again.

Tips for Bottle Feeding

You can make your baby's feedings consistently successful and happy by remembering to do a few simple things:

♦ Hold the baby in a semireclining position during feedings. If his head is too low, the milk will pool back in his throat around his eustachian tubes (which extend from the back of his throat to his ears). This pooling can cause middle-ear infections.

♦ Hold the baby sometimes with your right arm, sometimes with your left arm to promote normal eye muscle development (the baby will look toward you as he feeds).

♦ Burp your baby after every one to two ounces when he is little, and about halfway through a feeding as he matures.

♦ Trust your baby to let you know how much he needs to eat. He will not always be interested in taking the same amounts. Do not coax him to empty the bottle if he seems satisfied. When he rapidly and consistently finishes his feedings, he may be ready to have another ounce added to his bottle.

♦ Make feeding your baby a special time. Be sure to cuddle him. Do not prop his bottle and leave him alone for feedings. Interacting with a loving person during feedings helps him thrive emotionally and develop trust in you and those who care for him.

Cautions

If you feed water to your baby, do not mix honey in the water, and do not dip a pacifier in honey before giving it to your baby. Feeding honey (cooked or uncooked) to a baby under one year of age has been associated with infant botulism.

Though it may seem tempting to coat the bottle nipple or pacifier with sugar or juice to entice your baby to feed, most babies refuse the bottle simply because they are not hungry. Adding additional sugar to formula is not recommended either because it may cause diarrhea.

Conclusion

Feeding your baby has far greater significance than simply providing nutrients and calories for physical growth. A baby whose hunger cries are consistently answered develops a sense of trust, security, and well-being. A baby who is smiled at, talked to, and cuddled develops a sense of emotional security. And holding your baby close stimulates the senses of touch, smell, and taste. All these things occur during feeding. Feeding provides many opportunities for your baby to express affection toward you and appreciation by cooing, grinning, patting, and other endearing behaviors. Feeding time is an important catalyst for the emotional development of the infant and the strengthening of family ties.

—photograph by Lise Alexander/Beginnings

Feeding time means more than nourishment—it means love, comfort, and fun.

Chapter 15
Preparing Other Children for Birth and the Baby

If you are expecting your second child (or third or more), you will want to prepare your older child for the birth of a sibling—a baby brother or sister. You will need to teach your child about pregnancy, birth, and life with a newborn in a realistic and age-appropriate manner. This chapter offers a variety of suggestions for preparing your child. Some will be more appropriate than others, depending on the age and maturity of your child and your plans and desires. Several books listed in Recommended Resources can also help prepare you and your child for another baby.

Preparations before the Birth

When to Announce the Pregnancy

When is it best to tell your child you are pregnant? If you are especially tired or are vomiting each morning, you might announce the pregnancy early in order to relieve a child who may be worried that you are ill. On the other hand, announcing it very early means a long waiting period for a young child who has no concept of time.

Some parents prefer to announce the pregnancy after the first trimester when the likelihood of miscarriage is reduced. Others put it off until later, when the pregnancy becomes obvious. Linking the expected birth date to a special event or season makes the wait more understandable. Making a special calendar together helps the child who repeatedly asks when the baby will come.

Some parents feel reluctant to announce the pregnancy because they worry about displacing the older child, but waiting does not diminish these feelings of displacement. Try to announce the pregnancy early enough to allow time to ease your child's adjustments by including her in the preparations and providing an opportunity to develop positive feelings and realistic expectations about the new baby.

Suggestions

The following suggestions will help involve and prepare your child before the birth:

♦ Discuss with your young child what "baby," "brother," and "sister" mean; give examples of families you know who have more than one child.

♦ Talk to your child about pregnancy and birth. Find out what your child already knows, correct misconceptions, fill in the gaps, and answer questions. Use appropriate terms or examples: the baby is in the "uterus," not the "stomach." However, you will want to avoid overwhelming a small child with too much information.

♦ Read books to your child about pregnancy, birth, new babies, and feelings about being a big brother or sister.

♦ Arrange to bring your child to one or more prenatal visits to meet your doctor or midwife.

♦ Let your child hear the baby's heartbeat and feel the baby move. Talk about fetal development with your child. Tell your child what the fetus can do (hiccup, suck her thumb, hear, wiggle, kick, for example).

♦ Attend a sibling preparation class if one is available in your area. Let your child see films, slides, or pictures of birth and newborns; a demonstration of a birth with a doll can also be helpful.

♦ Practice prenatal exercises with your child. Explain that these exercises help you feel better during pregnancy and afterward.

♦ Take your child on a hospital tour, if possible.

♦ Help your child make a picture book about pregnancy, birth, babies, big brothers, sisters, and families.

♦ Show your child photographs or videotapes of herself as a baby—especially ones showing you or her father caring for her as a newborn.

♦ Have your child see and interact with a friend's baby. Let her see how small and sometimes unplayful a baby is.

♦ Have your child help you pack your suitcase or the baby's bag for the hospital. If she will be staying with someone while you are in the hospital, have her pack her bag, including special gifts for those who will care for her.

♦ Make changes in room or sleeping arrangements several months before the birth to prevent your child from feeling suddenly displaced by the baby. Set up the new baby's sleeping area to give your child time to become accustomed to where the new baby will be.

♦ Safety-proof your home if you have not already done so, since accidents can happen when you are busy with the new baby.

♦ Follow your child's lead about how much and when to discuss birth and the baby. Be sensitive to the possibility of overloading your child with talk of a new baby.

Should Your Other Child Be Present When You Give Birth?

Many hospitals and birth centers today welcome the presence of children at birth, and many more invite children to visit their mother and baby sister or brother very soon after birth. They leave the decision to you. Caregivers and psychologists disagree in their opinions regarding children attending birth.[1] Most agree, however, that if a child spends time with his mother and the new baby soon after birth, it reduces separation anxiety and helps the child adjust to life with a new baby.

Some parents feel that it is too complicated and possibly disturbing to have their other child attend the birth. They are concerned about the logistics of caring for the child during labor, the gamble that the child will be in good health, and the possibility of having to interrupt the child's sleep. Or they are concerned about the child's reactions to his mother's pain and possible crying out, and to the presence of blood and possible use of instruments. They may feel their child is too young or will turn only to his mother for attention during labor, or may distract or disturb his mother or the staff.

Others feel that birth is a family event, and that if their child is well prepared and well cared for at the time, being at the birth will be a joyful and healthy experience. They feel a bond between the children is created and that positive healthy attitudes about birth will be encouraged.

The decision is a personal one, best made by you, your partner, and your child, if he is old enough to make such a decision.

Guidelines for Having a Child Present at Birth

If you decide your child will be present, the following guidelines will help ensure that it will be a positive experience for everyone, especially your child:

♦ Education for everyone involved is essential in providing understanding, accurate interpretation, and constructive responses.

♦ As parents, you must be prepared. Take childbirth classes or review what you learned in previous classes. You need to feel comfortable about birth and know how to relax and respond appropriately to contractions.

♦ Obviously, you (and your child, if he is old enough to make such a decision) must want him to be present. Do not allow yourself to be talked into it if you are uncomfortable with the idea.

♦ Assess your child's physical health and emotional readiness. The personality and maturity of your child are important considerations. If your child is ill and feels sick, he may not tolerate the birth experience well. If your child has had a recent painful, traumatic, or frightening experience involving his own body, doctors, or hospitals, he may not be ready to attend a birth.

♦ Arrange for a support person for your child—someone different from the mother's support person. A relative, a close friend, or sometimes the child's father can be there to look after the child's needs and help interpret and explain what is going on.

Preparing Your Child

In some areas, classes are available for children. Many books, films, and teaching aids are available, and family discussions are essential.

Familiarize your child with the following:

♦ The birth setting, equipment, and caregivers. A tour of the hospital and visit to the doctor's or midwife's office are a good idea.

♦ The sights and sounds of labor and birth: his mother unclothed; her face red with effort; the presence of blood; the baby's initial wetness, vernix, and dusky color; moaning, grunting, crying out, or straining by the mother; the baby's crying; the painless cutting of the cord; and so on.

♦ The appearance of a newborn, placenta, and umbilical cord.

♦ The duties of the mother, father, your child's support person, and your birth attendants.

♦ The tasks your child can perform: bringing a cool cloth for mom, giving back rubs, walking with mom, bringing fluids, taking pictures, playing music, being quiet when mom asks, and so on.

♦ What labor and birth is like—long, boring, exciting at times.

♦ The possible interactions between the older child and the newborn—touching, holding.

At the Birth Setting

♦ Provide an environment for the birth that makes your child's participation feasible and stress-free (room for your child, flexibility to come and go, clear guidelines).

♦ Make sure the labor and delivery staff (nurses, midwives, doctors) are supportive and will not be upset at having a child present. Find out in advance the hospital's policies regarding children's attendance at birth.

♦ Have an alternative plan to use if your child is sick, asleep (and does not want to wake up), bored, or changes his mind, or if labor complications develop and require that you transfer from the alternative setting to a standard labor ward or delivery room. Before your labor, explain these possibilities to your child, and prepare a plan for his care under such circumstances.

♦ Have realistic expectations of your child. One does not expect a two- or four-year-old to be transformed during labor. He will not suddenly become more calm, ask fewer questions, or begin to perceive birth as a transcendental experience. Children still fuss, need to go to the bathroom, say "no," argue, need cuddling, want to know where their toys are, and so on.

The point of all this is that children are children; they will not suddenly step out of character during labor or after the birth of a new baby. Children take birth in stride, responding as they would to any long-awaited, exciting event. With preparation and good support at the time, the birth of a new sibling can be a positive experience for your child. And with it exists the potential for developing long-term healthy attitudes about birth.

Guidelines for Care of a Child Who Will Not Be Present at the Birth

If you are planning a hospital birth with a typical one- to three-day stay, you will need to consider the possibility of separation anxiety, which sometimes occurs when a child is separated from one or both parents. When you leave to have your baby, your child's ability to tolerate the "separation" will vary depending on your child's age, how long the separation lasts, how comfortable she is with her caregiver and setting, how well she understands what is happening, how often she has been separated from you before, and how much contact she has with you while you are in the hospital. Most young children experience some degree of separation anxiety, including such reactions as fretting or crying for mother, sadness, clinging, irritability, sleeping difficulties, and tantrums. When they are reunited with their mothers, some children react in a positive way, others continue to react negatively and may even ignore their mothers. These reactions are the child's way of expressing her dismay at being left.

Suggestions

You can do several things to ease a child's anxiety over being left at home:

♦ At some point during the last weeks of your pregnancy, let your child know you will be leaving to go to the hospital for the birth. Tour the hospital with your child if possible. Tell your child where she will be (at home or visiting someone) and who will care for her while you are away. Your child will also be less anxious if she is familiar with the person who will care for her during your absence. A close friend, relative, or a favorite babysitter can make the separation less traumatic. When labor begins, tell your child when you are leaving and where you are going.

♦ Before the birth, increase the father's or other loved one's role as caregiver if he or she is not already responsible for much of your child's daily care, such as giving baths and putting the child to bed. Try to establish a routine that is not greatly disrupted by your hospitalization or the arrival of the new baby.

♦ Plan to have your child visit you and the new baby in the hospital. Sibling visitation has become recognized as valuable to the emotional well-being of the family, and most hospitals allow children to visit their mothers after the birth of a baby. Learn about the policies at your hospital. May you see your older child in your room, the hallway, or a visitor's lounge? Many hospitals welcome siblings in the room immediately after birth to see both mother and newborn.

What can you realistically expect when your child visits you in the hospital? She will probably be reassured by seeing you and the baby, responding in a positive way to the opportunity to visit. It is possible, however, that she may ignore you and the baby, cling excessively, or cry uncontrollably when it is time to leave. You may feel that it would have been easier on both of you to avoid the visit entirely. However, as difficult as it may be for a young child to see you for short periods and not be able to stay with you, it is healthier for your child to see you, even if only briefly, than to be separated for a longer period. The negative reaction shows that the child is under stress; the visit provides her with an opportunity to express her anger or frustration.

♦ If your child cannot visit you, you might try a "long-distance" visit with her: talk on the phone, or send Polaroid pictures, notes, and gifts home. Many mothers go home from the hospital within hours or a day after birth to minimize the time away from their families.

Adjusting to the New Baby

Besides the possible separation from his mother, an older sibling feels another traumatic change: the constant presence of a helpless, crying newborn who requires almost continuous care. Life is never the same for the older child after the arrival of a baby. Parents who once provided total atten-

tion and care for the older child are suddenly less available—all because of the new baby!

Your child may react in a variety of ways: temper tantrums; attention seeking behavior; return to outgrown behavior such as thumb-sucking, wanting a pacifier, feeding from bottle or breast, or wetting his pants; excessive preoccupation with the baby; withdrawal; aggression toward parents or baby (hitting, biting, throwing things); and changes in eating and sleeping patterns. Some parents have never seen such behavior in their child before and are caught by surprise. Sometimes the impact of the new baby on the child is immediate, but it may take weeks or months before the child seems to feel the impact of the intruder.

Suggestions

Perhaps the most important way you can help your older child adjust to the newborn is to accept whatever reaction he displays. Try not to be disappointed in him. Accept the behavior as a normal reaction and work from there. The following suggestions may also help ease your child's adjustment to a new baby in the family:

♦ Before and after the birth, read books to your child about living with a new baby.

♦ Give your child a doll so he has a "baby" to care for.

♦ Plan for time alone with your older child to do what he wants to do. This could be when the baby is asleep or when someone can watch the baby.

♦ Respond to your child's requests, comments, and actions. Ignoring him when you are busy may diminish his sense of self worth at this vulnerable time.[2]

♦ When your child behaves negatively, correct his behavior as you always have. If you feel guilty over bringing this "rival" into

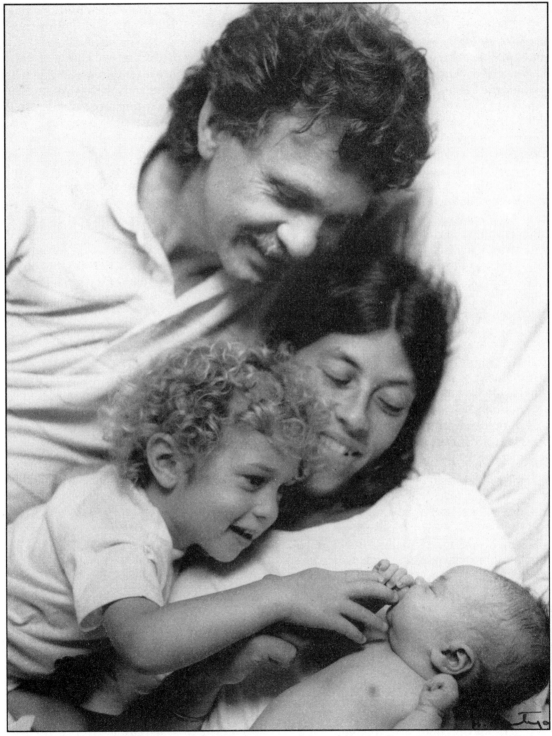

Although adjusting to the new baby may be hard, a lasting bond between siblings will develop.

—photograph by Harriette Hartigan/Artemis

your child's life, you may find yourself letting him break family rules or overstep the boundaries he has always had. This is not a good solution for either of you.

♦ Help your child express his feelings in words: "New babies sure make a lot of noise"; "Sometimes it seems that the baby never wants to sleep. It makes it hard for us to have our special time together, doesn't it?" "Sometimes it is hard to have a tiny baby around all the time."

♦ Have a birthday party after the birth with cake for all. Give a gift to your older child, and encourage your child to make or buy a gift for the baby.

♦ When visitors bring presents for the baby, your older child may feel left out. It may help to have him open them, to have special treats or gifts ready for him, or to delay opening them until he is not around.

♦ If he wants to help, include your child in baby-care activities that are appropriate to his age: holding the baby, helping with diapering, dressing or bathing the baby, helping feed and burp the baby, and entertaining the baby with smiles, singing, or talk.

♦ Allow your child to have nothing to do with the baby if that is what he wants.

♦ Think of activities that you and your child can do together and that will help him feel good about himself. Spend time on useful tasks (even small ones) that allow you to work together and allow him to feel successful.

♦ Use the time you spend feeding the baby to read, talk, play, or share a snack with your older child.

♦ Avoid statements like "You now have a new playmate" or "You're going to love the baby" when these are not very likely to occur.

♦ Provide new and stimulating activities or experiences that reinforce your child's awareness of his capabilities in comparison with the new baby, for example, planting seeds, blowing bubbles, making cookies, or washing dishes.

♦ "Tell" the baby about his special older siblings while they are with you and listening. For example, "Today, Eva Rose (the baby), Freddy, Charlie (the older children), and I are going to take you to the grocery store. We are going to pick out something very special for dinner, and maybe some of their favorite animal crackers. I always like going to the store with your brothers, don't you?"

♦ Take care of yourself. Try to rest when possible. This may not decrease your child's resentment or jealousy, but you will be able to cope better.

The age of your child has much to do with how and when he will react to the baby. Some children, particularly those three to four years or older, recognize immediately the impact the new baby has on their own relationship with their parents. Younger children tend not to recognize the threat for several months, until the baby begins crawling, interfering in play, and getting into things. Even children eight to ten years old feel resentment toward the baby, although it is usually accompanied by guilt and may be successfully hidden from the parents.

Remember that although adjusting to a new baby may be difficult, even traumatic, for a child, it is one of life's normal growth experiences. Your goal should not be that your child feel no displacement but that he adjust in a healthy and positive way. With time and your help, your child will find ways to adjust to the baby. A lasting bond between the siblings eventually will develop.

REFERENCES

CHAPTER 1

1. A.B. Bennetts and R.W. Lubic, "The Free-Standing Birth Centre," *Lancet* 8268 (13 February 1982): 378; J.P. Rooks et al., "Outcomes of Care in Birth Centers," *New England Journal of Medicine* 321 (28 December 1989): 1804.

2. Ibid.; M.W. Hinds et al., "Neonatal Outcome in Planned versus Unplanned Out-of-Hospital Births in Kentucky," *Journal of the American Medical Association* 253 (15 March 1985): 1578; W.F. Schramm et al., "Neonatal Mortality in Missouri Home Births, 1978-1984," *American Journal of Public Health* 77 (August 1987): 930; R. Campbell and A. MacFarlane, "Place of Delivery: A Review," *British Journal of Obstetrics and Gynaecology* 93 (July 1986): 675.

CHAPTER 2

1. M.L. Doshi, "Accuracy of Consumer Performed In-Home Tests for Early Pregnancy Detection," *American Journal of Public Health* 76 (May 1986): 512.

2. D.S. Kirz, "Advanced Maternal Age: The Mature Gravida," *American Journal of Obstetrics and Gynecology* 152 (1 May 1985): 7; G.S. Berkowitz et al., "Delayed Childbearing and the Outcome of Pregnancy," *New England Journal of Medicine* 322 (8 March 1990): 659; D. Gordon et al., "Advanced Maternal Age as a Risk Factor for Cesarean Delivery," *Obstetrics and Gynecology* 77 (April 1991): 493.

3. J.L. Shapiro, *When Men Are Pregnant: Needs and Concerns of Expectant Fathers* (San Luis Obispo, CA: Impact, 1987).

CHAPTER 3

1. J.M. Bowman, "Controversies in Rh Prophylaxis," *American Journal of Obstetrics and Gynecology* 151 (1 February 1985): 289.

2. S. Neldham, "Fetal Movements as an Indicator of Fetal Well-Being," *Danish Medical Bulletin* 30 (June 1983): 274; T.R. Moore et al., "A Prospective Evaluation of Fetal Movement Screening to Reduce the Incidence of Antepartum Fetal Death," *American Journal of Obstetrics and Gynecology* 160 (May 1989): 1075.

3. A. Grant et al., "Routine Formal Fetal Movement Counting and Risk of Antepartum Late Death in Normally Formed Singletons," *Lancet* 8659 (12 August 1989): 345.

4. B. Ewigman et al., "A Randomized Trial of Routine Perinatal Ultrasound," *Obstetrics and Gynecology* 76 (August 1990): 189; J. Neilson and A. Grant, "Ultrasound in Pregnancy," *Effective Care in Pregnancy and Childbirth, Part I*, edited by I. Chalmers, M. Enkin, and M.J.N. Kierse (New York: Oxford University Press, 1989); E.A. Reece et al., "The Safety of Obstetric Ultrasonography: Concern for the Fetus," *Obstetrics and Gynecology* 76 (July 1990): 139.

5. M.G. Rosen et al., "Caring for Our Future: A Report by the Expert Panel on the Content of Prenatal Care," *Obstetrics and Gynecology* 77 (May 1991): 77.

CHAPTER 4

1. B. Worthington-Roberts, "Maternal Nutrition and the Outcome of Pregnancy," in *Nutrition in Pregnancy and Lactation*, 4th ed., edited by B. Worthington-Roberts and S.R. Williams (St. Louis: C.V. Mosby Co., 1989): 108.

2. Ibid.

3. B. Abrams and J. Parker, "Maternal Weight Gain in Women with Good Pregnancy Outcome," *Obstetrics and Gynecology* 76 (July 1990): 1; B. Worthington-Roberts, "Maternal Nutrition and the Outcome of Pregnancy," 112.

4. B. Worthington-Roberts, 107.

5. M.M. Weigel and R.M. Weigel, "Nausea and Vomiting of Early Pregnancy and Pregnancy Outcome: An Epidemiological Study," *British Journal of Obstetrics and Gynaecology* 96 (November 1989): 1304.

6. M.A. Klebanoff et al., "Epidemiology of Vomiting in Early Pregnancy," *Obstetrics and Gynecology* 66 (November 1985): 612.

CHAPTER 5

1. C. Lecos, "Caution Light on Caffeine," *FDA Consumer* (October 1980): 6.

2. W. Scrisuphan and M.B. Bracken, "Caffeine Consumption during Pregnancy and Association with Late Spontaneous Abortion," *American Journal of Obstetrics and Gynecology* 154 (January 1986): 14.

3. T.R. Martin and M.B. Bracken, "The Association between Low Birth Weight and Caffeine Consumption during Pregnancy," *American Journal of Epidemiology* 126 (November 1987): 813.

4. C. Lecos, "Caution Light on Caffeine," 6.

5. American Medical Association's Council on Scientific Affairs, "Caffeine Labeling," *Journal of the American Medical Association* 252 (10 August 1984): 803.

6. J.L. Brazier et al., "Pharmacokinetics of Caffeine during and after Pregnancy," *Developmental Pharmacology and Therapeutics* 6 (1983): 315.

7. M.B. Morris and L. Weinstein, "Caffeine and the Fetus: Is Trouble Brewing?" *American Journal of Obstetrics and Gynecology* 140 (15 July 1981): 607.

8. J.W. Scanlon, "A Cup of Coffee and a Cigarette: Prolonged Caffeine Blood Levels in Healthy Babies," *Perinatal Press* 5 (July/August 1981): 87.

9. S. Schenker et al., "Fetal Alcohol Syndrome: Current Status of Pathogenesis," *Alcoholism: Clinical and Experimental Research*, 14 (September/October 1990): 635.

10. H.L. Brown et al., "Premature Placental Calcification in Maternal Cigarette Smokers," *Obstetrics and Gynecology* 71 (June 1988): 914; M.G. Pinette et al., "Maternal Smoking and Accelerated Placental Maturation," *Obstetrics and Gynecology* 73 (March 1989): 379.

11. N.R. Butler and H. Goldstein, "Smoking in Pregnancy and Subsequent Child Development," *British Medical Journal* 4 (8 December 1973): 573.

12. B. Zuckerman et al., "Effects of Maternal Marijuana and Cocaine Use on Fetal Growth," *New England Journal of Medicine* 320 (23 March 1989): 762; E.E. Hatch and M.B. Bracken, "Effect of Marijuana Use in Pregnancy on Fetal Growth," *American Journal of Epidemiology,* 124 (December 1986): 986.

13. J.R. Janke, "Prenatal Cocaine Use: Effects on Perinatal Outcome," *Journal of Nurse-Midwifery* 35 (March/April 1990): 74.

14. B.B. Little et al., "Methamphetamine Abuse during Pregnancy: Outcomes and Fetal Effects," *Obstetrics and Gynecology* 72 (October 1988): 541; K.M. Gillogley et al., "The Perinatal Impact of Cocaine, Amphetamine, and Opiate Use Detected by Universal Intrapartum Screening," *American Journal of Obstetrics and Gynecology* 163 (November 1990): 1535.

15. C. Kowalchik and W.H. Hylton, eds., *Rodale's Illustrated Encyclopedia of Herbs* (Emmaus, PA: Rodale Press, 1987).

16. K.L. Bunce, "The Use of Herbs in Midwifery," *Journal of Nurse-Midwifery* 32 (July/August 1987): 255.

17. A.K. Henry and J. Feldhausen, *Drugs, Vitamins, Minerals, Pregnancy* (Tucson, AZ: Fisher Books, 1989): 40.

18. Ibid., 16.

19. Ibid., 138.

20. J. Stellman and M.S. Henifin, "Video Display Terminals," *Office Work Can Be Dangerous to Your Health,* 2d ed. (New York: Fawcett Crest, 1989): 71.

21. R. Blackwell and A. Chang, "Video Display Terminals and Pregnancy: A Review," *British Journal of Obstetrics and Gynaecology* 95 (May 1988): 446; H.E. Bryant and E.J. Love, "Video Display Terminal Use and Spontaneous Abortion Risk," *International Journal of Epidemiology* 18 (March 1989):132; A.D. McDonald et al., "Work with Video Display Units in Pregnancy," *British Journal of Industrial Medicine* 45 (August 1988): 509; T.M. Schnorr et al., "Video Display Terminals and the Risk of Spontaneous Abortion," *New England Journal of Medicine* 324 (14 March 1991): 727.

22. M.A.S. Harvey et al., "Suggested Limits to the Use of the Hot Tub and Sauna by Pregnant Women," *Canadian Medical Association Journal* 125 (1 July 1981): 50.

23. M.B. Bond, "Reproductive Hazards in the Workplace," *Contemporary OB/GYN* (September 1986): 57; N. Roeleveld et al., "Occupational Exposure and Defects of the Central Nervous System in Offspring: Review," *British Journal of Industrial Medicine* 47 (1990): 580.

24. V. Kulikauskas et al., "Cigarette Smoking and Its Possible Effects on Sperm," *Fertility and Sterility* 44 (October 1985): 526.

25. P.B. Marshburn et al., "Semen Quality and Association with Coffee Drinking, Cigarette Smoking, and Ethanol Consumption," *Fertility and Sterility* 52 (July 1989): 162.

26. J.M. Friedman, "Genetic Disease in the Offspring of Older Fathers," *Obstetrics and Gynecology* 57 (June 1981): 745.

27. N. Roeleveld et al., "Occupational Exposure and Defects of the Central Nervous System in Offspring: Review," 580; J. D. Brender and L. Suarez, "Paternal Occupation and Anencephaly," *American Journal of Epidemiology* 131 (March 1990): 517.

CHAPTER 6

1. H. Varassi et al., "Effects of Physical Activity on Maternal Plasma Beta-Endorphin Levels and Perception of Labor Pain," *American Journal of Obstetrics and Gynecology* 160 (March 1989): 707.

2. R. Huch and R. Erkkola, "Pregnancy and Exercise — Exercise and Pregnancy: A Short Review," *British Journal of Obstetrics and Gynaecology* 97 (March 1990): 208.

3. American College of Obstetricians and Gynecologists (ACOG), *Exercise during Pregnancy and the Postnatal Period* (Washington, DC: ACOG, 1985).

4. V.L. Katz et al., "Fetal and Uterine Responses to Immersion and Exercise," *Obstetrics and Gynecology* 72 (August 1988): 225; R.C. Goodlin et al., "Shoulder-out Immersion in Pregnant Women," *Journal of Perinatal Medicine* 12 (1984): 173.

CHAPTER 7

1. P. Simkin, "Stress, Pain and Catecholamines in Labor, Part 1: A Review," *Birth: Issues in Perinatal Care and Education* 13 (December 1986): 181.

2. R.A. Harrison et al., "Pain Relief in Labour Using Transcutaneous Electrical Nerve Stimulation (TENS): A TENS TENS/Placebo Controlled Study in Two Parity Groups," *British Journal of Obstetrics and Gynaecology* 93 (July 1986): 739; P. Bundsen et al., "Pain Relief in Labor by Transcutaneous Electrical Nerve Stimulation: A Prospective Matched Study," *Acta Obstetrica Gynecologica Scandinavica* 60 (May 1981): 459.

3. C. Lenstrup et al., "Warm Tub Bath During Delivery," *Acta Obstetrica Gynecologica Scandinavica* 66 (August 1987): 709.

4. C.S. Mahan and S. McKay, "Are We Overmanaging Second-Stage Labor?" *Contemporary OB/GYN* (December 1984): 37.

5. M.D. Avery and L. van Arsdale, "Perineal Massage: Effect on the Incidence of Episiotomy and Laceration in a Nulliparous Population," *Journal of Nurse-Midwifery* 32 (May/June 1987): 181.

CHAPTER 8

1. A.P. Fuchs et al., "Oxytocin Receptors and Human Parturition: A Dual Role for Oxytocin in the Initiation of Labor," *Science* 215 (12 March 1982): 1396; D.M. Strickland et al., "Stimulation of Prostaglandin Biosynthesis by Urine of the Human Fetus May Serve as a Trigger for Parturition," *Science* 220 (29 April 1983): 521.

2. J.M. Carlson et al., "Maternal Position during Parturition in Normal Labor," *Obstetrics and Gynecology* 68 (October 1986): 443; J. Roberts et al., "Maternal Positions in Labor: Analysis in Relation to Comfort and Efficiency," in *Perinatal Parental Behavior,* edited by B.S. Raff, (White Plains, NY: March of Dimes Birth Defects Foundation, 1981):1.

3. C. Beynon, "The Normal Second Stage of Labour: A Plea for Reform in Its Conduct," *Journal of Obstetrics and Gynaecology of the British Commonwealth* 64 (June 1957): 815, reprinted in *Episiotomy and the Second Stage of Labor,* 2d ed., edited by S. Kitzinger and P. Simkin (Seattle, WA: Pennypress, 1986): 23.

4. R. Caldeyro-Barcia, "Influence of Maternal Bearing-Down Efforts during Second Stage on Fetal Well-Being," in *Epi-*

siotomy and the Second Stage of Labor, 2d ed., edited by S. Kitzinger and P. Simkin (Seattle, WA: Pennypress, 1986): 43; M.A. Rossi and S.G. Lindell, "Maternal Positions and Pushing Techniques in a Non-Prescriptive Environment," *Journal of Obstetrical, Gynecological and Neonatal Nursing* (May/June 1986): 203.

5. P. Simkin, "Active and Physiologic Management of Second Stage: A Review and Hypothesis," in *Episiotomy and the Second Stage of Labor*, 2d ed., edited by S. Kitzinger and P. Simkin (Seattle, WA: Pennypress, 1986): 7; M. Maresh et al., "Delayed Pushing with Lumbar Epidural Analgesia in Labour," *British Journal of Obstetrics and Gynaecology* 90 (July 1983): 623; D. Knauth and E.P. Haloburdo, "Effect of Pushing Techniques in Birthing Chair on Length of Second Stage of Labor," *Nursing Research* 35 (February 1986): 49.

6. M. Klein et al., "The McGill University of Montreal Multicentre Episiotomy Trial," presented at the Ninth Birth Conference in San Francisco, California, "Innovations in Perinatal Care: Assessing Benefits and Risks" (November 1990); J. Sleep et al., "Care during the Second Stage of Labour," *Effective Care in Pregnancy and Childbirth, Vol. 2* (New York: Oxford University Press, 1989); P. Shiono et al., "Midline Episiotomies — More Harm Than Good," *Obstetrics and Gynecology* 75 (May 1990): 765; D. Banta and S. Thacker, "Benefits and Risks of Episiotomy: An Interpretative Review of the English Language Literature, 1860-1980," *Obstetric and Gynecologic Survey* 38 (November 1983): 322.

CHAPTER 9

1. P.A. Dunn et al., "Transcutaneous Electrical Nerve Stimulation at Acupuncture Points in the Induction of Uterine Contractions," *Obstetrics and Gynecology* 73 (February 1989): 286.

2. L. Davis "The Use of Castor Oil to Stimulate Labor in Patients with Premature Rupture of the Membranes," *Journal of Nurse-Midwifery* 29 (November/December 1984): 366.

3. J.P. Elliott and J.F. Flaherty, "The Use of Breast Stimulation to Prevent Postdate Pregnancy," *American Journal of Obstetrics and Gynecology* 149 (15 July 1984): 628.

4. Y.M. Salmon et al., "Cervical Ripening by Breast Stimulation," *Obstetrics and Gynecology* 67 (January 1986): 21.

5. C. Kowalchik and W.H. Hylton, eds., *Rodale's Illustrated Encyclopedia of Herbs* (Emmaus, PA: Rodale Press, 1987).

6. J.G.B. Russell, "The Rationale of Primitive Delivery Positions," *British Journal of Obstetrics and Gynaecology* 89 (September 1982): 712.

7. V. Brocks et al., "A Randomized Trial of External Cephalic Version with Tocolysis in Late Pregnancy," *British Journal of Obstetrics and Gynaecology* 91 (July 1984): 1,339; A.W. Robertson et al., "External Cephalic Version at Term: Is a Tocolytic Necessary?" *Obstetrics and Gynecology* 70 (December 1987): 896; R. Marchick, "Antepartum External Cephalic Version with Tocolysis: A Study of Term Singleton Breech Presentations," *American Journal of Obstetrics and Gynecology* 158 (June 1988): 1339.

8. S.A. Myers and N. Gleicher, "Breech Delivery: Why the Dilemma?" *American Journal of Obstetrics and Gynecology* 155

(January 1986): 6; P. Bingham and R.J. Lilford, "Management of the Selected Term Breech Presentation: Assessment of the Risks of Selected Vaginal Delivery versus Cesarean Section for All Cases," *Obstetrics and Gynecology*, 69 (June 1987): 965; S.S. Christian et al., "Vaginal Breech Delivery: A Five Year Prospective Evaluation of a Protocol Using Computed Tomographic Pelvimetry," *American Journal of Obstetrics and Gynecology* 163 (September 1990): 848.

CHAPTER 10

1. R.P. Porreco et al., "The Cesarean Rate is 25 Percent and Rising: Why? What Can Be Done About It?", *Birth: Issues in Perinatal Care and Education* 16 (September 1989): 118; S.A. Myers and N. Gleicher, "A Successful Program to Lower Cesarean Section Rates," *New England Journal of Medicine* 319 (8 December 1988): 1511; R.P. Porreco, "High Cesarean Rate: A New Perspective," *Obstetrics and Gynecology* 65 (March 1985): 307.

2. L. Sanchez-Ramos et al., "Reducing Cesarean Sections at a Teaching Hospital," *American Journal of Obstetrics and Gynecology* 163 (September 1990): 1081.

3. E. Blair and F. Stanley, "Intrapartum Asphyxia: A Rare Cause of Cerebral Palsy," *Journal of Pediatrics* 112 (April 1988): 515; M.G. Rosen and C.J. Hobel, "Prenatal and Perinatal Factors Associated with Brain Disorders," *Obstetrics and Gynecology* 68 (September 1986): 416; K.B. Nelson and J.H. Ellenberg, "Antecedents of Cerebral Palsy," *New England Journal of Medicine* 315 (10 July 1986): 81; J.A. Low et al., "The Association of Intrapartum Asphyxia in the Mature Fetus with Newborn Behavior," *American Journal of Obstetrics and Gynecology* 163 (October 1990): 1131.

4. B.L. Flamm et al., "Vaginal Birth after Cesarean Delivery: Results of a 5-Year Multicenter Collaborative Study," *Obstetrics and Gynecology* 76 (November 1990): 750; ICEA Position Statement, "Cesarean Section and Vaginal Birth after Cesarean," (Minneapolis: International Childbirth Education Association, May 1989).

5. M.G. Rosen and J.C. Dickinson, "Vaginal Birth after Cesarean: A Meta-Analysis of Indicators for Success," *Obstetrics and Gynecology* 76 (November 1990): 865.

6. ICEA Position Statement, "Cesarean Section and Vaginal Birth after Cesarean."

7. A.R. Graham, "Trial of Labor Following Previous Cesarean," *American Journal of Obstetrics and Gynecology* 149 (1 May 1984): 35.

CHAPTER 11

1. J.J. Bonica, "Labour Pain," *Textbook of Pain*, edited by R. Melzack and P.D. Wall (Edinburgh, Scotland: Churchill Livingston, 1984): 377.

2. P. Simkin, "Stress, Pain and Catecholamines in Labor, Part I: A Review," *Birth: Issues in Perinatal Care and Education* 13 (December 1986): 181.

3. S. Kitzinger, "Pain in Childbirth," *Journal of Medical Ethics* 4 (1978): 119.

4. American Academy of Pediatrics Committee on Drugs, "Stilbestrol and Adenocarcinoma of the Vagina," *Pediatrics* 51 (February 1973): 297.

5. B.R. Kuhnert et al., "Disposition of Meperidine and Normeperidine following Multiple Doses during Labor, Part 2: Fetus and Neonate," *American Journal of Obstetrics and Gynecology* 151 (1 February 1985): 410.

6. B.R. Kuhnert et al., "Effects of Low Doses of Meperidine on Neonatal Behavior," *Anesthesia and Analgesia* 64 (1985): 335.

CHAPTER 13

1. A. Henningson et al., "Bathing or Washing Babies after Birth?" *Lancet* 1 (19-26 December 1981): 1401.

2. K. Barnard et al., "Early Parent-Infant Relationships," *First Six Hours of Life*, No. 1., Module 3 (White Plains, NY: National Foundation/March of Dimes, 1978): 21; T.B. Brazelton, *Neonatal Behavior Assessment Scale* (Philadelphia: J.P. Lippincott, 1973).

3. American Academy of Pediatrics, "Report of the Task Force on Circumcision—Policy Statement," *AAP News* (March 1989): 7.

4. Ibid.

5. T. Wiswell and R. Geschke, "Risks from Circumcision during the First Month of Life Compared with Those for Uncircumcised Boys," *Pediatrics* 83 (June 1989): 1011.

6. "SIDS Research: Putting It into Perspective," (Seattle: SIDS Northwest Regional Center at Children's Hospital and Medical Center): 1.

CHAPTER 14

1. D. Smith and R. Marshall, *Introduction to Clinical Pediatrics* (Philadelphia: W.B. Saunders Co., 1972): 52.

2. D. Smith and R. Marshall, *Introduction to Clinical Pediatrics* (Philadelphia: W.B. Saunders Co., 1972): 34.

3. American Academy of Pediatrics Committee on Nutrition, "On the Feeding of Supplemental Foods to Infants," *Pediatrics* 65 (June 1980): 1178.

4. J. Riordan and B.A. Countryman, "Basics of Breastfeeding," *Journal of Obstetrics, Gynecologic, and Neonatal Nursing* 9 (September-October 1980): 279.

5. A.S. Cunningham, "Morbidity in Breastfed and Artificially Fed Infants," *Journal of Pediatrics* 95 (1979): 685-89.

6. R.A. Lawrence, "Diet and Dietary Supplements for the Mother and Infant," *Breastfeeding: A Guide for the Medical Pro-*

fession, by R.A. Lawrence (St. Louis: C.V. Mosby Co., 1985): 233.

7. R.A. Lawrence, "Diet and Dietary Supplements for the Mother and Infant," *Breastfeeding: A Guide for the Medical Profession,* by R.A. Lawrence (St. Louis: C.V. Mosby Co., 1989): 233.

8. A. Hervada et al., "Drugs in Breastmilk," *Perinatal Care* 2 (19 February 1978): 19.

9. H. Vorherr, "Drug Excretion in Breastmilk," *Postgraduate Medicine* 56 (1974): 97.

10. J.R. Colley et al., "Influence of Passive Smoking and Perinatal Phlegm on Pneumonia and Bronchitis in Early Childhood," *Lancet* 2 (1974): 1031.

11. C. L'Esperance and K. Frantz, "Time Limitation for Early Breastfeeding," *Journal of Obstetric, Gynecologic and Neonatal Nursing* (March/April 1985): 114.

12. J. Riordan, *Practical Guide to Breastfeeding* (St. Louis: C.V. Mosby Co., 1983): 46.

13. B.C. Bowles et al., "New Benefits from an Old Technique: Alternate Massage in Breastfeeding," *Genesis* 9 (January 1988): 5; P.C. Stuttle et al., "The Effects of Breast Massage on Volume and Fat Content of Human Milk," *Genesis* 9 (April/May 1988): 3.

14. C. L'Esperance and K. Frantz, "Time Limitation for Early Breastfeeding," 114.

15. J. Riordan, *Practical Guide,* 208.

16. C. Engdahl et al., "Longterm Antibiotic Prophylaxis for Recurrent Mastitis," *Journal of Human Lactation* (1986): 72.

17. American Academy of Pediatrics Committee on Nutrition, "Human Milk Banking," *Pediatrics* 65 (1980): 854.

CHAPTER 15

1. R.S. Isberg and W.E. Greenberg, "Siblings in the Delivery Room: Consultations to the Obstetric Service," *Journal of the American Academy of Child and Adolescent Psychiatry* 26 (March 1987): 268; S. Van Dam Anderson and P. Simkin, eds., *Birth—Through Children's Eyes* (Seattle: Pennypress, 1981): 1.

2. M. Lewis and N. McCarthy, "A Child's Strength," *Mothers Today* (Nov/Dec 1984): 6.

RECOMMENDED RESOURCES

Following is a list of books, pamphlets, and tapes that provide additional background on many of the subjects covered in this book. Most of these materials are available by mail order from the Birth & Life Bookstore, P.O. Box 70625, Seattle, WA 98107, and the ICEA Bookcenter, P.O. Box 20048, Minneapolis, MN 55420. The following descriptions are from *Imprints,* the catalog of the Birth & Life Bookstore.

Pregnancy and Birth

Abrams, Richard S. *Will It Hurt the Baby? The Safe Use of Medications During Pregnancy and Breastfeeding,* 1990. Drug reference with risks and trade-offs of 700 drugs and chemicals.

Anderson, Sandra Van Dam, and Del Guidice, Georgeanne. *Siblings, Birth and the Newborn,* 1983. Four-page pamphlet assists parents in deciding whether and how best to include siblings in birth.

Armstrong, Penny, and Feldman, Sheryl. *A Wise Birth: Bringing Together the Best of Natural Childbirth with Modern Medicine,* 1990. How to find a setting that will make birth a healthy and positive experience.

Balaskas, J., and Gordon, Y. *Water Birth,* 1990.

Bean, Constance. *Methods of Childbirth,* rev. 1990. Practical information about available options for expectant parents: methods of preparation, relaxation, comfort techniques, hospital procedures, advantages and disadvantages of current technology, and other issues.

Bing, Elisabeth, and Colman, Libby. *Making Love during Pregnancy,* 1977. Illustrated guide dispels myths about having intercourse during pregnancy, describes difficulties and unexpected joys of sex during each stage of pregnancy.

Booth, Trish. *Before You Get Pregnant,* 1987. Helps expectant parents to a better outcome.

California Health Services & Coalition for Medical Rights of Women. *Natural Remedies for Pregnancy Discomforts,* rev. 1987. Alternatives to relieve common discomforts of pregnancy.

Colman, Libby and Arthur. *Pregnancy: The Psychological Experience,* rev. December 1990. Stages of pregnancy and labor in the context of feelings and experiences of expectant parents.

Campion, Mukti Jain. *The Baby Challenge: A Handbook on Pregnancy for Women with a Physical Disability,* 1990. Presents a positive and practical approach for women with a disability who are contemplating childbirth and for those who are involved in providing support.

Davis, Elizabeth. *Energetic Pregnancy,* 1988. A guide to achieving a harmonious balance in pregnancy and early motherhood.

Enkin, Murray, et al. *A Guide to Effective Care in Pregnancy and Childbirth,* 1989. Conclusions of comprehensive studies of all aspects of care in pregnancy and childbirth.

Gaskin, Ina May. *Spiritual Midwifery,* 3d ed., 1990. Accounts of home births in a farm community, with instructions for midwives.

Gilgoff, Alice. *Home Birth,* rev. 1988. Assesses the pros and cons of having a baby at home.

Goer, Henci, and Simkin, Penny. *Gestational Diabetes,* 1989. Four-page pamphlet clarifies current management of gestational diabetes, diagnosis, treatment, fetal surveillance and labor management, and methods of coping.

The Good Housekeeping Illustrated Book of Pregnancy and Child Care, 1990. Comprehensive, beautifully illustrated book of practical information.

Haire, Doris, et al. *The Pregnant Woman's Bill of Rights/The Pregnant Responsibilities,* 1975. Statement of the ICEA on informed consent and the equivalent responsibilities.

Hales, Dianne, and Johnson, Timothy. *Intensive Caring: New Hope for High-Risk Pregnancy,* 1990. Tests, treatments, and options available to high risk mothers and their babies.

Hoffman, Susan Greene. *Bedrest in Pregnancy,* 1985. Four-page pamphlet explains the reasons for and potential benefits of bedrest.

Johnston, Susan, and Kraut, Deborah. *Pregnancy Bedrest: A Guide for the Pregnant Woman and Her Family,* 1990. For women with a high risk pregnancy who are confined to bed.

Jones, Carl. *Mind over Labor,* 1987. Eight-step method of using mental imagery to reduce pain and prepare for a safe, happy birth.

Jones, Carl. *Visualizations for an Easier Childbirth,* 1988. Visualizations to help women relax, reduce fear and pain in labor and after.

Jones, Carl, et al. *The Labor Support Guide–for Fathers, Family and Friends,* 1984. Eight-page pamphlet for anyone who is helping a woman through labor describing how to be of support and assistance.

Kitzinger, Shelia. *The Complete Book of Pregnancy and Childbirth,* rev. 1989. Comprehensive, splendidly illustrated reference guide by an international expert.

Kitzinger, Shelia. *Sex after the Baby Comes,* 1980. Four-page pamphlet describes the unique postpartum physical and emotional adjustments and how they affect the sexual relationship.

Kitzinger, Shelia. *Sex during Pregnancy,* 1979. Four-page pamphlet provides information and practical advice to pregnant women and their partners on common concerns, changing sexual feelings, and the special needs of partners.

Kitzinger, Shelia, and Simkin, Penny, eds. *Episiotomy and the Second Stage of Labor,* rev. 1986. International perspective on management of labor to protect the perineum and fetal well-being.

Korte, Diana, and Scaer, Roberta. *A Good Birth, A Safe Birth,* rev. 1990. What women need to know about options in pregnancy, birth, and mothering to get what is best.

Lieberman, Adrienne B. *Easing Labor Pain: The Complete Guide for Achieving a More Comfortable Birth,* 1987. Causes of pain, how it is perceived, and the great variety of resources available to deal with childbirth pain.

McCartney, Marion, and van der Meer, Antonia. *The Midwife's Pregnancy and Childbirth Book: Having Your Baby Your Way,* 1990. Introduces parents to a less intrusive, more inclusive approach to healthy pregnancy and safe delivery.

McKenna, Nancy Durrell. *Birth,* 1989. Evocative photos of fouteen different birth experiences, with comments by parents and birth attendants.

Nightingale, Elena, and Goodman, Melissa. *Before Birth: Prenatal Testing for Genetic Disease,* 1990. A thorough overview of the issues parents face with genetic testing.

Nilsson, Lennert. *A Child Is Born,* 3d ed., 1990. Human reproduction from conception to birth, with outstanding photographs.

Odent, Michel. *Birth Reborn,* 1984. Description of birth at Pithiviers, France; how birth can be a normal, safe, and confident part of life.

Perez, Paulina, and Snedeker, Cheryl. *Special Women: The Role of the Professional Labor Assistant,* 1990. The newest member of the maternity care team —professionally trained to provide continuous physical and emotional support and sometimes private nursing care to women and their partners.

Reinke, Carla. *Herpes in Pregnancy,* 1990. Four-page pamphlet explains genital herpes and the problems it causes in pregnancy and birth.

Samuels, Mike and Nancy. *The Well Pregnancy Book,* 1986. Gives a holistic understanding of pregnancy and birth so parents can make satisfactory choices.

Simkin, Penny. *The Birth Partner: Everything You Need to Know to Help a Woman through Childbirth,* 1989. A complete and practical guide for partners to help make birth a fulfilling memory for everyone involved.

Wallerstein, Edward. *The Circumcision Decision,*1990. Four-page pamphlet explains the practice of routine nonreligious circumcision in the United States.

Wallerstein, Edward. *When Your Baby Boy Is Not Circumcised,* 1982. Four-page pamphlet on care and hygiene.

Weed, Susun. *Wise Woman Herbal: For the Childbearing Year,* 1985. How women can stay healthy during pregnancy and birth using common plants, simple ritual, and intuition.

Cesarean Birth

Ancheta, Ruth S. *VBAC Source Book: Vaginal Birth After Cesarean,* rev. 1990. Overview of VBACs for professionals and parents.

Cohen, Nancy Wainer, and Estner, Lois J. *Silent Knife: Cesarean Prevention and Vaginal Birth after Cesarean,* 1983. Powerful, impassioned, well-documented critique of the growing reliance on cesarean, and strategies to prevent needless cesareans.

Flamm, Bruce. *Birth after Cesarean: The Medical Facts,* 1990. Documented research on unnecessary cesarean sections.

Hausknecht, Richard. *Having a Cesarean Baby,* rev. 1991. Reasons for cesareans and what to expect.

Richards, Lynn Baptisti. *The Vaginal Birth after Cesarean Experience,* 1987. Covers a wide range of birthing issues through birth stories by parents and professionals.

Young, Diony, and Mahan, Charles. *Unnecessary Cesareans: Ways to Avoid Them,* rev. 1989. Ways to safely avoid a cesarean or make it a better personal experience.

Teenage Pregnancy

Brinkley, Ginny, and Sampson, Sherry. *Young and Pregnant: A Book for You,* 1989. Empowers teens to work toward having the healthiest baby possible.

Lindsay, Jeanne Warren. *Parents, Pregnant Teens and the Adoption Option,* 1989. Focuses on how parents can help their pregnant teenager.

Lindsay, Jeanne Warren. *Pregnant Too Soon: Adoption Is an Option,* rev. 1987. Teens talk about their choices.

Lindsay, Jeanne Warren. *School-Age Parents: The Challenge of 3 Generation Living,* 1990. For all families facing the dilemma of adolescent pregnancy and parenthood.

Simkin, Penny. *Cami Has a Baby,* 1990. A comic book written especially for pregnant teens.

Exercise and Yoga

Hughes, Helga. *The Complete Prenatal Water Workout Book,* 1989. Exercise in water offers a stress-free program for maximum benefit with minimum effort.

Jordan, Sandra. *Yoga for Pregnancy,* 1989. Ninety-two Iyengar poses chosen for safety and effectiveness in pregnancy.

Noble, Elizabeth. *Essential Exercises for the Childbearing Year,* 3d ed., 1988. Therapeutic exercises for pregnancy, postpartum restoration, physical changes in pregnancy.

Olkin, Sylvia Klein. *Positive Pregnancy Fitness,* 1987. Mental, physical, and spiritual preparation for pregnancy and birth, using yoga, exercise, and relaxation.

Pirie, Lynne, and Curtis, Lindsay. *Pregnancy and Sports Fitness,* 1987. For the athletic woman concerned about sports activities during pregnancy.

White, Rulena. *Fitness in the Childbearing Year,* 1990. Four-page pamphlet addresses the needs and concerns of pregnant women who are very fit and those who are just beginning a fitness program.

Family Planning and Infertility

Hatcher, Robert, et al. *Contraceptive Technology,* 1990-1991. Basic reference for health care providers.

Kass-Annese, Barbara, and Danzer, Hal. *The Fertility Awareness Workbook,* 1986. A well-organized explanation of natural family planning.

Winstein, Merryl. *Your Fertility Signals, Using Them to Achieve or Avoid Pregnancy, Naturally,* 1989. Well-illustrated, step-by-step instructions.

Twins

Alexander, Terry Pink. *Making Room for Twins,* 1987. Insightful guide to twin pregnancy and parenting.

Gromada, Karen Kerkhoff. *Mothering Multiples,* 1985. Practical guide for parents of twins, particularly for breastfeeding mothers of twins.

Noble, Elizabeth. *Having Twins,* rev. 1991. Comprehensive parents' guide to multiple births from conception through early childhood.

Novotny, Pamela Patrick. *The Joy of Twins: Having, Raising, and Loving Babies Who Arrive in Groups,* 1988. Medical, psychological, and sociological findings on all aspects of caring for two or more babies.

Fathers

Greenberg, Martin. *The Birth of a Father,* 1985. Gentle directives for new fathers to help them become "engrossed" and involved in baby's care.

Sears, William. *Becoming a Father,* 1986. The joys and problems of fatherhood.

Shapiro, Jerrold Lee. *When Men Are Pregnant: Needs and Concerns of Expectant Fathers,* 1987. To help expectant fathers make better sense of the experiences of the earliest days of fatherhood.

Postpartum Adjustment

Gruen, Dawn. *The New Parent: A Spectrum of Postpartum Adjustment,* 1988. Eight-page pamphlet explores the emotional side of new parenthood, "baby blues," postpartum depression, and postpartum psychosis.

Pacific Post Partum Support Society. *Post Partum Depression and Anxiety: A Self-Help Guide for Mothers,* 1987. Practical guide to what is happening and what can be done for postpartum depression.

Parenting and Child Development

Brazelton, T. Berry. *Infants and Mothers: Differences in Development,* rev. 1983. Variations in normal first-year development in three "typical" infants, includes single and working mothers.

Gruen, Dawn. *Babies and Jobs: Concerns and Choices,* 1986. Eight-page pamphlet includes survival tactics for both employed and at-home parents.

Klaus, Marshall and Phyllis. *The Amazing Newborn: Discovering and Enjoying Your Baby's Natural Abilities,* 1985. The development of baby's sensory perception in the first few weeks and months of life.

Myrabo, Jessica. *The First Days after Birth: Care of Mother and Baby,* 1983. Four-page pamphlet covers normal appearance and needs of the newborn and mother.

Pies, Sheri. *Considering Parenthood,* 1988. Deals with the issues of lesbian parenthood.

Sears, William and Martha. *300 Questions New Parents Ask,* 1991. Parenting information in a question-and-answer format.

For Children

Cairo, Shelley. *Our Brother Has Down's Syndrome: An Introduction for Children,* 1985. Jai's sisters explain how he is different but that mostly he is just like the rest of us (ages 4–8).

Carroll, Teresa. *Mommy Breastfeeds Our Baby,* 1990. A charming story for children to help them understand breastfeeding as a natural and special way to feed their new sibling (ages 3–10).

Kitzinger, Shelia, and Nilsson, Lennert. *Being Born,* 1986. Poetic text and magnificent photos make this book about conception and birth an instant classic (all ages).

Lindsay, Jeanne Warren. *Do I Have a Daddy? A Story about a Single-Parent Child,* rev. 1990. With a special section for single parents with suggestions for answering children's questions (ages 3–12).

Malecki, Maryann. *Mom and Dad and I are Having a Baby,* 1980. Picture book to prepare children to be present at a birth. Split text for short and long attention spans (all ages).

Breastfeeding

Lee, Nikki, and Edwards, Margot. *An Employed Mother Can Breastfeed When . . . ,* 1991. Four-page pamphlet contains necessary information on how mothers can continue to breastfeed while working outside the home.

Huggins, Kathleen. *The Nursing Mother's Companion,* rev. 1991. A lucid troubleshooting aid for the new mother learning how to nurse.

Kitzinger, Shelia. *Breastfeeding Your Baby,* 1989. Reassuring breastfeeding guide, with outstanding photos and illustrations, many in color.

Video Recordings

BirthSense Corporation. *A Birth Class: Focus on Labor and Delivery,* 1991, 115 minutes, five segments. Four pregnant women, their spouses and/or support persons are taught by childbirth educators Beth Shearer and Cathy Romeo.

Leach, Penelope. *Your Baby: A Video Guide to Care and Understanding with Penelope Leach,* 1990, 72 minutes. The author of *Your Baby and Child* demonstrates everyday baby care.

Vida Health Communications, Inc. *Baby Basics,* 1987, 117 minutes. Eight easy-to-find chapters with information on the first few months of infant care: the newborn at birth; caring for yourself post partum; your first days at home; daily care; feeding; health and safety; crying and sleeping; growth and development.

Loss and Grief

Borg, Susan, and Lasker, Judith. *When Pregnancy Fails,* rev. 1988. For families coping with miscarriage, stillbirth, and infant death.

Ilse, Sherokee. *Empty Arms: Coping after Miscarriage, Stillbirth, and Infant Death,* rev. 1990. Offers practical support for decision making at the time of loss and the days that follow.

Schwiebert, Pat, and Kirk, Paul. *Still to be Born*, rev. 1989. Helps consider options involved in a future pregnancy after a pregnancy that ends in a loss.

Schwiebert, Pat, and Kirk, Paul. *When Hello Means Goodbye*, rev. 1985. Sensitive booklet for parents whose child dies at birth or shortly after.

Premature and Ill Infants

Centerwall, Siegried, et al. *Low Birth Weight*, 1987. A twenty-four- page booklet for parents of small infants.

Goldberg, Susan, and Devitto, Barbara. *Born Too Soon: Preterm Birth and Early Development*, 1983. Key aspects of preterm infant development, focusing on the first three years of life.

Harrison, Helen, and Kositsky, Ann. *The Premature Baby Book: A Parent's Guide to Coping and Caring in the First Years*, rev. 1990. Comprehensive, well-illustrated guide to the emotional, medical, and practical issues following a premature baby's birth.

Adoption

Arms, Suzanne. *Adoption: A Handful of Hope*, rev. 1989. What adoption means to children, adoptive parents, and especially the birth mothers.

Gilman, Lois. *The Adoption Resource Book*, rev. 1987. A practical handbook on adoption today, options, procedures, and long-term factors.

Lindsay, Jeanne Warren. *Open Adoption: A Caring Option*, 1986. Adoption agencies and services facilitating honest, open relationships among all in the adoption triangle.

INDEX

Boldface numbers refer to pages on which definitions or descriptions of key terms will be found.

Abdominal examination, 47
Abdominal muscles
    during cesarean, 193
    postpartum changes in, 226
    postpartum exercises for, 230–34
    during pregnancy, 98
prenatal exercises for, 98–99
Abruption, placental, 51, **52**, 84, 191
Acetaminophen
    use for baby, 259
    use during pregnancy, 85
Active phase of labor
    during first stage, 143–48, 174
    during second stage, 152–53
Active relaxation techniques, 110–11
Acupressure, inducing labor with, 167
Adolescents. *See* Teen pregnancy
Aerobic exercise, 95–96
Afterpains, **159–60**, 225
    during breastfeeding, 273
    breathing for, 164, 225
Age, pregnancy and, 34–37
Airway
    clearing newborn, 172–73
    suctioning newborn, 17, 156, 166
Alcohol
    and breastfeeding, 271
    during pregnancy, 82–83
    use on nipples, 265
    use on umbilical cord, 241
Alcohol related birth defects, 82–83
Allergies, to food, 76, 270
Alpha-fetoprotein (AFP) test, 48
Amnesics, 208
"Amnihook," 184
Amniocentesis, 35, **60–61**
Amnioinfusion, 187
Amniotic fluid, **27**, 33
    loss of, as sign of labor, 138
    monitoring of, 166
    volume, 41–44, 63, 187
Amphetamines (crank, speed, ice), 84
Analgesics, **207**, 209–211. *See also*
        Acetaminophen; Aspirin;
        Ibuprofen
    postpartum use of, 216
    regional and local, 211–15, **214**
Anesthesia, **207**
    for cesarean birth, 19, 193
    continuous, **214**
    general, 210, **211**
    regional and local, 207, **211**, 211–15
"Angel kisses," **240**
Ankles, swelling in, 31, 43, 101
    to prevent or reduce, 96, 101
Anorexia, 76
Antibiotics
    and breastfeeding, 281, 283
    during post partum, 215
    during pregnancy, 55, 85

Apgar, 158
Areola, **29**
    when breastfeeding, 266, 267, 272,
        273, 279, 280, 281, 283
Arm exercises
    for baby, 256–57
    for mother, 233
Artificial insemination, **23–24**
Artificial rupture of membranes. *See*
        Membranes
Aspartame, use during pregnancy, 82
Aspirin
    use during pregnancy, 85
    use for baby, 260
Attention-focusing, 113, 117, 129
Auditory focus, **113**
Augmentation. *See* Labor,
        stimulation of
Auscultation, 15, **166**. *See also* Fetal
        stethoscope

Baby. *See also* Jaundice; Premature baby
    appearance at birth, 154–56, 160,
        239–41
    birth plan, care of, 11
    after birth without medical help,
        172–73
    breathing patterns, 253
    care, 239–62
        immediately after birth, 17–18,
            156–60
    circumcision of, 18, **250**–51
    communication cues from, 245
    development and growth of, 246–47
    exercise for, 256–57
    feeding, 263–88
        breast, 264–87
        formula, 264–65, 287–88
        guidelines for, 263–64
    illness in, 260
    immunizations for, 259–60
    medical care for, 259–61
    playing with, 256–58
    reflexes in, 247
    senses in, 244–45
    sleep-activity states, 248–49
    sleeping and waking patterns,
        247–48
    soothing cues from, 245–46
    tests and procedures, 17–18, 242–44
Backache
    comfort measures for, 100–101
    during early labor, 162
    after epidural, 212
    home remedies for, 86
    with occiput posterior position,
        175–76
    as sign of labor, 137–38
    during transition, 147
Bag of waters. *See* Membranes
Barbiturates, 208
Baths
    during labor, 115
    during post partum, 228
    during prolonged labor, 174
Bearing down, 16, 124–25, 130,
    149–54, 164, 173, 176–77.
    See also Pushing in labor

Beds
    for birth process, options for, 16
    for newborn, 222
Benzodiazepines, 209
Bilirubin, jaundice and, 249–50
Birth, 131–64. *See also* Cesarean
        birth; Labor
    bed for, 16, 151–52
    guidelines for practice for, 128–30
    medications during, 205–19
    options for, 7–9, 14–20
    pain in, 204–5
    positions for, 15, 123–24, 151–52
    place for, 7–8
    plan for normal, 10–12
    preparation for, 103–30
    classes, selection of, 6–7
    sibling, 289–90
    siblings present at, 290–92
    speed–up procedures for, 16,
        151–52, 176–77, 187–88
    without medical help, 170–73
Birth control, 230, 286–87
Birth defects, 11
    alcohol related, 82–83
    decisions about baby with, 181–82
    prenatal detection of, 48, 60–61
Birthing rooms, 5, 7
Birth plan, **9**–12, 14–20, 133–34
Bladder
    emptying of, during labor, 16, 174
Blastocyst, **27**
Bleeding. *See also* Lochia
    during cesarean, 194
    postpartum, 173, 180, 187, 210,
        218–19, 224
    pregnancy and, 51
    prevention of newborn, 242
"Blood patch," 196, 215
Blood pressure test , 47. *See also*
        Pregnancy-induced
        hypertension
Blood tests
    in newborn, 242–44
    during pregnancy, 46
"Bloody show," 44, **137–39**, 162
Body awareness techniques, 106–7
Bonding with baby. *See* Contact
between baby and mother/parents
Bottle feeding, 287–88. *See also*
        Formula feeding
    along with breastfeeding, 284–85
Bowel movements. *See also*
        Constipation; Enema
    during early labor, 162
    during birth, 171
    during post partum, 228
    in newborn, 252
    as sign of labor, 137, 138
Bowel stimulation, 167–68
Braxton-Hicks contractions. *See*
        Contractions, during late
pregnancy
Breast cups or shells, 266, 280
Breastfeeding, 264–87. *See also*
        Colostrum; Milk
    advantages of, 264–65
    breast milk composition, 268–69

after cesarean, 197, 271
diet and nutrition during, 72,
76–79, 228, 269–71
difficulties with, 273, 277–83
expressing and storing milk,
283–84
fertility and, 286–87
first feedings, 18, 160, 271–73
frequency of feedings, 274–75
growth spurts and, 275
guidelines for, 272–73
inducing labor with, 169
introducing bottle feeding with,
284–85
jaundice and, 250, **281**, 282
latch, 272–73, 278, 279–80, 281
leaking during, 282
milk production, 268, 275–76
"nipple confusion," 275, 284
on one breast, 277–78
positions for
alternate cradle hold, 278
cradle hold, **272**, 280
football hold, 197, 271, 280
side-lying, 271, 280
for premature infants, 19, 285
preparation for, 223, 265–67
relactation, 286
scheduled feedings, 18, 277
working mothers and, 285–86
Breasts. *See also* Areola;
Breastfeeding; Mastitis;
Montgomery glands; Nipples
anatomy of, 267
binding and icing of, 226
changes in, during pregnancy, 30,
32, 41–43
clogged ducts in, 233, 282
engorgement, **225**, 279
flat or inverted nipples, 47, 266–67
massage during breastfeeding, 276
on newborn, 241
during post partum, 225–26
prenatal examination of, 47
self-examination of, 229–30
Breathing. *See also* Afterpains;
Bearing down; Hyperventilation;
Pushing in labor
during first stage of labor, 142,
146, 147–48, 162–64
light (accelerated), **119**, 120, 162
newborn patterns of, 253
organizing breath, 111, 117,
119–20, 121, 124, 128
patterns, 116–26
relaxation and, 106, 109, 111–12
scramble, **121**, 122, 130
slow breathing, **117**, 119, 129, 162, 233
during second stage of labor. *See*
Bearing down
during third stage of labor, 156,
164, 172
variable (transition), **121**–22, 130, 162
Breech presentation, **135**, 178–79, 191
"Breech-tilt" position, 178
Bulimia, 76
Burping of baby, 253, 273–74, 277

Caffeine
and breastfeeding, 270–71, 278
interference with calcium intake
from, 70
during pregnancy, 81–82
Calcium, in diet, 70, 75, 77, 102, 270
Calendar of pregnancy, 41–44
Calories, 76
for breastfeeding, 269–70
in breast milk, 268
during pregnancy, 68, 71, 72, 75, **76**
Carbohydrates
in breast milk, 268
during pregnancy, 76
Cardiopulmonary resuscitation
(CPR), newborn, 173
Caregiver
for baby, 12–13
and birth plan, 9–12
choosing, 3–6, 205
communication with, 8–9
during prolonged labor, 174–75, 177
role of, in labor and birth, 143
when to call
during labor, 139–40, 163, 167, 171
during pregnancy, 51
during post partum, 224
with sick baby, 260
Car safety, for baby, 258
Castor oil, inducing labor with, 168
Caudal anesthesia, **212**, 214, 215
Central/diagonal lift exercise, 232–33
Cephalo-pelvic disproportion (CPD),
191
Cervix, **22**, 24
changes in
during labor, 137–39, 162
during early pregnancy, 41
during late pregnancy, 33, 44, 46,
132, 133, 136–37, 162
dilation of, 52, **136–37**, 140, 147, 149
effacement of, 34, 44, 132, **136**, 142, 162
during post partum, 225
ripening of, **34**, 44, 132, 136, 162
Cesarean birth, **189–202**
benefits and risks of, 189–90
birth plan for, 11, 18–19
for breech babies, 179
caregivers' philosophy about, 5
emergency cesarean, 192–93
emotions following, 197–98
incisions for, 193–94
planned (elective), 18, 192
reasons for, 190–92
repeat, 192
vaginal birth after cesarean
(VBAC), 189–90, 198–202
Chicken pox, 54, 55
Chlamydia, 54, 55
in newborn, 242
Chloasma, **30**, 42
Chorionic villi, **27**
Chorionic villus sampling (CVS), 35, **61**
Chromosomes, **24**
Circumcision, 18, **250**, 251
Classes
choosing childbirth, 6–7
for sibling preparation, 290–91

Clitoral stimulation, inducing labor
with, 168
Clitoris, **22**
Clothing, for new baby, 222
Cobalamin (B$_{12}$), 79
Cocaine (crack)
breastfeeding and, 271
pregnancy and, 84
Cold packs. *See* Ice packs
Colds
in babies, 260
during pregnancy, home remedies
for, 86
Colic, in newborn, 253–54
Colostrum, **30**, 43, 225, 268
Comfort measures. *See also*
Relaxation techniques
during labor, 112–16
during pregnancy, 99–102
Complications during childbirth,
165–88. *See also* Birth defects;
Cesarean birth; Death of baby
birth plan for, 11–12, 18–20
Computers, pregnancy and, 87
Conception, 23–26
Constipation
in newborn, **252**
during pregnancy, 74–75
during post partum, 228
Contact between baby and
mother/parents, 17, 18, 19, 20, 160, 164,
195, 235, 255, 264, 288
Contractions. *See also* Breathing,
patterns
during labor, 140–41, 143, 147
during late pregnancy, **33**, 43–44,
132–33
medication to stimulate, 218–19
nonprogressing, 138, 162
during preterm labor, 53
progressing, as positive sign of
labor, 138, 139, 162
to start or stimulate, 167–69
to stop preterm, 53, 217
timing, 139, 140
Contraction stress test, 62
Cordocentesis. *See* Percutaneous
umbilical blood sampling
(PUBS)
Corticosteroids, for fetal lung
maturation, 217
Coughing
after cesarean, 196
home remedies during pregnancy
for, 86
in newborn, 260
Couvade (Fathering) Syndrome, 40
Cradle cap, on newborn, 252
Cramps
intestinal, as sign of labor, 53, 137, 13
in legs and feet during pregnancy,
101–2
menstrual–like, as a sign of labor,
44, 53, 138, 162
Crowning phase of labor, 153–56
avoidance of pushing during, 125
during birth without medical help, 172
Crying, in newborn, 249, 253

Cytomegalovirus, 54–55

Day care, 14, 223
  breastfeeding and, 285–86
Death of baby, 11, 19–20, 181–82, 261
Delivery. *See* Birth
Depression, postpartum, 334–35
Descent, **134–35**, 153
  problem with, 176–77
Diabetes
  cesarean section and, 192
  gestational, 49, 55–56
  mellitus, 55–56
Diagnostic tests, during pregnancy,
  60–66
Diaper rash, 252
Diapers, arranging for, 222
Diarrhea. *See also* Bowel movements
  in newborn, **252**
Diet. *See* Nutrition
Dilation of cervix. *See* Cervix, dilation of
Displacement
  experienced by fathers, 39
  experienced by sibling, 294–95
Doppler blood flow studies
  (velocimetry), 62
Double hip squeeze, 176
Down's syndrome, 35, 48
DPT vaccine, 259–60
"Dropping." *See* Lightening
Drugs. *See also* Anesthesia
  for babies, 260–61
  benefits and risks of, 204, 206–7,
    208–10, 217–19
  in breast milk, 270–71
  after cesarean, 196, 216
  during cesarean, 196
  effects on labor, 206–207
  and expectant father, 88–89
  for fetal lung maturation, 217
  during labor, 203–15
  deciding on use of, 203–7
  narcotic antagonists, 209
  narcotics, 209
  during post partum, 215–16
  for preeclampsia and high blood
    pressure, 218
  during pregnancy, 73–75, 81–86
  sedatives and hypnotics, 208
  to stop preterm labor, 217
  for suppression of lactation, 219
  systemic, **208**–10
  to stimulate uterine contractions,
    218–19
  tranquilizers, 208–9
Due date, calculation of, 25–26
Early labor record, **140**, 143
Eclampsia, **56**
Ectopic pregnancy, **50**, 51
Edema, **96**. *See also* Ankles, swelling in
Effacement of cervix. *See* Cervix,
  effacement of
Effleurage, 104, **113**
Electronic fetal monitor. *See* Fetal
  heart rate monitoring
Embryo, **27**, 41
Emergency delivery, 170–73
Emotions

during active phase of labor, 143, 164
  on baby's death/illness, 181–82
  during birth, 156, 164
  following cesarean, 197–98
  during early labor, 141–43, 163
  of expectant fathers, 39–40
  in first trimester, 28–29, 41
  near term, 34, 44, 163
  during postpartum period, 44,
    234–38
  during recovery, 160, 164
  in second trimester, 30, 42
  in third trimester, 32–34, 43
  during transition, 147–48, 163
  during vaginal birth after cesarean
    (VBAC), 199–202
Endometrium, **23**, 27
Enema
  inducing labor with, 167–68
  as option in birth plan, 14
Engagement, of baby's head, **33**, 44,
  132, **135**
Engorgement. *See* Breasts,
  engorgement
Environmental agents, 86–89
Epididymis, **21**
Epidural anesthesia, 193, 211–12,
  214–16
Episiotomy, 16, **154**, 155, 156, 187.
  See also Perineal massage
Erythromycin. *See* Eye care for
  newborn
Estriol studies in pregnancy, 48, 63
Estrogen, **23**, **26**, 41, 226
  effect on labor, 31, 43, 131–32
Examinations. *See also* Vaginal
  examination
  postpartum, 229–30
  prenatal, 45–49
Exercise
  aerobic, 95–96
  for babies, 256–57
  with baby, 233–34
  for backache, 100–101
  after cesarean, 196–97
  conditioning, 96–99
  during postpartum, 230–34
  during pregnancy, 91, 94–102
Expulsion techniques, options for,
  16. *See also* Bearing down
External version, 178–79
Eye care for newborn, 17, 55, 242
Eyes, newborn, 239

Facial rash, on newborn, 252
Faintness, 25, 41
Fallopian tubes, **22**, 23–24
Families
  baby's impact on, 237–38
  as helpers during post partum, 223
  involvement of, in breastfeeding, 276
  preparation of, during pregnancy,
    289–95
Family-centered maternity care, 7
Family physicians. *See also* Caregivers
  for postpartum care, 13
  for prenatal care, **3**–4
Fathers. *See also* Partners

drugs, environmental hazards and,
    88–89
  during pregnancy, 39–40, 41–44
  during post partum, 235
  as sibling caregivers, 292–94
Fatigue
  breastfeeding and, 278
  during early pregnancy, 28–29, 41
  during post partum, 44, 226–27
  relaxation techniques to reduce, 105
Fat, in pregnancy, 71–72, 76
Fats, in breast milk, 268
Fears during pregnancy, 29, 32, 37–39
Feeding of baby, 263–95. *See also*
  Bottle feeding; Breastfeeding
Fertility, breastfeeding and, 286–87
Fertilization, **23–24**
Fetal alcohol syndrome (FAS), 82–83
Fetal biophysical profile (FBP or
  BPP), 63
Fetal distress, 166, 191. *See also* Fetal
  heart rate monitoring
Fetal heart rate (FHR)
  contraction stress test and, 62
  fetal stimulation and, 166, 186
  medication and, 207–9, 213,
    217–18
  nonstress test and, 64
Fetal heart rate monitoring, 47, 166,
  184–86
  electronic fetal monitoring
    (EFM), 166, 185–86
  options for, 15
Fetal maturity tests. *See*
  Amniocentesis
Fetal movement counting, 58–59, 63
Fetal scalp blood sampling, 166, 187
Fetal stethoscope, monitoring with, 184
Fetal stimulation test, 166, 186
Fetus, **28**
  effects of drugs on, 206–7
  in first trimester, 27–28, 41
  lung maturation in, 132, 217
  maturity of, 131–32, 192
  in post-date pregnancies, 34
  in second trimester, 29, 42
  in third trimester, 30–31, 43–44,
    132–33
Fever
  with mastitis, 282–83
  in newborn, 259–60
  during pregnancy, 50, 51, 87–88
First stage. *See* Labor, stages of, first
  stage
Fluids
  with breastfeeding, 269–70
  intake of, during pregnancy, 69, 73, 76
  intravenous (IV), 183
  during labor, 15, 116, 117, 142, 146,
    163
  during post partum, 228
  to stop preterm labor, 53
Fluoride
  breastfeeding and, 269
  formula feeding and, 287
Focal point, **104**, **113**
Folic acid, 70, 78
Fontanels, **239**

Food. *See also* Nutrition
  allergies in pregnancy, 76
  food groups, 68–69
  during labor, 15, 142, 163
  for newborn, 263
  sensitivities, breastfeeding and, 270
Football hold, for breastfeeding, 197, 271, 280
Forceps delivery, 177, **188**
Formula feeding, 263–65, 275, 281, 287–88. *See also* Bottle feeding
Formulas, composition of, 287
Fraternal twins, 57
Fundus, **29–30**. *See also* Massage, fundal

Galactosemia, test for, 243, 265
Gas. *See also* Burping of baby; Colic
  abdominal, after cesarean, 197
  bubbles, in baby, 277
Gate control theory of pain, 105
General anesthesia. *See* Anesthesia, general
Genital herpes, 55
Genitals, on newborn, 241. *See also* Reproductive anatomy
German measles. *See* Rubella
Gestational diabetes. *See* Diabetes, gestational
Glucose screening, 49, 55–56
Gonorrhea, 54–55, 242
Groin pain, 42, 102
Group B streptococcus, 54–55, 242, 283
Growth spurts, 275

Hair, on newborns, 239. *See also* Lanugo
Hands and knees labor position, 118, 123, 144, 151, 175
Hay fever, remedies for, 86
Headache
  from anesthesia, 196, 212, 215
  home remedies for, 86
  as warning sign during pregnancy, 51, 55
Head lift exercise, 231
Hearing
  in fetus, 31, 178
  in newborn, 244
Heartbeat, fetal. *See* Fetal heart rate (FHR)
Heartburn, 31, 43, 74–75
Heat use. *See also* Hot packs
  heat lamps, 227
  during labor, 115
HELLP syndrome, 56
Hemophilus influenzae biotype IV, 242
Hemorrhage. *See* Bleeding
Hemorrhoids, 31, 43, 75, 228
Hepatitis B virus, 54–55, 265
Herbicides, pregnancy and, 86–87
Herbs (tinctures, teas, capsules), 84, 169
Herpes virus, 54–55, 143, 192, 242, 265
Hib vaccine, 259–60
High blood pressure. *See* Pregnancy-induced hypertension
High-risk pregnancies, 49–58
  nutritional concerns, 75–76
  in older women, 35, 37

prenatal testing, 58–66
Hip walking (twist) exercise, 234
Hoffman's technique, 267
Home births, 8, 146
  emergency births, 170–73
Home remedies, for common ailments, 86
Honey, avoidance of, for new babies, 288
Hormones
  changes in, during pregnancy, 26
  effects of maternal, on newborn, 241
  onset of labor and, 43–44, 131–32
  postpartum changes in, 226
Hospital
  arrival at, 143, 145–46
  choosing, 7
  discharge from, 6, 17, 19, 228–29, 294
  emergency transfer to, 8
  packing for, 133–34
  when to go to, 143
Hot packs, 115, 154, 163, 175, 227
Hot tubs, pregnancy and, 87–88
Household help, 13, 223, 229
Human chorionic gonadotropin (hCG), 25, 26, 41, 48
  morning sickness and, 28
Human immunodeficiency virus (HIV), 54–55, 265
Human placental lactogen (HPL), 56
Hyperemesis gravidarum, **50**, 51, 74
Hypertension. *See* Pregnancy–induced hypertension
Hyperventilation, avoidance of, 116–17
Hypnotics, 208
Hypoglycemia, in newborn, 56, 243
Hypotension. *See* Supine hypotension
Hypothyroidism, in newborn, 243

Ibuprofen, use during pregnancy, 86
Ice packs
  during breastfeeding, 279–80, 283
  during labor, 115, 175
  for perineum, during post partum, 159, 164, 227
  to prevent milk production, 225–26
Immunizations, for babies, 259–60
Induction. *See* Labor, induction of
Infections
  in breast. *See* Mastitis
  cesarean section and, 192
  from labor interventions, 186, 187
  in newborn, 241, 242, 259–60
  during post partum, 224, 227
  during pregnancy, 46, 54–55, 88
  from ruptured membranes, 139, 184
Insecticides, pregnancy and, 86–87
Internal focus, **113**
Interviews
  with baby caregivers, 13
  with maternity caregivers, 4–6
Intravenous (IV) fluids, 175, **183**, 193, 214
In vitro fertilization, **24**
Involution, 159, **224–25**
Iodine, 77

Iron, 77
  in breast milk, 269
  in pregnancy diet, 70
Jaundice, 242, 249–50, 281–82

Kegel exercise, 97, 127, 227, 228. *See also* Pelvic floor contraction
Kneeling, during labor, 118, 144, 175

Labia, **22**, 225
Labor. *See also* Bearing down; Birth; Breathing, patterns; Descent; Emotions; Position of fetus; Pushing in labor
  active phase of, 142, 143–46, 162–63, 174
  birth plan for normal labor, 10–11, 14–15
  breathing patterns for, 116–26
  comfort measures for, 112–16
  complications during, 165–88
  control in, 112
  induction of, 15, 166–69, 183–84, 218
  interventions, 182–88
  latent phase of, 141–43, 162–63, 173–74
  in second stage, 150, 153
  medications during, 203–19
  without medications, 205–7
  monitoring techniques for, 165–66
  onset of, 15, 131
  positions for, 15–16, 115–16, 118, 123, 125–26, 129, 144–45, 146, 150–52, 163–64, 174–76
  practice for, 127–30
  precipitate (short), **170**
  preterm, **52**, 53, 138, 179–80, 217
  prolonged, 173–77, 191
  relaxation techniques for, 105–12
  signs of, 137–40, 162–63
  stages of, **137**
    first stage, 117–19, 137–48, 162–63, 173–76
    fourth stage, 137, 159–60, 164
    second stage, 137, 149–56, 164, 176–77
      expulsion breathing for, 122–26
      interventions in, 187–88, 154–56
      positions for, 15, 123–24, 151–52
      prolonged, 176–77
    third stage, 137, 156–59, 164, 180–81
  with stillbirth, 19, 181–82
  stimulation of, 16, 115–16, 167–69, 174–76, 183–84, 218
  support person, 14, 18, 199–202, 205
  transition phase of, 142, 147–48, 162–63
  with twins, 180
  during vaginal birth after cesarean (VBAC), 200–202
  variations in, 165–81
Lacerations, during delivery, 154, 155, 180
Lactation. *See also* Breastfeeding; Relactation

medication to suppress, 219
Lactiferous ducts, in breast, **267**
Lanugo, **29**, 42, 43, **239**, 254
Layette, preparation of, 221–23
Legs, cramps in, 101–2
Leg sliding exercise, 232
Leopold's maneuvers, **31**
Let-down reflex, **268**, 272–73, 275, 277
  breast pain with, 281
  difficulties with, 271, 278
Lifting, during pregnancy, 92–93
Lightening, 33, 132, **135**
Light sleep
  in mother, 33, 43, 86, 132
  in newborn, 248
Linea nigra, **30**, 42
Liquids. *See* Fluids
Listeriosis, 54, 55
Lithotomy position, **152**
Lochia, 44, **159**, 224, **225**
Lying down. *See also* Labor, positions for
  for breastfeeding, 271, 272, 280
  during labor, 118, 145
  during pregnancy, 93–94
  during second stage, 123, 151
Lyme disease, 54, 55

Magnesium, in diet, 78
Magnesium sulfate, 53, 217–18
Malpresentation or malposition, 177, 179, 191
Marijuana, 84, 271
Mask of pregnancy, 30, 42
Massage. *See also* Perineal massage
  for baby, 257–58
  of breasts, 168, 276
  fundal, 159, 164, 172
  during labor, 110, 113–14, 163, 174, 175
Mastitis, **282**, 283
Meconium, 42, **252**
  in amniotic fluid, 166
Medical intervention. *See* Labor, interventions
Medications. *See* Drugs
Membranes, 31, **33**, 132
  artificial rupture of (AROM), 15, 169, 184
  prolapsed cord and, 140, 177
  rupture of, 15, 44, 51, 139–40, 162, 163, 169, 184
  stripping of, 169, 183
Menstruation, **23**
  postpartum return of, 226
Midwives, **3**–4. *See also* Caregivers
Milia, 240
Milk. *See also* Breastfeeding
  breast
    composition, 268–69
    drugs in, 270–71
    foremilk, **269**
    hindmilk, **269**, 276, 277
    production of, 268
  formulas, composition of, 287
Milk intolerance
  breastfeeding and, 270
  pregnancy and, 75
Minerals, 70, 77–78
  in breast milk, 269

Miscarriage, **49–50**, 51, 55, 82, 84, 86–88
MMR (measles, mumps, rubella) vaccine, 259–60
Molding, of newborn head, 184, **239**
Mongolian spots, **240–41**
Monitoring fetal heart rate. *See* Fetal heart rate monitoring
Montgomery glands, **29**, 265, 267
Morning sickness, 28–29, 73–74. *See also* Nausea and vomiting
Morula, 24, **27**
Multigravidas, 37, 289–95
  labor in, **134**, 136, 143
  nutrition for, 75
Multiparas. *See* Multigravidas
Multiple pregnancy
  labor and delivery with, 180
  nutrition during, 75
  placenta in, 28

Narcotic analgesics, 209, 212, 214, 216
Narcotic antagonists, 209
Naturopaths, 3, 13. *See also* Caregivers
Nausea and vomiting
  during labor, 147, 208
  in newborn, 251–52, 260
  nutrition and, 73–74
  during pregnancy, 25, 28–29, 41–42, 51
Nesting urge, as sign of labor, 44, 132, 138
Newborn. *See* Baby
Niacin, 79
Nipples. *See also* Areola; Breastfeeding
  flat or inverted, 266–67
  soreness, with breastfeeding, 279–81
  stimulation, inducing labor with, 168–69
  stretching exercises, 266–67
Nipple shields, 280
Nonstress test (NST), 64
NutraSweet. *See* Aspartame
Nutrients, chart of, 76–79
Nutrition, 67–71
  for breastfeeding, 76–79, 269–71, 278
  infant, 263–64, 287
  during post partum, 228
  pregnancy and, 5, 67–79
  special pregnancies and, 75–76

Obesity, maternal, 71–72, 194
Obstetricians, **3**–4. *See also* Caregivers
Occiput anterior position, **135**
Occiput posterior position, **135**, 175–76, 191
Occupational hazards, pregnancy and, 87–89
Older women, pregnancy and, 35–37
Orgasm
  inducing labor with, 168
  risks associated with, 38
Ovaries, **23**, 24
Ovulation, **23**, 25, 44, 286–87
Ovum, **23**–25, 27, 41
Oxytocin, **31**, 44, 131–32, 168, 169, 180, 226. *See also* Pitocin

challenge test (OCT), 62
  let-down reflex and, 268

Pacifiers, 253–54, 275, 278
Packing for hospital stay. *See* Hospital, packing for
Pain. *See also* Afterpains
  breastfeeding and, 279–83
  after cesarean birth, 196
  in childbirth, 204–5
  gate control theory of, 105
  medication for, 205–16
  relief of, 15, 149, 204–5
  techniques to reduce, 103–30
  as warning sign, 51, 224
Paracervical block, 213
Parenting, 1–2
  adjustments to, 234–38
Partners. *See also* Fathers
  experiences during pregnancy, 39–40
  help during birth without medication, 205
  participation during labor and birth, 14, 17, 141, 143, 146–48, 152, 156, 158, 160, 163–64
  perineal massage by, 127
  during post partum, 235
  practicing for labor with, 107–8, 110, 114, 127–30
  presence of, during cesarean, 18, 192, 193, 195
  during labor, 14
  role of, during labor variations, 170–78
  as sibling caregivers, 292
  during vaginal birth after a cesarean, 200–202
Passive relaxation techniques, 108–10
Patient-controlled analgesia (PCA), 216
Patterned breathing, **116**, 117–30
Pediatricians, selection of, **12**–13
Pelvic examination. *See* Vaginal examination
Pelvic floor contraction exercises, 96–97, 227, 231–32
Pelvic tilt exercises, 98–100, 232
Penis, **21**
  circumcision and, 250–51
Percutaneous umbilical blood sampling (PUBS), 64
Peri bottles, 227
Perinatologists, **3**–4. *See also* Caregivers
Perineal massage, 126–27
Perineum, **22**. *See also* Episiotomy
  options during birth, 16
  postpartum care of, 227
  relaxation of, 126–27
Phenothiazines, 208–9
Phenylketonuria (PKU), tests for, 243
Phosphorus, 77
Pitocin, 169, 174–75, 180, 183, 214, 218, 242
Pituitary gland, **21**, 23, 268
Placenta
  abruption of, 51, **52**, 84, 191
  accreta, 181
  delivery of, 156–59, 172

in first trimester, 28, 41
and onset of labor, 131–33
in post-date pregnancies, 34
previa, **50**, 51, 191
retention of, 173, 180–81
in second trimester, 29, 42
in third trimester, 31, 32–33, 43, 132
weight of, 32, 71
Playing, with baby, 233–34, 256–58
Polio vaccine, 259–60
Position of fetus, **135–36**
malposition, and cesarean, 191
occiput posterior, 135, 175–76
Positions in labor. *See* Labor, positions for
Postmature baby, 34, 255–56
Postpartum period
depression, 235
early recovery in, 159–60, 164
emotional adjustments during, 44, 234–38
exercise during, 230–34
medications during, 215–16, 219
physical adjustments in, 44, 223–30
planning for, 12–14, 221–23
self-care during, 226–30
warning signs during, 224
Posture, during pregnancy, 91–92
Precipitate (short) labor, **170**
Preeclampsia (toxemia), 47, 51, **56**, 167
medication for, 218
Pregnancy, 23–44. *See also* Drugs, during pregnancy; Prenatal care
complications during, 49–58
confirmation of, 25, 46
early signs and symptoms of, 25
nutrition in, 67–79
warning signs during, 51
Pregnancy-induced hypertension (PIH), 47, 51, 56, 167, 218
Pregnancy tests. *See* Prenatal care, diagnostic tests; Prenatal care, routine exams and tests
Premature baby, **254**–55. *See also* Preterm labor
birth plan for, 19
breastfeeding and, 285
labor and delivery, 179–80
Prenatal care, 45–66
choosing caregiver for, 3–6
diagnostic tests, 58–66
routine exams and tests, 45–49
Prenatal risk profile (triple screen), 48
Presentation of baby, 134, **135**
breech, 178–79
difficult presentations, 177–79
malpresentation, 191
Preterm labor, 51, **52**, 53. *See also* Premature baby
detection of (tocodynamometry), 65
medications to stop, 53, 217
Prickly heat, 252
Primigravidas, **134**
Progesterone, **23**, 26
effect on labor, 31, 43, 131–32
Prolapsed cord. *See* Umbilical cord, prolapsed

Prostaglandin gel, 169, 174, 183, 219
Prostaglandins, **31**, 43, 131–32, 137, 167, 168
contraction stimulation with, 219
Protein, 77
in breast milk, 268–69
need for, during pregnancy, 68–70
Psychoprophylaxis, **103**
Pushing in labor. *See also* Bearing down; Labor, stages of, second stage
breathing to avoid, 122, 125, 154, 171–72
directed, 125–26, 130
prolonged, 126, 177
in second stage, 122–26, 149, 152–54, 171–72, 176–77
spontaneous bearing down, 124–126, 130, 149
urge to push, 122, 124–25, 149
Pyridoxine (B$_6$), 79, 270

Quickening, **29**

Radiation. *See also* X rays
pregnancy and, 87
Rashes, on babies, 252
Rectus muscles, 231.
Relactation, 286
Relaxation techniques, 105–12. *See also* Comfort measures
during post partum, 233
use in labor, 117, 119, 146, 148, 163–64, 174
Reproductive anatomy
female, 22–23
first trimester formation of, 27–28
male, 21–22
Rest
during post partum, 226–27, 273, 278
Rh incompatibility, 57–58, 61, 64
jaundice with, 242, 250
RhoGam injection, 57–58
Riboflavin, 79
Rickets, 269
"Rim of fire," **153–54**, 164
Ripening of cervix. *See* Cervix, ripening of
Rooting reflex, **247**, 272
Rotation of baby
during birth, 154–56, 188
in OP position, 175
Round ligament contractions, 42, 102
Roving body check, 111
Rubella, 54–55, 259–60
Rupture of membranes. *See* Membranes, rupture of

Saddle anesthesia, 213, 214–15
Salt, intake of, during pregnancy, 72–73
Saunas, 87–88
Scopolamine, 208
Scrotum, **21**
Second stage. *See* Labor, stages of, second stage
Sedatives, 19, 208

Self-administered medication (SAM), 215–16
Semilithotomy position, 152
Senses of baby, 244–45
Sex determination of baby, 24–25. *See also* Reproductive anatomy, first trimester formation of
Sexual function, 21–22
Sexual intercourse
conception and, 23–25
inducing labor with, 168
during post partum, 230
during pregnancy, 32, 37–39, 41–43
risks associated with, 38
Sexually transmitted disease (STD), 51–52, 54–55, 242
Shaving of pubic hair, 14, 193
Shoulder
circling exercise, 101
dystocia, 176
Showers
during labor, 15, 115, 142, 163, 174
during post partum, 228
Siblings
adjustment to new baby by, 294–95
preparation of, 289–95
presence at birth, 290–92
Sick baby, 19, 181–82, 260–61
Sickle cell anemia, tests for, 244
SIDS (sudden infant death syndrome), 261
cocaine use and, 84, 271
Silver nitrate. *See* Eye care for newborn
Single parent, 40, 237
Sit back exercise, 232, 234
Sitting
position for labor, 118, 144
during pregnancy, 92
position for second stage, 123, 150, 151
Sitz baths, **227**–28
Skin
changes during pregnancy, 30–32, 42–43
of newborn, 240–41
postpartum changes in, 226
Sleep schedules and states, newborn, 247–49
Sleeplessness
home remedies for, 86
as sign of postpartum depression, 235
Small for gestational age (SGA) baby, **255**
increased risk for, 56, 81–84
Smoking
during breastfeeding, 271
during pregnancy, 83–84
Sperm, **21**–22
Spinal anesthesia, 193, 211–16
Spitting up, by newborn, 251–52
Spontaneous bearing down. *See* Bearing down
Sports, participation in, during pregnancy, 94–96
Squatting
exercise during pregnancy, 97–98, 100

position for first stage, 145
position for prolonged second
  stage, 176
position for second stage, 123,
  150, 151–52
Standing
  following cesarean birth, 196–97
  position for labor, 118, 144
  during pregnancy, 92
Station, pelvic, **134**–35
Stillbirth
  birth plan for, 11–12, 19–20
  labor and delivery with, 19, 181–82
Stork bites, **240**
Stretch marks. *See* Striae gravidarum
Stress, relaxation techniques to
  reduce, 105–12
Striae gravidarum, **32**, 43
Sucking
  breastfeeding and, 272–80, 284–86
  lip blister from, 240
  nonnutritive, 278
  reflex, 247
  to stimulate milk production and
    release, 268, 277
Supine hypotension, 51, **93**, 145,
  151–52, 193
Supplemental Nutrition System
  (SNS), 275, 286
Support groups
  with premature or sick baby,
    19–20, 181–82
  for vaginal birth after cesarean
    (VBAC), 199–200
Swallowing reflex, 247, 254
Syphilis, 54–55
Systemic medications, 207, **208**–10
Tailor-sitting position, 100
Tea, 81–82
  herbal, 84–85, 169
  as treatment for sore nipples, 280
Tears, vaginal, 154, 155, 180, 187, 213
Teen pregnancy, 34–35
  nutrition during, 75
Testosterone, 21
Tests
  benefits and risks, 45, 49
  confirming pregnancy with, 25, 46
  of fetal well-being, 60–66, 184–88
  for newborns, 242–44
  prenatal diagnostic, 60–66
  routine pregnancy, 46–49
Tetracycline. *See* Eye care for
  newborn
Thiamin (B$_1$), 79
Thrombophlebitis, 51, **52**
Thrush (yeast infection), 54–55, 281
Tocodynamometry, 53, 65
Tocolytic drugs, 53, 179, 217
Touch relaxation, 110, 129. *See also*
  Massage
Toxoplasmosis, 54–55, **88**
Tranquilizers, 208–9
Transcutaneous electrical nerve
  stimulation (TENS), **114**–15, 176
  inducing labor using, 167
Transition phase. *See also* Breathing,
  variable (transition)

of labor, 142, 147–48, 162–63
of second stage, 153–56

Trimesters of pregnancy
  first trimester, 26–29,
  second trimester, 29–30, 42
  third trimester, 30–34, 43, 132–33
Triple screen, 48
Twins. *See* Multiple pregnancy

Ultrasound, **59–60**, 65
  to monitor blood flow, 62
  to monitor fetal heart rate, 62, 64,
    184, 185
  scan, 65
Umbilical cord, **33**
  clamping and cutting, 17, 158–59
  on newborn, 241
  prolapsed, 140, 177, 191
Upper body stretch, 101
Urethra, **21**–23
Urge to push. *See* Pushing in labor,
  urge to push
Urination
  and cesarean, 193, 197
  during labor, 116, 174
  during post partum, 227–28
  during pregnancy, 29, 33, 41, 43
Urine
  estriol content of, 63
  tests, 46
Uterine atony, 180
  drugs to treat, 218, 219
Uterus, **22**–23. *See also* Contractions

  changes in during pregnancy, 24,
    26–27, 29–31, 33–34, 37, 41–44,
    141
  incisions, for cesarean birth, **194**
  involution of, 159, **224**, 225
  maintaining muscle tone in, 17,
    159–60, 218–19
  massage of, 17, 159
  second trimester changes in, 42
  third trimester changes in, 43

Vacuum extraction, 177, **188**
Vagina, **22**
  postpartum, 225
Vaginal examination, 46
  during labor, 15, 136, 165–66
  during post partum, 225
  during pregnancy, 46
Vaginal birth. *See also* Birth
  after cesarean (VBAC), 189–90,
    198–202
  improving your chances for, 190
Vaginal/cervical smear, 46, 66
Variable breathing. *See* Breathing,
  variable (transition)
Varicose veins, 31, 43
Vascular spiders, **31–32**, 43
Vasoconstrictors, 215
Vasopressors, 214
Vegetarian diet, pregnancy and, 75
Velocimetry, 62
Vernix caseosa, **29**, 42–43, 240, 254, 255

Video display terminals (VDTs),
  pregnancy and, 87
Visual focus, 104, **113**
Vitamin A, 78
Vitamin B$_1$, 74, 79
Vitamin B$_6$, breastfeeding and, 270
Vitamin B$_{12}$, 75, 79
Vitamin C, 70, 79, 271
Vitamin D, 78
Vitamin E, 78
Vitamin K, 78
  for newborn, 18, 242
Vitamins. *See also* specific vitamins
  in breast milk, 269
  chart of, 76–79
  in pregnancy diet, 70–71, 78–79
Vomiting. *See* Nausea and vomiting

Walking
  following cesarean birth, 196–97
  position during labor, 15, 118, 144
  stimulating labor with, 167
Warmth of newborn, 17, 252, 253
Warning signs
  during post partum, 224
  during pregnancy, 51
Water
  in breast milk, 268
  exercise in, 95–96
  for newborn, 275, 287
  in pregnancy diet, 73, 76, 95
Water birth, 16, 115
Weight gain
  in newborn, 277–78
  during pregnancy, 71–72
  prenatal assessment of, 47
Weight loss, postpartum, 228, 269–70
Wharton's jelly, 159
Wide arm circles, 231, **233**
Witch hazel, 227, 228
Working mothers
  breastfeeding and, 285–86

X rays, **66**, 87

Yeast infections, 54–55, 281

Zinc, 77

Order Form

Quantity	Title	Author	Order No.	Unit Cost (U.S. $)	Total
	35,000+ Baby Names	Lansky, B.	1225	$5.95	
	Baby & Child Emergency First-Aid Handbook	Einzig, M.	1381	$8.00	
	Baby & Child Medical Care	Hart, T.	1159	$9.00	
	Baby Name Personality Survey	Lansky/Sinrod	1270	$8.00	
	Best Baby Name Book	Lansky, B.	1029	$5.00	
	Best Baby Shower Book	Cooke, C.	1239	$7.00	
	Child Care A to Z	Woolfson, R.	1010	$11.00	
	Dads Say the Dumbest Things!	Lansky/Jones	4220	$6.00	
	Discipline without Shouting or Spanking	Wyckoff/Unell	1079	$6.00	
	Do They Ever Grow Up?	Johnston, L.	1089	$6.00	
	Eating Expectantly	Swinney, B.	1135	$12.00	
	Familiarity Breeds Children	Lansky, B.	4015	$7.00	
	Feed Me! I'm Yours	Lansky, V.	1109	$9.00	
	First-Year Baby Care	Kelly, P.	1119	$9.00	
	Gentle Discipline	Lighter, D.	1085	$6.00	
	Getting Organized for Your New Baby	Bard, M.	1229	$9.00	
	Grandma Knows Best	McBride, M.	4009	$7.00	
	Hi, Mom! Hi, Dad!	Johnston, L.	1139	$6.00	
	How to Pamper Your Pregnant Wife	Schultz/Schultz	1140	$7.00	
	Joy of Grandparenting	Lansky, B.	3502	$7.00	
	Joy of Parenthood	Blaustone, J.	3500	$7.00	
	Moms Say the Funniest Things!	Lansky, B.	4280	$6.00	
	Mother Murphy's Law	Lansky, B.	1149	$5.00	
	Pregnancy, Childbirth, and the Newborn	Simkin/Whalley/Keppler	1169	$12.00	
	Very Best Baby Name Book	Lansky, B.	1030	$8.00	
				Subtotal	
				Shipping and Handling	
			MN residents add 6.5% sales tax		
				Total	

YES! Please send me the books indicated above. Add $2.00 shipping and handling for the first book and 50¢ for each additional book. Add $2.50 to total for books shipped to Canada. Overseas postage will be billed. Allow up to four weeks for delivery. Send check or money order payable to Meadowbrook Press. No cash or C.O.D.'s please. Prices subject to change without notice. **Quantity discounts available upon request.**

Send book(s) to:

Name _____

Address _____

City _____ State _____ Zip _____

Telephone (_____) _____

Purchase order number (if necessary) _____

Payment via:

☐ Check or money order payable to Meadowbrook Press (No cash or C.O.D.'s please.)

    Amount enclosed $ _____

☐ Visa (for orders over $10.00 only) ☐ MasterCard (for orders over $10.00 only)

Account # _____

Signature _____ Exp. Date _____

A *FREE* Meadowbrook catalog is available upon request.

You can also phone us for orders of $10.00 or more at 1-800-338-2232.

Mail to: Meadowbrook Press
5451 Smetana Drive, Minnetonka, Minnesota 55343
Toll-Free 1-800-338-2232

Phone (612) 930-1100   Fax (612) 930-1940